Implementing
Exchange Server

Other Titles By New Riders

Implementing Exchange Server

New Riders

201 West 103rd Street,
Indianapolis, Indiana 46290

Doug Hauger

Marywynne Leon

William C. Wade III

Implementing Exchange Server

Doug Hauger

Marywynne Leon

William C. Wade III

International Standard Book Number: 1-56205-931-9

Library of Congress Catalog Card Number: 98-87229

Printed in the United States of America

First Printing: October, 1998

2001   00   99   98   4   3   2   1

Trademarks

All terms mentioned in this book that are known to be trademarks or service marks have been appropriately capitalized. New Riders Publishing cannot attest to the accuracy of this information. Use of a term in this book should not be regarded as affecting the validity of any trademark or service mark.

Warning and Disclaimer

This book is designed to provide information about Exchange Server. Every effort has been made to make this book as complete and as accurate as possible, but no warranty or fitness is implied. The information is provided on an as-is basis. The authors and New Riders Publishing shall have neither liability nor responsibility to any person or entity with respect to any loss or damages arising from the information contained in this book..

Executive Editor
Al Valvano

Acquisitions Editor
Amy Michaels

Development Editor
Jim Chalex

Managing Editor
Sarah Kearns

Project Editor
Clint McCarty

Copy Editor
Gayle Johnson

Indexer
Craig Small

Technical Reviewers
Mark Adcock
Janice Howd

Book Designer
Ruth Lewis

Cover Designer
Brainstorm Technology

Production
Steve Balle-Gifford

Proofreader
Megan Wade

Contents

About the Authors

Doug Hauger is Director of Technology for a major Microsoft Certified Solution Provider in the Pacific Northwest. He consults regularly on the design and deployment of large scale network infrastructures, messaging systems, and BackOffice technology to Fortune 500 customers. Doug is a recognized leader in the Exchange community, and is a consistent contributor to Microsoft conferences and technical briefings. With close ties to the product group, Doug provides customers with expert product knowledge and the product group with practical insight to use of the technology. He has traveled and worked extensively abroad, including work in Morocco, Yemen, and Tacoma. Doug holds a BA from St. Olaf College and an MA from Boston University. He lives in Bellevue, Washington with his wife, Christine, and two children.

Marywynne Leon is a Seattle-based consultant specializing in the design, deployment, and intelligent use of messaging systems for large enterprises. With a focus on Microsoft technologies, she has consulted on LAN/WAN design, BackOffice integration issues, Internet connectivity, and network security. She holds a BSEE from the University of Washington and balances work with a aggressive schedule of tennis, water sports, travel, and the Northwest experience.

William C. Wade III has been a Microsoft BackOffice and network consultant for several years. From a big six consulting firm, Bill's interests and talents lead him into the MCSE and MCT channels. After establishing himself in the Exchange consulting community, he became one of the few Exchange trainers certified to teach Microsoft PSS how to support Exchange, and did so worldwide. Bill has subsequently worked on numerous Exchange architectures and deployments for organizations of all sizes and shapes. He frequently gives technical briefings for Microsoft, does work for the Exchange product group, and has presented at the Microsoft Exchange Conference. Bill and his wife Julie live in Issaquah, Washington with their 14 children.

About the Technical Reviewers

These reviewers contributed their considerable practical, hands-on expertise to the entire development process for *Implementing Exchange Server*. As the book was being written, these individuals reviewed all the material for technical content, organization, and usability. Their feedback was critical to ensuring that *Implementing Exchange Server* fits your need for the highest quality technical information.

Mark Adcock is a Program Manager with the Personal and Business Systems Division in Microsoft and is responsible for the technical development of Microsoft Official Curriculum materials that are delivered worldwide to Microsoft ATECs and Microsoft Technical Support. He has been working with Exchange Server since early EMS Days (when one component used to be called the Mailer Administration Daemon [you'll have to figure it out]). Before that, he worked as a trainer in the PSS group and also served time in the trenches supporting Mac Mail and PC Mail. In his non-existent spare time, he helps his family run the Northwest's #1 B&B on Lopez Island, Washington.

Janice Howd is the president of Hawk Technical Services Inc, a Microsoft Solution Provider located in Merritt Island, Florida. She began training Microsoft products in 1992 and has been a practicing MCSE and MCT since 1995. As an independent trainer specializing in Microsoft Exchange, Ms. Howd has worked for ATECs throughout the United States, Canada, and the Caribbean Islands. When she isn't training, Ms. Howd provides consulting services ranging from initial architecture planning to post-installation troubleshooting. In her spare time she can be found in the Microsoft News Groups as an MVP answering Exchange Server administrative questions.

Foreword

Art? Science?

These simple questions expressed in the context of Microsoft Exchange may be a bit melodramatic, but Exchange and the industry built around it have certainly made the dichotomy more evident for the people involved in making state-of-the-art mail and messaging possible in the world today.

Why another tome on Exchange? Egads! What more can be added to the existing body of knowledge on the subject? On a recent trip through Barnes & Noble I counted 20 books on Microsoft Exchange. The list is growing daily, and what is there—and getting deeper—does a pretty good job of listing every tip/trick/secret/strategy/workaround/fix/bug/whatever known to Exchange geeks around the world. Even though the essentials of Microsoft Exchange are covered in the aggregate, it might take two or three of those five-pounders to find the proper treatment of a critical issue.

What's not on the bookshelf but needing explanation and elaboration is the "art" of Microsoft Exchange. The product has become so complex that the interactions it has with other systems, hardware, and mission-critical processes simply can't be predicted from the "science" perspective, without practical experiences from which to draw. Unfortunately, many readers of Microsoft Exchange books seek understanding, perspective—the answer to *their* problem: How do I make this work here? To this end, the science books are less than successful. This book succeeds by presenting intimate product knowledge in combination with broad practical experiences.

This book was written right in Microsoft's backyard. The authors couldn't have been closer to the product without working on the development team at Microsoft. As Exchange practitioners working for a Microsoft Certified Solution Provider (MCSP), the authors have access to the traditional set of "virtual" tools—TechNet, Premier Support, Web tools, whitepapers, and so on—to use in delivering Exchange design and deployment services to big customers, little customers, and everything in between. Although, there is a wealth of information available in these repositories, the value of being in close physical proximity to Microsoft is immense. The "face-time" with folks from the product group, from Microsoft Consulting Services, wherever, amplifies the value of the authors' practical customer experiences.

So what? Well, if you're new to Exchange technology and have to design and implement an Exchange solution for your company and Chattanooga, Tennessee is home base, you're a long way from the Exchange support mechanisms that might exist in a larger metropolitan area. Even in the big-city, access to the necessary resources can be difficult. You might have access to the "virtual" toolset, and you might even have access to more "soft" support mechanisms, but what if you can't take advantage of those venues, or are reluctant to do so? Try finding the answers in the "science" book? Yeah, right. Suddenly, the prospect of sleeping restfully after migrating a dozen MS-Mail post offices to Exchange and re-wiring Internet mail connectors and X.400 connectors becomes problematic. The science books make it look like a no-brainer.

If you're about to deploy Exchange, the experiences of the artists—the authors—expressed in this book will help you to realize the value of the science you have on that Exchange CD in your hand. How you paint the Exchange picture in your organization will determine how effective mail and messaging will be for your colleagues and most likely a predictor of your continued employment. Seeing how others have successfully used Exchange should enhance your confidence in moving forward. Good luck!

Art. Science. Yeah, and it is cool.

Jeff Harriott

Two Dot, Montana

Acknowledgments

Doug Hauger

Thanks to Christine for her patience and support and thanks to my father for introducing me to computers.

Marywynne Leon and William C. Wade III

Marywynne and William would like to thank their family and friends for their patience and forbearance during the writing process and Excell Data Corporation for their flexibility. We would also like to extend a big thank-you to Mark Adcock and Janice Howd for their diligent technical reviews. They kept us honest and added tremendous value.

Tell Us What You Think!

As the reader of this book, you are our most important critic and commentator. We value your opinion and want to know what we're doing right, what we could do better, what areas you'd like to see us publish in, and any other words of wisdom you're willing to pass our way.

As the Executive Editor for the Networking team at Macmillan Computer Publishing, I welcome your comments. You can fax, email, or write me directly to let me know what you did or didn't like about this book—as well as what we can do to make our books stronger.

Please note that I cannot help you with technical problems related to the topic of this book, and that due to the high volume of mail I receive, I might not be able to reply to every message.

When you write, please be sure to include this book's title and author, as well as your name and phone or fax number. I will carefully review your comments and share them with the author and editors who worked on the book.

Fax: 317-581-4663

Email: `avalvano@mcp.com`

Mail: Al Valvano
   Executive Editor
   Networking
   Macmillan Computer Publishing
   201 West 103rd Street
   Indianapolis, IN 46290 USA

Introduction

Exchange is much more than an email application. It goes beyond the traditional roles of moving email messages between users in an organization. Exchange is a messaging *foundation*. Not only are typical messages sent between users upon this foundation, but applications can also be built that use messaging across the enterprise as a basis for their functionality. This enterprise-messaging environment, along with its evolving directory, makes Exchange a true *system*. The successful implementation of this system requires a methodology that addresses several aspects of an organization. This book attempts to address how to best approach that methodology and conceive a messaging architecture.

As you begin to develop your Exchange architecture, it is important to understand the broad role that Microsoft Exchange Server and Exchange clients, such as Microsoft Outlook, can play in an organization. By focusing on the full scope of functionality that Exchange Server has, you will be better prepared to develop and architecture for your organization that meets current needs and is easily extensible in the future.

This Book's Approach to an Exchange Architecture

This book is organized in a fashion that is similar to how we conduct our Exchange architecture projects. We first document the existing environment and gather messaging requirements. When then define a project team and work to build a solution that meets the customer's requirements. Once the services and functionality are defined that will meet these requirements, we design an Exchange architecture that will provide those services and functionality in the customer's environment. This is defined as the architecture.

Next, we build a migration and implementation plan that will take the customer from where they are to an environment that is defined in the architecture. Coexistence, migration methods, training, and schedules are all defined in the migration and implementation plan.

Finally, once implementation is well underway or complete, we work with the customer to document a Disaster Recovery Plan and Operations manual. The completion of these documents concludes our engagement with our customer.

In this book we take you through this process. We discuss how and what information to gather and how that data will affect an Exchange architecture. The components of an Exchange architecture are defined as well as the decisions that need to be made when constructing them. We also discuss the disaster recovery and operations aspects of the Exchange project and what processes and policies need to be put into place upon completion of the Exchange implementation. Finally, we conclude the book with two examples of Exchange architectures. These two varying organizations have typical Exchange implementations. We discuss the decisions they have made based on their current environment, and why they made those decisions.

We hope you find this book useful and it helps to make your Exchange projects successful. Please provide us feedback, good or bad, and tell us your experiences. Let us know how you found this book useful and how we can improve our methodology. Send comments to `theauthors@excell.com`

Conventions

There are several typographical conventions used in this book that you should be aware of:

Element	Style	Example
Command line command	Monotype font	`isinteg -patch`
Server tab	"in quotes"	"Advanced" properties of the mailbox
System directory name or path	<between carots> and in a monotype font	`<winnt>\system 32 directory`

Building an Exchange Server Architecture

AS YOU BEGIN TO DEVELOP YOUR Exchange Server architecture, it is important to understand the broad role that Microsoft Exchange Server and Exchange clients, such as Microsoft Outlook, can play in an organization. By focusing on Exchange Server's full scope of functionality, you will be better prepared to develop an architecture for your organization that meets current needs and is easily extensible in the future. This chapter discusses some of the initial design considerations you should have in mind when starting your Exchange Server project. In addition, we will provide some guidelines for selling Exchange as a collaborative computing solution to the end users in your organization.

Audience and Scope

This book is designed for a very specific audience. It is for people who are setting out to design, implement, and then administer an Exchange Server system. The scope of this book is limited to identifying the critical steps in developing a solid architecture and how to implement that architecture. This book also identifies some of the major issues that need to be addressed once an Exchange system is in place.

Exchange Architects and Planners

For many organizations, Microsoft Exchange Server is a radical departure from the simple flat-file messaging system they currently have in place. With the transacted nature of Exchange and complex relationships between intraorganizational and interorganizational messaging systems, Exchange requires more advanced planning and tuning than past systems. With the implementation of Exchange, many businesses take their first steps toward establishing a true collaborative computing environment. This means that in addition to having to design and maintain a complex client/server environment, Exchange architects and administrators will be required to provide levels of service significantly more demanding and less forgiving than ever before. Once businesses begin to rely on Exchange for workflow and collaboration, delays in e-mail and loss of data are unacceptable.

The sheer volume of data that today's knowledge worker receives every day is overwhelming. The balance between receiving data and analyzing data has shifted sharply to emphasize a need for technologies that enhance and simplify analysis. People don't need more data—they need better information. When implemented successfully, Exchange server and client technology enables analysis of data and automated delivery of information to individuals, workgroups, and organizations of every size.

Providing a system for data management is the promise of Exchange. But first that system must be built. Most Exchange books address the administration of Exchange in exacting detail, but they ignore the significant level of effort that is required to architect and implement an Exchange system. *This book is different.* Targeted to Exchange architects and consultants, it is a planning, design, and management guide for the architecture and implementation process of Exchange. While this book does address some of the day-to-day administrative tasks required to maintain an Exchange environment, it is not intended to be an Exchange administrator's guide.

Required Knowledge

In order to get the most out of this book, you should have knowledge of Exchange features and functionality and should be able to implement the details of the architectures described in this book. Specifically, you should know how to install and configure Exchange Server as well as have a good understanding of the Exchange connectors or similar messaging integration on other messaging platforms. You should be familiar with the following topics and tools:

- Exchange Server requirements and basic installation
- Exchange Performance Optimizer
- Exchange Load Simulator
- Configuring the Internet Mail Service
- Configuring the Connector for MS Mail
- Mailbox administration and maintenance
- Directory import and export
- Internet mail routing and DNS

- Windows NT security and operations
- Directory replication and synchronization

Not an Exchange How-To

This book will cover the strategies of Exchange design for heterogeneous network and messaging environments and give case-study examples of implementations for those types of environments. Specific attention will be given to identifying the factors that influence architecture designs, with discussion of the trade-offs made to meet performance needs of different organizations.

Several excellent books that have been published detail the steps required in setting up a simple Exchange environment. The goal of this book is to build on that collection of books and provide you with a detailed analysis of the critical decisions made when implementing Exchange in a real-world production environment. Although there are some step-by-step instructions, rudimentary implementation and configuration details are covered in other books, such as *Microsoft Exchange Server 5.5 Unleashed* (Sams Publishing).

Small-to-Medium-Sized Organizations

This book is written with small-to-medium-sized organizations in mind. Although the topics addressed are applicable to larger organizations, it is our intent to keep the focus on organizations that have 2,000 or fewer seats.

Profile of a Small Organization

A small organization has 50 to 500 users. These users could be located in one, or multiple, physical locations with one or more messaging servers. Most small organizations have centralized administration of the network and messaging systems. In a small organization, it may be possible to consider a cut-over to Exchange in a single step with all users being migrated to the new platform at once. It is likely, however, that the process will be more complex and will require a phased migration with groups of users being migrated over an extended period of time. Both migration alternatives are discussed in this book.

A small organization typically has budget and support limitations that require special consideration when the Exchange architecture is designed. While budget is a consideration for all organizations, many small organizations cannot afford substantial investments in hardware and support. These organizations often need to configure a single server to support the file/print, application, messaging, and collaborative computing needs of multiple people. Exchange can be configured to perform well under these constraints.

Profile of a Medium-Sized Organization

A medium-sized organization as addressed in this book is an organization that has 500 to 2,000 seats. These seats will most likely be distributed across multiple physical locations and multiple messaging servers. These organizations typically have some distribution of administration of the network and messaging systems.

In medium-sized organizations, administrative tasks are segmented between central administrators who are responsible for maintaining organization-wide services and local administrators who perform administrative tasks for local workgroups. These tasks include creating, modifying, and deleting accounts, monitoring local performance of systems, and assisting users with day-to-day issues. Due to the distributed nature of the computing environment and the amount of data to be migrated, it usually isn't possible to migrate a medium-sized organization to Exchange in a single step. When migration is phased in over time, the complexity of the migration process can increase dramatically.

LAN and WAN Considerations

When developing an Exchange architecture, it's important to take into consideration the physical topology of the network on which the architecture will be implemented. The performance of Exchange, more than that of many client/server applications, can be radically affected by network topology.

Connections Within the Organization

Most companies deploy Exchange servers on physical networks that are distributed and that typically include multiple local high-speed segments linked by slower-speed connections. This combination of Local Area Network (LAN), Metropolitan Area Network (MAN), and Wide Area Network (WAN) computing can dictate specific design requirements for the Exchange architecture. This book addresses the challenges that you face when you're designing architectures for a distributed computing environment.

In addition to complex physical network connections, organizations also have other messaging systems that affect the design of an Exchange architecture. These messaging systems may remain in place only until the end of the Exchange implementation or may coexist with Exchange indefinitely. This book addresses both of these cases, with specific focus on the complexities of a long-term coexistence between Exchange and other messaging systems.

Connections to the Outside World

In today's interconnected world, it is rare to implement a messaging solution that doesn't connect to the Internet or some other external network. These networks are in most cases outside of the control of the Exchange administrators. This book addresses the design constraints and considerations necessary when you're connecting Exchange to other messaging and networking systems. In order for Exchange to be successful as a messaging and collaborative computing platform, it is essential that it coexist with a vast array of systems.

Project Orientation

You should approach developing an architecture for Exchange the same way you approach any other infrastructure project: A project team should be established, specific roles and goals should be outlined and assigned, and responsibilities for team members should be clearly identified. The team also needs to have a clear understanding of the project phases and how each team member will play a role in each phase.

Project Process

Critical to the success of an Exchange architecture is the process by which it is designed and deployed. The project phases described in Table 1.1 are used in this book.

Table 1.1 **Exchange Design and Deployment Project Phases**

Phase	Purpose
Gathering requirements	The Exchange project team gathers and gains consensus on the business needs that drive the Exchange architecture. This phase is critical for team unity and consistent communication. In addition, it is essential that the initial architecture design be driven by business requirements rather than technological constraints.
Architecting the solution	Based on the requirements gathered, the Exchange architecture is developed. The architecture includes the physical network requirements, the security context, and the Exchange organization and site configuration. Depending on the scope of the architecture project, client configurations may also be included in the architecture. Once the architecture is established, it should be reviewed in the context of the initial requirements. This will help ensure that the final implementation will meet the needs of the end users. This is an iterative process that should be repeated until the business requirements and the technical design are in alignment.
Testing the architecture	The testing phase provides the opportunity to verify that the Exchange architecture addresses all of the design requirements and that it functions as expected in a real environment. Implementation details for client rollout are also tested at this time.
Pilot implementation	The first opportunity to see the Exchange architecture in a production environment, the pilot implementation phase is a final sanity check for the architecture. It is also the phase in which the support team can test their knowledge and understanding of the Exchange solution. Once the pilot implementation is complete, any changes to the Exchange architecture should be included and documented.

continues

Table 1.1 **Continued**

Production implementation	The production implementation phase is the rollout of Exchange to the user community. Critical to the success of this phase are team cohesiveness, end-user communication and training, and operations procedures to handle the additional support load due to the change.
Project wrap-up	Following implementation, the team should gather for a wrap-up phase. This phase provides an opportunity to document any anomalies that occurred during the implementation phase. In addition, the initial architecture should be reviewed, and any inconsistencies with the final implementation should be noted. It is essential that the final design as implemented be documented.
Future planning	This phase allows the team to plan for the future of the messaging platform. As organizations become more familiar with Exchange, they will seek to extend the messaging architecture to increase functionality. It is critical that every Exchange architecture and deployment project include a final planning phase that addresses future functionality needs and the methodology by which those needs will be incorporated into the Exchange environment. It is important at this point to plan for the growth, tuning, and optimization of Exchange. All of the discussions that take place during this phase should be documented for use by the project team when the next iteration of the Exchange architecture is designed.

The Importance of Planning

Although it's possible to install Exchange in an afternoon, it is unlikely that such an installation will meet the needs of an organization in the short term or long term. In many cases, unplanned installations of Exchange require a reinstallation and therefore cause interruption of service for the users. Planning is emphasized in this book, because it is critical to making Exchange an organization's enterprise messaging and collaboration platform. In addition, proper planning also facilitates the most effective use of hardware, software, and employee resources to install, configure, and manage Exchange.

Defining Business Needs for Messaging

Electronic messaging has become a critical technology for success in today's business environment. At a very basic level, electronic messaging systems provide structure for the exchange of information. Business colleagues need not be concerned with the technical details of communication as long as the messaging systems they are utilizing to communicate with each other are standardized and are connected in some way. As messaging becomes more critical to business, the business needs that are affected by messaging become broader. It isn't inconceivable that businesses may rely on messaging for such diverse applications as tracking time on projects, transferring orders from an e-commerce Web site to an inventory application, or managing all the workflow decisions in an online helpdesk application. Consequently, it has become increasingly more difficult to identify business needs that can be addressed with a messaging solution.

What Are Valid Business Needs?

At the broadest level, any business need that has a component of collaboration or information exchange can map to a specific electronic messaging technology. To design the best messaging support system, you need to discover the business need behind the collaboration component. In addition, it is critical that the project team identify future business needs while asking users about current business needs. This is important because in most cases it will be easier to design an architecture that can accommodate future modification if the future needs have already been identified. In addition, some future needs may not be able to be accommodated without redesigning and implementing the Exchange system.

Separating Business Needs from Technical Needs

When Exchange is selected to meet an organization's messaging needs, the reasons for the selection are often expressed in technical terms rather than business terms. The selection team may identify Exchange's scalability as a selection criteria, or its single-instance message store. While it is often the technical merits of the product that drive the selection of Exchange, you must define the business needs for the messaging platform in order to design the best Exchange solution. It is the role of the Exchange solution architect to step back and look at the strategic business issues and requirements that are part of the current business environment. Does the business have a distributed sales force? Are users seeking a way to collaborate more effectively on projects? Are budget cuts affecting the technology team's ability to administer the existing environment? Is the expansion of the business driving technology partnerships with external companies? Examples of common business requirements are outlined in Table 1.2, along with the commonly associated technical requirements.

Table 1.2 **Business Versus Technical Requirements**

Business Requirement	Technical Requirement
Roaming/roving users	Server-based storage with .ost files locally or .pst files on the client, and/or HTTP
Collaborative computing environment	Integrated electronic forms and distributed public folder replicas
Required reduction in the total cost of ownership	Centralized and distributed administration of the Exchange organization
Group access to similar data	Public folder support

continues

Table 1.2 **Continued**

Assurance of message delivery	Message tracking, server and link monitors, multiple MTA routes using independent physical network links and protocols
Single authentication scheme	Integration with NT security
Managed growth of messaging platform	Mailbox limits
Seamless operation while transitioning to Exchange	Integration with legacy mail systems, including connectors for MS Mail, cc:Mail, Lotus Notes, and Office Vision
Messaging access across a heterogeneous desktop environment	Outlook for Windows and Macintosh, Outlook Web for browser access on UNIX, POP3 and IMAP4 server support
Access to public data when WAN is unavailable	Replicated public folders

Business requirements usually aren't specific to a product or feature but can be associated with a business cost. If you deploy an effective collaborative computing environment, you know that your overall project cost will go down. If you can centralize administration of your messaging system, you will be able to lower your total cost of ownership. Once collected, the business requirements can be used to better limit the scope of issues that the architecture will address, enabling a successful architecture design process.

Distinguishing Business Needs from Opinions

Business needs often appear in the form of opinions of the administrators, user community, or executive committee. Instead of driving the Exchange architecture from these opinions, it is important to discover the business needs underlying them. Opinions are not foregone conclusions in most cases and are sometimes not the best solution to a business need. Once the true business needs are uncovered, the Exchange architecture team can do a better job designing the solution.

An example of this scenario is the selection of public folders for multiple user access to the same data. Is this driven by the need for several users to open the same mailbox? If so, could it possibly be solved by assigning a Windows NT group of those users to the mailbox? Or is this driven by the need to have threaded discussions and therefore would most appropriately be designed as a public folder solution? Once the business needs are gathered and separated from the technical requirements and organization opinions, it is possible to proceed with the architecture of the environment.

Exchange as an E-Mail and Collaborative Computing Platform

As part of the process of identifying the business needs for Exchange, one of the steps to be taken is to identify the extent to which Exchange will be implemented as a messaging solution and to what extent it will be utilized as a collaborative computing platform. In nearly all cases, it is prudent when designing an Exchange architecture to take into account Exchange's collaborative computing aspects. As noted earlier, if an Exchange system is designed and implemented in a way that doesn't take future business needs into account, it may be costly and time-consuming to modify the design at a later date.

Integrating Exchange into Current File/Print and Intranet Environments

With so many technical solutions to business problems arising in the current market, it is possible to inundate users with too many solutions to a problem. It is therefore critical to integrate Exchange with the current environment. In many organizations, public folders on the messaging system compete with file servers and intranet Web servers for document storage. Integrating the technology with the policies in place for the organization will help the users and technology be more successful.

Project Scope Should Include the Extended Functionality of Exchange

Exchange offers an extended feature set of collaborative computing and Web integration applications. These features are likely to be used at one time or another within an organization, so the project scope of Exchange and the architecture should include consideration of these features. Design should include not only the feature set at the time of deployment, but also the expansion of environment and services.

Environment Discovery

PERHAPS THE MOST CRITICAL STEP in an Exchange architecture project is discovering and defining the environment in which Exchange will function. This discovery mainly entails asking the appropriate people in each department or group questions about the computing environment. The answers to these questions are used to make delicate decisions during the actual Exchange architecture design.

After this series of questions about the current computing environment is answered, the next series of questions refers to the requirements of the new messaging system. In Chapter 1, "Building an Exchange Server Architecture," we discussed business requirements. Usually these business requirements exceed the capabilities of the current messaging system and are the driving force behind implementing a more robust messaging system, such as Exchange. Documenting these requirements, as well as which Exchange services will satisfy those requirements, ensures that they are addressed in the Exchange architecture.

In the next two chapters, we will discuss the questions you should ask your users when you are developing an Exchange architecture. In this chapter, we will discuss the questions to be asked about the existing computing environment. In Chapter 3, "Gathering Requirements," we will discuss the questions that you should ask regarding the requirements for the new messaging system. There is a list of questions at the end of each main section in these chapters. These questions can be copied and used as a checklist when you complete your own Exchange Server architecture project.

In subsequent chapters, we will address each of the questions raised in Chapters 2 and 3 and will provide guidance on how to utilize the information you will gather when designing your Exchange architecture.

Environment Discovery

The approach taken in this information-gathering exercise is to address the computing environment as it loosely relates to the OSI model. We start with the network, discovering its topology and bandwidth. Next, we move to the operating system, where we learn what types of server and client operating systems are in place and the roles they play. In addition, we document any existing Windows NT domain architectures. After that, we look at the current messaging system and how it functions, as well as any other applications that will be replaced or augmented by Exchange, such as any calendaring or faxing applications.

When addressing environment discovery, here are the main categories covered:

- The current LAN/WAN environment
- Protocols used on the network and IP networking strategy
- Server and client hardware profiles
- Internet connectivity, including security configuration
- The Windows NT domain architecture
- The current administration model

Current LAN/WAN Environment

Starting with the networking layer of the OSI model, we ask questions about the current LAN and WAN environment. Who will answer these questions depends on the size of the organization and the size of the Information Systems group. Typically, as the size and complexity of an organization's information services grow, so does the staff. In medium-to-large organizations, it's important to pinpoint the best person in the IS department to answer, or find the answer to, the posed questions. In a small organization, all questions can most likely be answered by the one- or two-person IS staff.

WAN Environment

Starting from a bird's-eye view, we first document the WAN environment. Small organizations often have a single point of contact for all LAN and WAN configuration knowledge, and it is seldom documented. However, this person or persons might not know much about current bandwidth consumption. Research into how much bandwidth is being consumed, by way of router statistics or carrier-supplied statistics, will have to be done to properly answer this critical question. Medium-to-large organizations will usually have a group responsible for WAN services. This group should have these statistics readily available.

Geographic Profile

For your Exchange architecture, create a geographic profile. This profile will be useful throughout your architecture as a reference for each location. This geographic profile is an illustrated view of your organization, with all the physical locations and the WAN segments that link them. Figure 2.1 shows an example of a medium-sized organization's geographic profile.

WAN Circuit Type

In Figure 2.1, frame relay services are used as the primary method for connectivity between sites. The access rate to the frame relay service provider at each site is a T1 speed of approximately 1.536 Mbps. There are permanent virtual circuits (PVCs) between Seattle and all other locations except Bellevue. Bellevue doesn't participate in the frame relay service. Instead, it has a 10 MB MAN TLS (transparent LAN service, based on ATM) link to Seattle. For your WAN, draw a similar diagram, showing the physical locations, the circuits that join them, and their relative speeds.

As well as documenting the geographic profile, document the types of WAN circuits established between each physical location.

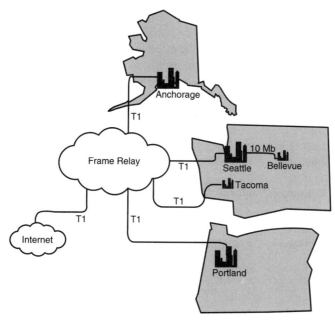

Figure 2.1   An example of a medium-sized organization's geographic profile

Current Available WAN Bandwidth

When you're developing an Exchange architecture, it is important to establish what the available bandwidth is between geographic locations. The answer to this question can greatly affect the Exchange architecture. The available bandwidth between each location will determine where Exchange site lines will be drawn. Therefore, it is important to be relatively confident in the answers to this question.

In the geographic profile just discussed, the digital circuits between Seattle and the other frame relay sites are full duplex. The consumed bandwidth in and out of these sites, from Seattle, is documented in Table 2.1.

From this information we can determine the amount of available bandwidth between sites. Even though we have a 10 MB pipe from Bellevue to Seattle, it is quite possible that the bandwidth across that circuit is limited. If the bandwidth were limited across that circuit, it would most likely alter our Exchange architecture. Hence, it is important to evaluate each WAN connection.

Small and medium-to-large organizations with WANs must gather the same type of information. Your WAN carrier might be able to provide you with these statistics. Otherwise, you will need to gather this information from the routers used for connectivity between sites.

LAN Topology

Small organizations, which consist of a single subnet, have a simple topology that will not affect the Exchange architecture. However, small and medium-to-large organizations that have multiple subnet LANs need to look at the location of their Exchange servers in relation to the groups of users that they will support.

Again referring to the geographic profile discussed a moment ago, document the media at each location. Where appropriate, specify the media speed—for example, 4 MB token ring as opposed to 16 MB token ring, or 10 MB Ethernet as opposed to 100 MB Ethernet.

Table 2.1 **Consumed Bandwidth Between Geographic Locations**

City	Line Speed	CIR*	Access Rate	Average Used Bandwidth Inbound**	Average Used Bandwidth Outbound**
Anchorage	T1	128 KB	128 KB	13.74%	15.11%
Tacoma	T1	1,544 KB	1,544 KB	1.06%	1.59%
Portland	T1	96 KB	128 KB	15.21%	20.26%
Bellevue	10 MB	N/A	N/A	1.13%	1.13%

*Committed Information Rate
**Average based on available network bandwidth between Seattle and each city during business hours.

Protocols

The network protocols that exist on each LAN will help determine which protocols will be supported on the Exchange server. For example, in a small organization that uses only NetBEUI, it isn't necessary to install NWLink on the Exchange server. Whether or not these protocols are supported across the WAN will dictate whether additional protocols are needed.

Determine the protocols running across the LANs in your organization. If necessary, use a network-monitoring application (promiscuous) such as NetMon, which is bundled with Microsoft Systems Management Server. The version that ships with Windows NT doesn't run in promiscuous mode and won't give you a complete picture of the protocols running across your network.

It is quite possible to have IPX/SPX as the protocol being used between the current Lotus cc:Mail clients, to have Novell server hosting the cc:Mail post office and to have TCP/IP as the protocol being used between the existing Windows NT servers and clients. Exchange architectures typically don't require protocol reconfiguration. However, this exercise will help determine which protocols will be used.

It is important to note that if a protocol reconfiguration is required, the best time to do so is prior to rolling out Exchange. Changing protocols can be a time-consuming and troublesome issue once Exchange is implemented and client applications are configured to connect to the server using a specific protocol.

Exchange will communicate between physical locations across the WAN, as well as on the local network. Consequently, the Exchange servers will need to be configured with a routed protocol such as TCP/IP that can be routed between geographic locations.

LAN Segmentation

It is easiest to document LAN segmentation using an illustration. If your organization doesn't have a current copy of its LAN topology, take a few moments to draw one for each physical location that has more than a single subnet. Figure 2.2 shows a semi-complex LAN topology.

Existing Server and Client Hardware Specifications

It is important to know the client hardware specifications because the default Exchange client, Outlook, is a full-featured application that requires significant hardware resources. Many existing messaging clients are "light" and do not consume the client resources that the Outlook client consumes.

In a small organization it is possible that existing hardware will be used for the Exchange server. Hence, it is important to know the specifications of that hardware. Simply document the CPU, clock speed, amount of RAM, and amount of disk space requirements of the existing messaging clients.

The same specifications should be gathered for the Exchange server hardware. Document the number of CPUs and their speeds; the amount of RAM and what it's expandable to; and the number of disks, their sizes, and their configuration (RAID level).

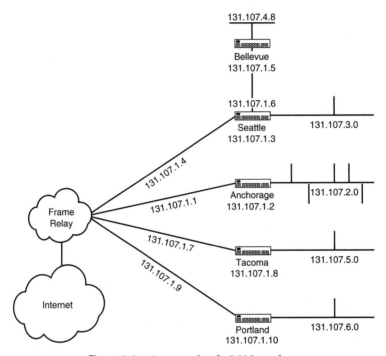

Figure 2.2   An example of a LAN topology

TCP/IP Strategy and Topology

Today it's uncommon to find an organization of any size that doesn't use TCP/IP. Since a messaging system relies on the network and its protocols, it's important to understand an organization's TCP/IP strategy when designing an Exchange architecture.

Subnets

Using a copy of the geographic profile, document the current and allocated subnets that exist at each physical location.

Take the geographic profile and add the TCP/IP network addresses of each LAN, as well as the addresses of the WAN, as shown in Figure 2.3.

DNS

Because it's uncommon to find an organization that doesn't use TCP/IP, it's also uncommon to find an organization that isn't connected to the Internet. DNS services are an important part of a TCP/IP network and will be more heavily relied upon with the coming Windows NT 5.0. Where the DNS server is located, who manages it, and what clients are configured to use it are all important questions.

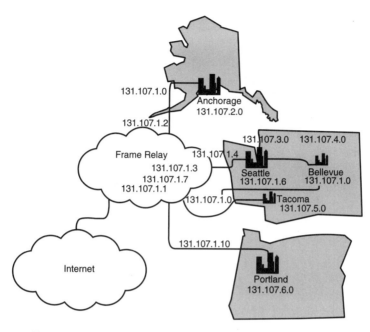

Figure 2.3   The LAN topology mapped to the geographic profile

Often in small organizations an ISP will manage the organization's few DNS entries at the ISP's DNS server. But in medium-to-large organizations it is not uncommon to find an internal DNS that forwards queries it can't resolve to the ISP. The people who manage this DNS should be involved in the Exchange architecture and perhaps the implementation, so finding out who these people are and contacting them about the pending project is a good idea.

If a workstation has TCP/IP configured as the primary networking protocol, the Outlook client will try to resolve the Exchange server host name to an IP address using DNS services during startup. If DNS services are not available, the Windows operating system will eventually resolve the name using resolution to a host file, a broadcast, or the Windows Internet Naming Service (WINS).

WINS

Alongside DNS in the name-resolution arena is WINS. Whereas DNS resolves host names to IP addresses, WINS resolves NetBIOS names to IP addresses.

Using the geographic profile, document the location of the WINS servers and which WINS servers are responsible for resolving each subnet's NetBIOS names.

Additionally, note which WINS servers have replication relationships. Figure 2.4 shows the WINS server topology for our ongoing example.

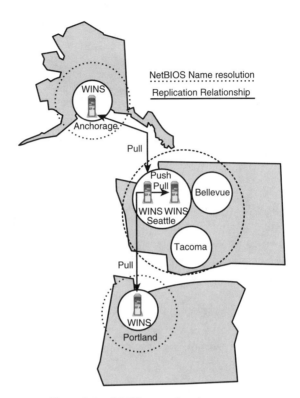

Figure 2.4 WINS server locations

Internet Connectivity

Exchange is becoming more and more integrated with Internet-based protocols and standards. Many of Exchange's proprietary protocols and interfaces are giving way to Internet protocols and standards. Hence, it is important to define how your organization is connected to the Internet and how Exchange will become a part of that equation.

WAN Connection to the Internet

Small organizations might not have a permanent connection to the Internet. Instead, they might have a dial-up analog or ISDN modem that periodically dials the ISP and sends and receives Internet messages. Medium-to-large organizations most likely have a permanent connection to the Internet. Whichever the case, the connection to your ISP needs to be documented.

Firewalls

Any organization permanently connected to the Internet needs a firewall. If your organization is permanently connected to the Internet and you don't have a firewall or proxy service, or at least router filtering, make that project your top priority. The well-being of your organization, not to mention your own job, might lie in the balance. Once the firewall is in place, document its configuration and relationship to the current messaging system.

Some of the most common ports to have enabled are listed in Table 2.2. For a complete listing of IP port numbers, see **http://www.isi.edu/ in-notes/iana/assignments/port-numbers~**.

Web Services

Document the nature of the Web services offered by your organization. Most small organizations that have a Web page typically host that page at an Internet Service Provider. Medium-to-large organizations often have their own Web servers and maintain their own Web site either inside the firewall or in the firewall's demilitarized zone.

One of the coming trends in business computing is to have information and business processes available to users through an HTML interface. Exchange is an excellent mechanism for facilitating this trend. Document any existing internal workgroup applications that have been developed in HTML, and identify which groups developed them.

There are two reasons we suggest documenting the Web services that exist in your organization. First, it is important for the Exchange project team to have a complete understanding of what applications are utilizing HTTP on the network in order to better troubleshoot issues if they should arise when Outlook Web is implemented with Exchange. Second, it is helpful when implementing Outlook Web to have a comprehensive understanding of how your organization utilizes Web services. Many corporate cultures don't foster rapid acceptance of new applications such as Outlook Web. If that is the case with your organization, it is important that the project team understand this from the outset and plan accordingly. That may include providing additional training for the people who will be using Outlook Web for remote access to Exchange, adding an Outlook Web help page to the company intranet, or providing workgroup presentations on the use of Outlook Web.

Table 2.2   **Common IP Port Numbers**

Protocol	Port Number
HTTP	80
HTTP over SSL	443
SMTP	25
POP3	110
IMAP4	143
FTP	20/21

For more information on how to set up a firewall, refer to *Internet Security Professional Reference, Second Edition* (New Riders, 1997).

Internet Client Access Methods

You should document any Internet messaging protocols, such as POP3 and IMAP4, as well as whether any protocols are being used to access the current messaging system from the Internet. This is important as part of the process of identifying which messaging protocols should be supported as part of the implementation of Exchange. If no users in your organization are currently utilizing POP3, for example, it isn't necessary to implement that protocol as an element of the initial Exchange deployment. It may be an option that you will implement as part of a second phase. Once again, it is important to reiterate that users will expect Exchange to provide them with (at a minimum) the same functionality that the old messaging system did.

Security Policies

Organizations have different levels of information security policies. Some companies don't allow external data communications. This is typically the case with organizations that deal with proprietary or sensitive information, such as the banking industry. Other organizations have permanent connections to the Internet with virtually no security. Document the level of security that your organization adheres to.

Your organization's security policies will dictate the level of access that you can provide to Exchange. For example, does your organization allow access from the Internet to Web sites on the corporate network? If not, it might not be possible to implement access to Exchange by using Outlook Web. Does your organization allow mail destined for internal corporate recipients to be transmitted unencrypted across the Internet? If not, it might not be possible for recipients to send and receive messages by using a POP3 or IMAP4 client unless the client supports SSL.

Summary Questions for a LAN/WAN Environment

Table 2.3 contains a list of the questions to be addressed when gathering information on the current LAN and WAN environment. These questions are designed to serve as a reference while addressing the issues discussed in the LAN/WAN sections.

Table 2.3 **Preexisting LAN/WAN Question Checklist**

Planning Category	Question
Wan Circuits	What types of WAN circuits connect the physical locations?
Available Bandwidth	What is the amount of *available* bandwidth between each physical location during business hours?
Media for Each Physical Location	For each physical location, document the type of network medium used—for example, 10 MB Ethernet or 16 MB token ring.
Protocols Used for Each LAN	List the protocols that exist on each LAN. This includes protocols that are not currently used between the messaging server and messaging clients.

Planning Category	Question
Protocols Used Between Messaging Clients and Servers	Of the protocols found on each LAN, which protocols are currently being used to communicate between messaging clients and messaging servers?
Protocols Routed Between Physical Locations	Of the protocols found on each LAN, which ones are routed between sites?
Client Hardware Specifications	What is the hardware specification of the existing messaging clients?
TCP/IP Addressing Strategy	What is the TCP/IP addressing strategy?
Managing DNS Services	Who is responsible for and capable of manipulating the DNS database?
Clients Configured to Use DNS	Which clients are configured to use DNS? This will help isolate name-resolution problems at startup.
WINS	Where are the WINS servers located?
Internet Connection	How is your organization connected to the Internet? What is the speed of that connection?
Firewall Configuration	How is your firewall configured? List the ports that are open on your firewall.
SMTP and the Firewall	How is SMTP traffic handled at the firewall? Does the firewall pass the SMTP port 25 packets through to a single SMTP host, or does the firewall itself act as an SMTP host, receiving messages and then forwarding them to the messaging gateway?
Internet Web Services	If your company has a Web page, is it hosted by your ISP or on an internal Web server?
Intranet Web Services	Do internal Web applications and services exist? If so, what kind are they, and who developed them?
Internet Messaging Protocols	What Internet protocols (POP3 or IMAP4) are being used to access the messaging system?
Internet Clients	If users are accessing their messaging system via the Internet, what clients are being used?
Web Policy	Is there a policy regarding Web access from the Internet to servers on the intranet?
SNMP Policy	Is there a policy regarding SMTP (unencrypted) company e-mail traveling across the Internet?

NT Architecture

Now that you have a good understanding of the network infrastructure, it's time to focus on the existing Windows NT architecture that will support Exchange. Microsoft Exchange is a Windows NT BackOffice product that relies on several Windows NT subsystems for its functionality. One of those subsystems is the security subsystem represented by an NT Domain topology.

Existing Domain Overview

Using the geographic profile you established in the preceding section, the next step is to document the existing domain topology. Show existing trusts between domains. An example is shown in Figure 2.5.

This example shows a single domain. Our NT architecture places backup domain controllers in Portland and Anchorage to satisfy the local domain authentication and places the primary domain controller and a backup domain controller in Seattle to satisfy the authentication requests of Seattle, Bellevue, and Tacoma.

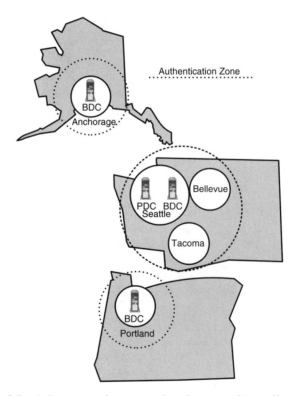

Figure 2.5   A domain topology mapped to the geographic profile

Existing Security Structure

The domain model will tell you a lot about the existing security structure. However, it is important to document the reasons for the existing domain architecture.

If an organization has a distributed administrative model, a complete trust NT domain relationship is usually the only domain model that will satisfy that requirement. However, most complete trust domain models are not designed and implemented in a formal NT domain implementation project. Rather, the complete trust NT domain usually evolves uncontrollably from several NT domains being created in an organization that need to share resources.

Domain Controller Physical Locations

Document the physical location of each domain controller and the role it plays in the domain. As we have done in our NT domain architecture example (shown in Figure 2.5), show which domain controllers are responsible for authenticating which groups of users.

Existing NT Policies and Profiles

NT policies and profiles are a sign of an organization that is taking full advantage of Windows NT's feature set. In addition, policies and profiles are typically a sign that an organization has a more sophisticated level of administrative support, because policies and profiles can be challenging to administer. Document how your company has implemented policies and profiles with Windows 95, Windows 98, and/or Windows NT Workstation clients.

Existing Naming Conventions (Devices and User)

Because our sample organization will also be using Internet resources, we have defined our NetBIOS names to be compatible with the DNS (Domain Name Service) host name specification. DNS names are restricted to a to z, A to Z, 0 to 9, and - (hyphen). DNS names may not contain blank spaces. For these reasons, we recommend the following computer-naming convention:

Use workstation names that begin with a three-letter city code (the three-letter airport codes work well), then a hyphen followed by a unique five-character asset number.

Format: *<city code><-><unique five-digit number>*

Examples: SEA-00001, PDX-00003

Table 2.4 lists the three-letter city abbreviations that we have selected for use in our example. You should select appropriate abbreviations for your geographic locations.

Table 2.4 **Sample Abbreviations**

City	Abbreviation
Seattle	SEA
Bellevue	BEL
Anchorage	ANC
Tacoma	TAC
Portland	PDX

The server names in the example are derived from a three-letter city code, then server function (a three-character abbreviation), followed by a unique two-digit number. Although hyphens are X.500- and DNS-compliant, they are not implemented in server names because of support issues with SQL Server.

Format: *<server location><server function><increment>*

Examples: SEASQL04, PDXEXC01, ANCBDC01, TACFPS01

Table 2.5 gives examples of some appropriate three-letter abbreviations for server roles. If a server has multiple roles, choose the predominant one.

The host name is the native TCP/IP name given to a workstation or host. Host names will be the same as the computer NetBIOS name in lowercase characters. Windows NT Servers should also have the domain name configured as the TCP/IP domain name. The Fully Qualified Domain Name (FQDN) for each Windows NT server will then be `servername.ourdomain.com`.

In a Windows NT domain, resources are kept secure by assigning them permissions based on user accounts. Before access to a resource is granted, the user's account must have permissions to access that resource. Furthermore, the type of access to the resource can also be defined and limited. All users who want access to the domain resources such as Exchange will log on to the domain with their own accounts. Account names will be derived from the user's name. When two or more people have the same name, middle initials will be used to ensure a unique NT account name.

Full Name Format: *Last name, first name middle initial*

Example: Smith, John D.

Username Format (NT account name): *<first initial of first name><last name>*

Example: Jsmith

Client Software Installation Points

Client software installation points are used to distribute software. Document any existing client installation points that may be used during implementation of the Outlook client. In addition, it is important to document other software distribution methods that your company utilizes, such as Microsoft System Management Server. Documenting all distribution methods will provide a basis for selecting the best distribution method for Outlook and other associate Exchange software.

Table 2.5 **Server Role Abbreviations**

Application	Abbreviation
Domain Controller	PDC/BDC
Exchange: Generic	EXC
Exchange: Public Folder Server	PUB
Exchange: Private Folder Server	PRV
Exchange: Bridgehead Server	EBH
Exchange: Free/Busy Server	EFB
SQL Server	SQL
Communications	COM
Backup/Archive	BUS
File and Print Server	FPS

NetWare Integration

With the popularity of the NetWare network operating system, it is common for Exchange to be implemented in a NetWare environment that doesn't already have Windows NT. However, Windows NT is necessary to support the Exchange architecture. In these cases, it is important to know enough about the NetWare environment so that the two can coexist with minimal additional administrative overhead.

If NetWare and Windows NT exist on the same network, document the administrative tools used to ease the administrative burden of managing two heterogeneous systems. Tools such as Microsoft's Windows NT Directory Services for NetWare and Novell's Novell Administrator for NT are popular multidirectory management tools. Microsoft and Novell both have clients for Windows 95 and Windows 98 that are used to access Novell NetWare resources.

Summary Questions for an Existing Windows NT Domain

Listed in Table 2.6 are the summary questions for gathering information on your existing Windows NT domain environment.

Table 2.6   **Domain Environment Question Checklist**

Planning Category	Question
Domain Architecture	What is the NT domain architecture, including trusts?
Administrative Model	If your domain model is a complete trust domain model, document the technical reasons for the complete trust model.
NT Policies and Profiles	Are policies and profiles implemented? If so, do users have the ability to roam throughout the organization?
Workstation (NetBIOS) Names	What is the workstation naming convention?
Server Names	What is the server naming convention?
Host Names	What is the host name naming convention?
Usernames	What is the username naming convention?
Client Installation Points	Does your organization use client installation points? If so, pinpoint any client installation points that exist on your network.
NetWare and NT Coexistence Tools	Document any special tools used to manage the Windows NT and NetWare accounts.
NetWare Client	What NetWare client used by your organization is called upon by Windows 95 or Windows 98 to access the NetWare environment?

Current Messaging System

With the current network architecture defined, we now ask questions about the current messaging system. We will most likely have to coexist with the current messaging system—if not indefinitely, at least during the migration from the current messaging system to Exchange. Coexistence is a critical part of the messaging architecture, and its stability and efficiency can determine if users and management view the migration as a success.

Post Office Topology

To help determine where connectors between the current messaging systems and Exchange will be placed, we need to understand the current messaging topology. Existing messaging topologies typically fall into one of two categories: LAN-based or host-based. Of these two, the more common type found in small and medium organizations is LAN-based messaging. This chapter focuses primarily on LAN-based systems but also provides limited discussion of host-based systems.

The first step in understanding the existing messaging system is to document the logical and physical configuration of existing post offices. In addition, document the MTAs that move messages between the post offices. This information will be critical to identifying the message flow that will be implemented when Exchange is implemented.

In the case of a host-based system, it is important to identify the logical and physical location of the host and the connectivity method by client applications. This will help when identifying the location of Exchange servers and the transport protocol that will be used for connectivity between servers and between Exchange clients and the servers.

Figure 2.6 documents the cc:Mail post offices that exist at each of the physical locations, along with the MTAs that move messages between them.

SMTP Services

Another component critical to the coexistence and migration is the SMTP gateway. How SMTP messages will flow, uninterrupted, between the Internet, the current messaging system, and Exchange will most likely be answered by how the current SMTP services are configured. In our fictional example, the organization's DNS mail exchanger record points to the firewall, which runs UNIX sendmail. If the firewall is up and running, Internet messages are received by the firewall and then passed along to a cc:Mail SMTP gateway, which in turn delivers the message to the cc:Mail system. If the firewall is down, a second MX record points to an SMTP host at the organization's ISP (see Figure 2.7). If for some reason the firewall is temporarily down, messages will be delivered to the ISP's SMTP host. Then, periodically, the ISP will try to deliver the message to our organization's SMTP host.

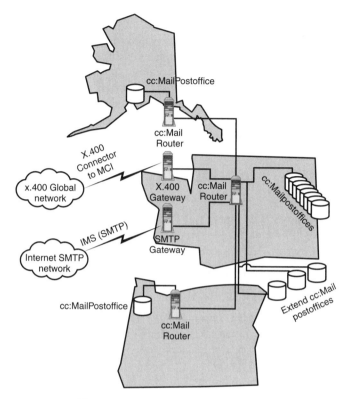

Figure 2.6 Existing post office topology

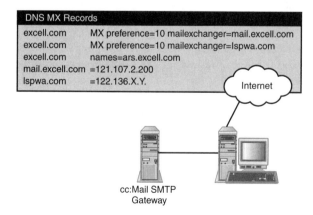

DNS MX Records

excell.com	MX preference=10 mailexchanger=mail.excell.com
excell.com	MX preference=10 mailexchanger=lspwa.com
excell.com	names=ars.excell.com
mail.excell.com	=121.107.2.200
lspwa.com	=122.136.X.Y.

Figure 2.7 DNS MX Records

When Internet messages are sent from cc:Mail, they are delivered to the SMTP gateway, which, as a relay agent, forwards them to the SMTP host running on the firewall. The SMTP host then does a DNS lookup and delivers the message to its final destination. This is an example of the flexibility of the Exchange Internet Mail Service. In your own organization it is possible to architect your Exchange systems with an IUMS that delivers directly to the Internet, delivers to a relay host, or delivers to the Internet through a firewall.

Administrative Structure

In small organizations, one or two people might administer the current messaging system. Medium-to-large organizations might have a group of administrators who all share administrative responsibilities. There also might be different types of administrators segmented into several different groups. One group might be responsible for creating and deleting mailboxes. Another group might be responsible for backing up a set of messaging servers, and yet another group might be responsible for server maintenance and MTA availability.

Automated Services That Use the Messaging System

If any automated or *batch* processes use the current messaging system, it is important to identify them before the migration takes place.

List all the known applications or batch processes that use the messaging system. Most often, these batch processes automatically deliver reports generated by a host system. The host system will spit out a report to disk, and then, at a scheduled time, a batch process will run that delivers the message to a list of recipients. These processes will have to be individually addressed in the Exchange architecture.

Remote User Services

Remote users are people who either work from home, travel, or work at a remote office without their own messaging server. These users typically dial into the messaging system or the network to send and receive messages. You should identify how users access their mailboxes.

With MS Mail, for example, remote users dial directly into the MS Mail MTA (external) application to send and receive messages. How users access their mail remotely, and the resources they use to do so, might have to be reallocated with the introduction of Exchange.

Next, identify the number and type of remote users in your organization. The number of remote users might dictate the type of "off-LAN" access you provide to your Exchange system. If there are a limited number of users, for example, you might be able to provide dial-in access to the LAN. If there are a large number of users, however, supporting a large modem pool for dial-in access might not be possible. In this case, you might need to consider an outsource or consider providing Outlook Web access via the Internet. As the number of users increases, you will also experience an increase in the amount of time needed to provide administrative support.

Recipient Group Structure and Public Folder Strategy

Many messaging systems have a shared folder system and the capability to group users into distribution lists. Here we need to document how the current messaging system is configured to use shared folders and how it organizes its distribution lists.

Document a hierarchy, if one exists, of the current shared folder system. Some implementations of shared folder systems, or public folders, are created using a defined hierarchy. When you document this hierarchy, it can be revised and implemented into the Exchange architecture.

When documenting the hierarchy, identify which shared folders have content that needs to be migrated. For example, a shared folder for personal advertisements might not warrant migration, whereas a shared folder with the company handbook or insurance program documentation probably will.

For those shared folders in the current messaging system hierarchy, identify which ones need to be migrated. One of the major challenges during migration between some messaging systems and Exchange is the synchronization of shared folders to Exchange public folders. When a user posts a message in a shared folder, that message also needs to be posted into the Exchange public folder. When an Exchange user posts a message into an Exchange public folder, that message also needs to be posted to the current messaging system's corresponding shared folder. This can be tricky to configure and can require constant attention. Determine how important it will be to synchronize the shared folder systems.

Many client/server messaging systems have evolved from a single post office and have seen multiple messaging administrators, so there is rarely any structure to the distribution lists of an existing messaging system. If your system is one of the organized few, document the structure here.

Summary Questions for an Existing Messaging Environment

Table 2.7 lists summary questions for gathering information on your existing messaging environment.

Table 2.7 **Existing Messaging Environment Question Checklist**

Planning Category	Question
Post Office Topology	What is the current messaging system's post office topology?
SMTP	How do SMTP messages currently flow between the organization and the Internet?
Messaging System Administration	What is the administrative structure for the current messaging system?
Automated or Batch Processes	Do any automated or batch processes use the messaging system?
Remote Users	In the current messaging system, how do remote users send and receive messages?
Type and Number of Remote Users	How many remote users consistently work from home? How many remote users are traveling remote users?
Shared Folders	Does the current messaging system utilize a shared folder system? If so, how is that system organized?
Migrating Shared Folders	Does the current messaging system contain shared folders that don't need their content migrated?
Shared Folders During Migration	How important is it that the shared folders on the current messaging system be synchronized with the Exchange public folder system?
Distribution Lists	Is there a formal structure as to how users are grouped into distribution lists?

3

Gathering Requirements

AFTER WE HAVE GATHERED THE INFORMATION for the current infrastructure, network operating system, and messaging system, we move on to gather the extended requirements for the Exchange messaging environment and any third-party solutions that will be deployed with Exchange.

Exchange Architecture

This portion of the information-gathering process focuses on how your organization intends to implement Exchange, the requirements that will drive that implementation, and the standards you wish to adopt. It is important to draw these out so that they can be incorporated into the Exchange architecture. Some of these questions will undoubtedly need to be answered by committee or upper management due to their inability to be changed after implementation.

This chapter addresses the following:

- Naming conventions
- User classifications
- Administrator classifications
- Mailbox quotas and limitations
- Exchange information store protocols

- Public folder strategies
- Distribution list strategies
- Custom recipient issues
- Third-party solutions

As you read through this chapter and address the summary questions at the end, you should begin to identify the key technical elements of your Exchange architecture. As with any architecture, requirements, discovery, and analysis should drive the design.

Naming Conventions

Exchange naming conventions are a standard part of an Exchange architecture. Here we discover what preferences your organization has in naming the various levels of the Exchange X.500 directory.

Organization Name, Site Name, Server Name

The organization and site names are decisions that should be made by a group of managers who can bear the responsibility if the names need to be changed. Changing the organization and site names of an Exchange organization is currently extremely difficult. Although this functionality might be introduced in later versions of the product, at this time it is important to choose a name that is appropriate and that won't need to be changed.

In today's culture of corporate buyouts and mergers, an organizational name change is not uncommon. This makes it difficult to choose an organization name that you are sure won't change. It can also be difficult to build consensus and decide on a single organization name. The U.S. Army named its organization *Organization* to avoid limiting on who could join. If the U.S. Army and U.S. Navy wanted to join Exchange organizations, and each had a unique organization name, this task would prove difficult. However, if both had organizations named *Organization*, the task would be much easier.

The next version of Exchange that will integrate with the Active Directory of Windows NT 5.0 should eliminate this dilemma. However, organizations that are implementing Exchange 5.5 today should plan their organization with a naming convention that will meet their needs for the next several years. This will allow for organizational expansion without forcing a migration to new versions of Exchange and Windows NT. It is clear that the next version of Exchange will require Windows NT 5.0 in order to take advantage of Active Directory integration. When Windows NT is available, your organization might not be at a point where it is prudent or even possible to adopt a new network operating system. You may have to exist on Windows NT 4.0 for an extended period of time.

The Exchange site name is another difficult directory parameter to change. Site names generally reflect a geographic region serviced by the Exchange site. But just as organizations can change their names, they can also move. Avoid naming sites after buildings or towns. If possible, use regions such as *Puget Sound* or *Southern Alaska.* Another approach is to name sites after the function of the office, such as *Headquarters* or *Arizona Call Center.*

Exchange server names should adhere to whatever server-naming conventions your organization incorporates. If your organization doesn't have a preexisting naming convention, the project team should create one. See the section "Existing Naming Conventions (Devices and User)" in Chapter 2, "Environment Discovery," for suggestions on server names.

Mailbox Display Names and Aliases

Mailbox display names are the normal representation of a user name and are presented in address book displays. The display name format can be the user's first name, middle initial, and last name, or portions thereof, in any order.

The mailbox display names for our sample organization are constructed from the user's first name, middle initial, and last name.

Display name: <first name> <middle initial> <last name>

Example: John B. Smith

The mailbox alias is the alias that Exchange uses to try to match the Exchange mailbox with the NT account during the addition of the account or during migration. Using the same naming convention for both the mailbox alias and the user name alias will simplify this process. In addition, in order to simplify security authentication when using POP3 or IMAP4 clients, it is prudent to match the NT account to the POP3/IMAP4 account name.

SMTP Aliases

SMTP aliases provide the unique element of the user SMTP address, as in `alias@ourdomain.com`. When migrating from an existing messaging system connected to the Internet, where users already have assigned SMTP addresses, it is easiest to keep the same format. If the format changes, things such as return addresses and business cards are no longer valid.

In our organization, the SMTP alias is the user's first initial followed by his complete last name. When two or more users have the same name, the middle initial will be used to ensure a unique SMTP address.

SMTP alias: <first initial first name><last name>@ourdomain.com

Example: `jsmith@ourdomain.com`

When migrating from an existing messaging system, where coexistence will be established, Exchange uses a connector that relies on the existing system's address format for message routing. Identify the proper address format of the existing messaging system for the Exchange users. After that, you can create an Exchange secondary proxy address for that messaging system. This will let you map an existing legacy e-mail address to a new recipient mailbox on Exchange. In this way you can preserve message delivery to Exchange users from the legacy system while at the same time changing a legacy addressing scheme that you might not be happy with.

If you were migrating from cc:Mail, you would need to support a cc:Mail connector between the Exchange system and cc:Mail. Thus, the cc:Mail address format that each of our Exchange mailboxes will be assigned will need to be identified.

cc:Mail format: <last name>, <first name> <middle initial> at <postoffice>

Example: Smith, John B at EXCHPOST1

Custom Attributes

Exchange has the underutilized ability to define custom attributes. With future versions of Exchange, this functionality will expand greatly due to integration with the Windows NT 5.0 Active Directory. Identify any custom attributes that your organization might want displayed in the address book. For example, the U.S. Navy has defined the custom attribute of *Rank* in its Exchange organization. This allows Exchange users to view and search for addresses by rank as long as the display template for addressing has been modified to display this property.

Public Folder Names

Some organizations have shared folders that are specialized and must be part of the Exchange Public Folder system. If your organization has any specialized or specific public folders, such as Corporate Policies or Benefits, specify those here.

SMTP Alias Different Than Mailbox Alias

It is possible to change the SMTP alias generation to use a different convention than the mailbox alias. To do this, open the Exchange administrator and choose Configuration | Site Addressing and then choose the Site Addressing tab. Highlight the SMTP proxy and select Edit. From here you can change not only the domain information but also the username information with the following symbols:

%%	Single percent sign
%s	Surname
%g	Given name
%i	Middle initial
%d	Display name
%m	Mailbox (default option)

%rxy   Replace all subsequent characters x with y in the username. If x==y, the character will be deleted.

Invalid characters will be removed from the name unless they are explicitly replaced with the %r formula.

In addition, if a number is added to the formula, it is possible to customize the number of characters included in the alias. For example, %1g%7s would generate an alias that included the first letter of the given name and the first seven letters of the surname.

Distribution List Names and SMTP Addresses

As with public folders, many organizations that have a messaging system also have specific groups or distribution lists that need to be incorporated into the Exchange architecture. What's more, with Exchange these distribution lists can, by default, include an SMTP address alias and can receive mail from the Internet as long as an Internet Mail Service is configured. Distribution lists that should not be accessible from the Internet should be identified. It may be appropriate, for example, to disallow Internet messages to the *Everyone* distribution list. This can be accomplished by removing the SMTP e-mail address from the properties of the distribution list. Other distribution lists, particularly those that contain Custom Recipients Internet users, may require Internet availability for their usefulness.

User Classification

User classification is very useful when you're trying to size servers for an organization. The most reliable method for sizing a server is to classify users into three groups: light, medium, and heavy. With these classifications, configure Loadsim, an Exchange utility, to see how many of each classification a candidate server can support while providing adequate performance. Hardware has become inexpensive enough, and Exchange has become efficient enough, that this tool is much less important than it used to be. However, it is still a useful exercise to provide some validation to an Exchange architecture. In addition, this is a valuable tool for determining the number of users that a specific server hardware profile can support.

Definition of Light, Medium, and Heavy Messaging Users

Different organizations have different definitions of light, medium, and heavy. Microsoft, for example, is a very heavy user of electronic mail. A light e-mail user at Microsoft might be considered a heavy e-mail user at an organization that has implemented e-mail for the first time. The reason that this is irrelevant is that Loadsim lets you define your own levels of light, medium, and heavy users and apply those definitions in varying numbers to candidate Exchange servers. As a starting point, however, we recommend that you utilize the definitions of light, medium, and heavy as defined by Loadsim. This will give your organization a baseline against other standard organizations.

Our sample organization has had cc:Mail for several years. However, it is used only for electronic mail, not calendaring or other workgroup applications. Hence, we foresee the utilization increasing among each group of users. Currently, our e-mail users are classified as shown in Table 3.1.

Table 3.1   **User Classifications★**

Type of User	Messages Sent Per Day	Messages Read Per Day
Light	5	23
Medium	14	66
Heavy	31	119

★For a much more exhaustive definition of light, medium, and heavy users, see the Loadsim white paper, published by Microsoft and available on its Web site.

Number of Light, Medium, and Heavy Users Per Physical Location

With the definition of light, medium, and heavy users complete, the next step is to put user counts at each physical location for each user type.

Again, in our sample organization, we have put numbers to the three different classifications of users, as shown in Table 3.2.

Type of Messaging Traffic and Load

It is also useful to determine the type of messaging traffic and load. By far the most common message is an electronic message. But now and again you will find organizations that have Exchange integrated with a voice-mail system, or who use Exchange as a means of moving large files (document repositories), in the form of messages, from one group to another. These types of electronic messaging have an impact on the performance and specification of your average Exchange server. Therefore, if you know that you will be supporting these types of messages or data transfer, you can design your architecture accordingly. Loadsim allows you to take a sample voice mail, for example, for use during the simulation. It's even possible to configure how often these types of messages are sent.

Administrator Classification

Exchange is a very secure messaging system, allowing you to define several levels of security for various types of administrators. Here we determine the types and numbers of Exchange administrators.

Table 3.2   **User Classifications and Head Counts**

Type of User	Percentage of Users	Seattle	Portland	Anchorage
Light	25%	50	10	40
Medium	50%	100	40	40
Heavy	25%	50	50	20

Number of Administrators and Permissions Administrators

Exchange has two major classifications of administrators: Permissions Administrators and Administrators. Permissions Administrators have total control over the objects they are assigned. They can add, delete, and modify all objects under the security context for which they are given permissions. Administrators have the same power. The only subtle, but important, difference is that Administrators can't change the permissions on an object under the security context for which they have permissions. This means that an Administrator can add, delete, and modify any parameter in the tree for which he has permissions, except the permissions parameter. This keeps administrators from being able to grant themselves permissions on a user mailbox.

Therefore, it is important to keep the population of Permissions Administrators to a small group and to assign Administrator rights to most Exchange administrators.

Mailbox Quotas and Limitations

Exchange gives you the ability to set mailbox quotas and limitations. Limitations focus mostly on the protocols that the user can use, but it can also include who the user can send e-mail to and receive e-mail from.

Mailbox Size Limits

This feature was very important before Exchange 5.5, when the Information Store had a 16 GB size limit. An organization could put 320 users on a system with a 50 MB mailbox quota, and if every user utilized the full limit of his mailbox (not taking into account the single-instance store), the store would be at its limit.
With Exchange 5.5, the Information Store has increased in total capacity to 16 TB per database, so running out of storage space is no longer a practical consideration (today!). However, disk space will always be limited. That same company that had 320 users with a 50 MB limit with Exchange 5.5 can increase the number of users to 500 given adequate CPU and memory size, but it will have to support a 25 GB information store. A 25 GB information store isn't easy to defragment or restore. Hence, organizations are still imposing mailbox quotas on their users to keep the Information Store size manageable.

With all that said, choose mailbox limits for your users. The most common size limits are around 50 MB.

Deleted Item Retention Policy

With Exchange 5.5, users can undelete items from their deleted items folder. After a user deletes an item and it's moved into the deleted items folder and the folder is emptied, the user can retrieve the message by using the undelete function. As an administrator, you need to decide if you will enable this functionality, and, more importantly, how long you will retain deleted items in the Exchange folders. Deleted messages that have been retained don't count against the user's mailbox size quota.

Enabled Protocols

By default, all protocols are enabled for each user. These protocols can be disabled individually by site or server. It is generally recommended that these protocols be disabled unless needed. Here are the protocols and the level at which they can be applied:

- POP3. Site, server, and mailbox.
- IMAP4. Site, server, and mailbox.
- LDAP. Site and server only.
- HTTP. Site and mailbox only.

Exchange Information Store Protocols

Of the protocols you choose to enable, how will they be used? It's important to understand how your organization, and the different clients supported in your organization, will interact. The first step in understanding this is to know which protocols and clients will be used, and by whom.

POP3

The vastly popular POP3 protocol is most commonly used on the Internet, with its roots extending from UNIX. Many organizations have another form of UNIX for users who use POP3 clients. Many times, the easiest way to migrate those users is to provide them with a POP3-accessible mailbox in the Exchange organization.

IMAP4

IMAP4 is the replacement protocol for POP3. IMAP4 is the natural evolution of POP3, although it is a different protocol from POP3. allowing for an industry-standard protocol that has the features that today's e-mail users demand. IMAP4 allows for private folders and the traversing of folders on a server-based mailbox. POP3 was a message download protocol only.

LDAP

In addition to requiring access to messaging and folders on the server, messaging applications need access to the directory. Borrowing from the X.500 family of protocols, LDAP is an industry-standard protocol that lets a POP3 or IMAP4 client read from and write to the directory.

Web (HTML)

With the operating system's UI moving in the direction of HTML, Exchange is no different. A common tool, the Web browser, allows users to access their mailbox via HTTP through the Internet Information Server. Outlook Web access looks, and somewhat feels, like the Outlook application. This is a very powerful feature, not only for UNIX users who are tired of POP3 and who have a browser, but also for roaming and remote users who have access to the Internet.

Although Outlook Web Access is an excellent tool for leveraging Exchange across a broader set of operating systems, you should be cautious about distributing access to a large number of users. This is due to the architecture of Outlook Web Access. The browser on the desktop provides access to the server but doesn't assume a large amount of the application's processing impact. Instead, the processing occurs on the Internet Information Server that executes the Active Server Page script that builds the Outlook Web Access view. Consequently, the server might suffer a performance hit if a large number of users access Outlook Web Access simultaneously.

Public Folder Strategy

Public folders are best implemented in a premeditated hierarchy. If the public folder system grows unchecked, its usefulness will diminish with each new folder created. To keep the public folder system efficient and well-tuned, a hierarchy needs to be created and maintained, and policies should be put into place for the creation, replication, and deletion of public folders.

How to Group Public Folders

Public folders are best grouped from a general to a more granular scale. This way, not only is information easier to locate, but permissions are more manageable (see Figure 3.1).

With the top-level public folders representing each location in the organization, replication can be more easily managed. A group of users from Portland may be working on a project with a group of users from Seattle, but that project folder can be replicated between sites on an as-needed basis. This hierarchy will reduce the overall number of public folders that are replicated.

Public Folder Permissions

Public folder permissions can be set by both the Exchange Administrator and the client. However, the Exchange administrator determines who can create top-level public folders. It is recommended that the list of users who can create top-level public folders be limited to the permissions administrators. These administrators can in turn define who in each tree off the root can grant permissions on their specific public folder tree.

Public Folder Replication Policy

As with a public folder hierarchy policy, a strict policy should be defined for the public folder replication policy. Even though users can't configure public folder replication from the client, often in organizations that have several administrators, public folder replication can be difficult to control. With Exchange 5.5, it became easier to limit who could configure public folder replication. A policy should be put in place that requires administrators or users to request that a public folder be replicated. An administrator with proper permissions would then replicate the requested public folder.

Public Folder Affinity

Public folder affinity allows clients at one site to reach out across the WAN to another site and search for the contents of a public folder. Whether or not this capability is configured depends on the amount of available WAN bandwidth and RPC connectivity and whether your organization needs this functionality.

For public folders that are rarely accessed but that change often, public folder affinity can actually save bandwidth. However, once public folder affinity is enabled for a site, it is enabled for all folders at that site. With public folder affinity enabled, public folders that are being accessed often from another site should be replicated to that site. The problem is that there is no easy way to monitor public folder activity from users at another site. These are but some of the things you should consider when deciding whether to set up public folder affinity.

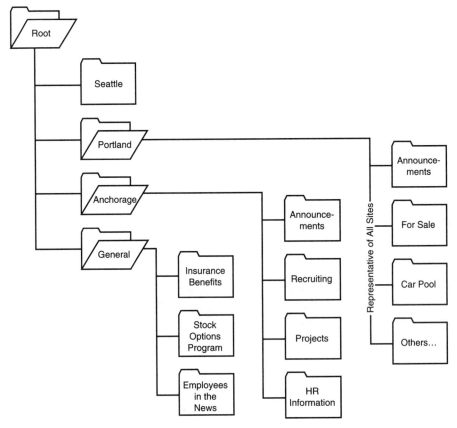

Figure 3.1   Public folders.

Distribution List Policy

Distribution list policy, like public folder policy, is something new to many organizations. Also as with public folders, distribution lists need structure in order to remain manageable.

Distribution List Structure

Distribution lists can be nested, and it is with this nesting that we build a distribution hierarchy. At the top of the distribution list hierarchy is a global group, such as Everyone. Other groups are the only members of this Everyone group. Usually, these Everyone member groups are departmental or geographical. These groups contain groups within the department, or individual users. If a user is a member of multiple groups, and both groups are sent a piece of e-mail, the user will receive only a single message. For example, in Figure 3.2, if a message is sent to the Everyone group, the user Julie Hope will receive only one copy.

The Exchange architecture should include a distribution list structure.

Distribution List Creation Policy

Outlook and Exchange clients can't create public distribution lists. Public distribution lists must be created by an Exchange administrator. After they are created, one or more users can be designated owner of the distribution list and can manage its population. A distribution list creation policy and process should be developed and included in the Exchange architecture.

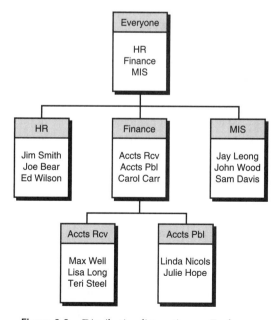

Figure 3.2   Distribution list nesting on Exchange.

Distribution List SMTP Address Issues

As mentioned earlier, distribution lists by default can be mailed to the Internet. This may be undesirable for most distribution lists. It is necessary for distribution lists that contain custom recipients, which are Internet addresses. The custom recipient can't respond to the distribution list if it doesn't have a valid SMTP address.

Custom Recipient

Different organizations use custom recipients in different ways. They are almost always used during coexistence. Other organizations continue to use them for contractors, customers, and vendors. Nevertheless, a policy and procedure for the management of custom recipients should be defined in the Exchange architecture.

Custom Recipient Creation Policy

Unlike distribution lists, Outlook and Exchange clients can't create custom recipients. The Exchange administrator is used to create publicly accessible custom recipients. A procedure should be defined for the creation of custom recipients.

Summary of Questions for Exchange Requirement Gathering

Following is a summary of the questions that should be asked regarding gathering requirements for the Exchange architecture. Each of these questions addresses a specific topic raised in this chapter.

- **Exchange Organization Name**

  Question   What Exchange organization name will be used?

- **Exchange Site Names**

  Question   Although the sites have not yet been defined, what general theme will be used when naming sites?

- **Exchange Server Names**

  Question   Does your organization have a server naming policy that the Exchange servers can adhere to? If not, define an Exchange server naming policy.

- **Display Name Format**

  Question   What is the display name format?

- **Alias Name Format**

  Question   What is the alias name format?

- **SMTP addresses**

  Question   What is the SMTP address format?

- **Foreign Messaging System Address Format**

  Question   What is the address format of the messaging system with which you will coexist?

- **Custom Attributes**

  Question   Are there any custom attributes that your organization would want displayed in the address book?

- **Public Folder Names**

  Question   Should any specific public folders be created upon the initial configuration of the Exchange organization?

- **Light, Medium, and Heavy Users Definition**

  Questions   What is the messaging utilization of a light e-mail user?

  What is the messaging utilization of a medium e-mail user?

  What is the messaging utilization of a heavy e-mail user?

- **Numbers of Light, Medium, and Heavy Users**

  Questions   How many light e-mail users does your organization have?

  How many medium e-mail users does your organization have?

  How many heavy e-mail users does your organization have?

- **Type of Messaging and Load**

  Questions   Will any special applications be supported by Exchange? If so, would it be possible to get an average sample of one of these applications' messages?

- **Numbers of Permissions Administrators and Administrators**

  Questions   Who will the administrator be?

  How many Administrators will there be in each location?

  How many, if any, Permissions Administrators will there be in each location? (You must have at least one Permissions Administrator.)

- **Mailbox Quotas**

  Question   What mailbox quotas will you impose?

- **Protocols**

  Questions   Enable or disable POP3?

  Enable or disable IMAP4?

  Enable or disable LDAP? (Site and server only, not mailbox.)

  Enable or disable HTTP? (Site and mailbox only, not server.)

- **POP3**

  Question   Will you support POP3 access from the Internet?

- **IMAP4**

  Questions   If you are enabling IMAP4, which IMAP4 client do you plan on supporting? Will you support IMAP4 access from the Internet?

- **LDAP**

  Question   If you are enabling LDAP, which LDAP client do you plan on supporting?

- **HTML**

  Question If you are enabling HTML, will you support the browser on the Internet, or just the intranet?

- **Public Folders**

  Question What public folder hierarchy best suits your organization and how its users work together?

- **Public Folder Permissions**

  Questions Who are the Exchange Permissions Administrators?

  Who are the Exchange Administrators?

- **Public Folder Replication**

  Question Who will be responsible for the configuration of public folder replication?

- **Public Folder Affinity**

  Questions Will you enable public folder affinity between sites? If so, which sites?

- **Distribution List Structure**

  Question What is the most useful method of grouping users into distribution lists?

- **Distribution List Creation**

  Question Who will be responsible for creating distribution lists?

- **Distribution List SMTP Addresses**

  Question Which distribution lists will be able to receive messages from the Internet?

- **Custom Recipient Creation**

  Question Who will be responsible for managing custom recipients?

Questions for Third-Party Services

Any third-party services that will be included in the initial implementation of Exchange should be included as an element of the Exchange architecture. The following is an initial list of third-party solutions you should gather information for.

- **Third-Party Services**

  Questions What third-party services are you planning on implementing along with Exchange?

  Paging?

  Faxing?

  Virus protection?

  Electronic forms?

4

The Project Team and Project Phases

T HE PEOPLE WHO COMPRISE YOUR TEAM as you deliver your Exchange project are critical to the success of your deployment. Without the right people, you will have a difficult time successfully completing your Exchange implementation. In addition, it is important to understand the project phases, as well as how the team member map fits into each phase and which team member is ultimately responsible for delivery in each phase. This chapter examines the roles of the team members and maps those roles into each project phase.

Who Should Be on an Exchange Team?

This section defines the roles and responsibilities of the Exchange project team and describes the involvement of the team members throughout the project life cycle. Defining the right team for the Exchange architecture project is very important to a successful Exchange implementation. Without all the right members, it is likely that the project will be less successful—usually in communication and coordination with the organization. A project team without executive sponsorship runs the risk of designing an architecture that doesn't meet the needs as perceived by management. A team that doesn't include a representative of the infrastructure group might not clearly understand the topology and therefore design a solution that isn't optimized for the network infrastructure.

It is possible that one person might represent several of these team roles or that several persons make up one of the roles, depending on the organization's size and structure. In either case, make sure that all the project team members understand their roles on the team.

It is important to include all the team members throughout the project life cycle. This doesn't mean that every team member will participate in all the meetings. It means that they will be aware of their involvement and the process throughout the project.

The members of the Exchange team should include the following:

- Executive Sponsor
- Project Manager
- Migration Team Lead
- Exchange Architect
- Exchange Administrator
- Trainer

There may be additional members on the team, but these are the key jobs that need to be addressed. This chapter examines the roles that these people play during the project.

Executive Sponsor

The executive sponsor of the Exchange project team is the team member who has executive buy-off for the project. The executive sponsor usually either initiates the Exchange project or is brought in for approval at the outset. Although the executive sponsor won't be involved in the day-to-day design decisions, he will be responsible for the following actions:

- **Project charter.** The direction and scope statement for Exchange in the organization.
- **Project budget and timeline.** The budget for the hardware, software, implementation staff, support staff, and rollout timeline.
- **Feature set review.** The final review of the feature set decisions.
- **Environment restriction decisions.** Approval for the restrictions placed on the Exchange environment, such as mailbox limits and the scope of data migrated from legacy messaging systems.

It is critical that this role be identified and filled from the very beginning of the project. Even if executive approval isn't necessary for budget or staff, the scope of the Exchange project must be communicated to and approved by the management team. The executive sponsor role isn't usually filled by a technical person, but more often someone with a good business perspective of the organization's messaging needs.

Project Manager

The project manager for the Exchange architecture project is the linchpin of the process and the team. This role can be filled with one or more people. Sometimes the responsibilities are divided between geographic locations or between a consulting organization and the client organization. Although sometimes it gets more complicated with more than one project manager, the responsibilities for this role are as follows:

- **Project plan**. Plan for all phases and processes of the Exchange architecture and implementation.
- **Communication plan**. A plan that details the communication schedule and content to the end-users, help desk staff, administrative staff, training staff project team members, and the executive sponsor.
- **Project status meetings**. Regular meetings for communication of project status and "to-dos."
- **Coordination of hardware, software, and staff resources**. Overall management of all resources for the project, even if another role has budgetary or implementation responsibility for the resource.
- **Project timeline and rollout schedule**. Managing the project to the project plan timeline and driving responsibility for the rollout groups and schedule.
- **Interaction with the executive sponsor**. Point contact for the executive sponsor on status, budget, and decision points.
- **Change management**. Management of changes to scope and schedule.

Migration Team Lead

The Exchange migration team lead is the person who leads the migration team throughout the migration process. This person is responsible for communicating process or architectures to the migration team, clarifying any questions that arise during the migration, and communicating any technical or process difficulties to the project manager.

The migration team lead plays a role similar to that of the project manager. In some cases, this role may even be filled by the project manager. On larger projects, the differentiation between the project manager and the migration team lead is clearer: The project manager is focused on the entire project and on interfacing with the client throughout the project, and the migration team lead focuses on the migration process and on interfacing with the other members of the migration team. This collaborative interaction between the two roles allows for more oversight and management of process during the migration.

Exchange Architect

The Exchange architect is the person or persons responsible for the design of the Exchange server and client environment. The individual in this role will use knowledge of the Exchange architecture process (as described in this book), business requirements, and technical information and requirements gathered from the project team to design the Exchange solution.

Exchange Administrator

The Exchange administrator will administer and monitor the Exchange environment once it is deployed. It is important that the Exchange administrator be involved throughout the design and implementation process so that he understands the environment that he will be administering. This person will most likely maintain the current messaging environment and will fill both the Exchange administrator role and administer the well-known services of the organization in which Exchange is being implemented. Well-known services can be classified as technology services that are standard elements of an organizational infrastructure. These services include both passive and active network components such as switches, routers, and hubs, as well as Windows NT domain controllers, standard application servers, and file and print servers.

Well-Known Services Administrator

Well-known services as they relate to an Exchange project are file and print services, security and authentication services, name resolution services, desktop design services, and support services. All of these services play integral roles in the Exchange architecture process, and their input and coordination is vital to project success. The well-known services administrator is the LAN administrator who will administer these systems on a daily basis.

File and Print Services

File and print services provide a backbone for the client rollout. The networking client and protocols that have been established on the desktop usually originate from the file and print services connection requirements. Additionally, the file and print services team has most likely set the standards for backup software and procedures and other server standards within the organization. The file and print services role in the Exchange architecture is to provide information about the current networking connectivity environment, coordinate with the placement of the Exchange client source files, help with decisions regarding the network storage of Exchange client files (such as personal address book files and personal store files), and coordinate server decisions between the Exchange servers and the file and print servers.

Security and Authentication Services

Closely tied to the file and print services are the security and authentication services. These services include networking client authentication, firewall implementations, security standards for Internet and interorganizational communication, and desktop security standards. These services are critical to many of the Exchange architecture decisions, such as Internet Mail Service design and implementation, single authentication scheme for the client, and encryption design for the Exchange environment.

Name Resolution Services

Name resolution services includes both NetBIOS name resolution services and host name resolution services. Because the initial implementation of NT into an organization has often been at a workgroup level, these services are often fragmented between operational groups. As organizations prepare for NT 5.0, unification of the name resolution services becomes more important. Whether these services reside in one group or more than one group, name resolution is important to the Exchange architecture process because of client-to-server name resolution, Internet mail host resolution, and connector resolution.

Desktop Design Services

Desktop design services play a large role in the design of the Exchange client implementation. This service team has the history of the desktop environment, the technical specifications for the desktop environment, and usually also a good idea of the user technical and resilience levels. Because the Exchange client is so tightly integrated with other desktop applications, these services are key to the successful design and rollout of the messaging client environment.

Support Services

Support services teams such as the help desk team or user group champions are vital to the Exchange project team for two reasons—proactive communication to the end-user, and support requirements for the migration process and architected environment. Involving the support services team throughout the entire design process instead of just before the client rollout will help them be more successful in supporting the users. It will also provide the design team with critical user information.

Infrastructure Architects

The Exchange server design and the network infrastructure are tightly integrated, so including the network infrastructure team (including the infrastructure architects) throughout the project is critical. The infrastructure team will be responsible for providing network utilization statistics, network topology information, and traffic data pattern statistics. This team might also assist in implementing Exchange monitoring tools and assist with the correct placement of the Exchange servers. Most organizations are growing and changing their network links, hardware, and redundant paths because of the increased reliance on network performance in organizations today. Working together, the Exchange architects and network infrastructure architects can plan for the current and future direction of the network and messaging infrastructure.

Project Phases

Now that we have reviewed the members of the team, we will examine the phases that people go through when executing an Exchange project. These phases include the following:

- Architecture
- Lab
- Pilot
- Migration
- Training
- Wrap-up

Architecture

In the architecture phase of the Exchange project, the Exchange architect works with the well-known services teams and infrastructure team to gather requirements and develop the Exchange architecture. The first step is to develop a feature set list and environment controls list for review by the executive sponsor. After approval from the executive team, the Exchange environment is designed to meet the requirements and features. Once the architecture is drafted, it should be reviewed by the entire project team and revised as appropriate.

Lab

The Exchange architect and the migration team lead pair up for the lab phase of the Exchange architecture process cycle. This phase gives the architect the chance to see Exchange working in the environment and gives the migration team lead the chance to test the migration process. It is important in this phase to get an idea of how long the migration process will take, as well as what kind of errors you should expect for the migration data. The best way to get this information is to replicate the current environment on a lab server and perform a test migration.

Once the lab tests have been performed to the satisfaction of the architect and migration team lead, the results need to be gathered and the architecture revised as necessary. The Exchange architect takes the lead in this portion of the lab phase.

Pilot

The pilot phase is the gray area between lab and production. At the time of the pilot, the Exchange servers should be built and tested as specified by the architecture with no expectation of rebuild between the pilot and production rollouts. The migration process should be finalized, and the end-user communication and training plans should be ready for execution. The migration team lead has primary responsibility for this phase of the process. This is of primary importance so that the migration team lead can prepare for the implementation of Exchange in the production environment. Through experience gained in leading the pilot effort, the migration team lead can refine and tune the production implementation plan. In addition, the Exchange architect, the well-known services teams, and the infrastructure team will be greatly involved.

Once the pilot group has been selected, the communication, training, and migration plans are executed. The migration team lead gathers results from the end-users and the migration team and delivers those results to the project team. At this point, there should be only minor changes to the Exchange architecture (if any). The Exchange architect will make those modifications.

Migration

The migration phase is led by the migration team lead in close conjunction with the Exchange administrator monitoring and maintaining the Exchange environment. This is usually a repetitive and tiresome phase. It is critical that the migration team lead continue to gather results and feedback from the end-users and the migration. In most cases, changes shouldn't be made to the architecture process or migration process, because too many variables are being changed in this phase. If a change is necessary, the entire project team should review the requirements and the suggested change.

Training

The project manager has primary responsibility for the training phase. This phase is really continuous throughout the project, because there are several types of training: administrator, support staff, and end-user. The project manager works with the Exchange architect, desktop design services team, and migration team lead to define the training needed. Once these are defined, the project manager manages the training development and delivery.

Training can, and should, be implemented in several different ways. For example, you may want to send the support staff to a formalized Exchange class at a local authorized training center. Following that, you might conduct a customized class to train them on your specific environment. For end-users, you can provide organized group classes or online help deployed via the Web.

Here are some of the key types of training:

- Formal classroom training
- In-house group training
- One-on-one training
- Online self-paced training
- Customized training

Your decision as to what type of training to utilize might be affected by the size of your training budget, the distributed nature of your end-user community, or the pre-existing skill level of your support staff. The key is to realize that there are many different options for you to choose from.

Wrap-Up

Once the migration process has ended and the environment is stabilized, the project manager leads the wrap-up phase of the project. This phase is a chance to review the project process, gather architecture requirements for the next phase, and celebrate team success. During the wrap-up phase, the executive sponsor should be involved for a project review, as well as a summary of the budget, timeline, and successes and failures. Project failures are just as important to examine and document as the successes. Looking at failures will help project team members deliver a better product or solution the next time around.

Figure 4.1 shows the project phases and the Exchange project team primary and secondary involvement levels throughout the life cycle. The project manager will lead throughout the project and will look to the identified primary and secondary roles to be the contacts for each phase. Note that the project manager is identified as having primary responsibility across all phases of the project. In the phases of the project where other people are also identified as having primary responsibility, there should be a collaborative sharing of responsibility.

	Architecture	Lab	Pilot	Migration	Training	Wrap-up
Executive sponsor	░					
Project manager	▓				▓	▓
Exchange architect	▓	▓	░		░	
Exchange administrator				░		
Migration team lead		░	▓	▓	░	
Infrastructure team						
File and print services	░					
Security and authentication services	░					
Name resolution services	░					
Desktop design services	░				░	
Support services			░	░		

Legend
Primary responsibility
Secondary responsibility

Figure 4.1   Project phases and primary and secondary involvement levels.

5

How to Sell Exchange as a Messaging and Workgroup Solution

I N ADDITION TO BEING AN EXCELLENT enterprise messaging solution, Microsoft Exchange is also evolving into a solid collaborative computing platform. Once the technical team has identified Exchange as the appropriate solution to meet the organization's collaborative computing needs, the next step most often taken is to begin planning the architectural design and implementation of Exchange. While this may initially seem logical, it is actually not the best step to take next. It is necessary to first build consensus with the business teams before moving forward with design and implementation. Building consensus can often be the most difficult process in the entire project. Although business unit managers usually agree that the existing messaging system is inadequate, they often can't agree on the needs and requirements to be addressed by the new system.

The most common pitfall when trying to build consensus with the business unit managers is to sell Exchange as simply an upgrade to the existing electronic mail system. Exchange may have been brought into the organization as a tactical fix for an ailing mail system, but it is critical that the project team sell Exchange to the internal customers as a collaborative computing platform. Exchange has the potential to provide robust workgroup solutions to users throughout the company.

Exchange lies at the heart of a collaborative computing component architecture. When fully implemented, this architecture can provide substantial gains in productivity by workgroup teams and can extend the cost/benefit ratio of an Exchange Server implementation. It is important that the project team have a clear and precise understanding of each element of the architecture in order for the project to be successful.

The different elements in the collaborative computing component architecture are Exchange Server, Internet Information Server, Outlook, Outlook Web Access, and Internet Explorer.

All of the elements in the collaborative computing architecture should be implemented in the context of a collaborative computing best practices framework. This framework should include the following:

- Organizational integration and collaboration techniques
- Common organization document formats
- Document storage locations, such as a Web server directory, Exchange public folders, and a file server directory
- Conflict resolution processes to be followed when multiple parties modify the same document simultaneously
- Contact information for technical staff members who are responsible for the collaborative computing platform, such as the Exchange help desk, network administrators, mail administrators, and IT architecture group

In addition to the high-level collaborative computing component architecture just described, there are many benefits that help make Exchange Server an excellent collaborative computing platform:

- Extensibility and accessibility of the Exchange directory
- The integration that Exchange has with Internet Information Server
- Integration with Windows NT security
- Integration with the Microsoft Office suite of applications
- Data replication and control features
- The server Event Service, which allows applications to run on the server even while client computers aren't connected. The Event Service is the main element that lets Exchange be a true workflow engine

Accessibility to the Exchange Directory

With Microsoft Exchange versions 4.0, 5.0, and 5.5, the directory is an integrated part of the product. With the next version of Exchange, the directory will be integrated into the operating system as the Active Directory is deployed with Windows NT Server 5.0. In both cases, the directory can contain large amounts of data about the users of the Exchange system and can be easily accessed.

Exchange Administrator's Raw Mode

An excellent way to explore the database schema of the Exchange directory and to see what the schema of the Active Directory looks like is to run the Exchange Administrator program in *raw mode*. To start the administrator in raw mode, choose Start | Run and execute the command `admin.exe /r` from the `exchsrvr\bin` subdirectory on the Exchange server (type `c:\exchsrvr\bin\admin /r`).

Once the Exchange directory has been migrated to Windows NT 5.0 and integrated into the Active directory, you can access and modify the directory and manage users by using a snap-in in the Microsoft Management Console. In the meantime, Exchange can be administered by using the Exchange Administrator program or by using scripting and command-prompt access. It can also be accessed and modified by using CDO (Collaborative Data Objects) and ASP (Active Server Pages), as shown in Figure 5.1, and by using Exchange clients, such as Microsoft Outlook. In addition, the Exchange directory and the Active Directory in Windows NT 5.0 are Lightweight Directory Access Protocol (LDAP) version 3-compliant and can support read and write access from any LDAP client.

Because the directory can be easily accessed and manipulated, it is an excellent repository for data about users in the organization. The directory can store phone numbers, pager numbers, and information about the reporting hierarchy. In addition to all of the standard fields, or attributes in the directory, 10 fields in the directory can be customized and populated with additional data about users in the organization.

In Chapter 2, "Environment Discovery," we discussed establishing standard naming conventions for your organization. One of the most difficult tasks of planning and implementing Exchange Server is gaining consensus on a standard naming convention for objects in the Exchange directory. Organizations typically have inconsistent or cryptic naming conventions for the objects and users in the legacy mail system. The implementation of Exchange is an excellent event to help drive a reconfiguration and standardization of the organization's naming conventions.

Exchange can seamlessly handle multiple namespace conventions for users, thus making the transition easier. For example, your organization may have adopted a nonstandard naming convention for SMTP addresses. Exchange lets you define multiple SMTP address aliases for individuals. For example, a user may have an existing SMTP address of `dhauger@mailrelay.smtp1.excell.com`. You want to change this to something easier, such as `dhauger@excell.com`, but you don't want to reject mail that is delivered to the old address. In Exchange, you can create multiple address aliases for recipients, thus providing for down-level integration and for modification to a new address space.

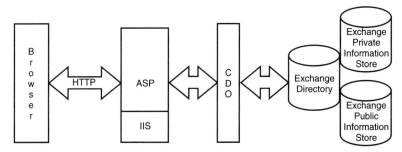

Figure 5.1   The Exchange directory can be accessed and manipulated by using CDO imbedded in an ASP page.

Despite Exchange's flexibility, it is often the case that users in the organization have grown accustomed to the existing naming convention and will resist the change to the new system. Elsewhere in this book we will discuss methodologies for implementing a new naming convention while at the same time keeping users happy.

Integration with IIS and Security

As Exchange has migrated from a proprietary platform to a collaborative messaging solution based on Internet standards, Exchange and Microsoft Internet Information Server have become more integrated. The Outlook Web access component is supported using ASP pages that run only on IIS. The Exchange public folder system can now be accessed by using HTTP or NNTP. The Internet mail server functions as a relay host for all messaging clients.

In Exchange 6.0, Internet standards integration continues. The most evident change in version 6.0 is that the default connection type utilized between servers, even servers in the same site, will be SMTP. As part of the move toward implementing SMTP as a connection protocol between servers, the Internet Mail Service has been tuned to provide more efficient transfer of data, including directory information. Initial tests indicate that the SMTP connector will be more efficient than the standard RPC Site Connector.

The move toward standards and the integration with Internet Information Server helps make Exchange an excellent collaborative computing platform. The goal of a collaborative computing platform should be to facilitate the exchange of information between individuals or workgroups to help people do their jobs better and more efficiently. Exchange can achieve this goal in part because of the tight integration with IIS. At the most basic level, users can access their mailboxes using a Web browser. Public folders can also be accessed using a Web browser. Beyond this basic functionality, Exchange can be extended to support the most complex intranet/Internet applications.

Security

Security is always a concern when you're implementing an enterprise-wide application such as Microsoft Exchange. The project team must address the security of the server application, the security of the client application, and the security of data sent from and received by the server. When defining the services on Exchange, you must address all the elements of security. Because of the tight integration that Exchange has with Windows NT, the security of your Exchange implementation depends heavily on the security of your Windows NT domain.

Every Exchange architecture project should start with an examination of the existing Windows NT domain structure. It may be necessary to modify the existing structure in order to address new security issues that arise with the implementation of Exchange. The most typical domain model implemented under Windows NT 4.0 is a single master domain with a resource domain for Exchange servers and a second domain for other resources, such as computer accounts, SQL Server, and other application servers. In Windows NT 5.0, organizational units within a single domain may replace the resource domains.

By placing the Exchange server machine accounts in a separate domain or in a separate organizational unit, you can segment security between network administrators who have access to all resources on the corporate network and mail administrators whose primary function is to add, delete, and modify mailboxes. Appropriate domain models for different organizations are addressed in Chapter 7, "Design of Associated Services." However, if you are implementing Exchange 5.0 and there are less than 100,000 resources and users in your organization, it is likely that you will configure a single domain with organizational units for Exchange servers and separate organizational units for other resources, such as applications servers (see Figure 5.2).

The integrated security model of Exchange and Windows NT can be a selling point when positioning Exchange as a collaborative computing platform. Because of integrated security, it is possible for users to log into Windows NT once and gain access to all workgroup applications based on Exchange without having to provide credentials used for authentication multiple times. Internet Explorer provides authenticated Web access to Exchange-based workgroup applications based from multiple types of client platforms, including Macintosh and UNIX.

Server Security

As noted in Chapter 2, Exchange Server security is based on the Windows NT security model. Network users with domain accounts can be granted and/or denied specific rights and permissions on objects in the Exchange directory tree. Special attention needs to be paid to the way that permissions are configured in the directory tree. All permissions configured at the organization, site, and configuration container levels in an organization will be inherited below that level. In addition, permissions can be assigned at the site or configuration level without previously being assigned at the organization level.

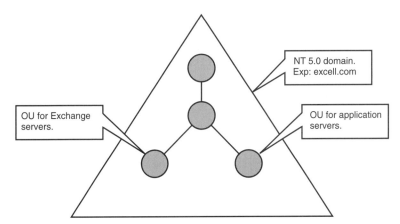

Figure 5.2   In a Windows NT 5.0 domain structure, the most likely scenario will include a single domain with organizational units (OU) for Exchange servers and separate OUs for other application servers.

User Security

User security is another compelling reason to migrate to Exchange. Since each Exchange recipient mailbox and resource is assigned a specific Windows NT domain account as a primary security account, it is possible to track all events, control access, and assign permissions by network user name. This is an advantage even if the organization that is deploying Exchange doesn't use Windows NT as a primary network operating system. Since the security of Exchange is integrated with the Windows NT operating system, all security events are logged in the event viewer and can be monitored via SNMP if desired.

One-Stop Management of Directory Information

Since the directory for Exchange is replicated and distributed, it is easy to manage directory modification. Whether your organization is implementing versions of Exchange prior to Windows NT 5.0 and Exchange 6.0 or implementing Exchange 6.0 with integration to the active directory, all the attributes for any specific recipient or resource can be managed from a single administrative interface. That interface can be the Exchange Administration application, Microsoft Management console, or a custom-built Web application accessing the directory via LDAP.

Sample Application Suggestions

As the number of Exchange seats deployed grows, so does the number of applications designed to provide collaborative computing functionality on top of the Exchange platform. Many of these applications are available for download for free from the Internet. A large number of applications can be found at `http://www.microsoft.com/ithome/resource/exchange`. This site has sample scripts to be utilized with the Exchange Scripting Agent, as well as Exchange Routing Objects. Routing Objects are a set of COM components that run on top of the Exchange Event Service. In addition, there are applications that enable Web-based modification of the Exchange directory, applications for managing help desk requests, and applications that manage authenticated and anonymous logon to an Exchange server via the Web.

Here are some other application suggestions:

- Expense reports
- Travel requests
- Vacation requests
- Purchase order requests
- Corporate library management
- Project management (integrated tasks with MS Project tasks)
- Status reports (integrated with tasks)
- Timesheets

You Already Have the Distributed Platform

One of the best arguments for convincing organizations to use Exchange for collaborative computing is that Exchange provides a distributed, organization-wide platform. Exchange is the "plumbing" that can be leveraged to distribute information and applications to every member of the organization. Two main sets of data are replicated throughout the Exchange organization: directory data, and public folder contents and hierarchy.

Directory Replication

The Exchange directory is a replicated and distributed directory. Replication of the directory between servers within a site is automatic. Replication between sites can be configured to be automatic or manual. However, it is always recommended that the directory be replicated automatically between sites. Depending on the replication cycle, you may chose to occasionally perform a manual replication cycle. Changes to the directory can be affected on one server in a site. Those changes will then be replicated to all servers in the organization in a controlled manner. Since the directory contains current details about all the recipients and resources in an organization, it is an excellent source of information for collaborative computing applications.

By using the Exchange directory to distribute information about recipients to distributed applications, you don't need to build a replication method into the applications themselves. For example, you could construct an application that uses a recipient's pager PIN number to send an alpha page over the Internet. First, the custom attributes for the user are modified to include a field called Pager PIN. Next, an ASP page is constructed that queries the Exchange directory for that PIN by using CDO or LDAP. The ASP page then takes that PIN and constructs a *send form* that sends an alphanumeric page to the recipient. The ASP page can be run against any Exchange server in the organization, no matter which server hosts the recipient's mailbox. This is because once directory replication is configured between sites, the directory on each server will always contain information on each user as current as the last completed replication cycle.

Public Folder Replication

Public folder contents can be configured for replication to every server in an organization or to specific servers in an organization. The public name space of the public folder hierarchy is automatically replicated to every public folder server in the Exchange directory tree. Changes made to items in public folders are replicated to all other replicas of the public folder within the organization. Changes made to the folder properties or to the public folder hierarchy are replicated to all public folder servers in the organization, even if they don't contain a replica of the folder.

Public folder replication provides an excellent method of distributing collaborative computing applications. You can build a script, publish it in a public folder, and then replicate that folder throughout your organization. In that way, collaborative computing applications become available to every member of the organization in a timely and controlled manner.

The replication of public folders can be scheduled in two different ways. The public information store on each Exchange public folder server can be configured to pull replicas from other public folder servers at a specified time each day, or each specific public folder can be configured to replicate to selected public folder servers at a specified time each day. This flexibility in replication scheduling helps minimize the impact that public folder content replication has on the network.

It is important to note, however, that the actual method of replication of public folder data is identical whether the replication schedule has been configured from the "pull" interface or the "push" interface. These two ways of configuring replication are essentially different administrative views of the same scheduling matrix. In Exchange versions 5.0 and later, administrators can limit access to public folder replication schedules by administrators who don't have access to the folder home server. This prevents an unauthorized administrator from replicating public folders to servers where replicas shouldn't be located.

Server Capabilities

Exchange 5.5 included the Exchange Event Service and the capability to build and deploy active scripts for both private and public folders. The Scripting Agent and Event Service are the two applications that provide this functionality. The Scripting Agent is a script engine that executes scripts that have been configured for specific folders and provides CDO session, folder, and message objects to the script. The Event Service is a server-based Windows NT service that monitors events in folders on Exchange servers.

Data Replication Control and Tuning

One of the key components of making Exchange scalable is its capability to adapt to many diverse environments—not only diverse in protocols and user demands, but also in network architecture and capacity. Data replication between sites, of both public folders and the directory, gives Exchange administrators some control over network utilization.

Public folders can be tuned to replicate at an interval suitable to both the network capacity and the users' needs for timely information.

Parallel Event Handling

The Exchange Event Service processes events in parallel. In other words, when the Event Service is processing events against items in the information store, it doesn't block access to items by other processes. This means that a workflow script may be in the middle of processing an item, and the item could still be deleted by a folder assistant rule before the script completed the process. This limitation is important to note when you're building applications. There is no guarantee, especially in a high-volume situation, that the Event Service will be able to process all the items that enter a folder.

Additionally, intersite directory replication can be configured to take place at times more prone to light usage or higher levels of available bandwidth.

It is important to keep in mind that regardless of the interval between replication cycles, changes to public folders, public folder hierarchy, and the directory will replicate and will consume bandwidth. It's with the replication schedule, and tuning that schedule, that Exchange administrators can begin to tune intersite messaging system consumption.

Site-to-Site Tuning

Exchange connectors pass messages between sites over their respective messaging protocols. These messaging protocols themselves are encapsulated into network transport protocols. When you're tuning site-to-site traffic, the messaging and transport protocols are points of focus.

When connectivity and stability problems occur with an X.400 connector that is running over TCP/IP, you start with the transport protocol, TCP/IP, and try to create stability there. By manipulating the sliding-window protocol of TCP/IP, it might be possible to make the connection more stable.

When connectivity and stability problems occur with an X.400 connector that is running over TP4 or X.25, the transport protocol doesn't have runnable parameters. Therefore, Exchange lets you manipulate its own sliding-window protocol. By manipulating the sliding-window protocol of the X.400 connector, it might be possible to make the connector more stable.

6

Design of the Exchange Server Environment

THIS CHAPTER COVERS THE ELEMENTS of the Exchange server architecture, focusing on the pieces of the architecture that can't be changed after they are installed. This chapter also focuses on elements that are integral to an organization's Exchange servers communicating with one another. Specifically, we will examine the steps you need to take when determining how to establish your Exchange sites, how to choose the connectors to use for connectivity between sites, and which services to deploy once you have your Exchange architecture in place.

Determining the configuration of the sites within your Exchange organization can be challenging. Should you divide sites according to administrative or geographic boundaries? When choosing a connector, should you use X.400, SMTP, or the standard site connector? Should your connector topology be a star, a partial mesh, or a full mesh? How do you decide when to migrate from one to another? Once Exchange is deployed, which services should you activate, and which services will provide the most benefit for your users? Should you implement LDAP and IMAP4 access to the directory and folders? We will address these questions and more in this chapter. In addition, we will walk through developing a public-folder strategy and talk about replication configurations.

General Design Approach

The approach for the Exchange architecture is to define a solution that meets business requirements, technical requirements, today's needs, and tomorrow's plans. It's too often the case that one of these four ingredients is overlooked during the design process. In the following sections, specific issues concerning each of the four areas are addressed in the context of the architecture process, and decision matrices are presented as a guide to the design process.

Key Decision Points

The backbone of the design process is defining the key decision points and designing to those points. Many of the limiting factors for an Exchange implementation aren't technical. They may be procedural or organizational issues. The key to designing to actual needs is to find both the technical and non-technical decision points. Here are some non–technical decision factors:

- The administrative division of the environment
- User expectations of performance and limits
- Security policies
- Administrative assistant roles for executive support

It is critical to identify all the non-technical factors before proceeding with the architecture.

Technical factors also drive the decision-making process as you design your architecture. These factors may include the following:

- Distributed administration due to network bandwidth limitations
- Workstation hardware limitations
- Limitations in firewall technology securing the organization from the Internet
- No IP-based remote access for off-site workers

These are just a few examples of the types of factors that will play a role in your design process.

Decisions That Are Difficult to Change

Although Exchange is a very flexible and configurable messaging platform, there are certain decisions that, once implemented, are very hard to change. Using the answers to the requirements listed and information gathered in Chapter 2, "Environment Discovery," the foundation of the Exchange architecture is formed. These difficult-to-change decisions fall into two categories: naming conventions and administration implementation. Naming conventions are the most visible of these decisions. This is because not only are there technical limitations to doing so, but these decisions also affect the end-user directly. Here are the questions from Chapter 2 concerning naming conventions:

- What is the server-naming convention?
- What Exchange organization name will be used?

- What general theme will be used when naming sites?
- If your organization doesn't have a server-naming policy, what will the policy be?
- What is the display name format?
- What is the alias name format?
- What is the SMTP address format?

Exchange Server, site, and organization names are difficult to change after they are implemented because they are components of the distinguished name of every Exchange object. Although there are some creative ways to work around the problems encountered when changing these names, none are without significant effort or risk.

The display name, alias name, and SMTP address formats are difficult to change from a user consistency standpoint. Once users become familiar with the client, start using the address book, and publish their SMTP addresses. Changing the primary SMTP address is ill-advised. This is because recipients external to your organization may enter these addresses in their personal address books. If these addresses change, these external recipients won't be able to send mail to recipients on Exchange. It is important to note, however, that it is easy to add a second SMTP address to the properties for a recipient mailbox.

User perception is another reason why it is difficult to change the public folder implementation. Users become attached to their public folders in a very short time, so changing the hierarchy, naming conventions, or accessibility from the Internet can cause user distrust and dissension. Public-folder implementation decisions are discussed later in this chapter.

The second major area of difficulty concerning changing decisions is in the administration of the environment. Here are the Chapter 2 questions relating to this arena:

- Does your organization want any custom attributes displayed in the address book?
- Who will be responsible for creating and maintaining distribution lists?
- Which distribution lists will be able to receive messages from the Internet?
- Who will be responsible for managing custom recipients?

These decisions directly affect the environment's usability and flexibility and therefore should be kept consistent.

Setting User Expectations

It is important to start communicating with the end-user at the beginning of the design process. This has two primary benefits to the Exchange project: It creates a partnership between the Exchange team and the end-user community, and it allows communication of product features in as positive a light as possible. It is critical that differences between previous mail systems and Exchange be presented as features of the product rather than limitations or bugs.

Using communication to create a partnership between the Exchange team and the end-user community helps facilitate the information-gathering and expectation-setting process. A two-way flow of information allows trust to be established throughout the organization. End-users who don't feel as though they are a part of the Exchange implementation process won't be encouraged to help the project be successful. However, it is important to carefully balance the flow of information gathering to balance what is realistic for the project implementation with what is desired by the user community.

Communicating Exchange functionality, particularly the functionality of the client, as a set of features and not limitations or bugs is essential to the success of the Exchange project. An example of this is the contrast between Microsoft Mail and Exchange in automatically adding new addresses to the personal address book. In Microsoft Mail, the default configuration was to have unknown addresses added to the personal address book. This isn't possible with Outlook. To offset any possible perception of lost functionality, the Exchange project team should tell the users about issues such as this and let them know the advantages, such as fine-tuned management of the personal address book.

Although communication plans and methods will vary a great deal based on the organization and company culture, an end-user communication plan should include the elements listed in Table 6.1.

Table 6.1 **Communication Plan Components**

Communication Plan Component	**Description**	**Suggested Communication Method**
Project overview	General description of the project, goals, and timeframe	Email or company newsletter
Client design and functionality overview	Overview of the look and feel of the client and new feature definition	Brown-bag sessions
Migration process overview	Overview of the migration process and what impact it will have on the end-user	Email or memo
Migration process to-do's	List of tasks that end-users need to do before migration	Email or memo
Migration process reminder	Reminder message right before user migration	Email or voice mail
Migration wrap-up and information gathering	Help information and survey of user feedback	Written form left on desk
Communication wrap-up	Summary of project success and user feedback	Email

Planning for the Future

When you're in the throes of creating an Exchange architecture, it can sometimes be difficult to foresee how the architecture or organization will grow over time. In all but a few cases, growth is guaranteed. Although several features of Exchange help manage growth, messaging services will grow as a result of increased usage, increased functionality, or increased organizational growth. Because of this inevitable growth, it is necessary to have a proactive plan for the Exchange architecture. Here are the planning decisions necessary for growth:

- A naming convention that will expand for additional servers and accommodate naming conflicts
- A plan for how servers will expand with the number of users or the size of mailboxes
- A view toward future implementations and standards
- A tuning plan for Exchange as the network infrastructure changes

Keeping these points in mind during the initial Exchange design process will ensure that decisions can be made to help effectively manage the growth of the Exchange environment.

Geographic Profile

The organization's geographic profile plays a large part in the Exchange design decisions. The ultimate goals are to limit administrative costs, divide administrative responsibilities as necessary for divergent groups, and optimize performance and functionality for the end-user. These goals tie back to the design process in three main areas:

- Correct design of the site boundaries
- Division of the Exchange organization among administrative teams
- Optimizing the Exchange database for users and functionality

Language Requirements

Exchange Server comes in a number of different language versions. This lets worldwide organizations communicate more effectively. Instead of having a single language email system, organizations can implement Exchange with support for all the language preferences that exist.

Users

Outlook 98 comes in many language versions. Each of these versions can be loaded on the desktop and connect to a server database in any of the server languages. For special-character support, it is necessary to implement those characters on the desktop.

Administrators

Exchange Server 5.5 comes in many language versions. It is possible to launch an English-language version of Exchange and administer an Exchange database that is in a different language. The same is true of the other language versions of the Exchange Administrator. You can launch a French version of the administrator program and administer an English version of the database. This allows for distributed administration of a single database, or centralized administration of distributed databases.

This distributed administration model allows a lot of flexibility in design choices. For example, the design of Exchange for the network infrastructure and requirements shown in Figure 6.1 has two primary solutions, as discussed in a moment.

- 5×24 administrative support for all offices

- All Exchange administrators belong to one team and share administration

- The organization has one NT domain

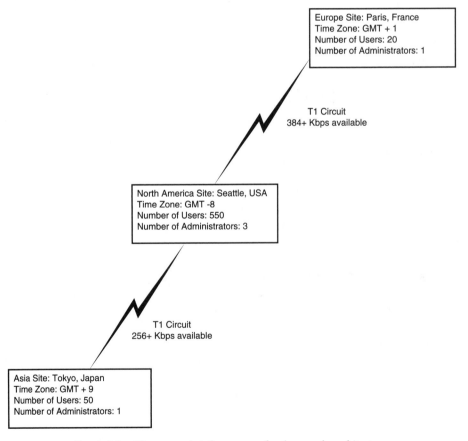

Figure 6.1   The network infrastructure for the sample architecture.

With this infrastructure and these support requirements, there are two likely design possibilities. The first is to install servers in every location in the appropriate language version. Administrators in every location would load their preferred language version of the Exchange Administrator and share administrative and support responsibilities. The second design possibility is to install only one Exchange server in the North American site. Administrators in every location would load their preferred language version of the Exchange Administrator and share administrative and support responsibilities. Both of these design possibilities are possible because of Exchange's multiple-language support features. The choice between the two models depends on the other design requirements gathered.

Drawing Site Lines

Deciding where the site lines will fall is a critical step in the Exchange design process. Two factors will help you make this decision: the network considerations and the administrative model. Sites are a powerful tool within the Exchange organization; multiple sites are often required. However, the more sites an organization has, the more complicated it is to maintain and administer.

Network Considerations

The number of sites and servers implemented across an organization is determined in large part by the network connections between physical locations. This section will look at the determining factors of those WAN situations. In Chapter 2, we gathered much information about the network infrastructure design and implementation. That information will now be used to make decisions about the Exchange site design. Here are the Chapter 2 questions referred to in this section:

- What type of network circuits connect the physical locations?
- What is the amount of *available* bandwidth between each physical location during business hours?
- For each physical location, document the type of network media used—for example, 10 Mbps Ethernet or 16 Mbps Token Ring.

The network considerations of site design will be based on the answers to these questions.

Available Bandwidth

The standard recommendation on available bandwidth necessary for servers within one site is 64 Kbps. There is much debate around this figure, because there have been implementations of one-site organizations with less available bandwidth that have worked and implementations of one-site organizations with more available bandwidth that haven't worked. Production data suggests that the available bandwidth within a single site should be 128 Kbps or more. This amount of bandwidth will allow the servers within a site to communicate messages, directory changes, and server information without getting bogged down.

With the current version of Exchange, version 5.5, it is still difficult to move users from one site to another. Although this limitation shouldn't be the case in Platinum, it is still a factor now. This problem affects our site design in two ways. First, if there is a case where users are commonly moving between physical locations, it is much easier to move their mailboxes to a different server within the same site than to move them between sites. This encourages a common site design between these locations. Second, making the wrong decision about site design is painful. Study the available bandwidth, administration, and move patterns carefully before drawing site lines.

Control of Connections

One factor that can affect the latitude of how much available bandwidth is necessary within a site is the control of the connections between the physical locations. This is a factor for three reasons: the ability to tune the physical link, the availability of link usage statistics and traffic information, and the reliability of link availability. If the WAN link between your physical locations is under your control, it is possible to tune your network to a single protocol, track all traffic and usage information, and make sure that the WAN link can deliver the promised committed information rate. Since having full control of a WAN link is more of an exception than a rule for most organizations, evaluate how much control and information you have for these three areas if a third party is providing your WAN link.

Administrative Considerations

Administrative divisions are the next concern for the site design. The information gathered for the following questions from Chapter 2 will lead to the necessary site design:

- What is the administrative structure for the current messaging system?
- How many Administrators are in each location?
- How many, if any, Permissions Administrators are in each location?

The answers to these questions, along with the factors considered in the network considerations sections, will help finalize the site line decisions.

Centralized/Decentralized Organization

The major administrative factor in making a site line decision is the Exchange Administrator support team model. In a centralized organization where all servers are managed by one team in one physical location or one team distributed across physical locations, it is recommended that you have a single site administration model (if allowed by the network considerations). If your organization has a decentralized support team for the messaging environment, using sites to divide the administration among those teams is an easy way to solve the administrative control dilemma.

The centralized versus decentralized model usually also extends to the architecture of the NT domain. Because all servers within any site use the same service account, it is necessary to have authentication for the NT domain local to the Exchange server physical location.

If the organization is using a single NT domain or a single accounts domain across all the physical locations, it is easier to use a single-site Exchange model across those locations, as long as at least 128 Kbps of bandwidth is available between servers. The administrative division of the Exchange organization is important because of the three levels of Exchange permission assignment—at the organization, site, and configuration container levels. Permissions can be granted at more granular levels, but not without a lot of maintenance and auditing of the permissions. For any given site, it is recommended that there be two NT groups used to assign permissions. The first NT group will be for Exchange administrators who can administer the organization but not change permissions for any given object. The second NT group will be for Exchange administrators who can administer the organization and change permissions for all objects. Using this model of administration for the Exchange organization, map the organization administrators to the Exchange administrators and divide the organization into sites where there are groups that want or need autonomous control of their sites.

Administrative and Support Hours

Another factor in dividing the organization into sites is the administrative support and support hours. In organizations with several time zones, it is sometime preferable to augment support of a physical location with support staff from other physical locations. This model can extend the support coverage hours that the messaging administrative staff can provide. If your organization can take advantage of backup support by administrators at other geographic locations, it is recommended that these locations be in the same Exchange site to ease the assignment of permissions.

Use these considerations, along with the network considerations and the distribution level of the administrative staff, to make the appropriate site line decisions. Table 6.2 lists the design decision factors for a fictional organization.

In this scenario, Seattle and Paris would be in a single site, and Tokyo would have its own site. This would be the case because the net available bandwidth between Seattle and Tokyo is 128 Kbps and the Exchange administrator for Tokyo is based in Tokyo. The Exchange administrator for Paris is based in Seattle.

Table 6.2   **Site Design Factors**

Physical Administrative Location	Available Bandwidth to Seattle	Control of Connection	Administrative Model	Backup Team
Seattle	Not applicable	Not applicable	Seattle team	None
Paris	256 Kbps	No—using telco provider	Member of Seattle team	Seattle team
Tokyo	128 Kbps	No—using telco provider	Tokyo team	None

Choosing Connectors

Typically, choosing where to draw your site lines is more difficult than deciding which connector to use. This decision is often driven by many of the same reasons you choose to draw a site line: either limited available bandwidth or a separation in the organization's administrative structure.

Drawing a site line and connecting sites with a connector gives you the ability to queue and control the flow of messages between sites. This makes messaging between limited-bandwidth locations more reliable and manageable. The connector also lets you change messaging protocols, and in some cases transport protocols. As Exchange evolves, sites are becoming larger and larger, with fewer connectors needed. What is considered limited available bandwidth is dropping with each version of Exchange. In addition, network bandwidth is becoming more affordable, and organizations are implementing more-robust distributed systems.

After site lines have been drawn, you can follow Figure 6.2 to help decide which connectors to use between sites.

The Site Connector

When site lines are drawn for administrative reasons, and limited available bandwidth between sites isn't an issue, the Site Connector is typically used. The Site Connector is also chosen when there is adequate available bandwidth between physical locations. It can be tricky to decide when to use a Site Connector over an X.400 connector. The *adequate available bandwidth* depends on the messaging environment. The size of messages, the number of messages, and the number of message recipients can all play a part in the utilization of a connector and the amount of bandwidth required.

Here is some additional information about Site Connectors that may assist you in your decision:

- The Site Connector uses remote procedure calls to communicate. By default, any server on one side of the connector will open an RPC association and deliver messages to any server on the other side of the connector. Therefore, messages won't transit an intermediary server when a site connector is utilized. This communication traffic pattern is shown in Figure 6.3.

- The Site Connector can be scaled down from its default configuration to create a bridgehead server relationship between sites. Furthermore, servers in the destination site can be given a cost, used in a weighted average formula. Figure 6.4 shows the communication traffic pattern resulting from a bridgehead server configuration.

Microsoft is in the process of obtaining a patent for its weighted average formula. Hence, it is undisclosed at this time.

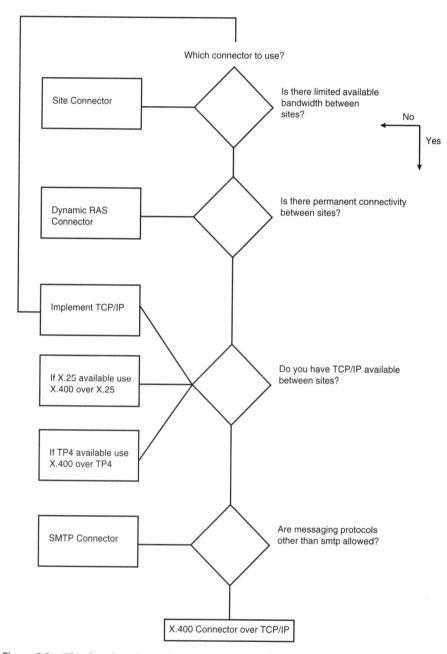

Figure 6.2   This flowchart shows the decision tree to follow when deciding on the appropriate connector to use between sites.

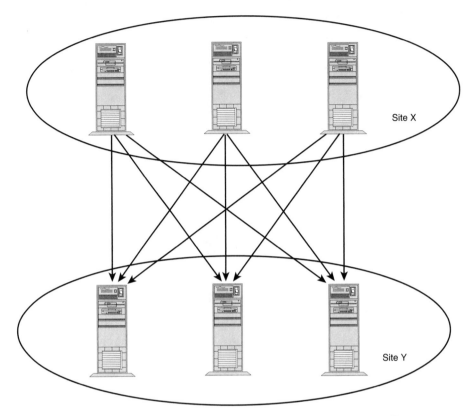

Figure 6.3 The default configuration of site connectors allows traffic between any servers in the sites.

- The Site Connector is the most efficient connector, because it assumes unlimited available bandwidth. If the connector messages queue exceeds the default limit, the Site Connector will open additional associations to the destination site, thus delivering multiple threads of messages at one time.

  While this makes email delivery between sites very fast and efficient, it can also cause problems when there isn't enough available bandwidth. Without available bandwidth, the queue on the Site Connector will build and eventually exceed the queue limit, opening additional RPCs across the limited bandwidth connection. Opening additional RPCs only adds to the problem. Another assumption that the Site Connector makes is, since it has all the bandwidth it needs, there is no need for a delivery schedule. Thus, the Site Connector is unschedulable.

- Some large organizations implement the site connector between sites with either a *connector backbone* or hub-and-spoke topology. In these cases, a server that resides in each site is physically located in the backbone or hub site, as shown in Figure 6.5.

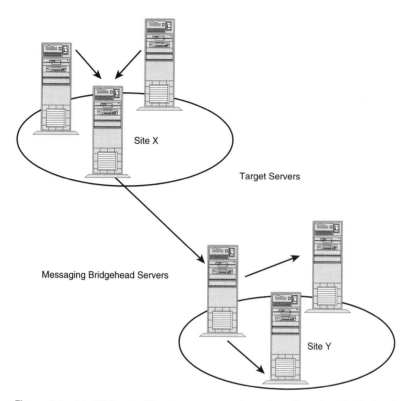

Figure 6.4   Modifying the Site Connector configuration allows for a bridgehead server relationship between sites.

■ From the spoke sites to the hub, the site connector is configured with a bridgehead. The bridgehead in the spoke site is configured to send messages to any server in the hub site. If there is a reason to steer messages from the spoke site to a particular direction, due to server location or typical message flow, costs are associated with the hub site's servers.

Site Versus X.400 Connector

When in doubt, most organizations choose the X.400 connector over the Site Connector. The X.400 connector, although not as fast and efficient as the Site Connector, is usually a remarkable improvement in delivery time when compared to the existing messaging system. This, coupled with the stability and ease of configuration that the X.400 connector provides over limited bandwidth situations, makes the X.400 connector the preferred connector in many situations.

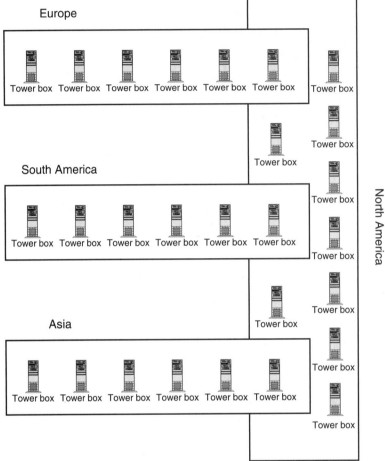

Figure 6.5 Servers that are members of the Europe, South America, and Asia sites are physically located in the North America location.

The X.400 connector is schedulable and is always in a bridgehead relationship between opposing sites. It is possible to have multiple X.400 connectors between sites, but these are usually configured for fault tolerance rather than increased efficiency. Another advantage of the X.400 connector is that Exchange is a native X.400 messaging system. This means that all messages (including directory replication messages) between servers in a site are in the form of an X.400 interpersonal message. Therefore, no efficiency is lost with the use of the X.400 connector, because it doesn't have to convert messages to X.400.

Although Exchange 5.5 and earlier versions were based on X.400, future versions of Exchange may be based on more-popular protocols. With Windows NT 5.0 employing LDAP for directory access, and the popularity of SMTP and IMAP4 as mail transport protocols, Exchange may abandon the X.400 protocol standard in favor of IP-based protocols such as ESMTP and LDAP.

Routing

With all the connectors chosen, it is possible to manipulate their costs to cause mes-sages to flow in a particular direction. Unless there is a reason to change the cost of a route between two sites, it is a good idea to leave all costs at the default of 1. Figure 6.6 shows a partial-mesh Exchange organization with all connectors at their default values.

In this topology, the route from Site A to Site C has a transitive cost of 2 in either direction—through Site B or Site D. If a user in Site A sends a message to a user in Site C, and all connectors are healthy, the messages has an equal chance of traveling through Site B or Site D to get to Site C.

If, for reasons of available bandwidth or communications costs, you wanted mes-sages to typically flow from Site A to Site C through Site B, increasing the cost of the connector to Site D would have that effect. The route from Site A to Site C through Site D (cost = 3) would be traveled only if there were a problem with a connector between Site A and Site B, or Site B and Site C. This cost configuration is shown in Figure 6.7.

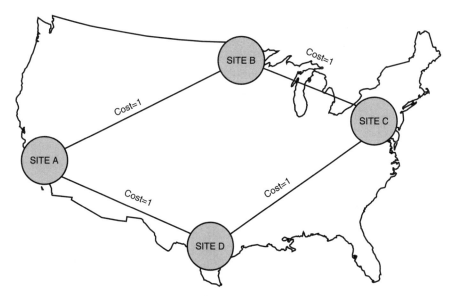

Figure 6.6   The default cost of 1 is used between all sites in this partial-mesh configuration.

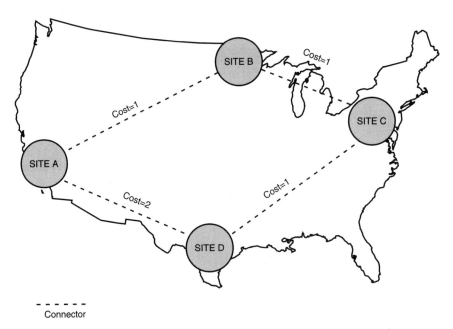

Connector

Figure 6.7   Raising the cost configuration between Site A and Site D to 2 results in a preferred path through Site B when messages are sent from Site A to Site C.

With Exchange having a multi-master directory, where each server in the Exchange
organization has a complete copy of the Exchange directory, each site learns of the
other site's connectors and their costs. The site then incorporates those connectors and
their costs into its own routing table. This way, the routes throughout the organization
are automatically built. In some situations, you might not want other sites to know of
a particular route. A good example of this is with the SMTP connector. If an organization has the Internet Mail Service configured at a site in Europe and at another site in
North America, as shown in Figure 6.8, there will be two possible routes to the
Internet. The least-expensive route to the Internet will be the site's local SMTP connector. The secondary route to the Internet will be through the other site.

To keep SMTP messages from being rerouted to Europe in the event that the
North American IMS is down, the SMTP route in Europe is hidden from North
America by configuring the SMTP route in Europe as a *hidden route*. That way, if the
IMS in North America is temporarily down, the messages will queue in North
America until the IMS is back up. The messages won't be rerouted to Europe. This
configuration is shown in Figure 6.9. It is important to note that this is a route config-
uration picture from the vantage point of the North American site. The route will be
available for servers in the European site.

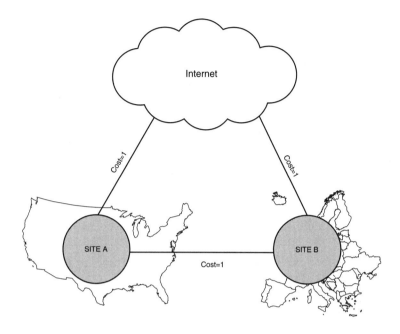

Figure 6.8 All SMTP messages from Site A will be delivered by the North American IMS. If the IMS is down, messages will be delivered via the next lowest-cost route, which is through Site B in Europe.

Networking Infrastructure

When you're designing a connector topology, it is very important to first study the network topology. If at all possible, place connectors over existing network paths. It's possible to configure connectors between two sites that don't have a direct network connection. Although this is necessary in some circumstances, it gives control of the message flow to the IP network, which might not be desirable.

To illustrate this example, refer to Figure 6.10, which shows an organization's WAN topology.

If we were to ignore the WAN topology and make Atlanta the messaging hub, even though we had no direct network connectivity between Atlanta, Chicago, and Boston, the IP packets containing the message would flow through San Francisco, as shown in Figure 6.11. This might not be desirable.

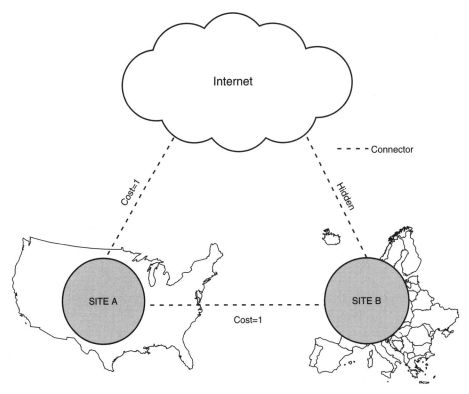

Figure 6.9 All SMTP messages from Site A will be delivered by the North American IMS. If the IMS is down, messages will queue in North America because the SMTP route through Europe isn't visible to Site A.

Impact on the Network

When studied closely, many organizations are surprised to find how much of their network bandwidth is consumed by message traffic. Of course, the amount of consumption depends on the company's messaging culture, the number of message-based applications, and how groups within an organization are dispersed across Exchange servers.

When an organization migrates from a basic store-and-forward messaging system, such as MS Mail or cc:Mail, to Exchange, the initial impact on the network is minimal. But as time goes by and users begin to utilize the parts of the messaging system not available in the legacy system, and as the organization implements message-based applications, the amount of bandwidth consumed by Exchange increases. It is a good practice to periodically monitor available LAN and WAN bandwidth as Exchange usage evolves in an organization.

Figure 6.10   The WAN topology is a hub and spoke to the San Francisco location. There are no network connections between the other sites.

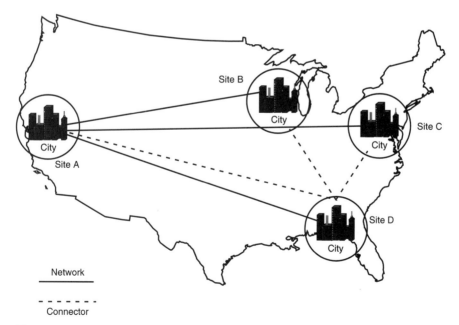

Figure 6.11   With Atlanta as the messaging hub and San Francisco as the network hub, all message traffic between the Atlanta and Chicago sites would flow over the network through San Francisco, even though this is a direct messaging link.

Network Performance

As mentioned, as Exchange evolves and consumes more local area and wide area network bandwidth, the performance of network applications, such as Exchange, can be affected. It is common to see weak or inadequate network topologies crumble under the stress added by a robust messaging system. If Exchange users experience performance problems, it might not be that the Exchange architecture is flawed. Instead, the network infrastructure needs reinforcing to support the increased load.

Connector Topology

As illustrated in the section "Networking Infrastructure," the connector topology may be dictated by the network topology. Nevertheless, three common topologies—full mesh, partial mesh, and hub-and-spoke—are implemented in an Exchange architecture.

Full Mesh

Full-mesh Exchange topologies, like full-mesh NT Domain topologies (complete trust), are usually derived over a period of unchecked growth of an application or system. Rarely, except in small Exchange organizations, are full-mesh Exchange topologies successful.

A full-mesh topology may be appropriate in an organization with limited sites that are all connected to a frame-relay cloud and that have PVCs (permanent virtual circuits) defined between all sites. With this topology, there is a single hop between sites. This topology is illustrated in Figure 6.12.

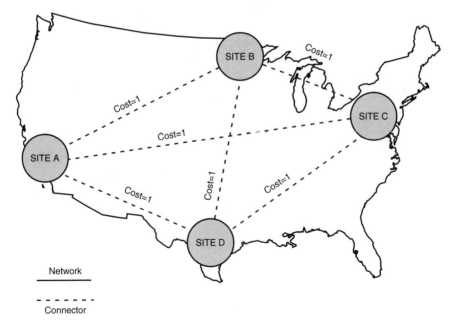

Figure 6.12   In this topology, each site is configured to communicate directly with every other site.

The problem with this topology becomes evident when a network outage occurs. When a message from Site A is sent to Site C, but the network connection from Site A to Site C is down, Exchange will reroute the message to Site B or Site D. If the network problem originates at Site C, the messages being delivered to that site will bounce around from site to site, as Exchange attempts to deliver the message, until the network problem at Site C is resolved.

Partial Mesh

Partial-mesh topologies, when designed properly, can be the best solution for organizations that have a dispersed network topology. A partial-mesh topology is illustrated in Figure 6.13.

In Figure 6.13, a single hub-and-spoke messaging topology would likely cause additional network overhead as messages traveled across the West Coast. This hub-and-spoke messaging topology is shown in Figure 6.14. When a Site A sends a message to Site B, there are only two connector hops, yet the IP packets would travel through the network to Site C and then back across the same WAN connection to Site B.

With a dual-hub or partial-mesh topology, this would be avoided. A message from Site A to Site B would simply travel through Site D, as shown in Figure 6.15.

As illustrated by the unnecessary network traffic created in Figure 6.14 and the optimized network traffic design shown in Figure 6.15, it is important to evaluate your network infrastructure to discover the best connector topology.

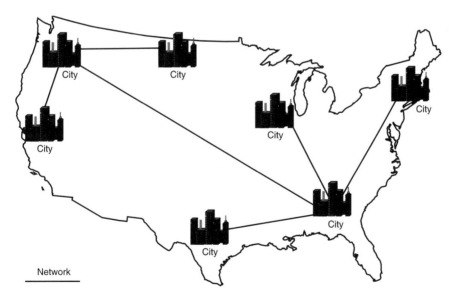

Figure 6.13 A partial-mesh topology with WAN connections between each office and the major network hubs, Atlanta and Seattle. Atlanta and Seattle are then connected directly.

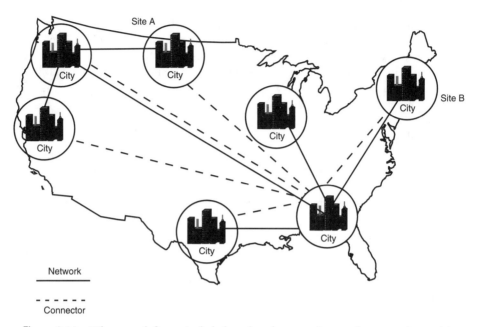

Figure 6.14   When you define a single hub-and-spoke messaging topology over the partial-
mesh network topology, message traffic isn't optimized for the network links.

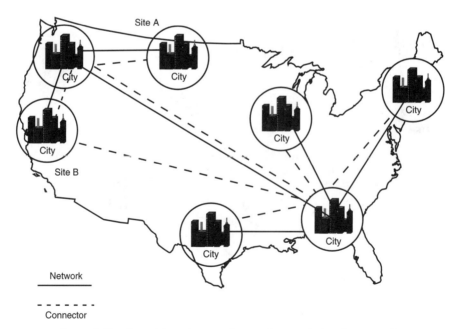

Figure 6.15   A partial-mesh messaging topology optimizes the network
traffic for the partial-mesh network topology.

Star or Hub-and-Spoke

The star or hub-and-spoke topology is, in most cases, the most reliable and manageable topology. Following the hub-and-spoke network architecture, the Exchange connectors originate from the network hub, as shown in Figure 6.16. While this forces the MTA in the hub site to manage messages traveling between all sites, it simplifies the routing table and keeps messages from bouncing around the organization in the case of a network outage.

Defining Services

Exchange has a rich protocol suite. These protocols let a variety of messaging clients access the Exchange directory and information store. These protocols include the following:

- MAPI
- POP3
- IMAP4
- LDAP
- HTTP

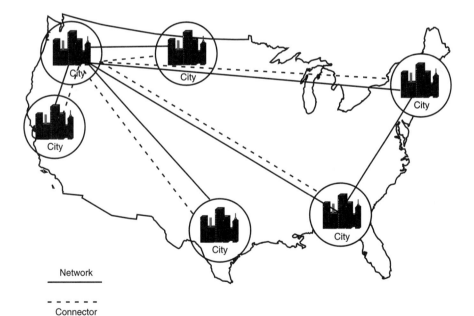

Figure 6.16   All messaging and network traffic flows through the hub site in
Seattle, with all other offices as spoke sites.

Client Design

Exchange 5.0 was the last version of Exchange to ship with the original Exchange client. Exchange 5.5 and later versions utilize Microsoft Outlook as the default Exchange client. The deployment of this useful and productive client is covered extensively in Chapter 8, "Design of Client Services." In addition to the Outlook client, Exchange supports numerous third-party clients that are based on Internet standard protocols. You decided which clients to support in Chapter 2. Here we will evaluate your decision and the services needed to support those clients.

- **Internet clients**. If users are accessing their messaging system via the Internet, what clients are being used?

- **Internet messaging protocols**. What Internet protocols (POP3 or IMAP4) are being used to access the messaging system?

If you have users who require ongoing support of their Internet clients, the protocols these clients use need to be implemented on the Exchange server. These protocols were supported by Exchange as of version 5.0. Mapping the clients you intend to support to the protocols they require will indicate which protocols need to be enabled or disabled in the Exchange organization. Protocols include the following:

- POP3
- IMAP4
- LDAP
- HTTP

By default, all the protocols that ship with Exchange are installed and enabled during implementation. These protocols can be disabled on a site or server basis (except for HTTP, which can only be configured on a site or mailbox level).

POP3 and IMAP4

The two popular Internet message retrieval protocols, POP3 and IMAP4, let users of POP3 and IMAP4 clients access their mail from an Exchange server. If access will be enabled from the Internet, the appropriate TCP/IP ports need to be enabled on existing firewalls and routers. Your network administrators should analyze the security risks of doing this. When analyzing the use of these protocols for Internet access, it is also prudent to evaluate whether the Outlook Web client could replace these legacy clients and provide additional functionality.

It is also important to note that POP3 and IMAP4 are mail-retrieval protocols only. These clients use SMTP to deliver mail to the server. Hence, when using these clients, you must implement an Internet Mail Service in the site. The client must be configured to retrieve its mail from the server that houses its mailbox, and then configured to deliver messages to the server that houses the Internet Mail Service. The connections established by IMAP4 and POP3 clients to send and receive mail are shown in Figure 6.17.

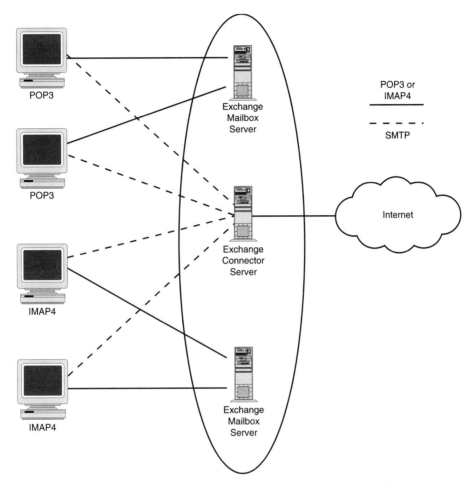

Figure 6.17   IMAP4 and POP3 clients establish connections with their mailbox server to receive mail and establish connections with the IMS server to send mail.

LDAP

Today's Internet client uses LDAP to access directory services. Exchange 5.0 and 5.5 support LDAP to give these clients access to the Exchange directory. These services are usually limited to read-only and sometimes allow for searches. If you plan on supporting Internet clients that use LDAP for directory services, LDAP will need to be enabled in the Exchange organization. In addition, you will need to decide which LDAP clients you will support in your organization. LDAP clients connect directly to their Exchange mailbox server, as shown in Figure 6.18.

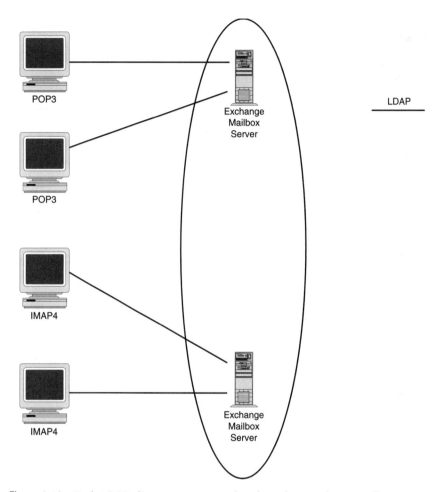

Figure 6.18   Each LDAP client communicates directly with its Exchange mailbox server or with an Exchange server that is LDAP-enabled and has a copy of the directory available.

With the next version of Exchange, and Windows NT 5.0, LDAP will have an expanded role. Inter-server directory management and Exchange client access will be LDAP-capable.

Web Services

Although Web-enabled email isn't a traditional means of messaging, the popularity of the Web and the widespread implementation of Web browsers make Web access to post offices an essential service provided by a modern messaging system. Exchange, which defines the modern messaging system, offers a rich Web client that is becoming more similar to the actual Outlook client with every version. As time goes by, it is likely that the two different clients will continue to converge.

There are a couple of additional benefits of installing Web access internally:

- Clients that do not, or cannot, support the Outlook client, such as UNIX clients, can take advantage of messaging services with Web clients. The Web client offers these users calendaring and scheduling functionality beyond those offered by POP3 and IMAP4 clients.

- A user, regardless of who is logged into the workstation, can easily access his messages without creating an Exchange profile. This is often used in kiosk and shared workstations. Enabling Web access to an Exchange server requires the implementation of Microsoft Internet Information Server version 3.0 or greater. Internet Information Server can reside on the Exchange server itself or can be installed on any server in the organization. Due to the single-hop authentication of LAN Manager challenge and response, IIS must be installed on the Exchange server if LAN Manager challenge and response will be used. If IIS is installed on a different server than the Exchange server, only clear-text authentication can be utilized.

The Exchange server doesn't actually support HTTP access, nor does it understand HTTP. IIS acts as a translator between HTTP and MAPI. Figure 6.19 shows the components involved in providing Web access to an Exchange server. To fully understand this process, refer to Figure 6.19 and the following steps:

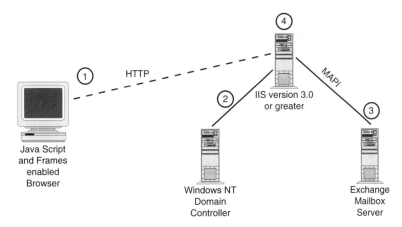

Figure 6.19 To provide Web access to the Exchange server, four components must interact.

1. A JavaScript- and frames-enabled browser opens the \\NTServer\Exchange page on the Web server. The Web user sees an Exchange Web page that lets him access the public folders configured for Web access or enter an alias name to access a mailbox. The user enters his alias. He is prompted to enter his domain, alias, and password.

2. The IIS takes the authentication information and contacts a domain controller, retrieving the user's credentials.

3. With these credentials, the IIS makes a MAPI call to the Exchange server associated with the IIS. If the user's mailbox is on a different server, the IIS is directed to that server. Otherwise, the Exchange server returns the contents of the user's mailbox to the IIS in the form of a MAPI response.

4. The IIS takes the MAPI response from the Exchange server, renders it into HTML, and returns it to the Web browser via HTTP.

Public folders can be configured for anonymous or authenticated access from the Web. Web public folder access is becoming popular with the use of other Web-based workgroup applications. Through the use of Collaborative Data Objects, you can exploit the Exchange messaging system for far more than simple messaging. Public folders, as a mechanism for storing objects for workgroup access, are a part of the Exchange messaging system currently used by many organizations in their Web workgroup application strategy.

Does your organization have a policy regarding HTTP access from the Internet to servers on your internal network? If so, implementing this policy might preclude recipients from gaining access to their Exchange mailboxes by using a Web browser.

If the Exchange system is the first set of servers directly exposed to the Internet through your firewall, it is prudent to evaluate the security risk that this new access imposes on your system.

If you plan to allow remote users to access their mailboxes using the Web client from the Internet, there are two main considerations:

- Security
- Firewall configuration

Security should be the first issue you address when setting up Outlook Web access. One of the most common ways of securing access is to configure the Outlook Web server with an SSL certificate and set the logon page to accept only secure connections. This will limit access to browsers that support SSL. However, it will ensure that all password and messaging data is transferred in a secure format.

The second consideration is firewall configuration. Unless you will be allowing full Outlook client access to your Exchange server, you should configure your firewall to allow only TCP and UDP port 80 for HTTP to your Exchange server. If you are using SSL, configure TCP and UDP port 443 for the SSL session.

NNTP

Along with the Internet client access protocols (POP3, IMAP4, SMTP, and LDAP), Exchange also supports NNTP (Network News Transport Protocol). NNTP is the protocol used on the Internet's UseNet for the synchronization of newsgroup postings across the globe.

NNTP provides two major functions to Exchange:

- It allows Exchange to participate in UseNet.
- It allows Internet news clients to access Exchange public folders.

Enabling NNTP Access to Public Folders

In order for certain public folders to be accessible using NNTP, they need to be configured for access. Using the Exchange Administrator, you select the public folder to publish via NNTP and the type of access you will provide.

- All public folders have access permissions assigned by default. These permissions can be modified using the Exchange Administrator or the Outlook client. From the Exchange directory, users are added to the access list and are assigned rights to the public folder.
- When an NNTP client accesses the Exchange public folder system, the user can be required to provide NT Domain user credentials. Based on these credentials, the user is permitted access to public folders based on his public folder permissions.
- When NNTP was introduced as a supported protocol in Exchange 5.0, an additional unique user was added to the public folder user access list. The anonymous user can be granted rights on a public folder. This lets anonymous NNTP and Web clients access the public folder information. What the anonymous user can do in the public folder depends on the type of access granted to him.

SMTP for Clients

As mentioned in the section "POP3 and IMAP4" and illustrated in Figure 6.17, common Internet clients that use POP3 or IMAP4 for message access use SMTP for message delivery. While these clients must be configured to retrieve mail from the server that houses their mailbox, they can be configured to deliver mail to any SMTP host. The Exchange Internet Mail Service is typically the SMTP host.

The Internet Mail Service, Our SMTP Host

SMTP has been supported by Exchange since its introduction in 1994. Initially provided by the Internet Mail Connector, its functionality and efficiency have been improved with each version in what is now called the Internet Mail Service.

The Exchange Internet Mail Service is RFC-compliant and is considered an SMTP host. Its rerouting functionality, introduced in Exchange 5.0, classifies the IMS as a Smart Host, giving it the capability to store and forward SMTP messages.

As Exchange can be configured to support organizations of many shapes and sizes, so too must the IMS be able to support a wide variety of Internet mail demands and environments.

Exchange Event Service

The Exchange Event service is a new feature with Exchange 5.5. This service triggers server-side scripts based on events that occur on server folders, including mailboxes. The caveat with this service is that it shouldn't be used for events that are message-based, or the server will soon be overloaded. In addition, scripts that are run by the scripting agent service will run as the Exchange service account, which could marginalize Exchange Server security.

Public Folder Strategies

Public folders are a function of Exchange that was introduced at the wrong time. Just as organizations began fully implementing Exchange and public folders, the Web became the shared information medium of choice for many organizations. Hence, public folders are often underutilized, and Web servers perform much of the shared information functionality public folders were meant for. Today, public folders are finding their place in organizations by supporting Web access to shared information and as easily configurable share points accessible by the Outlook client.

Public folder strategies can vary as much as messaging connector strategies. The size of the organization, as well as how the organization intends to utilize public folders, will help define how public folders are implemented.

Managing Public Folders

Managing public folders is a task proportionate to the size of the public folder hierarchy and the number of users who can create public folders.

It is always recommended that users who can create top-level public folders be limited to a few administrators, and that the creation of top-level public folders be dictated by the public folder section of the Exchange architecture.

After permissions are set on top-level public folders, the number of users you allow to create public folders will dictate the amount of public folder management that will be necessary. This is because there is no effective way for an administrator to manage a user's public folder—that management is up to the user. For example, if a user creates a dozen public folders somewhere deep inside the hierarchy and then leaves the company, there is no way for the Exchange administrator to know what public folder the user created. Hence, the public folders and their content continue to reside on the public folder system until a manual audit is done to find unused public folders.

Smart Host functionality was necessary to support POP3 clients. POP3 and IMAP4 clients deliver messages using SMTP. The Exchange IMS had to be able to reroute those incoming SMTP messages from POP3 clients to the Internet.

Here is one approach to identifying public folders that have no owner because the person who created the folder has left the organization: Export the list of public folders from the Exchange directory and include the public folder owner in the export file. Sort the list on the owner object and note all of the folders that are ownerless. This list can then be used to assign a new owner to folders or to delete folders.

For large organizations, this can become a nightmare. One organization in particular, which is especially proficient in the use of Exchange, has over 70,000 public folders. With several hundred users leaving the company daily, each person leaves behind his own contribution to the public folder cancer that grows out of control and becomes unmanageable.

What can we learn from this? Closely monitor the creation of public folders. Many organizations won't allow a public folder to be created unless an electronic form is submitted to an IS group. The IS group notes which users own which public folders. When a user leaves, his public folders are reassigned proper owners or deleted, depending on content.

Homegrown processes and mechanisms such as this are necessary to effectively manage the public folder system.

Client Access to Public Folders

Before designing a public folder system, you must understand how the Outlook client accesses the content of a public folder. Every Exchange server with a public information store has and replicates the public folder hierarchy, but the content of a public folder only resides on the public information stores it has been configured to replicate between.

Our hypothetical organization has several public information stores. Each one contains the complete public folder hierarchy. The content of the public folders can exist on one or many public information stores.

When a client goes to open a public folder, the following process unfolds, as shown in Figure 6.20 and as described in the following steps:

1. The Outlook client knows the location of the user's assigned public information store by the assigned value associated with the user's private information store. The Outlook client browses the hierarchy on the user's assigned public information store. When the user clicks a public folder, the Outlook client searches for the content of the public folder, first looking at the assigned public IS.

2. If the content of the public folder isn't found on the assigned public IS, the client looks at all the public folder information stores that have the same public folder location as the assigned public IS.

3. If the content of the public folder doesn't reside on any public information store in the public folder location, the client searches the rest of the public information stores in the site.

   If the content of the public folder isn't found on any of the remaining servers, the client returns an error to the user.

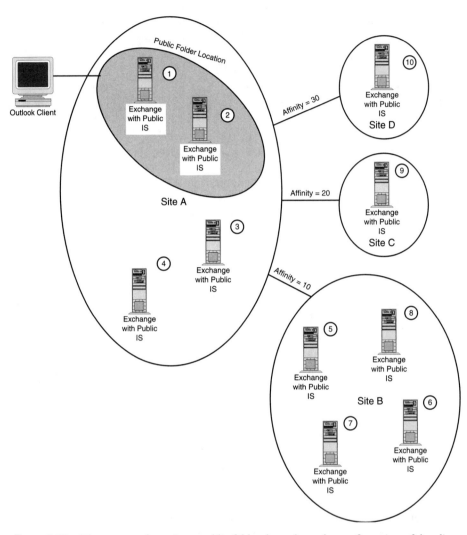

Figure 6.20   The process of opening a public folder depends on the configuration of the client and the configuration of the public folder hierarchy.

4. If affinity is configured between sites, the client reaches out across the site and searches all the public information stores in that site.

5. The client continues to search through all the sites in the organization, when affinity is configured, until it finds the content of the public folder.

You can see from this process that without a sound public folder architecture, an incredible amount of WAN bandwidth could be consumed by clients looking for the content of public folders. Solutions to this potential problem revolve around limiting the number of public information stores and even creating dedicated Exchange public folder servers, and replicating key public folders that are often accessed by users but that don't change regularly.

Public Folder Hierarchy

This section helps you determine which public folder hierarchy best suits your organization and how your users can best utilize that hierarchy. The public folder hierarchy will begin with the public folder root, followed by the top-level public folders. These typically will be segregated by

- Geographic location
- Business unit or organization
- User communities

The hierarchy should also try to reflect the locations of the public information stores. For example, if you have a geographic location of Atlanta, this will dictate that the public stores that contain the content of this folder and its subfolders will reside in Atlanta.

On the other hand, if you have a public folder that represents a business unit, such as Engineering, the content of this public folder isn't committed to a geographic location. Rather, the content of this public folder and its subfolders will likely be replicated between multiple sites. A sample public folder hierarchy is shown in Figure 6.21.

If you're migrating from your current messaging system and you intend to migrate the legacy system's shared folders, identify where in the public folder hierarchy the shared folder content would reside. In addition, try to answer the following questions:

- Does the current messaging system utilize a shared folder system? If so, how is that system organized?
- Should any specific public folders be created upon initial configuration of the Exchange organization?

Aside from the top-level public folder hierarchy, include any public folders you have identified that would be useful to the organization. Place these public folders under the appropriate branch of the hierarchy.

Public Folders in Small Organizations

When implementing public folders in a small organization, it is still important to define a logical public folder hierarchy, but it might not be necessary to implement a dedicated public folder server. It may also be impractical to configure public folder affinity, depending on the amount of available network bandwidth.

If available WAN bandwidth isn't abundant for the amount of public folder usage you foresee, you might decide to restrict public folder access to clients that exist in a particular site. If access to a public folder from another site is deemed necessary, configure that public folder to replicate to the site. You can easily restrict clients from reaching out across the WAN by not configuring public folder affinity. This configuration is shown in Figure 6.22. Here, clients only access public folders in their own sites, and replication is configured for public folders that need to be accessible to both sites. With this configuration, it isn't necessary for the clients to access an Exchange public folder on a server that is across a slow link.

If there is sufficient bandwidth available to allow users to access public folder content across sites, configuring public folder affinity will let users access all public folders in the hierarchy. If you sense that clients in a site are regularly reaching out across the WAN to access a particular public folder, you might decide to replicate that public folder to their site. This will grant them local access to the public folder.

Deciding to replicate a public folder when you have affinity configured is usually based on intuition. Unfortunately, there is no tool to monitor public folder access. Furthermore, it might not be wise to replicate a public folder, depending on the number of changes made compared to the amount of access.

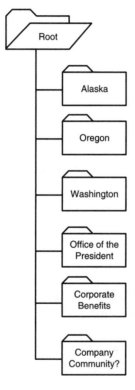

Figure 6.21 Public folders can reflect either geographic locations or business units.

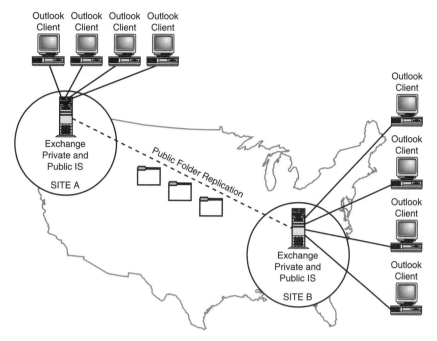

Figure 6.22   Here, public folder affinity isn't configured.

For example, a public folder that keeps track of stock exchange prices will be constantly changing. If clients in other sites visit this public folder 30 times a day, it would be worth analyzing whether bandwidth would be saved by replicating this public folder. During this analysis, it is found that in order for the public folder to remain useful, it would have to be replicated 96 times a day (every five minutes) to each site. The conclusion is that less bandwidth would be consumed by allowing users to reach across the WAN to access the public folder than by configuring the public folder for replication. Common sense and experience are what is usually relied upon when deciding to replicate public folders.

It is recommended that the number of public folders created be kept to a minimum. This will keep the public folder system manageable for administrators and useable to clients.

Public Folders in Large Organizations

Implementing public folders in large organizations raises many of the same issues as implementing public folders in small organizations. However, considering the potential size of the hierarchy, the number of users with an object in the Free and Busy public folder, and the need to centralize public folder content, certain strategies can be deployed to ease the burden that public folders have on the Exchange organization. A large organization must deal with a couple of issues when it comes to public folders:

- When the Outlook client starts, it must contact its Free and Busy public folder. The client will hang if it can't contact this public folder.

- The client will contact the public information store defined by the client's private information store.

- In organizations with 10,000 to 15,000 users, the Free and Busy public folder replication schedule must be tuned so that the public folder has time to replicate all changes between intervals. The public folder must also keep Free and Busy times synchronized enough to be useful to users.

Hierarchy and Free and Busy Public Folder Servers

The Hierarchy and the Free and Busy public folder servers have the sole purpose of providing the following services:

- Clients are evenly divided within each site to contact a particular Hierarchy public folder server. These servers contain no public folder content except for that of the Free and Busy public folder.

- The Free and Busy public folder resides on this server because the client must contact its Free and Busy public folder upon startup. With the Free and Busy public folder on this server, the client need not contact a content public folder server.

- This server doesn't contain a private information store.

Content Public Folder Servers

Content public folder servers are just that. They aren't directly associated with any clients, like the Hierarchy servers. Instead, they hold the content of the public folders. In sites with thousands of users, and potentially thousands of public folders, multiple Content public folder servers may be necessary, all configured to replicate with each other.

Free and Busy Public Folder

When combined, the public folder system in a large organization takes advantage of each public folder server role to provide efficient public folder services while maintaining manageability. Figure 6.23 shows a public folder configuration for a large organization. In Figure 6.23, Outlook clients in the Hub Site A contact their respective private folder servers when starting. From the private folder servers, they obtain their respective Hierarchy server, where they store their Free and Busy times. When a client in Site A browses the public folder hierarchy, it gets the hierarchy from its assigned Hierarchy server. When the client opens a public folder, it contacts a Content public folder server. Since all Content public folder servers are replicating all public folders, the client finds the content of the public folder it's opening.

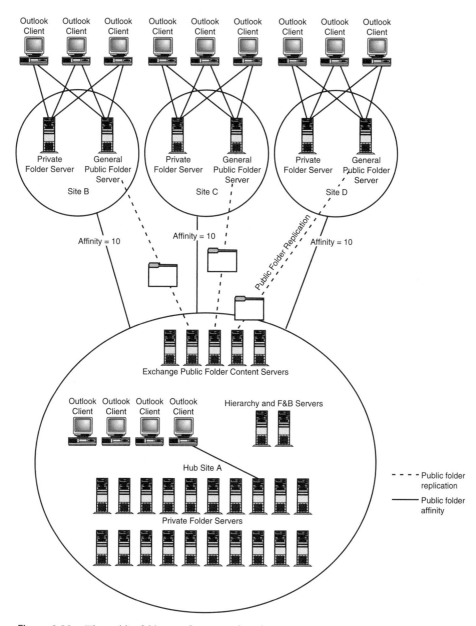

Figure 6.23   The public folder configuration for a large organization includes configuring the appropriate affinity, replication, and public store home configuration for each client.

The Exchange administrator can divide the private folder server's Hierarchy server association evenly. This spreads the load of Free and Busy objects across the Hierarchy servers.

In spoke sites B through D, the General public folder servers contain the hierarchy, the Free and Busy public folder for their site, and any replicated public folder that is relative to that site. If a user in a spoke site opens a public folder that doesn't reside on the site's public folder server, the client will reach across to the hub site and find the content of the public folder on the first server it contacts. Again, all public folders are replicated to each Content public folder server in the hub site.

Replication

As mentioned, public folder replication is a useful and efficient means of sharing information across sites. Users spread across sites can share information and collaborate on projects.

If left unchecked, replication can become a considerable consumer of WAN bandwidth. Therefore, it is prudent to devise a process by which public folders are replicated only when justified. Especially in large organizations, where many Exchange administrators at various sites may have the ability to configure public folder replication, centralizing the responsibility of replication to a few administrators who know the ramifications of replication can maintain the manageability of the public folder system.

Affinity

Companies are depending more and more on wide area network technology. Thus, WANs are becoming faster, more reliable, and fault-tolerant. When an organization has implemented a WAN that can support the bandwidth requirements of various applications and is monitored for utilization, public folder affinity can be implemented to extend the availability of public folders throughout the organization.

The ideal public folder implementation has public folder servers in each site that contain the public folder content that is relevant to that site. Content that is infrequently accessed is then available to users across the WAN to other sites via public folder affinity.

7

Design of Associated Services

BECAUSE MICROSOFT EXCHANGE IS A CLIENT/SERVER application, it depends on several operating system components and networking system components for its functionality. If Exchange isn't configured with these associated services in mind, or vice versa, the effect can be to limit the efficiency and reliability of Exchange. In this chapter, we will examine some of these underlying subsystems, their effect on Exchange, and ways to improve their performance.

Network Architecture

The typical network architecture is often built over time as an organization expands. It is important to periodically reevaluate local and wide area network architectures to ensure that they are meeting the needs of the systems they support.

Microsoft Exchange is one of those systems supported by the network. If a WAN link is unreliable, the Exchange architecture should account for that in the appropriate design decisions, such as choice of connector, configuration of alternative routes across other WAN links, and configuration of server monitors. If the WAN link becomes more reliable, those architecture decisions should be reviewed to take advantage of the new network configuration.

Available Bandwidth

The tolerance of a messaging bridgehead server dealing with a WAN connection with limited available bandwidth depends on the connector used. As mentioned in Chapter 5, "Defining Extended Services," the site connector's tolerance is not that of the X.400 connector. This makes the X.400 connector more desirable in limited-bandwidth networks. Measuring and expanding the amount of available bandwidth will increase the efficiency of an Exchange organization.

Many organizations don't know the amount of available bandwidth over their WAN links because the WAN links are provided by a third party. In this case, it's important to work with the third-party provider to provide usage and availability statistics. This discovery process often uncovers service issues that haven't been readily apparent before, such as a circuit availability that is less than the promised committed information rate (CIR) due to an oversubscribed circuit or outage situations caused by the third-party provider. By working with the provider to gather this information, you can improve both the service from and the partnership with the provider.

Total Bandwidth Versus Available Bandwidth

When viewing your network architecture, don't simply look at the size of the pipes connecting your physical organizations. Also look at the amount of available bandwidth in those pipes during business hours. The Exchange bridgehead server doesn't see how big the pipe is when it's communicating across the WAN to another site. Rather, it creates an association with another Exchange bridgehead server and streams messages across the best it can. When the WAN pipe is restricted, or unstable, Exchange attempts to send the message packets across the pipe. If it fails, it returns the message to the routing and selection process for a try at another route.

When the Exchange server is unable to send across a link, numerous problems can occur. For example, consider the WAN and connector configuration shown in Figure 7.1. If message transmission fails on the Seattle-to-Atlanta connector, Exchange will review the Gateway Address Routing Table (GWART) and try to send across the Seattle-Boston-Atlanta route. Although this is desirable for fault tolerance, if it happens too frequently, the message queues between Boston and Atlanta could become overloaded because of the slow link speed between them. If this is the case, the routing should be reviewed to determine whether costs should be modified or secondary routes hidden.

Gateway Address Routing Table

All message-routing decisions are made based on the Gateway Address Routing Table (GWART). There are two ways of accessing the GWART: by using the Exchange Administrator program to view the Routing properties under Site Addressing, or by using a text editor to view the file contained in the \exchsrvr\Mtadata directory. Two files contain copies of the GWART: GWART0.MTA contains the active copy of the GWART, and GWART1.MTA contains a copy of the last GWART.

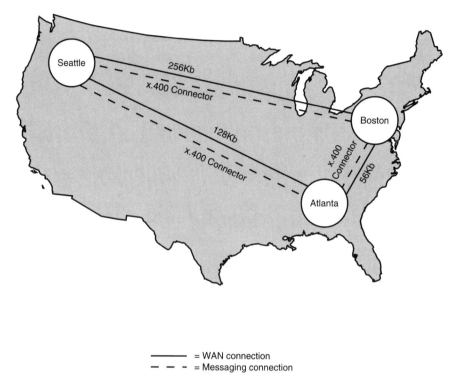

———— = WAN connection
– – – – = Messaging connection

Figure 7.1   This full mesh messaging configuration has a corresponding full mesh network configuration but has varying network speeds. If Exchange can't send a message from Seattle to Atlanta, it will try to send across the Seattle-Boston-Atlanta path. This could cause problems because of the 56 Kb speed between Boston and Atlanta. The routing configuration should be reviewed to make sure that messages aren't rerouted across a slow link unnecessarily.

While the available bandwidth is an important statistic to know for the associated Exchange design decisions such as connector type (as described in Chapter 5), knowing other WAN information such as the type of traffic, protocols, and service bottlenecks can help you tune the servers and network to better utilize the existing bandwidth. For example, if your network routes IP, IPX, and SAA traffic across the WAN, it won't utilize the routers and bandwidth as efficiently as a single-protocol IP network would. Also, you might discover that WINS replication is causing network bandwidth problems by coinciding with user logon bandwidth. Additionally, several server parameters can be tuned to optimize traffic across the WAN, especially when using the TCP/IP protocol. For most organizations, the default configuration should be used, but there could be special cases in which these parameters would be tuned. Table 7.1 lists some of the TCP/IP tuning parameters. All of these parameters are found in the HKEY_LOCAL_MACHINE\SYSTEM\CurrentControlSet\Services\Tcpip\ Parameters Registry key.

Table 7.1 **TCP/IP Tuning Parameters**

Parameter	Default	Description
TcpWindowSize	8760 (for Ethernet)	Defines the size of the sliding window that TCP uses to buffer data. Larger windows are better for high-bandwidth links because they send less-frequent ACKs. Smaller windows send more-frequent ACKs, which adds load to the network and computer.
DefaultTTL	32 seconds	Defines how long a packet can live on the network before being discarded. The TTL is decremented by the number of seconds the packet resides on each router. For slow links, increasing the TTL might be necessary to keep packets from timing out.
ForwardBufferMemory	74,420 bytes	Defines how much memory is used to store packets in the router queue. This is applicable only if IPEnableRouter is enabled, which shouldn't be the case for an Exchange server.
NumForwardPackets	50 packets	Defines the number of IP packet headers that can be stored in an IP router packet queue. This parameter is applicable only if IPEnableRouter is enabled.

Communication Patterns

Just as stock price patterns don't guarantee future prices, past communication patterns don't guarantee future patterns. On the contrary, as technology changes and users begin to accept and use the tools they are given, such as Outlook, communications patterns can and will change over time.

One of the few design decisions that can affect communication patterns is the grouping of users.

In most cases, when a user on an Exchange server e-mails one or more users on the same server, the message never leaves the information store. This reduces the load on the server and on the network and *decreases* delivery time. This is true except in a couple of cases. If a distribution list is used, the message is passed to the MTA for expansion. If the new journaling feature of Exchange 5.5 SP1 is enabled, each message is passed to the MTA for record-keeping.

While in some organizations (particularly large ones) it is very difficult and time-consuming to keep users grouped, this task can have value in medium organizations. Small organizations typically have only a single server per site, so grouping isn't an issue.

Depending on how easily your organization can benefit from grouping, this can affect the decision of how many servers to implement. A large number of small servers typically won't take advantage of grouping because of the increased likelihood that recipients will be on another server. On the other hand, a small number of large servers will benefit more from grouping.

Many legacy messaging systems, such as Microsoft Mail for PC Networks, made it very difficult to move users from one post office to another. When a user moved from one floor to another, or from one group to another, his mailbox stayed on its original post office. If the user changed physical locations, he would take his e-mail with him in a message file. The mail administrator would then remove that person's mailbox from its original post office and create for the user a new mailbox on the new post office. This usually caused address-list problems. These problems were caused by two factors: directory synchronization and the automatic .pab entry of sender addresses. In the directory synchronization case, issues arose because of the delay in directory synchronization, causing the first mailbox address to be used in the global address list until directory replication occurred. Secondly, by default the MS Mail client automatically added sender addresses to the .pab file. When a user was moved between post offices, clients still resolved the address to the original .pab location.

With Exchange, when a user changes from one department or group to another, the Exchange administrator can easily move the user from server to server within the Exchange site. The user isn't even aware of this change, nor are any desktop changes necessary, because the user's client software automatically reconfigures the profile with his new Exchange server. Unfortunately in the current version of Exchange, when a user moves from one Exchange site to another, the process isn't as simple. When moving between sites, the user must move his messages into a PST and take the PST with him to the new site. The mailbox is deleted from the site he is moving from, and a new one is created in the site he is moving to. He can then use the client to move messages from the PST back into his new server store mailbox. The process for moving between sites will become greatly simplified with the addition of some move server and move site utilities due out in late August of 1998.

Name Resolution

Each Microsoft Windows computer, configured with TCP/IP, has two names: the NetBIOS name and the host name. Within an NT domain, client and server computers must be able to resolve NetBIOS names to TCP/IP addresses and, in some cases, host names to TCP/IP addresses.

Each type of computer name, the NetBIOS name and host name, has its own distinct method for resolving its prospective names. Both also have a server-based service designed to facilitate and centralize these names to IP address mappings.

In order for the Outlook client to be able to contact the Exchange server, it must resolve the Exchange server name to an IP address. One of the methods discussed next must be able to provide this resolution, or the Outlook client will fail to start.

Domain Name System Services

Both Exchange servers and clients utilize DNS services to resolve host names to IP addresses. DNS is a good example of a network subsystem that Exchange relies on for its efficiency and reliability. It is important that domain name services be available to Exchange servers and clients. If your organization hasn't implemented DNS but is planning on migrating to NT 5.0, the Exchange project may be a good time to plan and implement DNS services. Not only do Exchange server and client utilize these services, but the Windows NT environment will rely heavily on DNS, because it displaces NetBIOS and WINS.

After identifying the person who manages DNS in your organization, identify the extent to which DNS services are available. Make sure that all the Exchange servers will have their host names registered in DNS and that the clients are configured to use DNS.

DNS services provide three major functions for Exchange: resolving the host delivering incoming SMTP messages, resolving hosts that will receive outgoing SMTP messages, and client connection support. As noted in Chapter 2, "Environment Discovery," the Mail Exchanger (MX) record with the lowest preference value in the authoritative DNS database for the Exchange determines to which server Internet mail will be delivered. The DNS configuration is important for the outgoing SMTP mail, because the Internet Mail Service will use DNS services to resolve the MX records for the outgoing SMTP mail unless it's configured to forward to an SMTP host. The SMTP relay configuration is described in detail in the section "The SMTP Delivery Process" in Chapter 9, "Internet Mail Service and Server Sizing Recommendations." The third function that DNS provides for Exchange is in client connection support. If TCP/IP is the preferred network transport, the client will use DNS to resolve the IP address of the Exchange server. The resolution of the name follows this process:

1. Check to see if the host is the local host.

2. Parse the local host file.

3. Query DNS.

4. Use the configured NetBIOS name-resolution method.

As with WINS, if your clients have difficulty resolving host names, reexamine your DNS topology and confirm which step in the DNS name-resolution process is returning the IP address. Configuring the client so that an earlier stage of the process resolves the name should reduce the time that it takes the client to connect to the server.

Windows Internet Naming Services

Today, with Windows NT 4.0 and earlier versions, Microsoft operating systems rely heavily on NetBIOS names. As with host names, NetBIOS names need to be resolved to IP addresses.

WINS services are used in varying degrees, depending on the implementation of DNS and protocols used in the organization. The two primary roles that WINS services play are resolution of domain controllers for domain authentication and resolution of the Exchange server address if NetBIOS is the preferred network transport for the client. If WINS servers are not available for either of these transactions, or if the WINS database is incomplete or inaccurate, clients will have difficulty authenticating and finding the Exchange server.

As with host name resolution, WINS server addresses need to be configured on each client. Whether clients are statically configured with WINS addresses or leased along with the TCP/IP addresses by DHCP, each client should be able to contact a WINS server to resolve a NetBIOS name to an IP address. If a DHCP client has a static WINS configuration and also has a WINS server entry in the DHCP lease, the client will use the DHCP lease entry. This is also the case for DNS server entries.

Although the name-resolution process can vary depending on how the client is configured, the NetBIOS name-resolution process typically goes as follows:

1. Check the local NetBIOS name cache.
2. Parse the LMHOSTS file.
3. Query the WINS server.
4. Broadcast for the name.
5. Parse the HOSTS file.
6. Query the DNS server.

If clients have difficulty resolving NetBIOS names, or NetBIOS name resolution is unreliable, confirm that the WINS topology of your organization meets the requirements for an organization of your design. Adding WINS servers or configuring replication between WINS servers might add efficiency in name resolution. This in turn will add reliability and increased user satisfaction with the messaging system.

Domain Architecture

Exchange depends on Windows NT security for its user and object authentication. One of the consequences of this is that all servers in an Exchange site must be in the same domain or a trusted domain. This is due to the fact that the Exchange servers in each site communicate with each other using a single Exchange service account that is common to all servers in the site. This, and the fact that user mailboxes are associated with NT Domain accounts, gives Exchange a dependency on the Windows NT Domain architecture.

In addition, the NT domain architecture affects the user implementation, especially the NT policies and profile usage. It is necessary to have domain support to implement roving Exchange user support.

Current NT Domain Architecture

It is typically difficult to change a domain architecture after it has been implemented. Usually a sound domain architecture based on one of the four standard domain models will easily accommodate an Exchange organization.

Here are the four standard domain models:

- **Single Domain**. All accounts and resources are located in one domain.
- **Single Master Domain**. All user accounts are contained in one domain. One or more resource domains contain resources such as file servers and print servers. These domains trust the account domain. Users from the account domain are assigned to resources in the resource domain.
- **Multiple Master Domain**. All user accounts are contained in several account domains. Every account domain trusts every other account domain. One or more resource domains contain resources such as file servers and print servers. These domains trust all the account domains. Users from the account domains are assigned to resources in the resource domain.
- **Complete Trust**. Several domains contain both users and resources in each domain. Every domain trusts every other domain.

Exchange Service Account Location

For small organizations that have a single domain, it's an easy decision where to create the Exchange service account. The service account for the Exchange site will reside in the one domain.

In medium-to-large organizations that employ a multiple-domain model, the options can vary, depending on which domain model is used. When choosing where to create the Exchange service account for an Exchange site, it is best to choose a Master Account domain that is trusted by all resource domains that will contain Exchange servers for that site, as shown in Figure 7.2.

If the Exchange service account isn't in an accounts domain that is trusted by all the other resource domains that contain Exchange servers in the site, intrasite communications between servers will fail to authenticate, and the site won't function (see Figure 7.3).

Analyze your domain topology and identify where each site's Exchange service account will reside.

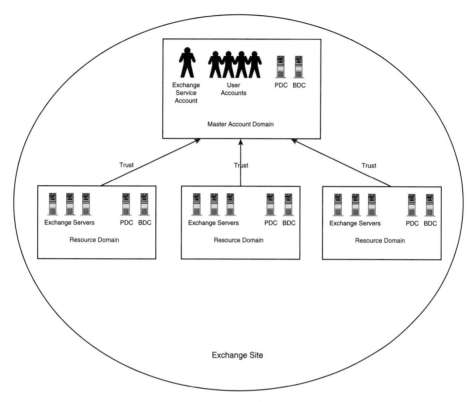

Figure 7.2 All of the resource domains that have Exchange servers for a site must trust the domain in which the Exchange service account resides.

If you are unfortunate enough to have to deal with a complete trust domain model that is greater than three domains, this might be a good time for you to reevaluate the domain topology and spin off a project to reorganize your domains, their relationships, and their trusts. The future of Windows NT, and the current Exchange project, both appeal for a simpler domain model than the complete trust. In addition to NT administration overload caused by the number of trust relationships that are necessary to maintain, the complete trust model is undesirable for the Exchange project because of the reliance on the trust relationships.

NT Policies and Profiles

Another aspect of the Windows NT domain implementation that can affect Exchange users is the implementation of Windows NT profiles.

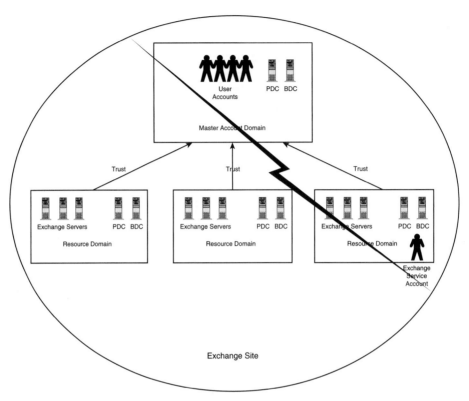

Figure 7.3 If the Exchange Server account doesn't reside in a domain that is accessible to all the Exchange servers within the site, intrasite communication won't work.

Through the use of Outlook client profiles, which are typically stored in the user's section of the Registry, the client knows which mailbox to access upon startup. When a user moves around an organization, so will the user's Exchange profile if the Registry is configured to rove with the user.

The proper implementation of roving Windows NT profiles can have the added benefit of allowing users to rove around the site and easily access their mailboxes from any workstation. Although this makes the client profile larger, it is very beneficial for users who use multiple workstations.

Planning Questions Answered

Many services work closely with Exchange servers to provide reliable messaging. These include the network architecture, domain name services, and NT domain architecture. It is important to review these services when designing the Exchange implementation.

In this chapter, we covered the answers to the following questions posed in Chapters 2 and 3:

- **Who manages the DNS services?** This person is responsible for and capable of maintaining the DNS database.
- **WINS**. Where are the WINS servers located?
- **Domain architecture**. What is the NT Domain architecture, including trusts?
- **Administrative model**. If your domain model is a complete trust domain model, document the technical reasons for the complete trust model.
- **NT policies and profiles**. Are policies and profiles implemented? If so, do users have the ability to roam throughout the organization?

8

Design of Client Services

THE REQUIREMENTS OF DESIGNING MESSAGING client functionality increase with complexity as the computing environment becomes more heterogeneous. This heterogeneous nature includes different client operating systems, different user access needs and locations, and different uses of the technology. These differences require messaging professionals to anticipate and plan for a multitude of user scenarios. The client design is critical in the Exchange design process because the client functionality is representative of Exchange as a whole to the end-user. In this chapter we will look at the design of the client services to meet today's complex messaging needs.

Defining User Types

Before you start the client design process, you must define the types of users accessing the messaging system. The types of users can be put into three groups: where the users access the messaging system, what the users will need access to, and how the users will use the messaging environment.

User Access to the Messaging System

User access to the messaging system falls into three types: single workstation access, roving access from multiple workstations, and remote access to the messaging system.

The final user group is how the users will use the messaging environment. This group classifies the volume of messaging functionality among clients, the usage of messaging within the organization, and the usage of messaging outside the organization.

This section covers all three user groups and the design decisions necessary to support them.

Single Workstation Client Access

The single-workstation client is not only the most frequent type of messaging client in most corporate environments but is also the building block for the roving and remote client design. This client design is for the user who consistently accesses his mailbox from the same workstation.

Client Services

To support the single workstation client, two services should be configured—messaging server service and address book service. For the Outlook 98 client, this would be the Microsoft Exchange Server service and the Outlook Address Book service. The support and functionality of these two services are described in Table 8.1.

The design of the client might determine the need for additional services, such as the personal folder store service.

Server Support

For the single workstation client, all functionality that is required for messaging can be implemented by using only the workstation and a single Exchange server. However, it might be necessary to utilize a network server other than the Exchange server to support service extensions on the Exchange client. For example, if you have decided to implement the Personal Address Book service for clients, it is recommended that the .pab files be stored on a file server that is backed up on a regular basis.

Table 8.1   **Services That Support Exchange Server**

Service	Functionality
Microsoft Exchange Server	Provides support for the sending and receiving of mail. This service also determines where messages are delivered and how addresses are resolved. Identifies the host name of the Exchange server to which the client must connect. By adding this service, it is possible to take advantage of the rich features of Exchange, such as Inbox Rules, Out of Office Autoreply, Outlook Today, and Shared Calendaring.
Outlook Address Book	The address book service stores addresses that are not part of the global address list.

Roving

Roving users are users who access their mailbox resources from multiple workstations on a single network or on multiple networks connected via dedicated connections. Solutions to match these requirements vary, from instructing users on how to create their own profiles on each new workstation to making their Exchange profiles available from the network. Storing Exchange profiles on the network in roaming Windows NT user profiles helps limit the impact that roaming has on users. Roving profile support is tied very closely to the client operating system and network operating system. To have full roving profile support, the client workstations must have implemented either Windows 95, Windows 98, or Windows NT Workstation. To support roving profiles, a full Windows NT domain design must be implemented.

Server Support

To support an Outlook 98 user with a true roving profile, the Windows NT domain to which he authenticates must have NT roaming profiles implemented. This requires that each user be assigned a user directory and that these directories be mapped to a drive letter at logon. In the case of both Windows 95 and Windows NT workstation, the user profile information is stored in the Registry settings that are replicated with the user data file. If user profiles are implemented, the user network directory must be available from any workstation that the user may authenticate from. In large organizations, this can be an issue if there are unreliable network connections between workstations and domain controllers.

For manual implementation of roving profiles, users must be able to set up a profile on any workstation to which they log on. This is necessary if the client operating system doesn't support Windows NT profiles or if Windows NT profiles haven't been implemented. In this scenario, users must know the name of a server within their organization, they must know their display name or alias name, and they must be able to set up a profile with those variables. Also, users must understand that files such as personal store files (.pst) and personal address book files (.pab) won't be accessible if stored on a workstation or added from the network. If the outlook.stf file is available on the workstation when the user launches Outlook, the user will be prompted for the information that is required for configuring Outlook. The outlook.stf file defines the services that will be configured for Outlook and that can be customized by using the Outlook Deployment Kit. If the outlook.stf file has included the Exchange Server service, the setup will prompt the user for information such as the name of the profile, the server's name or network location (IP address), and any configuration details for personal folders and address books.

Shared Desktop Environments

When users share client workstations for messaging access, the profile choices are different. Although it is then possible to store the appropriate Exchange profiles on the desktop, you should consider whether the profiles should be stored on the desktop or on the server. This is the same design decision that you face with single workstation access. The crux of this decision is the ability to back up and restore the Exchange profile. Most organizations don't back up individual workstations. In this case, profile information should be stored on servers so that the information can be restored.

Authentication

For roving user support, users must be able to authenticate to their own domain. This requires access to domain controllers across all physical locations to which users will roam, and WINS server support of the domain environment with a Windows NT 4.0 domain. With Windows NT 5.0, it will be possible to locate and authenticate to domains and server applications via DNS service records. In cases where there are slow links between the work site and the domain controller and the Exchange Server they are accessing, roving users will experience slow response time, and network bandwidth could be affected.

Remote

In this section we consider the needs of remote user client access to the Exchange environment. Remote users are defined for the purposes of this book as both users who occasionally access the Exchange servers from remote locations and users who always access the Exchange servers from remote locations.

Authentication

Authentication needs for remote users vary with the remote access solution implemented. With a Windows NT-based remote access solution such as Remote Access Services (RAS), a one-password implementation can be designed if the user is logging on to the same domain for RAS as Exchange. If the organization is using another remote access solution, such as a terminal server or an Internet Solution Provider (ISP), the authentication of the client takes on additional requirements. The password solution will differ with the remote access solution and client operating system. Some of the most common access methods and a suggested authentication design are listed in Table 8.2.

Table 8.2 **Authentication Methods for Remote Access Solutions**

Remote Access Method	Client Operating System	Recommended Authentication Design
Terminal server with terminal pop-up password screen	Windows 95, Windows NT	Use domain credentials for dial-up networking client password window. Enter terminal server credentials at password prompt.
RAS access in Exchange domain	Windows 95, Windows NT	Use domain credentials for dial-up networking client password window.

Remote Access Method	Client Operating System	Recommended Authentication Design
Access from Internet (through ISP or other third-party access)	Windows NT	Log on to workstation with domain credentials. Use ISP credentials for dial-up networking client password window.
Access from Internet (through ISP or other third-party access)	Windows 95	Use ISP credentials for dial-up networking client password window. Configure Exchange server client to prompt for authentication.

In the case of using a native Exchange client to access the Exchange server from outside the organization's firewall or network, RPC traffic must be allowed between the Exchange client and server.

Lessening Transfer Requirements

Transfer requirements and therefore transfer time can be reduced by lessening the amount of data that must be communicated between the client and the server. This is easiest to do for users who are only occasional remote users. In this case, the following client design decisions should be made:

- Encourage users to divide their mailbox data into subfolders and select only the necessary folders for offline synchronization.

- Encourage laptop users to synchronize their mailboxes before leaving the office and to work from the offline store when they are remote. When they need to send and receive messages, users should dial in and choose to only synchronize their Inbox, which will also send messages stored in the Outbox.

- Encourage users to download the address book once and then choose to only update the address book changes on an occasional basis.

- Only implement roaming profiles for clients who need the roaming functionality, because the larger profiles will add to the time necessary for authentication and logon over a slow link.

Offline Resources

The resources available to remote users when they are working offline will be all folders that have been selected for synchronization and that have been synchronized. (If an offline store file (.ost) has been configured for the client profile, all built-in folders are selected for offline access by default.) Additionally, the address book will be available if it has been downloaded to the client machine. When a user is working offline from an already-configured .ost file, folders that haven't previously been configured for offline use can be configured, and they will automatically synchronize the next time the client is connected to the network. This may be necessary if a user wants to sort mail out of the inbox while offline and hasn't synchronized all the folders in the mailbox. For users whose access to the network is only through dial-in, they should be advised to configure all of their folders for offline usage. In this case, they can always work from their .ost file and then synchronize as appropriate with the Exchange server. This will greatly reduce the transfer time for these permanently remote users.

The design decisions for the following questions from Chapters 2 and 3 were addressed in this section:

- In the current messaging system, how are remote users sending and receiving messages?

- How many remote users consistently work from home? How many remote users are traveling remote users?

User Resource Definition

It is also necessary to classify what messaging components users will need access to in the design process. The most common components are access to their own mailboxes, access to shared mailboxes, and access to extended features, such as public folders.

Shared Mailboxes

Users often want to share mailboxes in two scenarios. The first is multiple users who are responsible for managing the responses for a single mailbox or alias. The second scenario is an administrative assistant situation in which an executive wants the administrative assistant to be able to read and respond to messages that he or she has received.

Multiple User Access

It's very common in organizations for multiple mailboxes to be accessed by a single client application. This is usually necessary when a mailbox is implemented to receive group questions (for example, a suggestions mailbox or a webmaster mailbox) and a team of employees will be responsible for monitoring and maintaining this mailbox. There are two predominant ways to implement this functionality on the server side. The first is to implement a public folder for the group mailing and to grant owner access to all accounts that are maintaining the correspondence. Those users can then read, delete, and reply to messages that arrive in that public folder. The second method is to implement an Exchange mailbox for the group mailing and give user permissions to all accounts that are maintaining the correspondence. The public folder method is better for tracking which user responded to the correspondence. It also allows users to clearly separate their actions between their own personal mailbox and public folder response. The user permission method has the advantage of letting users work natively from a mailbox.

It is important to consider the return address of the respondent and the location of the message trail when configuring multiple-user access to a message store. Should the shared mailbox name or alias name be used in the reply so that any subsequent replies will be sent to the shared mailbox? Or should the individual user name be used in the reply so that any reply to the reply will be handled by that individual? In the case of responding with the shared mailbox name or alias name, the mail users will need to view and update the From field in the message composition to reflect the correct From address. A user must have permission to send as that user to fill in the From field. This prevents users from spoofing mail from other users.

The issue of how to reply to messages is simplified with the use of Outlook 98. With the Outlook 98 client, it is possible to configure the replies to messages in folders other than the Inbox to be saved in the same folder as the original message. This makes it easy to track the thread of a discussion, especially with multiple users using a single mailbox.

Granting Other Users Access to a Personal Mailbox

There are several ways to design other-user access to a mailbox, depending on the business needs and requirements. This is most commonly used in the case of an executive designating access to an administrative assistant. The first solution is to assign an alternative recipient for the mailbox. The alternative recipient can receive either the messages or a copy of the messages. In the Outlook client configuration, the executive can then grant Send On Behalf Of permissions to the administrative assistant. In this scenario, messages would appear in the administrative assistant's own mailbox with the sender's address on the From line. The assistant can respond on behalf of the executive as appropriate.

The second solution is to assign the administrative assistant user permission for the mailbox. This permission can be assigned only from the Exchange administrator program. The administrative assistant can then open the mailbox and send and receive messages as appropriate.

A third option is to have the original recipient assign permissions to his Inbox and other appropriate folders. This solution allows for multiple user access to new mail in the Inbox but can still ensure the privacy of the other folders. The mailbox owner can then establish a mailbox rule to automatically forward messages from senders that they don't want to share into folders that aren't shared with other users. To share subfolders of the Inbox, the Inbox must be shared as well.

Defining How Messaging Will Be Used

The third category that needs to be determined for the client architecture is how users will use the messaging system. This includes determining messaging volume and message traffic patterns.

Classifying Users for Server Sizing

In Chapter 2, users were split into three categories: light, medium, and heavy. The question was posed as to what each of these classifications meant for your organization in terms of messaging utilization. We will use those classifications in the following sections as we discuss the placement of users.

Enforcing Mailbox Limits

The number of users a messaging server can support is proportional to the mailbox limits enforced on that server. The mailbox limits that are realistic for users are related to the messaging utilization for those users. Many organizations set one mailbox limit for all users based on realistic numbers for heavy messaging users. Light and medium users usually never realize that there are restrictions in place. Some organizations set mailbox limits based on the utilization of medium users and grant exceptions for heavy users as appropriate. Whatever the philosophy used for setting limits, three levels of restriction are available for mailbox size limitation. These are listed in Table 8.3. Balancing the maintenance costs of unnecessarily large message stores against the needs of the user is delicate. Keep in mind that users will find other communication methods if they decide that the messaging system is unreliable (even if it is their own fault for exceeding limits). Instituting limits is a good practice to keep the messaging system functioning properly. Instituting an exception and review process for those limits is prudent for continued user satisfaction.

Message Traffic Flow

Optimizing message traffic flow within the organization can minimize network traffic and connector traffic. This is done at a basic level by placing users within the same flow of communication on the same Exchange server. Additionally, making sure that subsidiary offices have direct routing available to their home offices can streamline the message traffic flow within the organization.

Table 8.3 **Mailbox Limit Settings**

Restriction Level	Description
Warning	When the size of a mailbox has reached the threshold set for this restriction level, the Exchange server sends daily warning messages to the user.
Sending	When the size of a mailbox has reached the threshold set for this restriction level, the user is prohibited from sending messages until the mailbox has been reduced in size to beneath the send threshold.
Receiving	When the size of a mailbox has reached the threshold set for this restriction level, the user is unable to receive messages, and they are returned to the sender.

Some organizations have very dynamic work and department structures. In this case, it can be extremely time-consuming for administrators to continually move users between servers in order to ensure that workgroup members are all located on the same server. After the initial design and user placement has been done, set up a review process to decide how much time and effort will be spent conducting traffic analysis and moving users.

Outside Organization Message Flow

Traffic can also be optimized for message flow to and from recipients outside the organization. Typically, this traffic will be to and from the Internet. It's easy to pinpoint the workgroups that take advantage of this connectivity the most. Confirm that message flow from these workgroups to the Internet makes sense when placing these users on servers. If a specific group of users is sending and receiving large amounts of data through the Internet Mail Service, it is important that the architecture provide a server path to and from the Internet that minimizes the number of Exchange servers over which the Internet mail must travel.

The Outlook Client

The Outlook 98 client has many features that have been optimized to work in a corporate messaging environment and that can be designed to meet most of the diverse client needs. Here are some of those features:

- **Outlook Today**. A one-page view of the calendar, e-mail statistics (the number of unread messages, draft messages, and unsent messages), and tasks for the user.

- **Wide protocol support**. Outlook 98 supports the POP3, SMTP, IMAP4, LDAP, NNTP, MHTML, and S/MIME protocols.

- **HTML message support**. In addition to the RTF and plain-text format messages supported in previous versions of Outlook, Outlook 98 also supports HTML mail.

- **Drag and drop between components**. Outlook 98 commands for sorting and filtering information are the same across all modules. This enables drag and drop between components as well as searching across all components. A user can now drag a mail message to the calendar to create an appointment or a contact to the Inbox to start an e-mail message to that contact.

- **Enhanced offline store**. Outlook 98 takes the benefit of the offline store file (.ost file) a step further by automating synchronization when the user attaches to the server after working offline and lessening response time for events by working primarily from the offline store.

Deployment Strategies

The Outlook Deployment Kit is the tool that administrators use to configure installation files for distribution to the user. This kit replaces the STF editor released with versions of the Exchange client but includes and extends the functionality offered. Because Outlook 98 and Internet Explorer 4.01 are closely related, it is possible to customize and deploy Internet Explorer along with Outlook 98. Table 8.4 describes the most frequently customized Outlook 98 options that can be managed by the Outlook Deployment Kit.

Push

Push installations are those in which the deployment package is pushed to the desktop. This is done either through a systems management package or by sending the installation files to the user by e-mail. The Outlook Deployment Kit can configure a package for distribution by SMS. If an SMS package is deployed, it can be configured to require the user to execute the installation. This isn't the case with deploying the installation files through e-mail.

Table 8.4 **Outlook Deployment Kit Customization Options**

Option	Description
Services	Determines the list of services to be installed. Services include address book service, personal folder service, Microsoft Exchange Server service, LDAP service, and MSMail service.
Server Name	The Exchange server name. Set this to any server within the organization, and Outlook 98 will automatically update to the correct server for the user.
Mailbox	Set the default mailbox to use for the client. Use the %username% variable if you want Outlook 98 to use the user's NT username as the Exchange alias during setup.
Processing Items Behavior	Default settings for deleting Deleted Items upon exit, automatic name checking, auto-archiving, after move or delete action, and so on.
RPC Binding Order	Lets you change the binding order in the profile if the desired binding order is different than the default.
OST creation and synchronization	Lets you limit OST creation and caching and the setting of default synchronization settings.
Calendar	Settings for the default work week, default working hours, and the publishing of iCal information.
Tasks, Journal, and Reminder	Default settings for Tasks, Journaling, and Reminders.
Spelling	Lets you turn spelling on and off and set spell-check options.
Help settings	Lets you customize the location of help files.

Pull

A pull installation refers to a deployment that is launched from the desktop. Typically, the deployment team will configure an installation directory on a network server. This network share will include the outlook.stf file with all of the required user data. If the organization is configuring Outlook for users who will require multiple .stf file configurations, it is recommended that the deployment team configure multiple source directories with all the installation files and a different .stf file in each directory. Pull distribution is usually more successful than a push installation because someone—either a person on the migration team or the user—is launching and monitoring the installation. The Outlook Deployment Kit can be used to customize the installation files to be used on the network share.

Data Transfer

Chapter 10, "Coexistence and Migration," covers server data migration in great detail. However, if data from the existing messaging system is located on the desktop, it is necessary to address this migration from the client side. Depending on the legacy messaging system and messaging client, this could mean leaving the legacy messaging client on the desktop so that users can view their legacy mail without messaging functionality. If the legacy messaging client was Windows Messaging, an Exchange client, or an Outlook client, the client data transfer could consist of copying or moving the information from a personal store file (.pst) to the server mailbox after it is configured. In any case, the transfer of data must be considered during the design of the client installation method.

The design decisions for the following questions from Chapters 2 and 3 were addressed in this section:

- Of the protocols found on each LAN, which protocols are currently being used to communicate between messaging clients and messaging servers?

- What is the hardware specification of the existing messaging clients?

- What is the TCP/IP addressing strategy?

- Does your organization use client installation points? If so, pinpoint those that exist on your network.

9

Internet Mail Service and Server Sizing Recommendations

O NE OF THE PRIMARY ROLES THAT EXCHANGE Server plays in an organization is to connect the internal users with the rest of the world. This connectivity may take the form of Internet mail transferred between organizations, Web access to public folders, or X.400 messages sent via private or public networks. This chapter discusses the issues that need to be addressed when you're architecting external connections via the Internet Mail Service.

Internet Mail Service Strategies

Exchange has supported SMTP since its introduction in 1996. It was initially provided by the Internet Mail Connector. Functionality and efficiency have been improved with each version, and SMTP is now called the Internet Mail Service (IMS). The Exchange Internet Mail Service is RFC-compliant and is considered an SMTP host. The rerouting functionality introduced in Exchange 5.0 classifies the IMS as a Smart Host, giving it the capability to store and forward SMTP messages.

Smart Host functionality was necessary to support POP3 clients. POP3 and IMAP4 clients deliver messages using SMTP. The Exchange IMS had to be able to reroute those incoming SMTP messages from POP3 clients to the Internet.

Just as Exchange can be configured to support organizations of many shapes and sizes, the IMS can support a wide variety of Internet mail demands and environments. It is possible to construct an Exchange architecture that has a single IMS connecting it to the Internet, or one that has multiple connections to the Internet. It is also possible to restrict access to the IMS for sending and receiving mail.

When you're starting to design a strategy for implementing Internet mail, the first technical issue to address is the type of connection that your Exchange environment will have to the Internet.

Point of Entry for Internet Mail

Chapter 2, "Environment Discovery," addressed many of the questions that must be answered regarding configuration of the Internet Mail Service and connectivity to the Internet. The first of these is the speed and type of connection between the Exchange environment and the Internet.

There are typically two ways that the Exchange organization will be connected to the Internet: via a dedicated connection or via a dial-up service.

Dedicated Connection

Dedicated connections to the Internet are rapidly becoming the norm rather than the exception in today's business environment. As costs for frame relay and local point-to-point services drop and Internet Service Providers lower service fees, most companies are connecting to the Internet for mail as well as World Wide Web access and other public IP-based services.

When a dedicated connection to the Internet is configured, an organization typically configures a firewall—or, at a minimum, a filtered router—between the public Internet and an internal network. In either of these cases, the Exchange architecture can be configured with an Exchange server on the external side of the security device or on the inside of the security device. If an Exchange server is positioned on the external side of the security device, it should be a server that doesn't contain any user accounts and that should serve only as an SMTP relay host (see Figure 9.1).

Once you have identified where on your network relative to the connection to the Internet you will position your Exchange server, you can proceed with configuring the proper security between the Internet and your Exchange environment. The first step in doing this is to determine which IP ports are already open on your firewall or filtered router.

When a firewall exists between the Exchange server and the Internet, there are two common ways for the firewall to be configured.

The firewall can have an SMTP daemon enabled that passes all inbound SMTP traffic to the IMS. In addition, only the IMS can initiate an SMTP session to the Internet to deliver messages, as shown in Figure 9.2.

The firewall itself can be an SMTP host, as shown in Figure 9.3. This way, the firewall SMTP host receives all SMTP mail and forwards it to the IMS. The IMS is configured as a relay agent and forwards all SMTP traffic to the firewall SMTP host. The firewall SMTP host is then responsible for doing the DNS lookup and delivering the message.

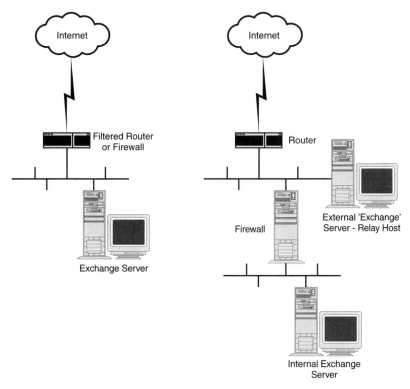

Figure 9.1 When connecting Exchange to the Internet, it is possible to configure an Exchange server inside or outside the firewall or filtered router. In either case, the Exchange server should be secured against attack.

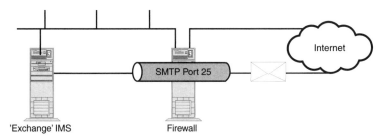

Figure 9.2 The firewall controls SMTP traffic by only allowing inbound SMTP traffic to the Exchange server and outbound SMTP traffic from the Exchange server.

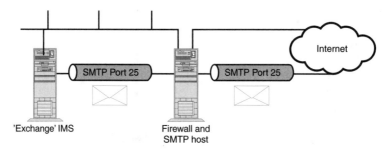

Figure 9.3 The firewall can be configured to act as an SMTP host for the organization. All inbound SMTP traffic is delivered to the firewall SMTP host, which then forwards it to the Exchange IMS. For outbound SMTP traffic, the IMS forwards all traffic to the firewall SMTP host, which then is responsible for the DNS lookup and delivery.

As mentioned, you need to decide how your organization will pass traffic to your Exchange server from the Internet. This decision should be based on the following:

- How is mail relayed to your existing mail system?
- What are your organization's security requirements?
- What access besides SMTP do you want to provide to external mail users?

If your organization currently utilizes a relay host located at an ISP for mail delivery, this might be the method of connectivity that will be implemented with the new Exchange architecture. Alternatively, the installation of Exchange can be used as an opportunity to modify the existing message flow.

Outlook Client Access from the Internet

In addition to providing SMTP access to the Exchange server, it is possible to configure your firewall and Exchange server for Outlook client access from the Internet. Supporting Outlook client access requires special configuration of the Exchange server. When an Outlook client connects to an Exchange server, it establishes an RPC session to the server on RPC listener port number 135. The Exchange server responds to the Outlook client with two random port numbers for connections to the information store and the directory service. These ports are normally chosen at random from port numbers above 1024.

When configuring an Exchange server for client access from the Internet, you must predetermine the information store and directory service port numbers so that they can be configured for access through the firewall. These ports can be set in the Registry of the Exchange server. The Registry keys are

```
HKEY_LOCAL_MACHINE\System\CurrentControlSet\Services\
↪MSExchangeDS\Parameters\
```

and

```
HKEY_LOCAL_MACHINE\System\CurrentControlSet\Services\
↪MSExchangeIS¦ParametersSystem.
```

In each of these subkeys, add the following entry:

```
TCP/IP port REG_DWORD
DATA: <port number to assign>
```

Do not assign ports immediately above the 1023 range.

The SMTP Delivery Process

When Exchange receives a message, it deciphers the message address, evaluates the route necessary to deliver the message, and sends the message on its way. When a message is bound for the Internet, the route will take the message through the Exchange IMS server with the lowest-cost route to the Internet.

The IMS can be configured to deliver messages in two basic ways:

- It can use DNS to resolve the SMTP domain name to a list of SMTP hosts that will receive messages for the recipient organization.

- It can forward all messages it receives to a predefined SMTP relay host. This configuration makes the IMS an SMTP relay agent.

Typically, unless a dial-up connection is used, the IMS will be configured to use DNS and deliver the messages directly to their destinations. This form of delivery is illustrated in Figure 9.4.

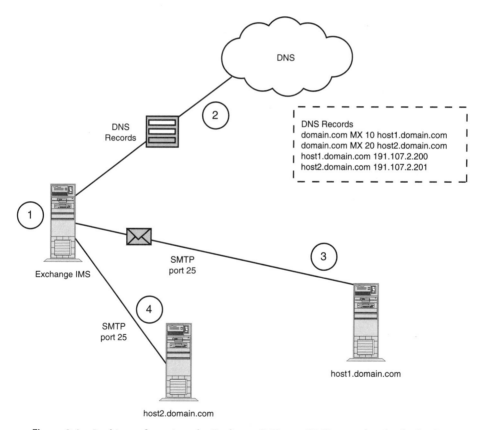

Figure 9.4 In this configuration, the Exchange IMS uses DNS to resolve the destination domain and then delivers the message to the host defined for that domain.

Here's how the process works:

1. The IMS receives a message destined for an SMTP host on the Internet.

2. The IMS contacts the DNS server designated in the TCP/IP configuration of the IMS server to resolve the MX records and A records for the destination SMTP domain. The DNS returns a list of eligible SMTP hosts that can receive SMTP messages for that domain. The Exchange server sorts the MX records and chooses the SMTP host with the lowest preference value. In this example, host1.domain.com has the lowest preference value (10).

3. The IMS then tries to open a TCP port 25 session with that SMTP host. In our example, this attempt fails.

4. The IMS then takes the next-lowest preference value SMTP host from the MX record, host2.domain.com. It opens a TCP port 25 session with that host and delivers the SMTP message.

If the IMS can't successfully deliver the message to any hosts in the MX record, the message will wait in the IMS queue until the configured timeout has expired. The message timeout is configured separately for urgent, normal, and non-urgent messages. The default configuration is 24 hours for urgent messages, 48 hours for normal messages, and 72 hours for non-urgent messages. It will then return the message to the sender. These messages waiting in the queue are often unwarranted cause for concern among Exchange administrators. A handful of messages stuck in the IMS queue doesn't indicate a problem with the IMS. Rather, the receiving domain of these messages might be down.

Troubleshooting IMS Problems

Although not the focus of this book, a few pointers in IMS troubleshooting will make your IMS experience more pleasant.

1. From the Exchange server, manually look up the MX records for the domain of the message stuck in the IMS queue.

   From a command prompt on the Exchange server, type
   ```
   nslookup-querytype=mx domainname.com
   ```
   If MX records are returned, proceed. If not, the domain name is wrong, or the organization is incapable of receiving SMTP mail. Another possibility is that your DNS is down.

   If MX records are returned, they will look something like this:
   ```
   domainname.com MX 10 server.domainname.com
   domainname.com MX 20 server2.domainname.com
   server.domainname.com A191.107.2.200
   server2.domainname.com A 191.107.2.201
   ```

2. Open a TCP port 25 session to the server returned in the MX record.

   Using the Telnet application, connect to server.domainname.com or 191.107.2.200 over port 25.

If the SMTP host at `server.domainname.com` answers over port 25, there might be a problem with the Internet Mail Service. Try stopping and starting the service. If one of these steps fails along the way, it is most likely a problem with the SMTP address or the SMTP hosts at the recipient's organization.

SMTP in Large Organizations

When implementing SMTP in large or dispersed organizations, it might not make sense to have SMTP traffic travel across the globe only to be delivered a few blocks away from where the sender is located. We saw earlier in this chapter how to configure multiple SMTP connectors that deliver messages based on the shortest route to the Internet. However, the MX records can be defined to deliver messages to multiple Internet Mail Services in a single site, with the other site only delivering outbound messages, as shown in Figure 9.5.

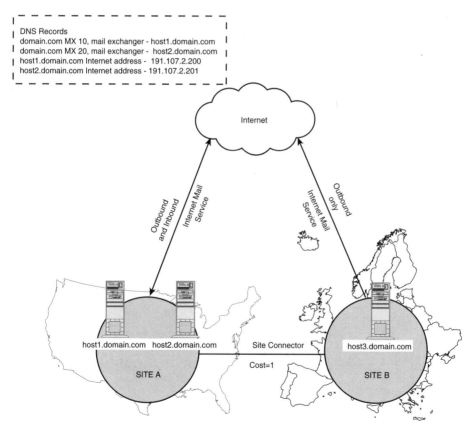

Figure 9.5   In this organization, outbound SMTP messages travel out the IMS on the server hosting the message sender. Inbound SMTP messages are delivered only to the North America site and are then routed within the organization to the users in Europe.

If both sites will accept SMTP messages, the MX records can be defined to send messages to any site, based on preference values (see Figure 9.6).

However, regardless of how many sites can receive inbound SMTP messages, a single site will always be the preferred site for the organization. If inbound messages need to be delivered to their respective sites, multiple domains need to be defined (see Figure 9.7).

It is also possible for organizations or sites that handle heavy SMTP traffic to define an IMS as the primary outbound SMTP host and another IMS as the preferred inbound SMTP host.

The primary inbound SMTP host is defined by setting lower preference values in the MX records. The primary outbound SMTP host is defined by setting lower connector costs. If the preferred inbound host is down, inbound messages will be delivered to the primary outbound host because that host is listed using MX records as the second preference. If the primary outbound host is down, the next-lowest-cost route, or the inbound host, will deliver the messages, as shown in Figure 9.8.

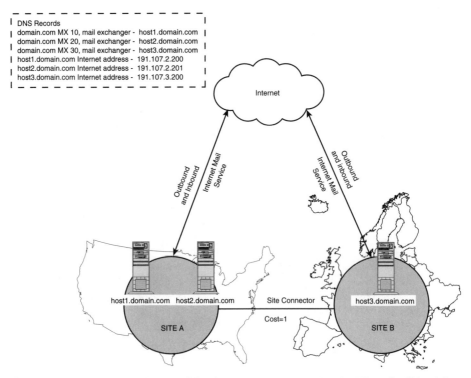

Figure 9.6   By adding an MX record for the Europe IMS, incoming SMTP mail will be delivered to Europe if the North American IMS servers are not available. If the North American servers are available, incoming SMTP mail will be delivered to them and routed within the organization to the Europe users.

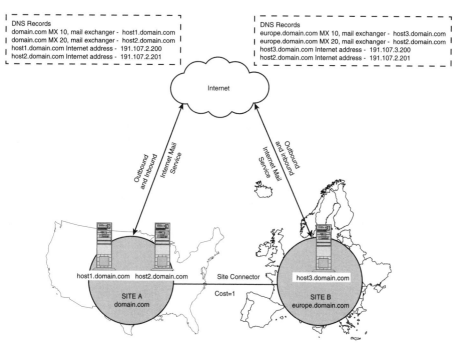

DNS Records
domain.com MX 10, mail exchanger - host1.domain.com
domain.com MX 20, mail exchanger - host2.domain.com
host1.domain.com Internet address - 191.107.2.200
host2.domain.com Internet address - 191.107.2.201

DNS Records
europe.domain.com MX 10, mail exchanger - host3.domain.com
europe.domain.com MX 20, mail exchanger - host2.domain.com
host3.domain.com Internet address - 191.107.3.200
host2.domain.com Internet address - 191.107.2.201

Internet

Outbound and Inbound Internet Mail Service

Outbound and Inbound Internet Mail Service

host1.domain.com   host2.domain.com   Site Connector   host3.domain.com

SITE A   Cost=1   SITE B
domain.com   europe.domain.com

Figure 9.7   In this organization, two DNS domains are defined. Both sites accept incoming
SMTP mail with the MX records in each location pointing to the appropriate domain and
IMS. The site connector then provides primarily intraorganization messaging transfer services.

Restricting Internet Mail Access

It is possible to restrict access to the Internet Mail Service in two ways: who can send
and receive Internet mail, and which Internet domains can send incoming SMTP
mail. In restricting who can send and receive Internet mail, access can be restricted to
only users from within the organization, or to only specific users. For the incoming
SMTP mail restriction, it is possible to specify domains and hosts on the Internet from
which mail will or will not be accepted.

The simplest way to restrict access to the IMS to only users within the domain is
to configure the IMS to not reroute SMTP mail. This will deny access to the IMS
submitted by POP3 and IMAP4 clients trying to use it as a relay host. If you have
configured your users with POP3 or IMAP4 access, you will have to configure the
IMS to reroute only mail for your domain.

To configure the IMS to reject mail from specific users or hosts on the Internet,
you must establish a *TurfList* of users and hosts from which mail is not accepted.
Messages received from hosts or users on this list are then moved to a directory on the
server called TurfDir and are not delivered to the intended recipients.

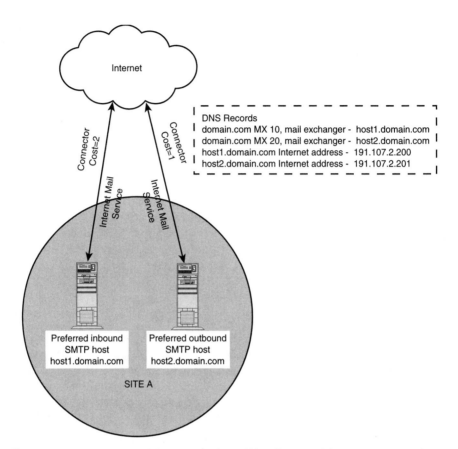

Figure 9.8 It is possible to define an IMS that will handle most of the incoming SMTP message traffic by assigning a lower DNS MX record preference for that IMS. It is also possible to define an IMS that will handle most of the outgoing SMTP message traffic by assigning a lower Exchange connector cost for that IMS.

To prevent unwanted messages from being delivered to local users, you must specify the directory where aborted messages are moved to and the messages that will be aborted. To do this, add the following values as shown in Table 9.1 to the Registry key:

```
HKEY_LOCAL_MACHINE\SYSTEM\CurrentControlSet\Services\
➥MSExchangeIMC\Parameters
```

Table 9.1 **TurfDir and TurfTable**

Value	Data Type	Description
TurfDir	REG_SZ	Specifies the directory where aborted messages are moved. It is recommended that you set this to Exchsrvr\ Imcdata\Turfdir, where Exchsrvr is the directory where the Microsoft Exchange Server files are located.
TurfTable	REG_MULTI_SZ	Specifies the messages that are aborted.

SMTP and Dial-Up Connectivity

In organizations that don't have permanent Internet connectivity, the IMS can be configured to dial up an Internet Service Provider and deliver and retrieve SMTP messages. The easiest configuration is possible when the ISP runs a version of Sendmail that supports the ETRN command. The ETRN command, which is the enhanced version of the TURN command, prompts the SMTP host at the ISP to deliver queued mail for the organization's domain. Both TURN and ETRN are automated SMTP store-and-forward services for SMTP mail. These services are defined by RFC 821 and RFC 1985.

When the Sendmail application at the ISP receives the ETRN command, Sendmail looks up the MX records using DNS and delivers the messages to the SMTP host with the lowest preference value. Since your organization is currently connected, which is necessary to issue the ETRN command, Sendmail can deliver the queued messages to your host.

When your SMTP host isn't connected, the sending SMTP host is unable to deliver messages to the SMTP host (your host) with the lowest preference value, so messages are delivered to the SMTP host with the next-lowest preference value (your ISP's Sendmail host). See Figure 9.9.

If the ISP's Sendmail application doesn't support ETRN, it is also possible to issue a Sendmail command to prompt the ISP's Sendmail host to deliver your domain's messages. The IMS can be configured to issue this command:

```
Rsh isp.com -l logonalias "user/lib/sendmail -q
➥-Ryourdomainname.com"
```

or this one:

```
Dequeue -m isp.com -d yourdomainname.com
```

This command causes the same chain of events to occur at the ISP as the ETRN command.

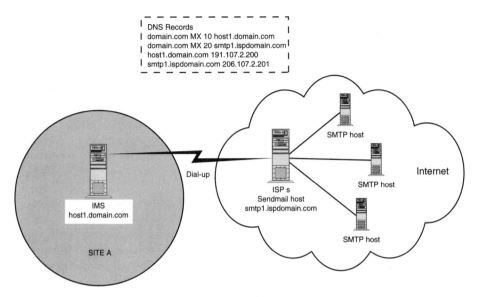

DNS Records
domain.com MX 10 host1.domain.com
domain.com MX 20 smtp1.ispdomain.com
host1.domain.com 191.107.2.200
smtp1.ispdomain.com 206.107.2.201

SMTP host

Dial-up

Internet

SMTP host

ISP s
Sendmail host
smtp1.ispdomain.com

IMS
host1.domain.com

SMTP host

SITE A

Figure 9.9   For organizations that have dial-up connectivity to the Internet, mail is delivered to the ISP's SMTP host as defined in the DNS MX records when the Exchange server SMTP host is unavailable.

Here are the questions from Chapters 2 and 3 that were addressed in this section:

- **Internet connection**. How is your organization connected to the Internet? What is the speed of that connection?

- **Firewall configuration**. How is your firewall configured? List the ports that are open on your firewall.

- **SMTP and the firewall**. How is SMTP traffic handled at the firewall? Does the firewall pass the SMTP port 25 packets through to a single SMTP host, or does the firewall itself act as an SMTP host, receiving messages and then forwarding them to the messaging gateway?

- **SMTP**. How do SMTP messages currently flow between the organization and the Internet?

Sizing Servers

Sizing the proper hardware for your Exchange organization can be a difficult task. This is because the number and size of Exchange servers required in any specific site and in the organization as a whole depend on several variables, some of which can't be determined during the architecture process. These variables include the following:

- The number and type of users in your organization
- The existing server hardware specifications

- Size limits to be imposed on mailboxes
- The projected number of public folders
- Gateways implemented between the Exchange organization and other mail systems

Once these variables are determined, the server hardware can be identified. When specifying server hardware, a rule of thumb for determining the number and type of servers in an organization is to purchase (when possible) a few large servers instead of many small ones. Increase the number of users on those servers to an appropriate limit. When the limit for that hardware is reached, buy a new large server. The reason for this is that server hardware capacity changes at a rapid pace. There is no point in investing in hardware now that won't be used until next year.

Users have the greatest impact on server hardware requirements. In Chapter 3, "Gathering Requirements," we discussed the different types of users and how many of each your organization has.

Depending on the percentage differential between the types of users in your organization, the number of users on your servers will vary. If you have a large percentage of light mail users, you will be able to place a much larger percentage of users on a server. This is because with light mail users it is less likely that the information store on the server will grow rapidly. Information store growth with heavy users will be less predictable and more likely to expand at a rapid rate.

When sizing servers for the information store, it is important to remember that defragmenting the information store requires at least the same amount of space as the information store on a local drive to which the temporary database must be written. This means that if your information store is 12 GB in size, you must have an additional 12 GB available to defragment your database.

Organization Policies and Restrictions

In order to check the growth of the information store and limit the performance impact on the Exchange system, it is possible to impose policies and restrictions on users of the Exchange system. When imposing limits, however, it is important to remember that the messaging system is there to serve the users and that any limits shouldn't inhibit the usual course of business operation.

Mailbox Quotas

One of the easiest ways to limit the growth of the information store is to impose a mailbox quota for users. As discussed in Chapter 5, "How to Sell Exchange as a Messaging and Workgroup Solution," it is possible to impose three mailbox limits: an *issue warning* limit, a *prohibit send* limit, and a *prohibit send and receive* limit. Although the sending limit will affect only the user, the receiving limit will affect everyone who is trying to send mail to that user. Consequently, it is recommended that the prohibit send and receive limit be imposed only when absolutely necessary.

Deleted Items Retention

Starting with Exchange version 5.5, it is possible to configure both public and private folders for deleted item retention. This means that if a user deletes an item from a folder, and that mailbox or public folder has been configured for deleted item retention, the item can be recovered. Although this is convenient functionality for users, it can adversely affect the size of the information store. The size of the deleted items doesn't count against the mailbox size limit for a user. This adds to the total size of storage necessary for a server. If there is a 50 MB mailbox limit and an average of 5 MB of retained deleted items, you will need to have approximately 5.5 GB available in order for the private information store to support 100 users. (This calculation assumes that there are no shared messages between the users on the server.)

If deleted item retention time is set too long, items will remain in the information store much longer than necessary. One way to avoid this is to configure deleted item retention to permanently delete items from the information store after they have been backed up. If your organization is backing up the information store on a regular basis (for example, incremental backups daily and full backups every week), this should help limit any impact that deleted item recovery will have on the size of the information store. If your organization doesn't do regular backups, this setting can actually increase the storage time for deleted items because it overrides the setting for deleted item retention and retains the deleted items until the store has been backed up.

Public Servers, Private Servers, Bridgehead Servers, and Distribution List Servers

When sizing servers for your organization, it is important to address the individual roles that the servers will play. There are four primary roles for servers in an Exchange organization: public folder servers, private information store servers, bridgehead servers, and distribution list servers. Each of these servers requires different hardware configurations. In addition, the servers must be set up differently with the Exchange Performance optimizer.

Public Folder Servers

Public folder servers are servers that maintain replicas of public folders and that don't have any recipient mailboxes or connectors configured. They are member servers in Exchange sites that typically include private information store servers and bridgehead servers.

Deleted Item Recovery is Not for Disasters

It is important that users and administrators not use deleted item recovery as a disaster recovery method. It is designed specifically for immediate recovery of a limited number of items that have been deleted from a folder by accident or without forethought. Deleted item recovery isn't meant as a way to recover from a catastrophic failure of an Exchange server, nor can it be used to recover a mailbox that has been deleted by an administrator.

Because they may potentially be serving information to a large segment of the Exchange users in the organization, it is critical that public folder servers have the capacity for high-speed network I/O. It is recommended that public folder servers be connected to the network with a high-speed NIC (100 Mbps or ATM). Depending on the distribution of user load on the network, it may be necessary to configure a public folder server on each segment of the LAN, and it may also be necessary to configure replicas of every public folder at every geographic location in the organization.

Configuration recommendations for public folders are discussed in depth in Chapter 5.

In addition to having a high-speed connection to the network, it is a requirement that public folder servers maintain a large amount of disk space. Most public folder servers are initially configured with a minimum disk space equivalent to the largest private information store in the organization. This is typically 16 GB. Whatever the initial size of the public information store, the server should be configured in such a way that the drive space can be expanded with limited impact to server performance. Hardware manufacturers such as Compaq and Hewlett-Packard have disk-management software that will allow the expansion of a RAID array while the server is online.

One other consideration for public folder servers is memory. If your organization is planning on utilizing workflow or collaborative computing applications, it will be necessary to increase the amount of memory in your public folder servers beyond the normal recommendation. Normally, a public folder server should have at least 128 MB of RAM. Depending on the number of public folder applications that are implemented in your organization, it may be necessary to increase the amount of RAM to more than 512 MB.

Private Information Store Servers

Private information store servers typically require a lot of hard disk space but aren't RAM-dependent. Disk size requirements vary, depending on the number of users deployed on a server and any limits that are set on mailbox size. It is possible to calculate the approximate size of disk required by taking into account the number of users to be deployed.

If 500 users are deployed on a server, and each user has an average of 50 MB of data in the private information store, this amounts to roughly 25 GB of data. Since Exchange is a single-instance store, meaning that a message sent to more than one recipient in the store will have only one copy in the actual private information database, the 25 GB of logical data may amount to only 16 to 18 GB of actual data in the database. This is approximately two-thirds of the logical data size. This ratio depends on the number of users per server in your organization and the grouping of users, as described in Chapter 7, "Design of Associated Services."

Bridgehead Servers

Bridgehead servers provide connectivity into and out of Exchange sites in the organization. They typically don't have any user accounts or public folders configured. Since these servers provide connectivity for multiple servers within the site, it is necessary that they have a high-speed connection to all of the servers in the site, as well as to the external bridgehead server to which it connects or to any other external messaging systems. For this reason, the bridgehead servers in a medium or large organization may have multiple NICs configured for connectivity to the LAN.

Bridgehead servers don't require large disks since they don't host private or public information stores. However, they do require adequate memory so that they can process routing calculations and effectively deliver messages into and out of the site and organization. Bridgehead servers should be configured with a minimum of 128 MB of RAM and, depending on the number of sites in the organization or the number of external connections, may need as much as 512 MB of RAM.

Distribution List Servers

When a message is sent to a distribution list, an MTA must expand that distribution list and route the message to all the recipients. In medium-to-large organizations it is possible to have very large or deeply imbedded distribution lists. The expansion of these distribution lists can actually cause a performance hit on an already-busy server. It is for this reason that Exchange gives you the ability to specify the server that will expand a distribution list. It is therefore possible to take the largest distribution lists in an organization and designate a single, perhaps underutilized, server to be responsible for expanding those distribution lists. If a distribution list expansion server has been defined, the message will first travel to that server for expansion and then be delivered.

Redundancy and Security

When planning connections between your Exchange organization and other organizations, it is important to consider both redundancy and the security of those connections.

Connectivity to the Outside

It is possible to configure multiple Internet Mail Service servers, as discussed in the section "Internet Mail Service Strategies." This provides redundancy for the organization's Internet Mail needs.

Digital Signing and Data Encryption

Digital signing of documents is a growing practice among businesses that communicate with each other over the Internet. When a digital signature is included with an e-mail message, it is possible for the recipient to determine exactly whom the message originated from. Outlook 98 supports digital signatures for messages sent to other recipients within the Exchange organization and to recipients on the Internet. Messages sent to the Internet can be signed by using S/MIME digital signatures.

> Prior to Exchange 5.0 Service Pack 2, very large distribution lists caused the MTA to fail. Exchange service pack 2 solved this problem.

In order to sign documents by using an S/MIME signature, it is first necessary for users to obtain a digital ID from a recognized security key provider, such as VeriSign, or be issued a key by a certificate provider internal to the organization.

In addition to digital signatures, it is possible to encrypt data being exchanged with recipients outside the organization. As mentioned in Chapter 3, one of the questions that needs to be answered during the architecture development process is whether or not mail will be encrypted when it is transferred over the Internet.

Growth Factors

Several factors affect how the server hardware needs will scale. These growth factors in no way replace actual data from the organization, but they can help predict what the server needs will be.

Single-Store Messages

Exchange maintains a single instance store for messages in the database. This means that if a message is sent to multiple users on the same server, a single copy of the message will be stored in the Exchange database, and pointers to that message will be copied to each of the user mailboxes that have received the message. When a user deletes the message from his mailbox, the message pointer is deleted. It isn't until the last user deletes the message that the actual message is deleted by the information store. The obvious advantage of a single-instance store is that if a large message is sent to several users on the same server, the impact to the information store will be limited. When a message is sent to users on several Exchange servers, one copy is made for each server on which a recipient is located.

The exception to the single-instance store is when data is migrated from a legacy mail system to Exchange. Even if the legacy system maintains a single-instance store, when messages are migrated to Exchange, there will be individual copies in the information store for each user who received a copy. Chapter 10, "Coexistence and Migration," covers ways to manage information store growth during migration.

Document Management Strategies

An excellent way to manage the growth of the information store in an organization is to encourage users to send small files when possible. Here are some of the ways to do this:

- Send shortcuts to documents that are located on servers instead of sending the entire document.
- Compress documents that need to be sent via e-mail.
- Send URLs to Web resources and other online applications rather than sending a copy of the entire Web page or online application.

When people in your organization exchange messages with users on the Internet or on messaging platforms other than Exchange, it is important to decide upon a standard document management strategy. In addition, a common encoding method must be negotiated for message attachments. The current encoding method for attachments is MIME. The previous standard was UUENCODE. There are still some organizations that use UUENCODE as an encoding method. Attachments from those organizations must be decoded using UUDECODE, and attachments being sent to them must be encoded with UUENCODE. It is possible in Microsoft Exchange to configure the encoding method on a per-domain basis rather than setting a default for all messages sent through the IMS. These settings can be configured on the Internet Mail Service's main property page.

Here are the Chapter 2 and 3 questions addressed in this section:

- **Light, medium, and heavy users definition**. What is the messaging utilization of a light e-mail user? What is the messaging utilization of a medium e-mail user? What is the messaging utilization of a heavy e-mail user?

- **Number of light, medium, and heavy users**. How many light e-mail users does your organization have? How many medium e-mail users does your organization have? How many heavy e-mail users does your organization have?

- **Mailbox quotas**. What mailbox quotas will you impose?

- **SMTP policy**. Is there a policy regarding SMTP (unencrypted) company email traveling across the Internet?

10

Coexistence and Migration

FOLLOWING THE DEVELOPMENT OF AN Exchange architecture, the first set of tasks that will be launched will focus on the coexistence of Exchange with the existing legacy mail system and then the migration of user resources and data from the legacy system to Exchange. Coexistence and migration often prove to be the most difficult time in any Exchange implementation project because it is necessary to maintain and connect two or more mail systems. For that reason, you must spend substantial time up front on planning for issues that will arise.

Coexistence with Other Messaging Systems

When implemented properly, Exchange can seamlessly coexist with other messaging systems. The tradeoff in maintaining multiple systems that coexist, however, is a high cost of configuration and administration. Before discussing coexistence in depth, it is important to define precisely what coexistence is.

For the purposes of this book, coexistence between two systems includes the following functionality:

- Originating messages between recipients on both systems
- Replies to messages between recipients on both systems
- Replies to replies between recipients on both systems
- Forwarding of messages between recipients on both systems

- Originating, replying to, and forwarding messages between recipients on both systems and recipients on foreign messaging systems such as the Internet or an X.400 network
- Full directory synchronization between the two systems

In some cases, coexistence may also include the following:

- Scheduling between the two systems
- Public folder, shared folder, or bulletin board synchronization between the two systems
- Workflow application integration

In summary, for true coexistence, recipients on one messaging system must be able to interact with recipients on the other messaging system as though they were all on a single system. Although this may initially appear to be a daunting task, this chapter will identify the critical success factors in making sure that this is possible.

Out of the box, Exchange provides coexistence support for multiple mail systems:

- MSMail for PC networks
- MSMail (AppleTalk), also known as Quarterdeck Mail
- Lotus cc:Mail
- Lotus Notes
- Officevision
- SNADS-compliant messaging systems

In addition, it is possible to build custom tools for coexistence between Exchange and other messaging systems, such as POP3/IMAP4, HP OpenMail, and Vines Mail.

MSMail

At first consideration, it would seem that MSMail should be the easiest system to coexist with. This is not the case, however. While there is an MSMail connector included with Exchange and an MSMail directory synchronization gateway, setting up true coexistence can be tricky. Due to the inherent instability in large MSMail installations, many subtle details need to be attended to before coexistence can be established.

The first step in establishing a plan for coexistence between MSMail and Exchange is to document in detail the existing MSMail environment. Many of the surprises that occur when synchronization between Exchange and MSMail is established are due to unknown complexities in the existing MSMail environment. Specific attention should be paid to the following:

- All direct and indirect routing relationships
- All directory synchronization requestors
- The current directory synchronization server and all previous directory synchronization servers
- All gateways into and out of the MSMail environment—specifically, the SMTP gateway and access component(s)

- Distribution lists and all recipients
- Local addresses
- Addresses in the MSMail global address list

Documenting this information in a diagram, as shown in Figure 10.1, helps you identify the MSMail components and their relationships.

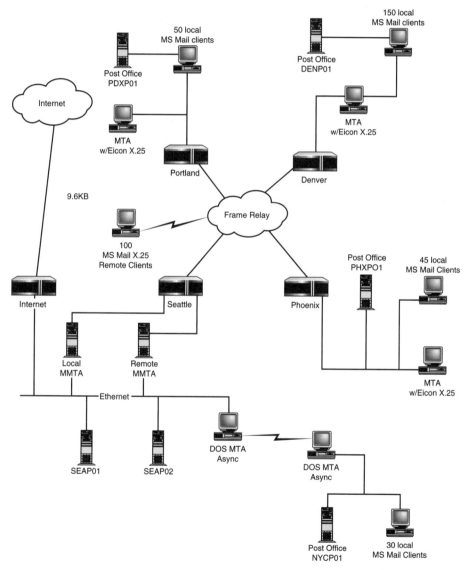

Figure 10.1 In most MSMail environments, a complicated web of routing and directory synchronization has resulted from years of growth. This example indicates a typical MSMail environment that needs to be fully diagrammed before being migrated to Exchange.

Once a detailed document of the existing MSMail environment has been established, it can be used as a road map for establishing Exchange connectivity. This road map can help identify possible roadblocks, such as the following:

- Potential problems with redirecting the directory synchronization relationships for the MSMail environment

- Integrating Exchange into an MSMail environment with multiple external gateways

- Migrating distribution lists from MSMail to the Exchange environment

- Modifying display names for internal and external recipients

- Connectivity to the MSMail environment from Exchange when the MSMail post offices are on NetWare servers

Coexistence, Connectivity, and Directory Synchronization

The first major step in integrating Exchange into the MSMail environment is to migrate directory synchronization server functionality from the MSMail DirSync server to Exchange. This involves first building an Exchange server and configuring the MSMail Connector so that messaging connectivity is established between the MSMail environment and Exchange.

Another approach is to configure Exchange as a DirSync requestor to the MSMail environment. This approach is easier and doesn't require as much interference with the already-fragile MSMail directory synchronization process. However, it isn't as robust a directory synchronization topology. Our recommendation when MSMail and Exchange will coexist for an extended period of time is to move to Exchange as the directory synchronization server at the beginning of the process, thereby making the DirSync environment more stable. However, if MSMail and Exchange will coexist for a limited period of time and DirSync is currently stable, make Exchange a DirSync requestor.

Once messaging connectivity between the MSMail environment and Exchange has been established, directory synchronization between MSMail and Exchange can be configured. The following is a checklist to be followed when implementing DirSync between Exchange and MSMail:

1. Shut down the MSMail MTAs in the MSMail system, and then shut down the MSMail Connector Interchange on the Exchange server. This will keep the MSMail and Exchange systems from transferring mail messages and DirSync messages until the DirSync system is completely configured.

MSMail Post Offices on NetWare Servers

Prior to integrating Exchange into an MSMail environment that is configured on NetWare servers, you must establish connectivity between at least one Exchange server in the organization and the NetWare environment. This means that it is necessary to load Gateway Services for NetWare (GSNW) on the Exchange server. Once GSNW is loaded on the Exchange server, a NetWare account with proper access rights to each MSMail share can be used to configure the MSMail connector.

2. Export the local address lists from each of the MSMail post offices. This will provide a basis for repopulating the address lists in the event of a problem with configuring DirSync with the Exchange system. To export an address list from an MSMail post office, run the MSMail Administrator's program and select Config, Dir-Sync, Requestor, and Export. When prompted to Export Local Users and Groups, click Yes. Then select from the same menu Config, Dir-Sync, Requestor, and Import, click Import, and confirm.

3. At this point, you should remove any MSMail recipients you may have configured in the Exchange environment during the pilot. It is important to note that when you remove these recipients, they will also be removed from all distribution lists and other resources to which you added them.

4. Configure the Exchange server to be the directory synchronization server by setting up a new Directory Synchronization Server object in the Exchange administrator program. As part of this step, you should configure remote directory synchronization requestor objects for each of the MSMail post offices that will participate in directory synchronization.

5. Reconfigure all of the MSMail post offices as DirSync requestors for the Exchange DirSync server. This will require launching the MSMail admin program and reconfiguring the requestor settings. In addition, you will have to reconfigure the former MSMail DirSync server as a requestor for the Exchange DirSync server.

6. Now restart the MSMail Connector Interchange on the Exchange server and the MSMail MTA in the MSMail system. Note that it is necessary to have an active process, such as the MSMail MTA or the external process, running in the MSMail environment in order for directory synchronization to work. Exchange will process inbound DirSync messages and will send the GAL updates to the MSMail post offices, but there needs to be an active process in the MSMail environment to drive the receipt of the DirSync messages by the MSMail post offices and the rebuild of the GAL on each post office.

7. To verify that the DirSync process is working, you can force the T1 time to occur in the MSMail environment by mapping a DOS drive to each MSMail post office and executing the command `reqmain -t` on each post office.

8. Shortly after the transmission of the directory updates, the MSMail recipients should begin to appear in the address list in Exchange. If this doesn't occur, it is an early indication that there might be problems with messaging connectivity or DirSync connectivity between the MSMail environment and Exchange.

9. If the MSMail recipients successfully appear in the address list, you can begin transferring the consolidated address list to the MSMail post offices. You do this by pausing the MSMail Connector Interchange in the Windows NT service list on the Exchange server.

10. Once the DirSync messages have been transferred from Exchange to the MSMail post offices, you should proceed with processing T3 time in the MSMail environment. To do this, map a DOS drive to each of the post offices and execute `reqmain -r` and a rebuild of each post office address list.

Once directory synchronization has been established between MSMail and Exchange, the MSMail recipients will show up in the Exchange global address list as custom recipients. Each of these custom recipients has a unique directory name created by Exchange that is a combination of his MSMail alias and some hexadecimal numbers. If the directory synchronization objects are deleted and re-created, the custom recipients will also be deleted and re-created, resulting in a new directory name for each object.

Gateway Configuration

Once directory synchronization has been successfully completed, the next step is to configure the Exchange server as the external gateway server for all the post offices in the MSMail environment. This entails reinstalling the gateway access component on each post office and selecting the Exchange connector post office (the post office that resides on the Exchange server and that is used by the Exchange MSMail Connector) as the downstream post office for all messages addressed to the gateway. One of the greatest advantages of implementing Exchange in an MSMail environment is being able to leverage the Exchange Internet Mail Service as an SMTP gateway for MSMail. The IMS provides significant advantages over the standard MSMail SMTP gateway. Here are some of the most significant:

- The IMS is multithreaded, providing high-speed transfer of thousands of messages over multiple simultaneous sessions
- Multiple SMTP alias support, facilitating address namespace changes during implementation
- UUENCODE and MIME support for attachments
- Encrypted session support between Exchange servers
- Encrypted session support between servers by using SSL and server certificates
- ETRN support for the storage and forwarding of mail with Internet Service Providers that also support ETRN

Once gateway support has been established between MSMail and Exchange, it is important to test full gateway functionality. To test this functionality, send a message from a foreign messaging system, such as the Internet, through Exchange to recipients on MSMail, and have the MSMail recipient reply to those messages and verify delivery to the foreign system.

Directory Synchronization on Earlier Versions of Exchange

For versions of Exchange before Exchange 5.0, you must make a Registry modification to be able to pause directory synchronization. This process is documented in Microsoft Knowledge Base article number Q147464.

Distribution Lists

With directory synchronization configured and the gateway traffic rerouted, the next step in Exchange/MSMail coexistence is management of the distribution lists. It is advantageous to migrate all the distribution lists to Exchange after directory synchronization is established and won't change but before the migration of any MSMail mailboxes for two reasons:

- Distribution list membership is defined by directory name. If the Exchange/ MSMail directory synchronization relationships are changed after the distribution lists are created, resulting in the change of the MSMail custom recipient directory names, the distribution lists will have to be re-created to include the new MSMail user directory names.

- Exchange manages distribution list membership during the migration to Exchange. As users are migrated, Exchange changes the distribution list membership to reflect the Exchange mailbox. If the distribution list was on MSMail, the distribution lists would need to be manually updated after each migration to reflect the migrated users' Exchange addresses.

Moving distribution lists can be an arduous task. When exported from MSMail, the distribution list memberships reflect the display name of the MSMail user. To correctly associate this with the MSMail custom recipient object in Exchange, the display name must be replaced with the directory name. The easiest way to accomplish this task is to export the MSMail custom recipient object information from Exchange and then use a tool such as Microsoft Access to substitute the directory name in place of the display name before importing the distribution lists into Exchange.

Shared Folders

Although it's possible to migrate MSMail shared folders to Exchange, there is no easy coexistence solution. After the folders are migrated to Exchange, the contents are visible to Exchange users, and MSMail users still have access to the shared folder. However, updates made on either side are not replicated between the systems. One coexistence solution is to migrate the shared folder to Exchange but prohibit write access to the Exchange public folder copy of the MSMail shared folder. On a nightly basis, delete the Exchange copy of the shared folder and migrate the shared folder again. This provides Exchange users with a daily update of the shared folder contents.

A better solution is to determine which workgroups use the particular shared folders and schedule the shared folder migration with the workgroup user migration. At that time, all the users will have access to the copy of the Exchange public folder, and the MSMail shared folder can be deleted.

Exchange Directory Names

Directory names are created by Exchange at the time of object creation and cannot be modified. To view a directory name, select the Advanced tab when viewing the details of any object.

cc:Mail

Integration between cc:Mail and Exchange is extremely straightforward to set up, but as with MSMail, it grows in proportional complexity to the complexity of the existing cc:Mail environment. It is very important to document and understand the configuration of the cc:Mail environment and foreign system connectivity before trying to establish connectivity and directory synchronization.

Coexistence, Connectivity, and Directory Synchronization

The cc:Mail connector on Exchange must be installed and configured with the location of a cc:Mail post office. As with the MSMail connector, if the cc:Mail post office database is located on a NetWare server, you must first install GSNW on the Exchange server so that you can map a network drive to the location of the post office database.

Before you set up the cc:Mail connector, you must place copies of the Import and Export utilities for cc:Mail in a directory accessible to the Exchange server. For version 6 of the cc:Mail database, you must use Import version 5.15 and Export version 5.14. For version 8 of the cc:Mail database, you must use Import and Export version 6.0, and you must place the ie.ri file in the winnt\system32 directory.

Gateway Configuration

It's important to note that you can only use the cc:Mail connector in Exchange to connect to a cc:Mail post office on a direct DOS drive mapping. This means that you can't have Exchange function as a router for a set of distributed cc:Mail post offices. If your legacy mail system includes multiple distributed cc:Mail post offices that connect via a cc:Mail router, you must include a local cc:Mail post office in your Exchange coexistence architecture, as shown in Figure 10.2.

Distribution Lists

As with MSMail, migrating distribution lists from cc:Mail to Exchange after directory synchronization has been established but before user migration can greatly ease migration troubles. Once the distribution lists are established on Exchange, the membership will be updated as cc:Mail objects are migrated to Exchange objects.

Shared Folders

When utilizing the Exchange Migration Wizard for migrating data from cc:Mail to Exchange, it is important to know that the Migration Wizard will migrate data from cc:Mail bulletin boards, but there is no way to synchronize bulletin boards with public folders in Exchange. It is possible to configure Exchange public folders with a rule to forward all new messages to a corresponding cc:Mail bulletin board, but there is no easy way to configure cc:Mail to automatically replicate new contents to Exchange.

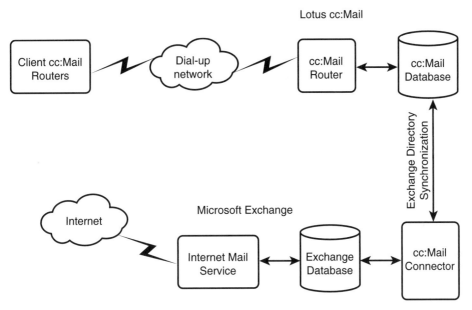

Figure 10.2 The Exchange server must connect to a local cc:Mail post office to communicate with the post offices connected by a cc:Mail router.

SMTP-Based Mail

Integration with SMTP-based mail systems is accomplished via the Internet Mail Service in Exchange. The IMS provides seamless integration between Exchange and any system that is compliant with the RFCs for SMTP.

Coexistence, Connectivity, and Directory Synchronization

The most straightforward method of connecting Exchange and an SMTP-based mail system is by using two different domain names and DNS MX records. For example, if the organization has a registered domain name of gapies.com, an MX record for gapies.com would be established to refer to the Exchange server, and an MX record for legacy.gapies.com would be established to refer mail to the legacy SMTP mail server.

Once the MX records are established so that mail flows correctly into each SMTP connection, Exchange custom recipient objects need to be established for all users on the SMTP-based mail system that point to the legacy mail MX record. This will allow mail to flow through Exchange to the users on the legacy SMTP mail system. For example, in the organization just described, a user with an SMTP alias of jsmith who resides on the legacy system would have an Exchange custom recipient object with a default SMTP address of jsmith@legacy.gapies.com and a secondary SMTP address of jsmith@gapies.com. This will allow Exchange to accept e-mail for this user and forward it to the legacy system.

Additionally, all Exchange users need to have recipient objects configured on the legacy SMTP system. Whether these objects are equivalent to Exchange custom recipient objects or accounts with forward files that forward the mail to the Exchange account depends on the type of legacy SMTP messaging system. This will allow messages to flow from the Internet through the legacy system to Exchange and also allow legacy users to address mail to Exchange users.

The configuration and messaging flow for this example are shown in Figure 10.3.

The drawback of integrating Exchange with an external mail system by using the IMS is that no standard facility is provided for replicating directory information between the two systems. Integrating Exchange with other systems by utilizing LDAP (Lightweight Directory Access Protocol) is one option. In addition, it is possible to import and export Exchange directory information from the command prompt on the Exchange server or via a script. Scripts can be built utilizing standard shell scripting languages or can be scripted in the Windows Scripting Host.

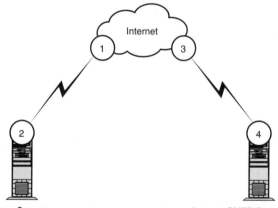

Exchange Server
Accepts mail for `gapies.com`
Has a mailbox object for `jdoe@gapies.com`
Has a custom recipient object for
`jsmith@legacy.gapies.com`

Legacy SMTP Server
Accepts mail for `legacy.gapies.com`
Has a mailbox object for
`jsmith@legacy.gapies.com`
Has a mailbox object for `jdoe@legacy.gapies.com`
with a forward file to `jdoe@gapies.com`

Message flow:
1. Message for `jsmith@gapies.com` is originated on Internet and DNS MX record points delivery to Exchange server
2. Exchange server accepts message for `jsmith@gapies.com` and forwards it to `jsmith@legacy.gapies.com`
3. DNS MX record resoution for `legacy.gapies.com` points to legacy SMTP server and message is delivered to that system
4. Legacy SMTP server accepts message for `jsmith@gapies.com` and delivers to mailbox

Figure 10.3 The configuration and message flow between Exchange and an SMTP-based mail system in one organization.

Distribution Lists

Without directory synchronization and established migration tools, distribution list management is much more difficult for environments in which Exchange and a legacy SMTP mail system coexist. The most common method of distribution list management for these environments is manual administration of the lists in each environment.

Other Messaging Systems

Starting with version 5.5, the Exchange Server enterprise edition provides messaging integration and migration support for IBM Office Vision, other SNADS-based messaging systems, and Lotus Notes. Many of the coexistence and migration strategies discussed in this chapter apply to integration with these messaging systems. For a complete discussion of integrating with OV, SNADS, and Lotus Notes, refer to the connectivity documentation included with Exchange Server version 5.5 Enterprise Edition.

Coexistence During Migration

The type and extent of coexistence necessary during migration depends to a large degree on how long coexistence is required. Gateway functionality needs may vary, for example, and recipients may require varying degrees of interoperability between the legacy messaging system and Exchange.

Short-Term Coexistence Strategies

If you can limit the time required for coexistence, you can limit the administrative burden required to support the system during coexistence. You may also be able to eliminate some of the modifications to both the legacy messaging system and Exchange when the coexistence is required over a long period of time.
Here are some of the advantages of a short coexistence period:

- Gateway support doesn't need to be shifted from the legacy messaging system to Exchange. In the case of MSMail, for example, this would mean that the gateway access component wouldn't have to be reinstalled on each post office.

- If the coexistence period is on the order of a week or two, full directory synchronization support doesn't need to be configured. Once again, in the case of MSMail, it would be possible to manually import an address into Exchange from MSMail and to import an address list into MSMail from Exchange.

- Support for multiple address formats need not be implemented. For example, multiple SMTP addresses wouldn't need to be supported.

- Scheduling integration between workgroups is less critical. It's possible for recipients to manually update schedules during a short coexistence period.

It is important for the migration team to note that while users may accept some inconveniences during a short coexistence period, these inconveniences may be unacceptable over a longer period of time.

Long-Term Coexistence Strategies

A long-term coexistence requires much more administrative support on the part of both the implementation team and the legacy and Exchange mail administration team(s). As with all computing systems, a heterogeneous messaging system demands more attention than a homogeneous one. Consequently, the implementation team should develop a strategy for providing ongoing assistance to the legacy and Exchange mail administration team(s). This strategy should include the following:

- Dedicated time from members of the implementation team to provide escalation support for help desk issues generated by the integration of the legacy messaging system with Exchange

- Exchange training for the mail administrators

- Access to Microsoft support channels for the administration team

In order for an implementation of Exchange to succeed with the users, it is critical that any long-term coexistence be as transparent as possible. The less inconvenient the coexistence is and the fewer interruptions of messaging functionality, the more tolerant the users will be of disruptions to the normal computing environment. Part of the key to successful coexistence is to provide broad integration between the legacy messaging system and Exchange, including the following:

- Full gateway support for all message types between Exchange and all foreign message systems, between Exchange and the legacy system, and between the legacy system and all foreign systems

- Complete and automatic directory synchronization between Exchange and the legacy system

- Access to the public folder data by users of the legacy system

Migration

There are several approaches to migration. The approach selected will depend on the configuration of the existing messaging system and the size of the organization that is being migrated. For organizations that can't migrate all the users at once, coexistence must be established before migration can proceed. For organizations that can migrate all the users at one time, it is not necessary to establish coexistence of the messaging systems.

Migration typically takes place over the course of several weeks or months. The complexity of the organization and the amount of data to be migrated from the legacy mail system to Exchange will dictate this time period.

The Exchange Migration Wizard provides for migration from several messaging products, as shown in Table 10.1. In addition, the Migration Wizard can import migration files that have been created with other tools.

Single-Phase Migration

A single-phase migration can be implemented only when the organization is small enough that all recipient data can be migrated in a single day or over a single weekend. This is typically not the case. Any organization much larger than 50 people will have to utilize a multi-phase migration.

If Exchange is implemented in a single-phase migration, the focus on Exchange testing and disaster recovery becomes critical. Because the Exchange messaging system won't have a gradual ramp-up of users but instead will be supporting all the users at once, Exchange Server and its integration with messaging systems outside the organization (such as the Internet) must be fully tested and completely reliable. Here are the steps for a single-phase migration:

1. Following the detailed specifications in the architecture, build the Exchange server. (Most organizations small enough to implement a single-phase migration will have only a single Exchange server.) The server should comply with all namespace recommendations in the architecture.

2. Establish connectivity between the Exchange server and the legacy mail system. In the case of MSMail, you will build the MSMail Connector and start directory synchronization. This is the same with all of the other mail systems for which connectors are provided. In the case of integration with SMTP-based messaging systems, integration will occur via the Internet Mail Service on Exchange. Directory synchronization needs to be established only if it is required as part of the pilot implementation.

Table 10.1 **Exchange Migration Tools**

System	Version
Microsoft Mail for PC Networks (Microsoft Mail (PC))	Version 3.x
Microsoft Mail for AppleTalk Networks (also known as Quarterdeck Mail)	Version 3.x
Lotus cc:Mail	Database versions DB6 and DB8
Verimation MEMO MVS	Version 3.2.1 or later
IBM Professional Office System (PROFS)/Officevision	All versions
Digital ALL-IN-1	Version 2.3 or later
Novell GroupWise	Versions 4.1 and 4.1a
Collabra Share	Versions 1.x and 2.x
Lotus Notes	Releases 3.x, 4.0, and 4.1
Lotus Domino server	Releases 4.5 and 4.6

3. Establish connectivity between Exchange and any external messaging systems that recipients in the organization will be communicating with. This usually means installing and configuring the Internet Mail Service on Exchange. In addition, it might mean setting up and configuring an X.400 connector for communication with X.400 systems external to the Exchange organization.

4. Identify a set of recipients to participate in a migration pilot. These recipients will be migrated first and will be used as a benchmark for the rest of the organization.

5. Isolate the legacy mail system so that recipients can't access it after their mailboxes have been migrated.

6. Migrate all the distribution lists from the legacy system to Exchange.

7. Launch the Migration Wizard and execute a single-step migration for the appropriate messaging system. Don't delete any of the recipients from the legacy messaging system until it has been verified that all recipient data has been migrated. Track the time it takes to migrate all the recipient data. This will be helpful when you're estimating the amount of time it will take to complete the actual production migration.

8. If all data has been migrated successfully, delete the pilot recipients from the legacy system.

9. Calculate the time needed for the complete single-phase migration.

10. Schedule a timeslot for the migration (a weekend or a service window).

11. Execute the production migration.

Once again, a single-phase migration typically isn't utilized unless an organization is relatively small and has a simple set of connections that need to be established with outside organizations.

Multi-Phase Migration

A multi-phase migration is the type of Exchange implementation that is used in most organizations. A multi-phase migration involves identifying multiple workgroups that can be migrated over an extended period of time. It offers the implementation team several advantages over a single-phase migration:

■ Discrete workgroups can be migrated in a controlled way.

■ Depending on the success of and time needed for migration of workgroups, the schedule for migration can be modified.

Single-Phase Versus Multi-Phase Migration

For the purposes of this book, we define a single-phase migration as a migration of a relatively small organization that can occur over a short period of time, such as over a single day or a weekend. A multi-phase migration is a migration that, due to the size of the organization, needs to be migrated over an extended period of time, such as over several weeks or months.

- If problems occur with the migration of any single workgroup, the member of that group can be given focused attention by the migration team.

- A gradual build of the load on Exchange servers allows administrators to tune the environment as users migrate.

Although a multi-phase migration is absolutely necessary for most organizations and provides many advantages, some aspects of a multi-phase migration can prove to be challenging and difficult to overcome.

The first step in a multi-phase migration is to identify the workgroups that will be migrated. When segmenting an organization population into workgroups for migration, it is important to take into account the inter-workgroup relationships that will be affected by a multi-phase migration. It might seem most logical, for example, to migrate the director of the IS department along with all of the members of the department. However, if the Director of IS works directly with the other executives of the organization and her schedule is maintained by a centralized administrative support staff, it might be more logical to migrate her along with the other members of the executive leadership.

As long as seamless messaging integration has been established between the legacy messaging system and Exchange, the most important issue to take into account when identifying workgroups to migrate is calendaring integration and management. People in the organization who need to manage each others' calendars should be migrated together. For example, it isn't possible for someone using Schedule+ and MSMail to manage the schedule of someone who has been migrated to Outlook and Exchange Server with the Schedule+ client application.

Once the workgroups to be migrated have been identified, the next step in the migration is to establish a schedule for the migration. As with many other aspects of the Exchange implementation, establishing the schedule has less to do with technology than with the work schedule of the organization being migrated. The implementation team should ask the members of the organization what their work schedule is. Specific attention should be given to any major projects or events that will occur during the migration window that won't be affected by downtime from the migration or that won't be put at risk by the potential failure of a migration.

Following the development of a migration schedule, the next step is to configure the server hardware needed to host all the recipient data that will be migrated to Exchange. Prior to the production migration, a pilot should be conducted. One of the results of the pilot will be a benchmark of how much space the data from the legacy system will take once it is migrated to Exchange. The legacy system-to-Exchange ratio will vary, depending on both the type of system being migrated from and the users' usage patterns.

Although Exchange is a single-instance store and the size of the store will decrease over time, the initial migration of data will create a single copy of each message for every recipient. This will be the case even if all the recipients of a message are located on the same Exchange server. As recipients begin to delete messages that have been migrated and send messages to multiple recipients who are on the same Exchange server, the size of the information store will begin to stabilize and eventually shrink from a logical storage perspective. To shrink the physical size of the database, an offline database defragmentation (or compaction) using ESEUTIL will need to occur.

The pilot data can be used to determine the size and number of servers required to host all the users in the organization. If the organization hasn't previously had limits on the size of recipient mailboxes, during the migration to Exchange is an excellent time to suggest implementing mailbox limits. While Exchange Server 5.5 can support an information store of up to 16 TB, the larger the information store is, the harder it will be to recover in the event of a disaster. Quite simply, the larger the information store, the longer it will take to restore from tape backup. During the restoration process, the entire server will be down. Although most organizations with very large databases use fault-tolerant hardware to reduce the possibility of having to restore the database, restoration time is still a factor.

Once server hardware has been sized and implemented, it is time to begin the actual migration from the legacy system to Exchange. Following the successful completion of a pilot, we suggest that the first workgroup to be migrated to Exchange should be the executive management team. There are a few reasons for this:

- If the executive team is the first to be migrated following the pilot, it will instill in the implementation team a sense of dedication that the pilot should be complete and should not be declared "over" until all the bugs in the migration process have been ironed out.

- Once the executive team is migrated, the members of the organization will realize that the migration is happening and that executive management is committed to it.

- Once the executive team begins to fully utilize Exchange and Outlook, they will most likely become champions for the migration to their respective workgroups.

Pre-Migration Mailbox Cleanup

It is important to note that the Exchange Migration Wizard won't limit the amount of data being migrated. Consequently, if the migration to Exchange is being used as an opportunity to impose mailbox limits, users must delete mail before it is migrated. Once recipient data is migrated to Exchange, the Exchange administrator can impose three different size limits on recipient mailboxes: a size limit for sending a warning to the recipient, a size limit for sending mail, and a size limit for sending and receiving mail. When a recipient mailbox that exceeds any of these limits is migrated, the limits immediately take effect. Therefore, users should be informed of the size limit policies and warned that if their mailboxes exceed the size limits at the time of migration, they might not be able to send or receive mail until they delete some of the contents of their mailbox.

Migrating Across Geographic Locations

When implementing Exchange in your organization, it might be necessary to migrate messaging system data across geographically distributed networks. This poses several challenges.

First of all, it is critical that the network be able to support the migration of data from the legacy messaging system to the Exchange environment. For example, you may be migrating from a centralized MSMail environment to a distributed Exchange environment. In your MSMail environment, recipients utilize MSMail Remote to access a post office located at a regional hub. As part of the implementation of Exchange, you have designed an architecture with Exchange servers at every geographic location in the organization. During migration, you will need to pull data from the MSMail server across the network to the Exchange server. If your network is comprised of frame relay connections with a low CIR, data migration might take an inordinate amount of time.

For example, in Figure 10.4, data is migrated from an MSMail post office in Baltimore to an Exchange server in New York by an administrator running the Migration Wizard on a workstation in Minneapolis. The migration of the data will be constrained by the 256 Kbps connection from Minneapolis to New York. It is recommended that the Migration Wizard be run from the Exchange server to which the data is being migrated.

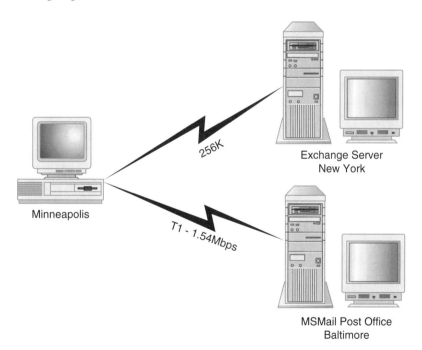

Figure 10.4 While migrating data from a legacy system to Exchange, it is important to consider the network links between post offices.

A second challenge faced by a distributed migration is how to manage the physical control of the legacy systems and the Exchange servers. Once Exchange is implemented, it can be managed from a central location and a single console. However, during the migration phase, it might be necessary to reboot Exchange servers or other resources in the legacy system. For that reason, it is essential to plan ahead to have local administrators available for support, or to send members of the implementation team to the distributed locations where support is required.

11

Monitoring and Optimization

ONE OF THE MANY ADVANTAGES of Exchange Server is its capability to actively monitor the server's messaging services and connectors. With the active monitoring functionality of Exchange, Exchange administrators often know of a network or server problem before the network administrator does. This is possible when the Exchange server and Link Monitors are properly configured and running in the Exchange organization.

Tools are also provided with Exchange that let Exchange administrators monitor the server's resource utilization. The Exchange administrators can then know when the performance of an Exchange server is declining due to lack of resources. This allows for the preemptive planning of additional servers or server resources.

This chapter discusses not only the ability to monitor Exchange, but also the ability of the Exchange administrator to actively tune the server to increase performance. The focus of this chapter is not the administration of monitors or how to run Performance Optimizer, but where to place monitors and the optimization schedule that should be included in the Exchange architecture.

Monitoring the Organization

To fully monitor Exchange as a messaging system, you must monitor the servers in a site, the connectors between sites, and the connectors to foreign messaging systems. To help you accomplish this, Exchange provides two types of monitors. The first,

Exchange Server Monitor, helps increase availability by alerting administrators of a service failure and attempting to recover a failed service. The second, Exchange Link Monitor, alerts administrators when a connection between Exchange sites or between Exchange and a foreign messaging system is down.

Both methods of availability monitoring are important in varying degrees, depending on the size of the Exchange organization and the business-critical nature of given services.

Server Availability

You monitor server availability by observing both the Exchange services and connectors that constitute an Exchange organization. Server Monitors actively monitor any NT services, including Exchange services, running on an Exchange server. When a service fails, preconfigured alerts are sent, and preconfigured actions are taken. With Link Monitors, messages are sent through both Exchange messaging connectors and gateways. When a monitor message isn't returned, a preconfigured alert is sent to warn Exchange administrators of a potential connector or network problem.

Exchange Administrator and the Monitors

Before we discuss the specific monitors, it is important to note that the Exchange monitors are a function of the Exchange Administrator application. Hence, the Exchange Administrator application must be running in order to have the monitors active. This means that you must decide not only what to monitor, but also from where it will be monitored.

The Exchange Administrator, with Exchange version 5.5 and earlier, is a Windows NT application and won't run on Windows 95 or Windows 98. Hence, with Exchange 5.5 and earlier, monitoring must be done from Windows NT servers or workstations. The Exchange Administrator application needs to have RPC connectivity to the servers it monitors.

With the next version of Exchange, code-named Platinum, administration has been moved to the Microsoft Management Console. The MMC can be run from Windows 95, Windows 98, Windows NT 4.0 Workstation or Server, or Windows NT 5.0 Workstation or Server.

Server Monitors

When deciding how to monitor your organization's Exchange services, it is important to understand how the Server Monitor works. When an administrator creates a Server Monitor, an object is created in the site's Monitors object container. This Server Monitor needs to be started in the Exchange Administrator before it will become active. When the administrator starts the Server Monitor, he is prompted for a server to connect to. This selection determines which Exchange server's System Attendant will be responsible for monitoring the services configured by the Server Monitor. Figure 11.1 shows a typical Server Monitor configuration.

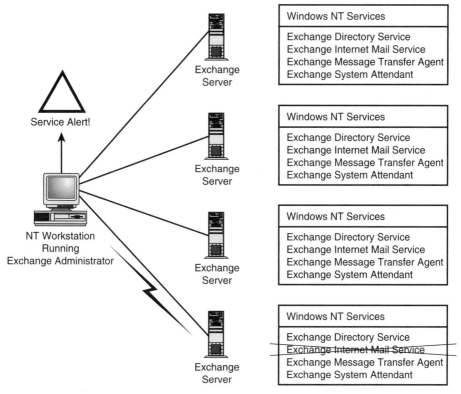

Figure 11.1   A Server Monitor alert occurs when the Exchange Internet Mail Service doesn't respond on one of the four servers being monitored.

Once started, the Server Monitors quietly keep track of the Exchange server's Windows NT services.

Services to Monitor

Create a Server Monitor in each site. Configure the Server Monitors to monitor all the core Exchange services, such as the System Attendant, the Information Store, MTA, and Directory Service, for all servers in the site. For servers that provide additional services, such as the Internet Mail Service or Internet News Service, also configure those services to be monitored.

Once all Server Monitors are configured, each server should have services configured in only one Service Monitor object.

Monitoring Locations

In organizations with centralized administration, it may be feasible to have a single Exchange Administrator monitoring the services of all the servers in the Exchange organization. However, this may not be possible in distributed administration organizations.

If your organization has only a few sites, and your Exchange administration is centralized to one of those sites, configure a single Exchange Administrator to run all the Server Monitors for your organization. If the network connection between sites fails, the Server Monitor and Link Monitor will both report failures and proceed with the alert actions. It is important to note that while the network connection between sites is down, the services in those sites won't be accurately monitored. When the network connection is restored, the Server Monitor will accurately report the status of the site's services. Figure 11.2 shows a Server Monitor configuration across two sites.

In organizations in which the possibility of network outages is greater, or organizations in which the Exchange administrative model is dispersed between sites, it is prudent to have an Exchange Administrator application in each site monitoring that site's Exchange services.

When there are multiple Exchange Administrators monitoring server services, it is a good practice to create a distribution list containing Exchange support personnel from each site. Each Server Monitor is then configured to send an alert to this distribution list. This distribution list could be used as the first notification contact or may serve as an escalation notification contact if the problem isn't resolved. When a service in a site fails, the Exchange support personnel distribution list receives a message reporting the outage. They can then respond appropriately. Figure 11.3 shows how a distribution list is configured for multiple sites and multiple monitor notification.

Link Monitors

As with Server Monitors, Link Monitors are created in the site's Monitors object container. When the administrator starts the Link Monitor, she is prompted for an Exchange server. The System Attendant on this server will be responsible for building the monitor messages and reporting on their transmission and return times.

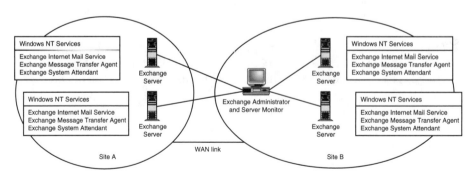

Figure 11.2 In this configuration, one monitoring location runs Server Monitor for two sites and four servers.

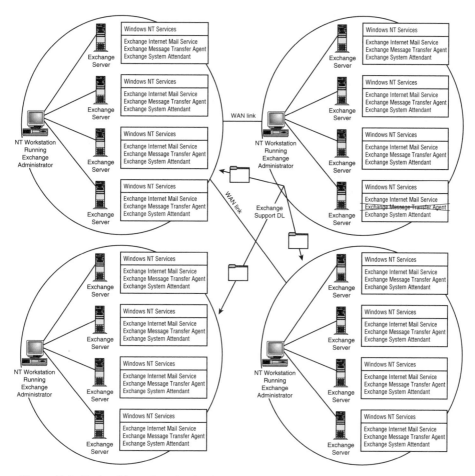

Figure 11.3   Each of these four sites has its own Server Monitor workstation that notifies the Exchange Support distribution list when an alert action occurs.

One of the functions of Link Monitors is to monitor connectivity between Exchange sites. In this case, the System Attendant sends a monitor message across the connector to the System Attendant in the opposite site. The System Attendant that receives the message returns a message to the sending System Attendant. The sending System Attendant uses this returned message as proof that a connector between the two sites is functional.

When a response isn't received from a site in the time allowed, a preconfigured alert is sent. Figure 11.4 shows a Link Monitor configuration.

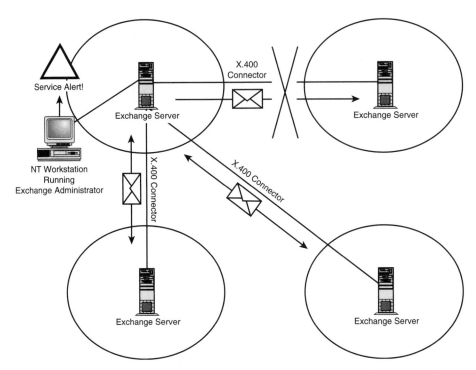

Figure 11.4 A Link Monitor alert occurs when the SMTP connection to the Internet fails to respond to the Link Monitor.

Monitoring Foreign Connectors

The other function that Link Monitors can provide is monitoring connections to foreign messaging systems, such as the Internet. A custom recipient is configured with a valid route out of the Exchange organization, but with an invalid individual recipient address at the destination route. The Link Monitor sends a test message to the custom recipient, which is routed to the foreign messaging system. The foreign messaging system receives the message but is unable to resolve the recipient and returns the message in a nondelivery report. The Link Monitor uses this NDR as confirmation that the link is functioning. The custom recipient should be hidden after the Link Monitor is configured.

For example, suppose that a Link Monitor is configured to send a message to noone@validdomain.com. The test message is successfully routed through the Exchange organization, out the Internet Mail Service, to validdomain.com. validdomain.com receives the message but doesn't have a user named noone, so validdomain.com bounces the message back to the System Attendant. The System Attendant receives the bounced message, which confirms that the link is functional, as shown in Figure 11.5.

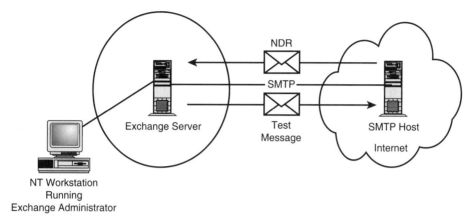

Figure 11.5   The Link Monitor in the Exchange site receives an NDR from the Internet SMTP host and thereby confirms that the link is functional.

Foreign connectors should have their own Link Monitor. This foreign Link Monitor can be run from the same Exchange Administrator that is running the Exchange site Link Monitors. This will allow for a different polling interval than that of the Exchange site Link Monitors.

Link Monitor Topology

The most efficient configuration of the Link Monitor applies to hub-and-spoke topologies, in which there is a single hop between the hub and all other Exchange sites. In this type of configuration, a single Exchange site Link Monitor can be configured in the hub site to monitor the connectors between the hub and all the Exchange sites, as shown in Figure 11.4. This single Link Monitor is configured to send test messages to each site. If a connector or network connection fails, a preconfigured notification is sent to the Exchange administrators.

If your Exchange topology isn't hub-and-spoke, it might be necessary to create multiple Link Monitors in each site that act as spokes. If a single Link Monitor is configured in a multi-hub topology, it might not be apparent which connection, across several hops, is down. In Figure 11.6, two Exchange site Link Monitors are created. The Link Monitor, not in the hub site, monitors only the connectors that are not directly connected to the hub site.

As mentioned, foreign connectors should have their own Link Monitor. If the foreign connector is in a remote site, the Link Monitor should be run from an Exchange Administrator in that site, as shown in Figure 11.7.

Choose a valid domain name for this address. It is best to choose a domain that has very high availability.

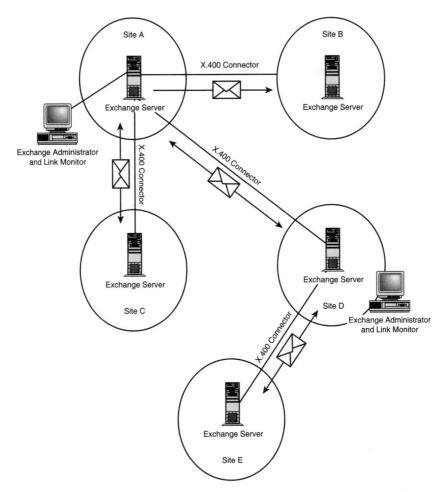

Figure 11.6 It is necessary to have multiple Link Monitors in sites A and D to effectively monitor the connectivity.

Running Monitors as a Service

It is possible to use the Srvany.e XE Windows NT Resource Kit utility to make the Exchange Administrator, with the monitors started, a Windows NT Service. The Exchange Administrator is started as a service with the appropriate switches that start the monitors. The service can log on as the Exchange service account at startup.

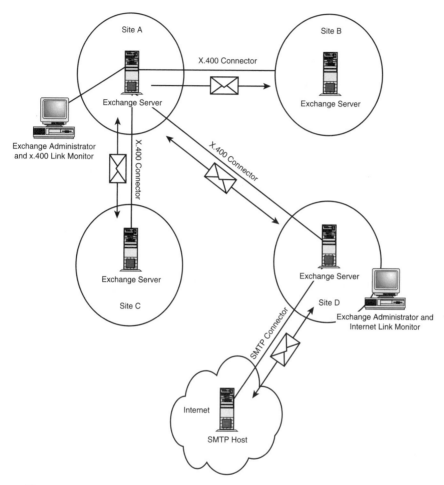

Figure 11.7 Site D, with the connection to the Internet, must have its own Link Monitor because of the multiple hub configuration.

The greatest advantage of running the Exchange Administrator and monitors as an NT service is that it isn't necessary to leave the Exchange Administrator running on the desktop. The Exchange Administrator running on the desktop poses a potential security risk. In order for the Exchange Administrator to start and run monitors, an Exchange administrator must stay connected to Exchange. This would let anyone approach the workstation and make changes to the Exchange organization as allowed by the permissions level of the account used to start the Exchange Administrator session. If you run the Exchange Administrator as a service, the monitors will run while all users are logged off the Windows NT workstation or server.

When the Exchange Administrator is run as a service, you lose the ability to view the monitors' status. You must rely on the configured alerts to notify Exchange administrators of service or connector failures.

Monitoring Availability Using SNMP

With Exchange 5.5, Microsoft shipped an SNMP MIB. This allowed Simple Network Management Protocol (SNMP) managers, such as HP Openview, to actively monitor the Exchange server.

SNMP is a TCP/IP protocol that allows for the simple monitoring of network resources, or SNMP agents, by an SNMP manager. Network resources, such as servers, printers, and workstations, can be monitored if configured as SNMP agents. SNMP software, such as that which ships with Windows NT, must be installed and configured before the network resources can be monitored by the SNMP manager.

The resources on an SNMP agent that the SNMP manager is aware of are defined in a Management Information Base (MIB). There are MIBs specific to products and applications, such as Exchange.

With the SNMP agent installed and configured on the Exchange server, it is possible to install the Exchange MIB that ships with Exchange Server. After it is installed, Exchange resources can be monitored for availability and statistics. The MIB counters available are listed in Table 11.1.

Message Tracking

Message tracking is another tool to ensure messaging integrity in the Exchange organization. When Exchange sites are configured to track messages, it is possible to trace a message throughout the Exchange organization. This capability helps pinpoint the trouble component in message delay and resolve delivery issues.

Message tracking is enabled on several components on a per-site basis. Once configured, the messaging activity is recorded as a message passes through each component. Here are the components on which to enable message tracking:

- **Information store**. By enabling message tracking on the General tab of the information store at the site level, message transfer to and from the information store on servers within the site will be recorded.

- **Internet Mail Service**. Selecting message tracking on the Internet Mail tab of all the IMSs will result in the IMS recording all SMTP mail transfers to and from the information stores, SMTP reroutes, and SMTP inbound receives from the Internet.

- **Connectors**. Enabling message tracking on all the other connectors and the MTA will create a log of connector message traffic.

Table 11.1 **Exchange MIB Counters**

Number	Svc	Counter	Number	Svc	Counter
1.1	MTA	Adjacent MTA Associations	2.1.13	MTA	Connections Current Inbound Associations
1.2	MTA	Messages/Sec	2.1.14	MTA	Connections Current Outbound Associations
1.3	MTA	Message Bytes/Sec	2.1.15	MTA	Connections Cumulative Inbound Associations
1.4	MTA	Free Elements	2.1.16	MTA	Connections Cumulative Outbound Associations
1.5	MTA	Free Headers	2.1.17	MTA	Connections Last Inbound Association
1.6	MTA	Admin Connections	2.1.18	MTA	Connections Last Outbound Association
1.7	MTA	Threads In Use	2.1.19	MTA	Connections Rejected Inbound Associations
1.8	MTA	Work Queue Length	2.1.20	MTA	Connections Failed Outbound Associations
1.9	MTA	XAPI Gateways	2.1.21	MTA	Connections Next Association Retry
1.10	MTA	XAPI Clients	2.1.22	MTA	Connections Inbound Reject Reason
1.11	MTA	Disk File Deletes/sec	2.1.23	MTA	Connections Outbound Failure Reason
1.12	MTA	Disk File Syncs/sec	2.1.24	MTA	Connections Inbound Messages Total
1.13	MTA	Disk File Opens/sec	2.1.25	MTA	Connections Outbound Messages Total
1.14	MTA	Disk File Reads/sec	2.1.26	MTA	Connections Inbound Bytes Total
1.15	MTA	Disk File Writes/sec	2.1.27	MTA	Connections Queued Bytes

continues

Table 11.1 **Continued**

Number	Svc	Counter	Number	Svc	Counter
1.16	MTA	ExDS Read Calls/sec	2.1.28	MTA	Connections Outbound Bytes Total
1.17	MTA	XAPI Receive Bytes/sec	2.1.29	MTA	Connections Total Recipients Inbound
1.18	MTA	XAPI Transmit Bytes/sec	2.1.30	MTA	Connections Total Recipients Outbound
1.19	MTA	Admin Interface Receive Bytes/sec	3.1	IMC	Queued MTS-IN
1.20	MTA	Admin Interface Transmit Bytes/sec	3.2	IMC	Bytes Queued MTS-IN
1.21	MTA	LAN Receive Bytes/sec	3.3	IMC	Messages Entering MTS-IN
1.22	MTA	LAN Transmit Bytes/sec	3.4	IMC	Queued MTS-OUT
1.23	MTA	RAS Receive Bytes/sec	3.5	IMC	Bytes Queued MTS-OUT
1.24	MTA	RAS Transmit Bytes/sec	3.6	IMC	Messages Entering MTS-OUT
1.25	MTA	TCP/IP Receive Bytes/sec	3.7	IMC	Messages Leaving MTS-OUT
1.26	MTA	TCP/IP Transmit Bytes/sec	3.8	IMC	Connections Inbound
1.27	MTA	TP4 Receive Bytes/sec	3.9	IMC	Connections Outbound
1.28	MTA	TP4 Transmit Bytes/sec	3.10	IMC	Connections Total Outbound
1.29	MTA	X.25 Receive Bytes/sec	3.11	IMC	Connections Total Inbound
1.30	MTA	X.25 Transmit Bytes/sec	3.12	IMC	Connections Total Rejected
1.31	MTA	Deferred Delivery Msgs	3.13	IMC	Connections Total Failed
1.32	MTA	Total Recipients Queued	3.14	IMC	Queued Outbound
1.33	MTA	Total Successful Conversions	3.15	IMC	Queued Inbound
1.34	MTA	Total Failed Conversions	3.16	IMC	NDRs Total Inbound

Number	Svc	Counter	Number	Svc	Counter
1.35	MTA	Total Loops Detected	3.17	IMC	NDRs Total Outbound
1.36	MTA	Inbound Messages Total	3.18	IMC	Total Inbound Kilobytes
1.37	MTA	Outbound Messages Total	3.19	IMC	Total Outbound Kilobytes
1.38	MTA	Inbound Bytes Total	3.20	IMC	Inbound Messages Total
1.39	MTA	Work Queue Bytes	3.21	IMC	Outbound Messages Total
1.40	MTA	Outbound Bytes Total	3.22	IMC	Inbound Bytes/Hr
1.41	MTA	Total Recipients Inbound	3.23	IMC	Outbound Bytes/Hr
1.42	MTA	Total Recipients Outbound	3.24	IMC	Inbound Messages/Hr
2.1.1	MTA	Connections	3.25	IMC	Outbound Messages/Hr
2.1.2	MTA	Connections Instance Name	3.26	IMC	Outbound Connections/Hr
2.1.3	MTA	Connections Associations	3.27	IMC	Inbound Connections/Hr
2.1.4	MTA	Connections Receive Bytes/sec	3.28	IMC	Total Messages Queued
2.1.5	MTA	Connections Send Bytes/sec	3.29	IMC	Total Kilobytes Queued
2.1.6	MTA	Connections Receive Messages/sec	3.30	IMC	Total Inbound Recipients
2.1.7	MTA	Connections Send Messages/sec	3.31	IMC	Total Outbound Recipients
2.1.8	MTA	Connections Queue Length	3.32	IMC	Total Recipients Queued
2.1.9	MTA	Connections Connector Index	3.33	IMC	Total Successful Conversions
2.1.10	MTA	Connections Inbound Rejected Total	3.34	IMC	Total Failed Conversions
2.1.11	MTA	Connections Total Recipients Queued	3.35	IMC	Total Loops Detected
2.1.12	MTA	Connections Oldest Message Queued			

Although message tracking is enabled on a per-site basis, the storage parameters are configured on a per-server basis. The System Attendant service is responsible for maintaining the message tracking log files and by default writes them to the exchsrvr\tracking.log directory. A log file is created for each day, and files older than seven days are discarded. To change whether log files should be automatically deleted by the System Attendant, or to change the number of days log files are retained, go to the General tab of the System Attendant for each server.

The directory that contains the message tracking logs on each Exchange server is shared. When an administrator tracks a message, the Exchange Administrator application parses the tracking log, finding the Exchange server that the tracked message was sent through. The Exchange Administrator application then accesses the tracking log directory *share* on the destination server and parses the log file on that server, finding the path of the message. The Exchange Administrator hops from share to share, tracking the message to its final destination while displaying the track for the administrator. Hence, the Exchange Administrator needs file-share access to servers in which it intends to track messages. If two sites are connected with an X.400 connector over X.25, or a dynamic RAS connector, the Exchange Administrator will be unable to track messages that enter that site, because it must have file-share access.

Server Performance Monitoring and Optimization

Monitoring and optimizing the Exchange organization allows proactive maintenance of the environment. Measuring performance helps you identify components that are failing and gives you the baseline performance for the system so that you can identify trends. When you optimize the Exchange environment, resources can best be utilized by Exchange.

Performance Monitoring

The Windows NT Performance Monitor, known as PerfMon for short, is a key component in maintaining and troubleshooting the Exchange Server environment. This tool enables monitoring of the physical components, Windows NT services, and Exchange services. As with the monitors, PerfMon needs to be running in order to gather data. This data can be used to see that a resource is being overextended or to find where the bottlenecks in a server exist. Several performance monitors are installed with Exchange. They can be used as examples of the types of resources an Exchange administrator can monitor.

Moving Message–Tracking Files

Message-tracking files can quickly become overly large, especially on bridgehead servers. If the drive on which the exchsrvr\tracking.log directory is located doesn't have the necessary disk space, you can move the directory to another drive. This can be done by moving the files, changing a Registry key, and sharing the new tracking.log directory, as documented in Microsoft Knowledge Base article Q169770.

Identifying Potential Problems

Identifying potential stop-server situations or bottlenecks is the first step in avoiding them. Most stop-server and bottleneck situations in Exchange are due to a lack of physical resources. Here are some situations to look out for:

- **Disk space**. Not having enough disk space for the transaction logs or database will quickly bring the Exchange server to a halt.

- **Memory**. Not having enough memory can cause excessive paging and can significantly reduce performance. By monitoring the amount of RAM used and the amount of paging, you can add additional resources before performance becomes a problem.

- **Queue lengths**. By monitoring queue lengths, you can see how well connectors are keeping up with demand. If the queue length on an IMS is always greater than 500 messages, it might be time to add an additional IMS.

Use the PerfMon counters described in the following section to identify potential stop-server situations before they occur.

Gathering Data

Several PerfMon charts are installed when Exchange is installed. These charts are configured with the components necessary to monitor the most common situations. The configured charts are described in Table 11.2.

Table 11.2 **Exchange Performance Monitor Charts and Update Frequencies**

Chart	Monitors	Update Frequency
IMS Queues	Number of messages in the inbound and outbound Internet queues	1 second
IMS Statistics	Inbound and outbound Internet messages since the IMS was started	30 seconds
IMS Traffic	Number of SMTP sessions and message movement between the MTS internal queues	1 second
Server Health	Percent of processor utilization total and per core component	1 second
Server History	User connections, page file usage, and outstanding messages in internal queue	60 seconds
Server Load	Address Book usage and message load	10 seconds
Server Queues	Number of messages waiting for processing or transmission in information store and MTA queues	10 seconds
Server Users	Total user connections	10 seconds

Although the included charts can be a great starting point for identifying trouble spots or usage trends, it is often necessary to create charts for the organization's specific monitoring needs. The most frequently used NT and Exchange Performance Monitor objects and counters are listed in Table 11.3.

Recognizing Trends

In addition to the troubleshooting capabilities that PerfMon provides, the data should also be used to track trends for the Exchange servers. By taking a snapshot of the server on a weekly basis using PerfMon's logging utility, you can extrapolate usage trends and proactively add components to the Exchange server or organization. Weekly PerfMon logs initialed by the NT scheduler one day per week, perhaps from 8:00 a.m. to 12:00 p.m., can automate data-gathering and provide a consistent sample set. Weekly tracking also provides the data necessary when you're justifying new hardware or maintenance expenditures.

Table 11.3 **Common Performance Monitor Objects and Counters**

Object	Counter
Processor	% Processor time
Processor	Interrupts/second
System	File read/write operations/second
Memory	Pages/second
Memory	Available bytes
Server	Bytes total/second
Physical disk	% disk time
Physical disk	Avg disk sec/transfer
Logical disk	% free space
Directory service	Pending replication synchronization
Directory service	Remaining replication updates
Information store private	Average time for delivery
Information store private	Average time for local delivery
Information store public	Message opens/second
MSMI (MSMail Interchange)	Messages received
MTA	Messages/second
MTA	Work queue size
MTA (PC) (MSMail-specific)	File contentions/hour
MTA (PC) (MSMail-specific)	LAN/WAN messages moved/hour
MTA connections	Queue size

Optimization

You can optimize the resources for the Exchange Server configuration through Performance Optimizer, which is installed at the time of the Exchange installation. Performance Optimizer examines the server hardware configuration and moves the Exchange Server files and logs to the optimal location and adjusts the thread, buffer, and cache settings.

Performance Optimizer can optimize the server based not only on the hardware information but also on the Exchange Server configuration information that the administrator provides. Specifically, Performance Optimizer asks for information on the number of users on the server, the number of users in the organization, and which Exchange services the server provides, such as public information store and private information store. Performance Optimizer then knows how to balance the services. For example, if a server is just a bridgehead server with no users, but there are 3,000 users in the organization, Performance Optimizer knows that this Exchange service will have very little information store usage and a lot of directory service usage.

Because it is necessary to stop the Exchange Server services while running the Performance Optimizer, it is not recommended or necessary that this utility be run frequently. However, Performance Optimizer should be run after you make server changes, such as adding memory, adding a processor, changing the number of Exchange users, adding or removing a component on the server, changing the role of a server, or adding a caching controller.

Performance Optimizer records all of its activity to the end of the log file in the winnt\system32 directory named perfopt.log. Check this file for changes made and the history of the Performance Optimizer changes if it has been run several times.

The Verbose Performance Optimizer

It is also possible to run the Performance Optimizer in verbose mode. This allows more granular tuning of the Exchange parameters, such as the ability to set the number of information store buffers and the minimum number of information store threads. Unless there is a specific setting to modify, it is best to let Performance Optimizer set these numbers automatically.

To run Performance Optimizer in verbose mode, change to the exchsrvr\bin directory at the command prompt and type perfwiz -v.

12

Implementation

THIS CHAPTER DISCUSSES THE PROCESS for implementing Exchange in an organization. All the design and planning decisions in previous chapters are put into context in
the planning, testing, and implementation process in this chapter.

Exchange Server Implementation Strategies

One of the most crucial parts of the implementation process is the server implementation. This includes planning, testing, piloting, and implementing the server architecture.
Whereas the client implementation phase carries risk due to the number of client
installations and different user types, the server implementation poses the greatest risk
for the project because of potential loss of service. Loss of service can affect the user's
perception of how the migration is going and how the final product might perform.
The key to a successful migration is the development of a sound implementation strategy and the management of user and manager expectations.

Creating an Architecture

Earlier chapters discussed gathering the necessary information for developing a messaging architecture. The architecture document details what the Exchange organization
should look like when implementation is complete. The first steps in the implementation

process are to define the business requirements of the messaging system and to define the current environment in which the messaging system is to be supported. The Exchange architecture is constructed so that the organization's business requirements are met in the current environment. In the implementation process, the information and design decisions are outlined in the architecture document. The architecture document contains the information necessary for the implementation, specific to both Exchange and the associated services needed to support Exchange.

Draft

The first step in creating an architecture document is creating the table of contents. Creating the table of contents sets the foundation for the document and establishes the basis from which architecture development assignments can be made to members of the team. Table 12.1 outlines a sample table of contents.

Table 12.1 **Sample Architecture Outline**

Table of Contents Heading	What It Contains
Executive Summary	Summary of project and charter
NT Domain Architecture	Design of the NT environment to support Exchange
Overview	Overview of the NT design: past, present, and future
Physical LAN/WAN Review	LAN/WAN topology
Naming Conventions	Naming conventions for physical locations
Domain Model	Browsing, policies and profiles, security, group assignment policies, shares
DHCP	Server addressing, scope ranges, DHCP server redundancies, option assignments
Time Synchronization Services	Authoritative time references
Security	Hardware level security, protocol level security, application level security, passwords, auditing policies
File Sharing Services	Network shares, software shares, workgroup shares, public shares, private directories
Printing Services	Printer shares and configurations
Backup Services	Backup strategy, software, schedule, and restore strategy
Integration with Other NOS	Administration, client
Name Resolution DNS	Domain, zone, primary name server, secondary name server, time-to-live, WINS integration
WINS	Server distribution, server replications, policies
Network Management	SNMP Manager, NT Server management, Exchange management
Hardware Description	Domain controllers, Server classifications
Exchange Messaging Architecture Overview	Architecture overview, implementation approach

Table of Contents Heading	What It Contains
Current Messaging Topology	PO topology, classification of user/disk space usage, SMTP services, foreign system connectivity, remote user services, message traffic analysis, administrative structure, distribution list, public folders
Exchange Naming Standards	Organization, site names, server names, user mailboxes, distribution lists, Exchange service account
Site Configuration	Site characteristics, topology, public folders, system folders/offline address book, distribution lists, custom recipients, mailboxes, recipient containers
External Connectivity	Internet Mail Service, X.400 connectivity, other connectivity
Client Strategy	Outlook, remote client, client feature sets, mailbox limits
Coexistence	Connector architecture, directory synchronization, recipient groups, foreign messaging system coexistence
Maintaining the Messaging Organization	Exchange backup, message tracking, link monitors, server monitors, periodic maintenance
Securing the Messaging Org	NT and Exchange Security, permissions, firewalls
Messaging Services	E-forms, virus protection, faxing, paging, crystal reports
Coexistence Issues/Strategy	Custom recipients for current messaging users, distribution lists, foreign system addresses for Exchange users
Training Requirements	Administrator, end-user
Appendixes	Messaging statistics, migration statistics, comments on draft

The scope of the architecture document will typically vary based on what other architecture documents have been written for the organization. Keep in mind when determining the scope of the architecture that this document will not only be used to communicate and define the current messaging project but will also be used as a reference for future messaging and networking projects.

After the table of contents for the architecture has been defined and agreed upon by the project team, assign the sections to the appropriate groups of people. The architecture should not be written by one person; rather, it should be written by the team, but one person should be responsible for consolidating the content into a single document.

Revisions

After a draft of the architecture document has been compiled, it should be distributed for review. The review audience should include the project team, the executive sponsor, and the staff responsible for associated services that are not on the project team. Setting clear expectations for review comments and review deadlines is vital to getting the correct feedback. Reviewers should understand the architecture process and the project scope and should be instructed to comment on not only what is in the document but also what is not in the document.

Ultimately, the architecture will proceed through the following steps: table of contents, draft, review, revision, and final format. Note that this process provides for only one iteration of the review and revision steps. It may be necessary to extend the review deadline or include later revisions after the first revision cycle is complete if critical information comes to light. Keeping these exceptions to a minimum will help keep the Exchange project on track.

Creating a Lab

When the architecture is complete and published, a lab environment is created to validate the design concepts. The lab also serves as a practice run for the implementation steps of the Exchange server and clients.

The lab should include, at minimum, an Exchange server and clients. The scope of the testing varies based on the organization's experience with Exchange and the complexity of the environment, but common lab tests include the following:

- **Client configuration.** Testing of client functionality, client connectivity to the Exchange server, software share configuration, file server storage of client support files (.PST's and .PAB's), calendaring support, and profiles.

- **Server configuration**. Testing of server connectivity, foreign system connectivity, backup and restore procedures, extended services (such as fax and paging), and coexistence.

- **Migration testing.** Testing of the migration process, especially focusing on data migration time and migration of such non-message objects as shared folders and distribution lists.

- **Load simulation.** Test the performance of the server under suspected load. If the architecture calls for 600 users on a server configuration defined in the architecture, simulate that load on the server to assure acceptable levels of performance.

Practical Versus All Permutations

Most small and medium organizations contain a variety of software and hardware configurations. It is usually not possible or recommended to test all of these configurations because the scope of the lab testing and the necessary time can become unmanageable. To limit the lab scope yet still provide valid testing, select the most common configurations for the primary testing platform. Depending on the organization, the number of primary configurations will vary, but it should not exceed four. If it's necessary to test more than four configurations, or if a rare configuration needs to be tested for compatibility, define a limited test set.

Test Methodology

Lab testing is only as good as the test methodology used. Performing multiple tests, having several people perform the testing, and not having a common feedback form are all factors that can invalidate a test. The following methods guidelines represent a sound testing methodology.

- **Consistent starting point**. For every test performed, use the same hardware and software configuration. This may require rebuilding the test platform between tests, but it reduces the possibility of invalidating the test because of inconsistent configuration on the test platform.

- **Test script**. Although the people performing the tests are probably knowledge-able about the platforms with which they are working, it is important that they follow a clearly defined test script. This eliminates the possibility that results will vary based on the person performing the test.

- **Results form**. Each defined test must have a predefined form for results. Keeping a consistent result format ensures that each test is performed with the same focus. In addition, gathering result trends and anomalies is possible if results are gathered in a consistent format and location.

Most organizations have already established testing guidelines and environments. Leverage these environments as well as the recommendations in the preceding list to create the best test environment for the organization.

Installing the First Server

Installing the first server in the organization should not differ greatly from the lab experience. The first production server will establish the Exchange organization as defined in the architecture.

- **Creating the Service Account**. If more than a single domain exists, the architecture should define which master user domain will contain the service account for the first site.

- **Defining the Exchange Administrators NT Groups**. Create global Windows NT groups to define who will act as Exchange Server administrators and permissions administrators.

- **Preparing Windows NT**. Install the proper service packs, option packs and patches, the Internet Information Server, Active Server components, and other NT services required to support Exchange.

- **Installing Exchange Server**. Install Exchange, creating a new site as defined in the architecture.

- **Configuring Permissions on the Directory**. Use the Exchange Administrator to apply the proper permissions in the three security contexts for the Exchange administrators and permissions administrators groups.

- **Creating the Initial Test Mailbox**. Use the Exchange Administrator to create a mailbox for the Administrator to test Exchange messaging functionality and configure client-only components of Exchange, such as Public Folders.

- **Limiting Top-Level Public Folder Permissions**. Use the Exchange Administrator to limit who can create top-level public folders to the Exchange Administrators.

- **Creating Recipient Containers**. Use the Exchange Administrator to create the recipient containers defined in the architecture.

- **Creating Distribution Lists**. Use the Exchange Administrator to create the top-level distribution lists defined in the Exchange architecture.

- **Creating Top-Level Public Folder Hierarchy**. Use the Outlook client to create the top-level public folder hierarchy as defined in the architecture.

- **Establishing Coexistence with the Current Messaging System**. Create necessary connectors to current messaging system, including directory synchronization configuration. These connectors should be tested using the test mailbox.

- **Setting Schedules for Automatic Processes**. Configure schedules for functions such as online maintenance.

- **Configuring Offline Address Book Containers**. Configure which recipient containers will be included in the offline address book.

- **Set Site Addressing Properties**. Configure the default site addressing to reflect the organization's standards.

- **Establish Foreign Messaging Connectivity**. Use the Exchange administrator to create the connectors necessary to provide the Exchange users the same level of foreign messaging service the current messaging users enjoy.

After the first server is installed and configured, it should be able to provide the functionality defined in the architecture. This server will house the first migrated users in the pilot group. Using the connector, these users should be able to interact with the current messaging system and should have access to a complete address book. These users should also be able to interact with any foreign messaging systems, such as the Internet.

If Exchange is to take responsibility for current gateway services, such as SMTP gateway services, from the current messaging system, it is wise to allow the Exchange server to function in this capacity for a period of time before users are migrated. This gives the administrators the opportunity to work through foreign messaging problems without affecting Exchange users.

Performing a Pilot

When the architecture has been validated with lab testing and the first server is up and running, the next implementation step is to perform the pilot. Rolling Exchange out to a pilot user group has three major benefits: It gives the migration and support groups the opportunity to work together as a team, it allows the support team to become comfortable with the frequently asked support questions, and it allows the architecture and project team to tune the production environment before the full implementation.

Full Exchange functionality is expected for the pilot, and no architecture changes are anticipated between the pilot implementation and the production implementation. Therefore, the Exchange server should be implemented as designed, and coexistence with any current messaging system and foreign connections should be established before the pilot begins.

Selecting the Right User Group

The value of the pilot is largely determined by the selection of an appropriate user group. Many organizations use the Information Systems department users for a pilot implementation, which gives the users who will be supporting and integrating with Exchange the chance to work with the product before the implementation. Although this is a logical decision and the IS users should be included in the pilot, it is recommended that the pilot group be extended to include users outside of the IS department. This will make the data gathered during the pilot more realistic and applicable to the production implementation.

The pilot group should also have client training before they are migrated. This will minimize confusion by pilot group members, reduce help-desk support, and help make the pilot successful.

In addition to selecting users outside of the IS department, here are the other selection criteria for the pilot user group:

- **Flexibility**. Pilot users should understand that although they will be supported, they will not be in a production environment and will need to be flexible to accommodate any service interruptions and changes that are necessary.

- **Technical ability**. The technical ability of the pilot group should be varied, including both advanced users who take full advantage of the current messaging system and beginning users who use only the basic messaging functionality. This ability and usage range will help the support team gather a good mix of support questions.

- **Interoperability**. The pilot group should be a workgroup (this is necessary so that they can all see and use the workgroup calendars during the pilot) that also has a fair amount of traffic with foreign mail systems and the current messaging system. The traffic to non-Exchange recipients will help the architecture and support team study and tune the Exchange connectors and gateways.

Gathering Feedback

Pilot feedback should be gathered in formal and informal ways. Migration process and notification to the user should be done as outlined in the communication plan in Chapter 5, "How to Sell Exchange as a Messaging and Workgroup Solution." In addition, pilot group users should be polled to solicit feedback on the migration process, the migration communication process, the Exchange messaging system functionality, and the support process. And finally, the support calls generated by the pilot group should be carefully tracked to determine usage and understand trends.

To gather informal feedback, the Exchange project team, especially the project manager, migration team lead, and support team lead, should have close contact with the pilot user group. Many comments that users do not take the time to write down can be gathered by proximity to the users. Spending time with the pilot user group also generates good will between the project team and the user group, which is a marketing advantage to the rest of the organization.

Both the formal and informal feedback should be recorded in a central location available to the entire project team. Because the architecture should be solidified at this point in the implementation, changes to the architecture should be made only on a critical-issue basis. Instead, the pilot feedback should be used to alter the migration process, training requirements, and next-generation Exchange architecture.

The results of the pilot should be a deciding factor in the rollout schedule. How many problems are experienced and the ability of the support team to recover from those problems can help dictate the number of users the organization is able to migrate at one time. Furthermore, if the pilot is not successful, the project team should feel comfortable postponing migration until all major problems are resolved. If necessary, a second pilot can be performed to ensure that the Exchange system and its components are stable and ready to support many users.

Training

A successful Exchange implementation is affected a great deal by the level of knowledge and understanding of the product and, therefore, by the training. The training requirements should be defined early in the Exchange implementation in order to allow plenty of time for training curriculum development.

End-User Training

It is important to find the right balance between offering too much detail and spending too much time on training and providing enough product knowledge. If the training is not balanced correctly, users will either not attend or not receive enough information to efficiently use the product. The other major end-user training challenge is providing the training as close as possible to the implementation so that users can practice what they learn. The end-user training strategy outlined in this section is proven to be practical and successful.

In correlation to selecting the migration workgroups (see the migration schedule section later in this chapter), select power users from each workgroup. The number of power users depends on the number and technical ability of people in a workgroup but should average one power user to 35 end-users. The power users receive in-depth training on the client functionality and support strategy, as well as thorough documentation on the messaging and calendaring client. After they have been identified and trained, these users serve as the first question-and-support point for users. These power users will also be in close touch with the Exchange project team and should be made aware of any migration challenges, timeframe adjustments, and support resources for advanced questions.

For other end-users, the training should cover the basic messaging and calendaring functionality of the Exchange client. This can be done in short, informal sessions such as brown-bag lunches. This training should provide the core knowledge but should not require an overwhelming time or understanding commitment. To reinforce the training, job-aid flyers such as tri-fold cue cards should be distributed to the end-users. This informal training should be delivered in close conjunction to the user migration date. For a workgroup of 30 people that will be migrated on a weeknight, 15 users can be trained the afternoon before the migration, and the other 15 users can be trained the morning following the migration.

If it's done carefully, users can be trained just before they are migrated. A migration cycle can be established in which users attend training and then return to find their mailboxes migrated and the Outlook client installed.

Table 12.2 outlines the suggested training content for the end-users and power users.

Help Desk Training

Training for the help desk requires two major components: client and messaging services. The client component of the help desk training should cover the same content as the power user training. The messaging services component should cover the basics of the Exchange server operation and functionality to give the support staff an understanding of the Exchange server environment. Included in the messaging services training are the following components:

- **Server connectivity**. An overview of the messaging topology, protocol binding order, mailbox and alias name, service functionality and configuration, and identifying client versus server issues.

- **User permissions**. An overview of how Exchange utilizes Windows NT security. An understanding of the relationship between the users' Windows NT accounts and their mailboxes.

- **Addressing and address book**. Discussion of address resolution order and address book views, foreign system addressing, migration of address book data from a legacy mail system, one-off addressing, and message format type (such as rich text format) to external recipients.

- **Interconnectivity with legacy calendaring**. Overview of migration and interoperability with a legacy calendaring system, as well as data conversion process and problems.

- **Tips and tricks**. Discussion of the tools and tricks for Exchange server and Outlook client, such as Inbox assistant, changing passwords, mailbox maintenance, offline synchronization, and moving mailboxes.

Table 12.2 **Suggested Training Content by Audience**

Audience	Content
End-user	*Messaging.* Sending and managing messages, addressing messages and address management, and mailbox limitations and management.
	Scheduling. Creating, inviting, and receiving appointments.
	Migration. What to expect from migrated objects and how to prepare for migration.
Power user	All end-user content.
	Client configuration. How to configure a messaging client and methods of connecting to the Exchange servers.
	Remote client. Overview of remote client support.
	Other services. Overview of additional client capabilities such as tasks, journaling, and contact management.

Depending on the distribution of account maintenance responsibilities and permissions, it might be appropriate to train the support staff on such Exchange administration tasks as mailbox creation and management and on how to add SMTP aliases if they will have permissions to do so.

Administrator Training

The training requirements for the Exchange administration group are much more stringent. A common approach for training the administration staff on Exchange is a combination of Microsoft Official Curriculum Exchange courses and custom curriculum specific to the functions they will perform. Such an approach teaches administrators how Exchange can be implemented, as well as how Exchange was implemented in their environment.

The following subjects should be covered as components of the administration training:

- **Administration**. Overview of creating mailboxes, distribution lists, custom recipients, and recipient containers by using directory import and export, raw mode administration (for experts only), Exchange server object review, and administration of servers in other sites.

- **Mailbox maintenance**. Discussion of moving mailboxes within a site, moving mailboxes to another site, moving custom recipients, and backing up and restoring individual mailboxes.

- **Monitoring and maintenance tools**. Overview of server monitors, link monitors, time synchronization, notification methods, event view, Inbox repair tool, RPC ping utility, Information Store consistency checker, MTA utilities, and Exchange database utilities.

- **Exchange resource kit**. Discussion of the most commonly used Exchange resource kit elements such as the administrative mailbox agent, backup tool, Event Log scan tool, mailbox cleanup agent, mailbox migration tool, ONDL tool, and Sentinel tool.

- **External connectivity**. Coverage of connectors and gateways (including X.400, SMTP, and legacy messaging system) and discussion of the GWART and connector costs.

- **Organization configuration and directory synchronization**. Overview of routing within and outside of the organization, calculation of routing using costs, and directory synchronization.

- **Message tracking**. How to track messages within an Exchange site, messages to other sites in the Exchange organization, X.400 messages, SMTP messages, and messages to the legacy mail system.

- **Security**. Information on how to configure permissions on the Exchange directory. The difference between mailbox access security, message encryption, and digital signatures.

- **Escalation Procedures**. Outline of the problem escalation procedures for the organization.

- **Public folders**. Discussion of replication, affinity, and homing of public folders.

The level of involvement of the administration staff in the Exchange design and implementation project will determine much of the focus and depth of the training requirements.

Developing a Migration Process

The migration process consists of the steps that the organization will complete to move from the legacy messaging system to Exchange. This section details the components of the migration plan. For information about the technical coexistence and migration details, review Chapter 10, "Coexistence and Migration."

There are two migration processes: the server process and the client process. The *server migration* process includes the migration of data from the legacy server to the Exchange server. The *client migration* process includes the steps taken on the client computers to migrate server connectivity and client-stored data.

The migration plan developed for an Exchange Server implementation project will contain the sections outlined in Table 12.3. The migration plan can be either delivered as a separate document or included with the architecture document.

Table 12.3 **Migration Document Outline**

Section	What It Contains
Overview	Overview of the server migration process
Migration of Connectivity and Routing	Verification of coexistence, reconfiguration of routing to current system, reconfiguration of router to foreign connectivity
Migration of data	Distribution lists, mailboxes, shared scheduling information, custom recipients, and shared folders
Remote Office Impact	Migration schedule, interoperability issues, and migration issues

Migration Limits

Migration to a new messaging system presents the perfect opportunity to clean up the messaging environment. One way this can be accomplished from the server is by setting limits on the data that is migrated. Although the parameters that can be changed vary based on the migration tool used, the following items are those most often limited:

- **Private messages**. Private message stores, or mailboxes, usually amount to the majority of the data that needs to be migrated. Limiting the data migrated based on date (only the past 180 days, for example) or mailbox folder (such as only those in the Inbox) is an effective measure for reducing the private message store. This is most easily accomplished by communicating to the users, in a series of e-mails, what will and will not be migrated. This gives the users an opportunity to clean up their mailboxes prior to the migration.

- **Personal address books**. Although it is an option to choose not to migrate personal address books, it is not a recommended method for reducing the amount of migrated data. Users might have personally gathered a lot of information in the personal address book that would take much effort to rebuild. Anyway, the address book files are small enough that they don't account for a large migration burden. Therefore, choosing not to migrate personal address books results in very little server savings while upsetting the user community.

- **Attachments**. Attachments to private e-mail messages account for much of the disk space usage. If attachments are not migrated, users can still keep all their e-mail messages, but the data to be migrated is greatly reduced. Using the Microsoft Mail Migration Tool, this is not an option. However, for tools that extract data into a packing list file, a primary file, and a secondary file, it is a simple procedure of stripping the attachments from the secondary file. This has to be done very carefully and should be thoroughly tested in the lab before it's performed on user mailboxes.

- **Calendaring objects**. Migrating calendaring objects is another option for the migration plan. The decision to migrate these objects depends largely on the usage of the legacy calendaring application. If the calendaring application has been greatly abused, a clean start might be warranted. Otherwise, calendaring information should be migrated. Migrating some calendaring objects, such as All-In-One objects, takes significant time and processing power. Again, thorough testing and planning should be done in these cases.

- **Shared folders**. The migration strategy for publicly available folders or shared folders is another consideration. Typically, this shared space has been abused in many organizations, and migration can be an excellent time to start fresh. In addition to consuming disk space and migration time bandwidth, shared folders often lose ownership in the migration process. This complicates both the cleanup process and the long-time vision for public folders. Another issue surrounding shared folders is coexistence. Many of the migration and connector tools (including MS-Mail tools) do not support any replication of data between the legacy folders and the Exchange folders. This forces a choice of which system the shared folders should reside on during the coexistence time period.

When the decision has been made about which objects to migrate, it is easier to map out the migration strategy based on the constraints and limitations for each object type.

Developing a Migration Schedule

Assuming that it is not possible to migrate the entire legacy messaging organization to Exchange at one time, it is necessary to define a schedule for the migration. As outlined in Chapter 10, many tasks, such as reconfiguring the routing, will be done well in advance of migrating users. The migration schedule focuses on the migration of users after the infrastructure changes have been made.

Network Considerations

Migrating data from one messaging system to another can generate a great deal of network traffic. It is important to consider the placement of servers and the time of day for the data migration when planning the migration schedule.

In addition to considering the amount of network traffic generated during migration, it is necessary to look at the operations schedule. The backup schedule for the servers can affect how long the migration can run on a nightly basis. Also, regularly scheduled network outages need to be coordinated with the messaging migration at the outset of the migration process.

Workgroup Considerations

The migration schedule should be defined around workgroups in the organization. This is the most effective migration schedule, because it allows workgroups to have full scheduling functionality during the time of migration, and it facilitates the workgroup power user support and training model.

Help Desk Considerations

Migration to a new messaging system will increase the number of help requests to the help desk during the actual migration period. In addition to providing the appropriate training to the help desk, it is necessary to consider the impact of these requests on the help desk and the help desk support infrastructure. If large groups of users will be moved over a weekend, it will be necessary to add staff to the help desk for the days following the migration, as well as to confirm that there are enough phone lines and sufficient help desk database capacity for the additional staff.

It is also useful for the help desk to send a designated technician the morning of the migration to provide immediate "hands-on" support for migrated users. This gives a more caring image and can reduce the number of calls into the help desk. People are willing to wait a few minutes for in-person hand-holding instead of calling the help desk. Of course, this only works if the migrated users are in close proximity and are a reasonable number.

Supporting Service Considerations

When migrating from one messaging system to another, it is important to consider the legacy system's supporting services and how those services and resources will be migrated. For example, in a migration from MSMail to Exchange, the resources that support MSMail remote users will have to be migrated to support the growing Exchange users. Modems that support MSMail remote users may have to be moved to the RAS servers that are to support the remote Exchange users.

Outlook Client Implementation

The Outlook client implementation is a key part of the planning process. Table 12.4 describes the components that should be included in the migration plan.

Client Profile Generation

The client installation files should be customized as appropriate for the client design (as described in Chapter 8, "Design of Client Services"). The Outlook Deployment Kit should be used to create the necessary files (.STF and .PRF files).

Authentication

One of the significant planning components of the client migration is authentication before, during, and after migration. Before migration, it is necessary that clients disable all local schedules, messages, and files that will be migrated by the migration team. If the clients will be responsible for migrating their own local files, this is not necessary. The authentication issues that occur during and after the migration center around client configuration and profile generation. Those issues and some suggested solutions are outlined here:

- **Storage of files on user share**. If the client design includes storage of associated client files, such as personal address book files (.PAB files) on the user's home directory, the home directory must be available during installation. For example, if the user's home directory is mapped to drive G, and the full path to the address book as designated in the default profiles is G:\apps\outlook.pab, the Outlook client will not install the Personal Address Book service if that path is not available. A suggested workaround is to place the empty .PAB file on the user share before the migration time and make sure that any G:\apps\ path is available during installation.

- **Configuration of the profile**. Using the `%username%` parameter in the default profile greatly simplifies profile generation. However, the profile that's generated then uses the NT username of the person logged on for the mailbox name when initializing the profile. If someone other than the designated user logs into the computer and launches the client for the first time, the profile will try to attach to the incorrect mailbox when the designated user tries to launch the client.

- **Mailbox security**. Mailbox security can be compromised during the migration. This is especially true if the NT account is generated at the same time as the mailbox. Often when a migration team visits the desktop for the client software installation, it is desirable for the migration team to be able to log in to the user's account and verify that the client mailbox connection works and that mail has been successfully migrated. One way to meet all of these requirements is to generate a list of random passwords before the migration. Communicate each user's password to him before the migration using voice mail or e-mail (only use e-mail if the client will definitely check his e-mail before the migration). During migration, set the NT account passwords to a password known to the migration team. Then, when the migration team finishes verifying the client configuration, reset the account password to the random password that the user knows and enable the option to change the password at first logon. Another option is to configure the Exchange Administrators group with *user* permissions on the Site. This will allow members of the Exchange Administrators group to open user mailboxes and test functionality.

These factors apply to all the installation types—push, pull, and desktop visit—and need to be resolved in order to establish a solid client migration process.

Table 12.4 **Sample Migration Plan Outline**

Section	What It Contains
Software Installation	Method for installation and configuration of messaging client software.
Migration of Desktop Data	Migration of files located on the desktop computer or on private user shares.
Authentication During Installation	Authentication of installation team for desktop visit during client configuration.
Calendaring	Migration issues from current calendar to Outlook calendar.

13

Exchange Server Operations

T HE FINAL PORTION OF A COMPLETE Exchange architecture goes beyond the building of an Exchange organization into the running of an Exchange organization. The Exchange disaster recovery plan and periodic operations, as defined in the architecture, set a precedent for maintenance and review of the Exchange organization. This precedent will help ensure a stable and fully functioning Exchange organization long after implementation is complete.

Disaster Recovery

Disaster recovery is defined as the steps taken to recover from a service failure. Service failures can be anything from a hard drive failure to a natural disaster that causes loss of hardware. The measures taken to minimize service failures, and the extreme steps taken once a failure occurs, depend on the organization and its tolerance for service outage. An organization in which e-mail is incidental won't go to the same lengths to ensure constant service as an organization in which e-mail is the primary means of communication.

The disaster recovery plan shouldn't be kept in a glass box, with a dangling hammer nearby in case of an emergency. Rather, the disaster recovery plan should be familiar to everyone responsible for having to recover from an outage. The disaster recovery plan should also be validated during scheduled exercises so that panic is minimized and support personnel are familiar with the procedures necessary to recover from a disaster.

The Exchange disaster recovery plan should be an additional component of a more-inclusive disaster recovery plan for the organization. For example, the organization's backups should be scheduled so that a backup is periodically taken offsite. The file and print servers, application servers, gateways, and workstations should all have sections in a disaster recovery plan. The Exchange section of the disaster recovery plan would integrate with this strategy.

Creating a Disaster Recovery Plan for Exchange

As mentioned, disaster recovery for Exchange can have varying levels of complexity, depending on the organization and its tolerance for periodic unscheduled service outages. Decisions need to be made on the downtime that is acceptable if an outage occurs. For example, if minimal outage is required, Exchange servers can be clustered so that if an Exchange server fails, another server will take over the failed server's responsibilities. Of course, there is a cost associated with this level of service. The deciding factor should be whether the costs of providing server redundancy exceed the cost in productivity if the Exchange server is down for several hours. If a server supports a thousand users whose productivity depends on the Exchange messaging system, redundancy has the potential of saving an organization money when an outage occurs.

The disaster recovery plan should reflect these business decisions. Exchange as a messaging system, along with Windows NT, is a very stable platform. If it is assumed (hypothetically) that an Exchange server will fail twice a year, the outage costs of the two assumed failures should be compared to the costs of redundancy. If it is determined that the redundancy provided by clustering isn't cost-effective, lower levels of redundancy will be considered. Having hot-spare parts or a hot-spare server available on which to restore Exchange if an Exchange server fails might be a more cost-effective way to recover from a disaster. The minimum level of disaster recovery is to have procedures in place to restore an Exchange server from backup once the server is repaired. In other words, if a backplane fails, the server will be down until the backplane is replaced, however long that takes. From this, three levels of recoverability emerge:

- **Server redundancy**. Clustering provides failover services if an Exchange server fails.

- **Hot-spare**. An extra server can be used to replace a whole server or parts of a server upon failure.

- **Restore**. All data on a server is backed up so that when a failed server is restored, it can be restored to the point before the failure.

High Availability for Exchange

High availability is a fancy term for fault tolerance, which is a fancy term for redundancy. Microsoft offers Exchange Server fault tolerance in the form of *clustering*.
Clustering is two servers that share a common physical drive space. The idea is that if one server fails, the other will be able to assume its services. Since they both share the same physical drive space, access to users or application data won't be interrupted beyond the time needed to start the services.

Microsoft began supporting clustering in Exchange 5.5. Microsoft Cluster Server (MSCS) allows independent Exchange servers to be accessible and manageable as a single system. With Exchange 5.5, the cluster is limited to two servers. These two *nodes* communicate to provide automatic recovery if one of the servers in the cluster fails. For example, suppose that two Exchange servers are configured in a cluster that shares a common disk array with 112 GB of storage space. One Exchange server in the cluster supports 1,000 users, and the other server is for redundancy. If the Exchange server with users were to fail, the second server would assume its responsibilities. Microsoft plans on expanding its cluster support so that both servers host users during normal operation. In this case, both servers are being utilized during normal operations.

Configuring a Hot Spare

The costs and complexities of high-availability servers might not be justifiable in some organizations. The next best thing to a backup server online is a backup server offline. If a drive in an Exchange server's RAID array fails, one is available from the spare. If a backplane fails, one is available in the spare. The idea is that a spare server makes parts available only if an Exchange server fails. While the Exchange servers are running, the hot spare may be used for lab testing, version verification, and administrator training.

Choosing a Backup-and-Restore Strategy

Saving server data to tape should be a requirement for most any server. The only exception would be the need to back up servers that don't store any private or public store data. While not considered an expedient form of disaster recovery, tape restorations with today's tape devices can be relatively fast. It is possible to restore around 30 to 60 GB an hour with Digital Linear Tape (DLT) technology. Hence, an organization may determine that one to four hours of potential downtime, in the event of a failure, is acceptable. This may become more acceptable with the next version of Exchange. Platinum will allow for multiple private information stores. Hence, a server with 1,000 users and 50 GB of private information store data can be broken up into five 10 GB private information stores. If a store becomes corrupted, it would only be necessary to restore the corrupted information store (10 GB), which would take approximately 20 minutes with DLT technology.

The Exchange database is a Joint Engine Technology (JET) database similar to the JET database used in many Microsoft products and services, such as Microsoft Access, Windows Internet Service (WINS), and Dynamic Host Control Protocol (DHCP).

JET is a transaction-based database: Database transactions are written to a transaction log and then posted to the mail database. Transactions are written to the *current transaction log*. This transaction log is approximately 5 MB in size. When the 5 MB is filled with transactions, it becomes a *previous transaction log*. The previous transaction logs, and the current transaction log, represent all database transactions since the last backup (if circular logging is disabled). Previous transaction logs are deleted only by an Exchange-enabled backup application. Hence, if backups are never run, or continue to fail, the disk space will be consumed by previous transaction logs, and Exchange will eventually shut down.

When curricular logging is disabled, there are three types of backups: full, incremental, and differential. Each requires a different amount of time to perform, both in backup time and recovery time.

- **Full backup**. This type of backup saves all information store data to tape and then removes all previous transaction logs. Full backups include all Exchange elements, as shown in Figure 13.1. Full backups take the longest to perform but allow for the quickest restoration.

- **Differential backup**. This type of backup saves only the previous transaction logs to tape and doesn't delete them. Restoring a database from differential backups requires that the last full backup and the latest differential backup be restored. For example, if a full backup is run Monday evening, differential backups are performed on Tuesday, Wednesday, and Thursday evenings (see Figure 13.2). If a server fails on Friday morning, the full backup from Monday would have to be restored, along with the week's transactions from the Thursday differential backup.

- **Incremental backup**. This type of backup saves only the previous transaction logs to tape and then deletes them. Restoring a database from incremental backups requires that the last full backup be restored, and then all incremental backups since the full backup are restored. For example, if a full backup is run Monday evening, incremental backups are performed Tuesday, Wednesday, and Thursday evenings, as shown in Figure 13.3. If a server fails Friday morning, the full backup from Monday would have to be restored, along with the week's transactions from the Tuesday, Wednesday, and Thursday incremental backups.

Circular Logging

Microsoft Exchange ships with *circular logging* enabled. This means that when the current transaction log becomes full, old transactions are discarded, and no previous transaction logs are created. This keeps the unknowing Exchange administrator from filling the Exchange server's disks with previous transaction logs and prevents incremental and differential backups from being possible. Circular logging should be disabled, using the Exchange Administrator, in most Exchange environments.

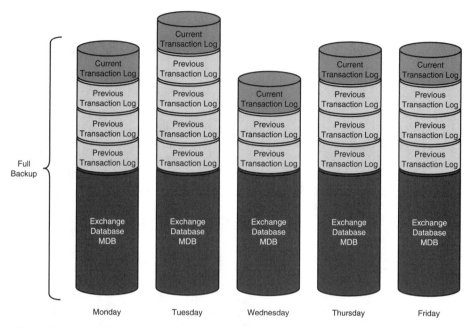

Figure 13.1 A full backup includes the Exchange database, previous transaction logs, and the current transaction log. The previous transaction logs are deleted after each backup.

Identifying Critical Data to Be Protected

Three types of data need to be addressed in the backup-and-recovery section of the disaster recovery document. The Exchange databases are usually where much of the focus is placed. This is the critical user data that exists only on these databases and their backups. The second type of Exchange data is the Exchange server configuration, which makes the Exchange server specific to the Exchange organization. It's stored in the Exchange directory database. Exchange uses a multi-master database, where each server has a copy of the directory. This database is included in each backup and is distributed throughout the organization on all the Exchange servers. The final component of the Exchange server configuration information is the portions of the Exchange server directory and Windows NT Registry that are specific to Exchange. This is the third type of data that needs to be addressed in the disaster recovery plan—the operating system and supporting systems that Exchange relies on for its operation.

By default, the Exchange databases and their supporting files reside in subdirectories of the \exchsrvr directory, as shown in Figure 13.4.

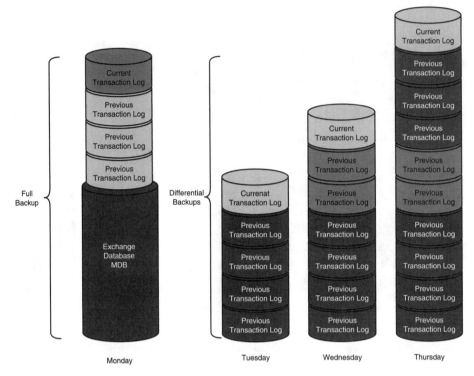

Figure 13.2 A differential backup doesn't delete the previous transaction log, capturing all the changes since the last full backup. A restoration after a differential backup requires restoring the last full backup and then restoring the most recent differential backup.

These file locations may change when the Performance Optimizer is run. As mentioned in Chapter 11, "Monitoring and Optimization," the Performance Optimizer will determine the best location for each portion of the database and will create the \exchsrvr directory at that location and move the files there.

Apart from the Exchange data stored on the server, the ability for Outlook users to *auto-archive* data to a personal store (.pst) file may also make it necessary to include these files in the backup strategy. This can be done in several ways. One example is to have an Exchange subdirectory in each user's home directory on the file server. The Outlook client is then configured to archive e-mail to a .pst file in the home directory. The .pst archives will then be backed up when the user's home directories are backed up.

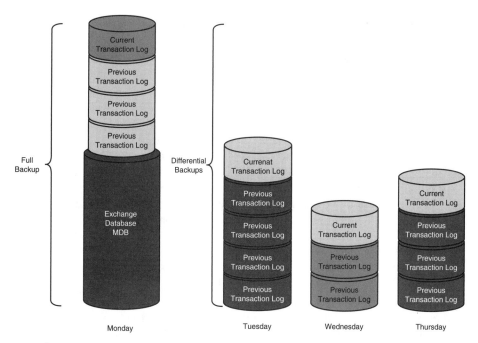

Figure 13.3 An incremental backup records the transaction logs since the last backup to tape and then deletes the previous transaction logs. While this solution takes the least time and space for backup, restorations from incremental backups are the most time-consuming.

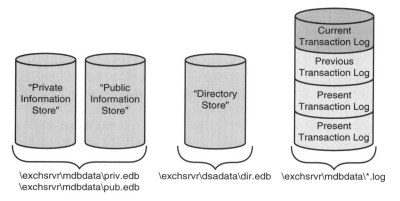

Figure 13.4 The Exchange databases and transaction logs are stored in subdirectories of the \exchsrvr directory.

Performing Disaster Recovery Exercises

Once a disaster recovery plan is in place, it's easy to file and forget. But as with any plan, it needs to be tested, or piloted. For this, it is necessary to run disaster recovery exercises. These exercises not only validate the plan, but they also familiarize staff with the steps that need to be taken and the associated tools and software that need to be ready when a failure occurs. It isn't uncommon for an organization, with disaster recovery plan in hand, to begin the recovery of an Exchange server only to find that they have misplaced the Exchange server software.

Performing disaster recovery exercises on lab or spare servers gives the support staff and administrators time to understand the steps necessary to recover from a disaster.

It is also important to use an actual backup tape for the exercise. Not only will this give you the opportunity to see how much time a restoration will take, but more importantly, it will verify that the backup tape actually contains good data.

Restoring a Complete Server to New Hardware

If a server suffers an untimely demise, from a major electronic failure, fire, theft, and so on, it will be necessary to recover the server's data from backup. The disaster recovery plan should include the steps necessary to recover a server to new hardware. The procedures for installing Windows NT with the proper service packs, installing the backup software, installing Exchange in Recovery mode, and laying down the databases off tape should be well-defined. For more detailed information on the specific steps for recovering an Exchange server, see the Microsoft Exchange Disaster Recovery white paper. The latest version can be downloaded from the Microsoft Web site.

Restoring Data to the Same Hardware

It is also possible that a portion of the Exchange database will become corrupted. This could be caused by many things, such as a failed disk drive, power surge, and so on. In this case, it is only necessary to recover the database, not the operating system or Exchange Server services. In this case, the missing portion of the Exchange database can be taken from tape. The transactions stored in the transaction log files will be replayed, and the database will be current. For example, if the RAID array that contains the private information store has a catastrophic failure and is unusable, it would become necessary to recover the database, not the operating system, transaction logs, or Exchange services. In this case, after repairing the RAID array, a restoration of the last full backup could be performed. The transaction logs still on the server would be replayed against this restored database, making it current.

Again, for more detailed information on the specific steps for recovering an Exchange server, see the Microsoft Exchange disaster recovery white paper.

Operational Procedures

It's easy for an Exchange administrator to focus on expanding the Exchange services for the organization once the initial implementation is complete. Building collaborative applications, developing Outlook forms, and integrating Exchange with other BackOffice applications can draw attention away from the operations necessary to keep an Exchange organization healthy.

The Exchange architecture should define daily, weekly, and periodic operations needed to keep the Exchange organization running smoothly.

Daily

Daily operations are tasks that are typically performed by operators or automated processes. While it may be possible to automate many daily operations, it remains necessary to monitor them on a daily basis for both success and analysis. Many daily operations include monitoring system resources to ensure adequate performance and capacity.

Backup

As mentioned, regular backups are necessary for a multitude of reasons—not just to recover from a failure, but also to recover from an operator or user error. Here are some guidelines to follow when creating your backup strategy:

- **Full backup**. Do a full backup if possible. Differential and incremental backups are a nice option. But with today's technology, a production system should be able to complete a full backup during the evening hours.

- **Disable circular logging**. Disable circular logging to enable differential and incremental backups. This will also keep all transactions throughout the day. If it becomes necessary to restore a database, the day's transaction logs will be available to replay.

- **Confirm that daily backups were successful**. Set up a process where daily backups are confirmed successful. If possible, configure e-mail notification. Make sure the notification is reliable. If e-mail notification of a failure is regularly sent out for successful backups, when a backup failure does occur, the e-mail will be ignored.

Gather Data

As mentioned in Chapter 11, gathering data using the Performance Monitor is useful for following trends in the Exchange environment. Using the Performance Monitor, data should be gathered daily to show trends in message traffic and server usage. The number of Internet messages sent, the number of NNTP news messages received, and the number of public folder replications are all the type of counters that should be gathered daily in order to reveal a trend. It isn't useful to once a week monitor the number of Internet messages sent, because trends aren't as visible when the data-gathering process is less frequent. Therefore, scripts should be developed that run the Performance Monitor for a period of time each day to collect data for later use.

Monitor Message Traffic

By gathering data on message traffic, an administrator can begin to understand how the Exchange topology is being used. The administrator can see how well users are grouped on servers in a site, as well as how much collaboration is taking place between sites. The administrator can see how much Internet resources are being utilized and make decisions on the number and placement of Internet services.

Table 13.1 lists a few of the Performance Monitor counters you may want to use to gather information on message traffic.

These message traffic counters will help document the utilization of the MTA on the monitored Exchange Server, as well as how much Internet protocols are being used to access message stores and the directory.

As an example of how daily monitoring of message traffic can prove to be business-critical, consider the case of an aerospace manufacturer that won a large contract with a defense contractor to build parts for a new airplane. The success of this project depended on the communication between the aerospace manufacturer's engineering group and the defense contractor's engineering group. During daily monitoring, the Exchange administrator saw a dramatic increase in the Internet messaging traffic, both inbound and outbound. When the Exchange administrator made some inquiries into the nature of the Internet traffic, he concluded that the Internet mail services provided by Exchange needed to have additional fault tolerance built in so that communication between the two organizations would be guaranteed. By reviewing the Internet messaging traffic, the Exchange administrator could proactively expand the level of service for an essential business function, and not wait for a failure to raise the importance of this functionality.

Table 13.1 **Messaging traffic counters**

Object	Counter
MSMI (MSMail Interchange)	Messages received
MTA	Messages/sec
MTA	Work queue size
MTA (PC) (MSMail-specific)	File contentions/hour
MTA (PC) (MSMail-specific)	LAN/WAN messages moved/hour
MTA connections	Queue size
Information Store Private	IMAP messages sent rate
Information Store Private	NNTP Messages posted rate
Information Store Private	NNTP Messages read rate
Information Store Private	POP3 Messages send rate
Directory Service	LDAP Searches/sec

Monitor Server Load

As with monitoring messaging traffic, monitoring server load should be built into the daily operations. Monitoring server load lets administrators anticipate and justify purchasing additional resources to meet user messaging requirements. This data can be consolidated into a report that shows where more resources are needed, how to better balance the load between existing servers, and general trends in the organization's messaging environment.

Table 13.2 lists a few of the Performance Monitor counters that you may want to use to gather information on message loads.

These counters will help document the server store utilization and its effect on performance. These counters can also expose bottlenecks in server performance.

Monitor Availability and Performance

Using the Performance Monitor to gather data is useful in calculating trends in the Exchange organization. The Performance Monitor can also be used daily to monitor availability and service performance. This can be useful for at-a-glance observation of queues when a support call is initiated by a user, or to help confirm a connector monitor alert message.

MTA Queue Monitoring

It is common to have a workstation running a Performance Monitor that monitors MTA queues. While the connector monitor will alert the administrators when a connector enters a warning state, the Performance Monitor can give you a feel for how much mail is running through the organization and how well the Exchange organization is keeping up with demand.

Table 13.2 **Messaging load counters**

Object	Counter
Processor	% Processor time
Processor	Interrupts/sec
System	File read/write operations/sec
Memory	Pages/sec
Memory	Available bytes
Server	Bytes total/sec
Physical disk	% disk time
Physical disk	Average disk sec/transfer
Logical disk	% free space
Directory service	Pending replication synchronization
Directory service	Remaining replication updates
Information store private	Average time for delivery
Information store private	Average time for local delivery
Information store public	Message opens/sec

System Monitoring

As mentioned in Chapter 11, Exchange can be monitored from a network management system. It is recommended that, in more-complex environments that contain several distributed network resources, a network management system be put into place. The MIB included since Exchange 5.5 can be a distributed resource. The daily monitoring of all network resources would also include Exchange.

Scan the Event Log

Scanning the event log daily is another way to learn of problems from the Exchange server, not the user. This process may be automated using the BackOffice Resource Kit utility evtscan.exe, which scans the event log for errors and alerts the administrator if an error is found. It is important to make sure that this notification occurs infrequently enough so that it is paid attention to when an important event is logged.

Check Disk Space

A sign of a poorly run Exchange organization is when an Exchange server fails because of lack of disk space. This shows inadequate planning and attention to system resources. To avoid being thought of as a poorly run Exchange shop, set up the processes necessary to ensure that an administrator is alerted when disk space becomes limited. These processes can be manual, where an operator checks daily, or automatic, where the Performance Monitor is run once a day and alerts the administrator when disk space becomes low.

Weekly

Weekly operations are more focused on the state of the Exchange organization and the consolidation of data collected during the week. There are also resources that an administrator may want to monitor for growth. This type of monitoring is meant to establish trends, not alert administrators of a problem, as the daily monitoring will.

Full Backup (if Taking Daily Incremental Backups)

If an incremental or differential backup is being performed, a full backup should also be performed at least once a week. Often, incremental and differential backups are being done because the information stores are larger than the backup system can successfully back up during off-hours. In this case, the weekend is typically the best opportunity to run a full backup.

Check Replication Activity

In organizations that contain several sites, it is necessary to review directory replication. Using the event log, check to make sure that replication between sites is successful and that there are no errors. It is also possible to confirm that new directory objects have been replicated throughout the organization. For example, choose a new mailbox or change to a mailbox that was made the previous day, and check the most distant site to ensure that the object was successfully replicated.

It is also prudent to make sure that no public folders have been configured for replication unnecessarily. Depending on the size of the organization and the number of Exchange administrators, this may or may not be necessary.

Gather Statistics

As messaging traffic grows and server load data is gathered throughout the week, it builds up in a series of log files. Once a week, those log files should be consolidated into a single file or report. These weekly log files will be periodically consolidated and analyzed to review trends and bottlenecks.

Document Changes

If changes are made to the Exchange organization configuration during the week, the architecture should be modified to reflect the changes. It is important to keep the architecture document useful by keeping it up to date. If the architecture should change and not be reflected in the architecture document, the document becomes much less useful.

Review Private and Public Information Store Usage

The private and public information store sizes should be checked on a weekly basis for significant size changes. An example of the usefulness of this activity is an organization that recently installed a digital scanner in its drafting department. Several engineers and drafters were working on the project for which this scanner was to be used. They agreed to utilize the powerful collaborative features of the public folder system during the project by posting specifications and drawings into the public folder system. The Exchange administrator, reviewing private and public information store usage weekly, noticed a significant increase in the public information store size. Using the Exchange Administrator, he could see which public folders were consuming the additional public information store space and validate its use. The decision was then made to add additional disk space to support this project. This is a fine example of how weekly reviews of information store utilization can be used to proactively add resources when additional demands are placed on the system.

Verify Server Health

As with reviewing information store utilization, a weekly review of server health can help you avoid problems. By looking at the Exchange Server process utilization, you can meet changes in the Exchange organization with additional resources or services. With Exchange 5.5 and the expanded information store size limit, it became possible to host many more users on each server. When servers host over 1,000 users, the Exchange processes that need to support this number of users can become very busy. Monitoring the utilization of these services weekly can provide the data necessary to add server resources or additional servers.

Periodic

Several Exchange utilities and activities need to be performed only occasionally. These operations often require the servers to be taken offline. When you set a schedule for periodic operations, users and management are forewarned of downtime. The frequency of periodic operations depends on the size and complexity of the organization, as well as the practicality of bringing the Exchange servers down. Some organizations that utilize Exchange servers 24 hours a day, seven days a week may be limited as to the number of times a year the Exchange servers can be shut down for maintenance. However, if possible, periodic operations should be performed at least once a year.

Compress Stores with ESEUTIL (Formerly Known as EDBUTIL)

The Exchange 5.5 databases have a scheduled nightly online defragmentation. For several hours early in the morning, the Exchange databases are defragmented. However, this online defragmentation doesn't reclaim disk space, nor does it guarantee that the database will be completely defragmented. Therefore, it is prudent to periodically take the Exchange server offline to do an offline defragmentation. There are several things to be aware of with an offline defragmentation:

- **Defragment all databases**. During the scheduled downtime, defragment the private and public information stores, as well as the directory database.

- **Schedule offline defragmentation**. If possible, schedule a quarterly or biannual offline defragmentation. ESEUTIL with Exchange 5.5 or EDBUTIL with Exchange 5.0 and earlier are the utilities used for this defragmentation.

- **Back up before and after defragmentation**. Back up the databases before the offline defragmentation. When defragmentation is complete, and the Exchange server is successfully brought back online, back up the defragmented database.

- **Time required**. The time required for an offline defragmentation depends on the size and amount of fragmentation of each Exchange database, as well as the speed of the Exchange server (CPU and disk speed). Exchange databases of around 15 GB may take several hours to defragment. To ensure that the time required is available during the scheduled outage, it may be necessary to copy a database to a lab Exchange server and defragment the information store in the lab to get a feel for the length of time required.

- **Have adequate disk space**. When sizing the amount of disk space an Exchange server should have, you must account for the disk space needed during defragmentation. An offline defragmentation essentially makes a copy of the database being defragmented. Therefore, if the private information store is 20 GB in size, there needs to be 20 GB of available disk space. The defragmentation utility can be run so that the copy of the database is redirected to a separate logical drive.

Run Mailbox Cleanup Agent

If a policy is in place to retain only mail of a certain age, configure and run the *Mailbox Cleanup Agent*. This is a component of the Exchange Resource Kit that moves messages based on age limits. Within each recipient container in a site, age limits can be set on the user's Inbox, Sent Items folder, Deleted Items folder, and all other folders as a group. The Mailbox Cleanup Agent can be run on a more-frequent basis if necessary, but if the policy is in place, it should be run quarterly at a minimum.

Run a Disaster Recovery Exercise

As mentioned earlier in this chapter, a disaster recovery exercise should be run periodically to validate the restoration process, the backup media, the location of software, and the necessary recovery procedures.

Install Service Packs

Windows NT and Exchange service packs that have been released for 60 to 90 days and that have been tested in the lab should be installed on the production systems during the periodic maintenance. Make sure the changes to the systems are reviewed and planned for. Make sure a validated backup of the complete server is done before you install any service pack.

Extend Server Functionality

If planned server functionality is to be added to the Exchange organization and has been tested in the lab, use the periodic downtime to implement and test this functionality. Extended functionality may be a new service, such as a voice mail or fax-connector, that would require the Exchange server to be rebooted. If problems occur during the installation, time should be allotted for a rollback or server restoration. As when making any change to the Exchange servers, make sure a successful backup of the entire Exchange server was done prior to the installation.

Change a Server's Role in an Organization

When a server is to be reconfigured to assume different responsibilities in an Exchange organization, the scheduled downtime for periodic maintenance can be the ideal time for this reorganization. When users are off the system, and controlled testing can be done, large numbers of mailboxes can be moved, connectors configured, and extended services installed without disrupting service to users and without having user activity extend the time required for the reconfiguration.

Six-Month Technology Review

Apart from daily, weekly, and periodic operations, you must review the overall Exchange architecture to see how it is meeting the demands of users and if it is taking advantage of current technology. A six-month review of the Exchange architecture will give you the opportunity to review the statistics gathered since the last review to ensure that the Exchange messaging system is meeting the needs of the users. The six-month review also provides the opportunity to evaluate changes in the organization's overall strategy and design, making sure the Exchange organization is in line with changes to the network and its services.

Assess Technical Developments

During the six-month review, examine all technical developments in the organization and their potential effect on the Exchange organization. Here are some areas of interest:

- **Windows NT design**. Because Exchange is dependent on the Windows NT architecture, changes to this architecture need to be closely scrutinized. For example, changing trusts between domains can affect the functionality of the Exchange servers and clients' access to it. No change to the NT environment better emphasizes this than the move from Windows NT 4.0 to Windows NT 5.0. This upgrade to Windows NT will have a significant impact on the Exchange environment. An Exchange administrator should be part of the team responsible for this upgrade. Furthermore, Exchange and Windows NT 5.0 coexistence should be thoroughly tested in the lab before Windows NT 5.0 replaces the Windows NT 4.0 domain.

- **Network design**. Changes to the network design can also affect the Exchange architecture. Site lines were drawn between physical locations because of available network bandwidth. If changes are made to the network, the criteria for the original Exchange organization decisions has changed. The Exchange architecture may be revisited to determine if the new network architecture could be better utilized by the Exchange organization. For example, consider an organization that has six physical locations, each with 200 users, all connected with heavily utilized 128 Kbps channels. Based on this network architecture, six Exchange sites were implemented. If this company were to expand its network services to include ATM between locations, the need for six sites could be reevaluated. It is possible that the six servers, one at each site, could be combined into one or two servers in a central site, with users accessing their mailboxes over the ATM network.

- **Exchange organization design**. Review the Exchange organization and be willing to make changes based on meeting the needs of the users, thus improving efficiency throughout the organization. If the architecture was designed right initially, changes in the Exchange organization usually are in the number and placement of servers, the location of connectors, and the replication schedule.

- **Client desktop environment**. Often the desktop is managed by a separate group than the application servers. It is important to review the changes that are taking place on the desktop, especially around the Microsoft Office applications, one of which is Outlook. How are changes to the desktop affecting user response and reliability? For example, when Outlook was first released, it contacted the user's free and busy public folders much more than the Exchange client did. This change to the desktop had an effect on server performance. Therefore, in many organizations, changes to the client had to go through the same testing process that changes to the server were subject to.

- **Operational practices**. During the six-month review, operational practices should also be reviewed. Is the desired data being collected, and is it being used properly? Are the services being protected adequately based on changing business requirements? For example, many organizations that first implement e-mail have limited utilization as users become accustomed to communicating electronically. But as time goes by, e-mail becomes more of a business-critical application. As this priority changes in the organization, the six-month review will allow for levels of service to be reevaluated.

Review Statistics and Predict Growth Patterns

The six-month review will also allow for a report to be generated on the utilization of the Exchange organization. The basis for this report can be the data gathered and consolidated during daily and weekly operations. The report should do the following (among other things):

- **Identify bottlenecks**. Patterns should emerge from weeks of data that show the system's bottlenecks. There will always be bottlenecks. Whether or not the resulting performance they limit the system to is acceptable should be the conclusion of the report. If a bottleneck is such that it affects the users' productivity, and resources can be added to alleviate the bottleneck, a project should be put in place to implement the solution to the bottleneck.

- **Foresee additional resource requirements**. Perhaps more difficult than identifying bottlenecks is foreseeing where resources will be needed in the future. But if the gathered statistics are reviewed with an experienced eye, it is possible to determine areas where additional resources will be needed. This is also the time to review the level of redundancy needed on critical systems. Again, if a service has become a mission-critical function for the organization because of its heavy use, redundancy may need to be added to help ensure undisturbed user service.

Verify Server Capacity

As everyone knows, server technology changes rapidly. Many organizations assign a three-year useful life to the servers that make up their organizations. With advances in application software, and reduced hardware costs, it is necessary to review the capacity of existing servers to determine if cost of ownership could be improved by increasing server capacity and reducing the number of servers. Maintaining 30 Exchange servers is more costly than maintaining 10. If Exchange can support the same number of users on 10 servers today, instead of the 30 servers required yesterday, it might be cost-effective to reorganize the Exchange server configuration.

Identify User Requirements for the Next Six Months

The six-month review isn't only to review what has happened in the previous six months, but also to look ahead to the next six months to determine if the architecture in place will support the users' growing needs. By extrapolating the trends found in the six-month review, you can predict future growth patterns. These future growth patterns can be mapped to the current environment to determine if the current environment will support the messaging system into the next six months.

For example, an organization may have migrated several hundred users to a single Exchange server. Once users become acquainted with the functionality of Outlook, group scheduling, and collaboration, the utilization of the server may increase dramatically when compared to when the migration was complete. The data gathered over a six-month period will expose this increased utilization and allow for the organization to either expand the resources of the existing server or add another server and split users between the two servers.

Lab Environment

One of the components of the Exchange organization that is necessary in order to ensure the reliability of an evolving software platform is a lab environment. Mentioned throughout this section is the need to test software and hardware before it is put into production. A lab gives you the opportunity to not only test software and hardware, but also to give administrators and operators the chance to work with new functionality and experiment with specific configurations.

A lab environment should be isolated from the production environment. The servers in a lab shouldn't be members of the production environment. It may even be necessary to have the lab physically separated from the production network, and perhaps only connected through a router with a firewall used to isolate the two networks. Many organizations learned this the hard way when upgrading from Exchange 4.0 to Exchange 5.0. Exchange 5.0 changed the directory schema so that no Exchange 4.0 servers could easily be added to the organization once Exchange 5.0 was installed into the Exchange organization. Many organizations that had their production and lab Exchange systems in the same Exchange directory installed Exchange 5.0 in the lab, only to find that they couldn't easily add additional Exchange 4.0 servers to their production Exchange organization.

Create a Realistic Lab

Not always easy to do, creating a lab that simulates the real world can be costly. If tests between two sites separated by a 56 Kbps channel are to be conducted, it is necessary to simulate a 56 Kbps channel in the lab. If at all possible, create a lab that accurately simulates the production environment. One method of simulating many users on a system is through the use of the Exchange Resource Kit utility Loadsim. Loadsim can be run on several clients to act like an organization's users. Performance tests can be run on the server as Loadsim simulates user activity. The results of the performance tests give the administrators an idea of how the server will perform in the production environment.

Components of a Lab

Here are some recommended components of a lab:

- **Connection to the organization.** As mentioned, isolating the lab from the production system is paramount. If the two networks are separated by a router and a firewall, the two can be connected using a foreign messaging connector such as the Internet Mail Service.

- **Runs new software.** The lab will be running new software. Run all new versions of the operating system, Exchange, and service packs in the lab until the administrators are comfortable in the stability, functionality, and supportability of the new software.

- **Duplicates the elements of the production environment.** The lab should be running the services offered in the production environment. If the production environment has a fax gateway implemented, for example, the fax gateway should be installed in the lab. This will ensure that new versions of software and service packs don't adversely affect the additional services that the production environment provides.

- **Runs the same hardware.** If possible, use the same server hardware in the lab as in the production environment. This will further validate the lab tests and also provide parts to the production server as needed.

14

Case Study: Small Organization

THIS CHAPTER PRESENTS A SAMPLE ARCHITECTURE for a small organization. The design document encompasses all the requirements and decisions necessary to implement Exchange in a small organization.

Company Profile

Grandma's Apple Pies (GAP) is a small manufacturer of tasty individual-sized apple pies and assorted treats. GAP has nine sites around the globe involved in the production and distribution of apple pies. In addition, numerous apple buyers access the network from remote locations. Table 14.1 shows the distribution of GAP locations and employees.

The two largest groups of users at Grandma's Apple Pies are the operations administrators at headquarters and managers in remote sites. Neither group are sophisticated users, yet they depend on email for interoffice communication, especially since they are spread across so many time zones.

The other users are plant managers, finance personnel, human resources employees, and apple buyers. The apple buyers group consists of about 35 users who work remotely. They depend on email as their primary means of communication and consider email a mission-critical application.

Table 14.1 **GAP office detail**

Location	Main Function	Number of Users
Yakima, WA	Headquarters, purchasing	500
Taipei, Taiwan	Production	100
Hong Kong, China	Production	100
Los Angeles, CA	Distribution	50
Kansas City, KS	Distribution	50
Newark, NJ	Distribution	50
Munich, Germany	Distribution	25
Lima, Peru	Distribution	25
Cape Town, South Africa	Distribution	25
Remote	Buyers	35

Currently, GAP uses Novell NetWare and cc:Mail for their basic IS needs. With the low prices of apples this season and the reduced labor costs of moving production overseas, Grandma's has the budget to upgrade their information systems. They have chosen to deploy NT and to migrate from cc:Mail to Exchange with the Microsoft Outlook client.

Business Case for Exchange

The need for a new messaging system became apparent when several employees, including a manager, were hired from a competitor. These employees insisted that they weren't as effective in their jobs because of the limited capabilities and efficiency of the GAP messaging system. This competitor, Cousin Ralph's Apple Pies (CRAP), utilizes Microsoft Exchange with the Outlook client. The ex-CRAPers and trade journals convinced GAP management that their business could benefit from an advanced messaging system upon which collaborative applications could be built. After diligent research, Microsoft Exchange was chosen as the messaging system. There were three prevalent reasons for the choice of Exchange:

- Many of the accounting/inventory packages that GAP is interested in migrating to are supported by Windows NT and recommend NT as the operating system of choice. Exchange fits into this strategy.

- Having a consistent front-office and back-office software vendor will ensure feature consistency and supportability into the future.

- The ability of Exchange to scale and tune for both the small and large locations would reduce the administration and maintenance costs for the organization.

Network Architecture

GAP's network architecture has evolved over the 10 years they've been in business. As offices and applications have been added, the network infrastructure, servers, and support devices have been expanded to meet their needs. Although this has been a functional approach, it has been more reactive than proactive.

This section describes the existing local area networks that make up the GAP enterprise, as well as the wide area network used to connect these LANs. The Exchange architecture will be built based on this understanding of the network infrastructure.

WAN Environment

Most of the day-to-day networking needs are addressed within each location. However, a WAN has been implemented over the years to accommodate data transfer and messaging traffic.

Geographic Profile

The GAP WAN uses frame relay services for connectivity between each site. All offices are connected to the frame relay service provider, although the access rate varies. The connection to the frame cloud from each office is shown in Figure 14.1.

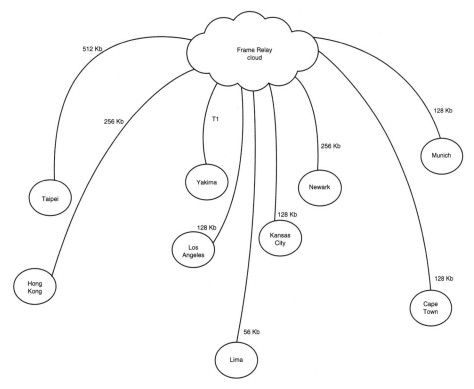

Figure 14.1 The GAP WAN is provided by frame relay services. Each office is connected to the cloud with varying access rates.

Table 14.2 summarizes the access rates from each location to the frame relay cloud.

Table 14.2 **Frame relay access rates for each location**

Location	Access Rate
Yakima	T1
Taipei	512KB
Hong Kong	256KB
Newark	256KB
Los Angeles	128KB
Kansas City	128KB
Munich	128KB
Cape Town	128KB
Lima	56KB

WAN Circuit Type and Available Bandwidth

Permanent Virtual Circuits (PVCs) are configured between each site and headquarters. Additionally, there is a PVC configured between Taipei and Hong Kong and another one between Munich and Cape Town (see Figure 14.2).

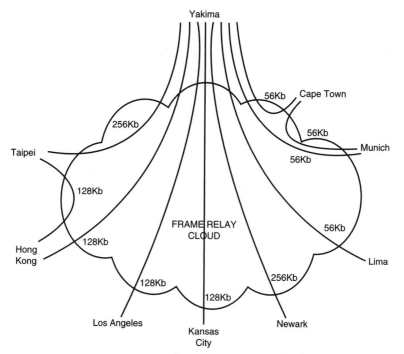

Figure 14.2   PVCs are configured between every location and Yakima, between Hong Kong and Taipei, and between Munich and Cape Town.

Table 14.3 summarizes the PVC committed information rate and available bandwidth average for each configured PVC. For more information on total bandwidth and available bandwidth, see page 102.

Table 14.3 **PVC committed information rate and available bandwidth**

City	Committed Information Rate	Available Bandwidth
Yakima – Taipei	256KB	128KB
Yakima – Hong Kong	128KB	64KB
Taipei – Hong Kong	128KB	64KB
Yakima – Los Angeles	128KB	96KB
Yakima – Kansas City	128KB	96KB
Yakima – Newark	256KB	64KB
Yakima – Lima	56KB	28KB
Yakima – Munich	56KB	28KB
Yakima – Cape Town	56KB	48KB
Munich – Cape Town	56KB	48KB

This configuration results in a logical topology. Figure 14.3 shows the CIRs for each link.

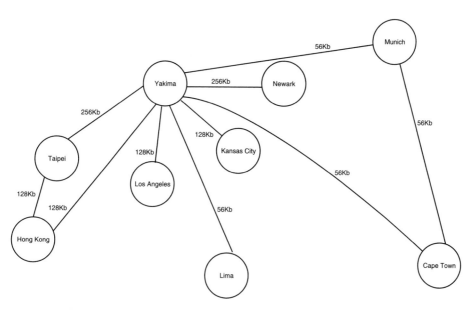

Figure 14.3   The resulting logical topology for the GAP WAN. Speeds shown are the CIRs for each circuit.

LAN Topology

This section describes the existing ocal area networks that make up the GAP enterprise offices. This information will be used to determine placement of servers and services as well as help optimize client-to-server connectivity.

Protocols

Two protocols are in use on the GAP network: IPX/SPX and TCP/IP. The long-term goal is to be an IP-only network. However, the workstations are currently connecting to the NetWare servers using IPX, and eliminating that protocol won't be possible until the NetWare-to-NT migration is completed.

LAN Segmentation

The GAP network has grown significantly in the past 10 years and has been an area of focus in the last two years because of the need to segment traffic and introduce intelligent devices on the network. This section describes the status of the LAN at each location, including initiatives that will occur during the same time frame as the messaging project.

Yakima LAN

The Yakima location has recently been divided into five segments that are networked with 100MB fiber Ethernet. Currently, the file, print, and messaging servers are located on their own 100MB Ethernet segment. TCP/IP and IPX are the two prevalent protocols, with TCP/IP being routed across several subnets. All workstations that will support the Outlook client will have TCP/IP connectivity to the Exchange servers.

There are five servers in the Yakima facility. The majority of these servers run Novell NetWare 4.11. Over time, the Novell NetWare services will be migrated to the Windows NT servers that will participate in the domain prescribed in this document.

Other Locations

The other locations in GAP each have local area networks:

Location	Description
Los Angeles	A Los Angeles LAN supports 50 workstations and one server. All workstations and servers are on one network segment.
Kansas City	The Kansas City facility is staffed with 50 people. These 50 workstations are on a single network segment with one server that provides file, print, and messaging services.
Newark	The Newark location has 50 workstations and one server on one physical network segment.
Lima	The Lima location has 25 users and one server on a single physical network segment.
Munich	The Munich location has 25 users and one server on a single physical network segment.

Location	Description
Cape Town	The Cape Town location has 25 users and one server on a single physical network segment.
Taipei	The Taipei location has 100 users and two servers. The workstations are on two physical network segments, and the servers are distributed between the two segments. One of the five servers hosts a production tracking application that is shared with the Hong Kong users.
Hong Kong	The Hong Kong location has 100 users and two servers on a single physical network segment.

Existing Server and Workstation Hardware Specifications

The inventory of existing server and workstation hardware specifications is necessary to determine the client architecture needs for the entire organization, as well as to make the decision on reuse of server hardware.

Workstations

Most of the workstations in the GAP organization were purchased in the last two years and are running Windows 95 or Windows NT Workstation 4.0. However, the workstations in the Lima office (25 workstations) are 486-class machines with 16 MB of RAM and are running Windows for Workgroups. These workstations aren't scheduled to be upgraded until after the messaging project is completed. Table 14.4 shows the breakdown of the workstation hardware and software configuration.

Servers

The hardware for the Exchange servers will be purchased new. There will be two classes of servers, depending on which services and in which location they will be installed. For more information on sizing servers, see page 136.

Table 14.4   **GAP workstation hardware and software configuration**

	Windows 95 Computers	NT Computers	WFW Computers
Number of workstations	800	100	25
Processor	Pentium/166	Pentium II/200	486/66
RAM	40MB	64MB	16MB
Hard drive space	2GB	4GB	1GB
Average hard drive space free	500MB	2.5GB	200MB
TCP/IP installed?	Yes	Yes	No
Microsoft clientinstalled?	Yes	No	Yes

Class A Exchange Server

This class of server is configured to host several mailboxes. This class of server is intended for the Yakima facility or a facility with several hundred Exchange clients (see Table 14.5). It is recommended that the implementation of Exchange at the Yakima facility begin with a single Class A Exchange Server. An additional Class A Exchange Server will be added to the Site when one of two thresholds is exceeded:

- The size of an information store exceeds 15GB. Exchange can support information stores in the terabytes, but maintenance and recovery of these very large information stores becomes cumbersome and impractical. When a compacted information store exceeds 15GB, it is recommended that an additional Class A server be added to the site and that a proportional number of users be moved to that server. For example, if two servers host 500 users each and are approaching the 15GB limit, an additional server would be added, and 162 users from each existing server would be moved to the new server.

- The performance of the server isn't acceptable. When slow performance occurs at the Outlook client, a performance audit should be performed. This audit would expose the cause of the poor performance. If the cause is determined to be overutilized CPUs or excessive paging, and additional resources can't be added to remedy the symptoms, an additional Class A server will be added to the site.

Class B Exchange Server

The second class of server, Class B, is configured to fit two roles in the GAP organization:

- A connector server and BDC for the Yakima facility. A Connector Server complements large mailbox servers because it offloads the responsibility of moving messages between sites, cc:Mail post offices, and the Internet. Furthermore, the Connector Server can be restarted without affecting the users, which adds to the total up-time of an Exchange organization. A single connector server/BDC is recommended for the Yakima facility.

- An Exchange server for the nonheadquarters locations. These locations have enough users to justify their own Exchange servers. The Exchange server at these locations would house the local user mailboxes as well as support a connector to the local cc:Mail post office and a connector to the hub Exchange site. They will also be BDCs for the GAP NT domain.

Table 14.5 **Class A Exchange Server specifications**

Resource	Specification
CPU	2, 266 Mhz Pentium
RAM	512MB
HDD	Hardware RAID 5; 36GB (4×9) for 27GB available
Tape	DLT

Table 14.6 defines this class of server.

Table 14.6   **Class B Exchange Server specifications**

Resource	Specification
CPU	1, 200 Mhz Pentium
RAM	128MB
HDD	Hardware RAID 5; 27GB (3×9) for 18GB available
Tape	DLT

TCP/IP Strategy and Topology

The TCP/IP strategy for the GAP organization has been defined for the implementation of the workstations and the migration to TCP/IP. GAP uses the private Class A IP address space of 10.x.x.x for all their LAN and WAN addresses. The firewalls perform Network Address Translation (NAT) for all packets coming from and going to the Internet.

Subnets

For the LAN and WAN subnets, GAP uses the first three octets for the network portion and the last octet for the host portion, creating a subnet mask of 255.255.255.0 for all addresses within the organization. Table 14.7 shows the allocation for the LAN and WAN subnets.

This IP address allocation results in a LAN and WAN IP address configuration, as shown in Figure 14.4.

DNS

The DNS services are currently being provided by the firewall at the Yakima location. This firewall is authoritative for the gapies.com domain and has records for the cc:Mail SMTP server and the Web server.

WINS

There are no WINS servers currently operating in the GAP network.

Internet Connectivity

The Internet connection for the organization determines the design of the SMTP mail and the service offerings to clients inside and outside the organization.

WAN Connection to the Internet

GAP has two Internet connections—one from the Yakima location and one from the Hong Kong location. The bandwidth of the Yakima Internet connection is 512KB, and the bandwidth of the Hong Kong Internet connection is 256KB.

Table 14.7 **LAN and WAN IP address allocation for the GAP network**

IP Subnet	Allocation
10.10.1.x	Yakima LAN
10.10.2.x	Yakima LAN
10.10.3.x	Yakima LAN
10.10.4.x	Yakima LAN
10.10.5.x	Yakima LAN
10.10.6.x	Yakima LAN
10.10.10.x	Yakima WAN
10.10.20.x	Munich WAN
10.10.30.x	Kansas City WAN
10.10.40.x	Cape Town WAN
10.10.50.x	Los Angeles WAN
10.10.60.x	Lima WAN
10.10.70.x	Taipei WAN
10.10.80.x	Hong Kong WAN
10.10.90.x	Munich LAN
10.10.100.x	Cape Town LAN
10.10.110.x	Lima LAN
10.10.120.x	Hong Kong LAN
10.10.130.x	Taipei LAN
10.10.131.x	Taipei LAN
10.10.140.x	Los Angeles LAN
10.10.150.x	Kansas City LAN
10.10.160.x	Newark LAN
10.10.170.x	Newark WAN

Firewalls

The GAP organization has a firewall for each of the Internet connections. Both of these firewalls are running firewall software that performs packet filtering, logging, and network address translation. Each firewall has an ISP-provided Class C IP address segment to use for the public address translation.

Web Services

The GAP Web services are currently housed off-site at the Yakima ISP location. Although GAP would like to increase the scope of its Web offerings from basic company information and job postings to the ability to order pies online, that project isn't scheduled for a year or more.

Internet Client Access Methods

The current messaging system doesn't support any client access from the Internet. With Exchange, the remote users migrate their remote access to an Internet Service Provider dial-up account and then access their mail through their Outlook client.

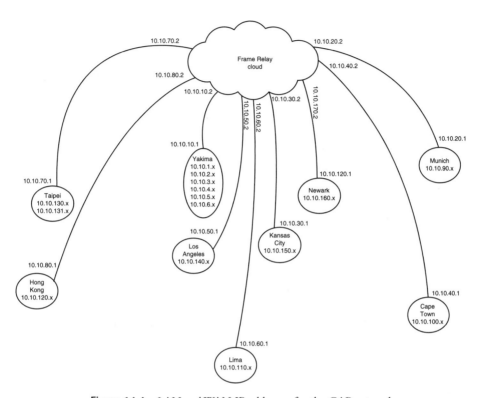

Figure 14.4 LAN and WAN IP addresses for the GAP network

Security Policies

The security policy at GAP requires that all passwords sent over the Internet be encrypted. No other security policies are defined at this time.

Existing Network Services

There is no existing domain topology at GAP. Currently the Yakima facility has three Novell NetWare 4.11 servers that run file and print services for headquarters. Collaboration between users in the various sites is accomplished by sharing file services across sites. This isn't done frequently or efficiently. The only Windows NT server running in the organization is a test installation installed in the lab. This installation isn't intended to be used in production.

Existing NetWare Applications

GAP uses a NetWare-based accounting/inventory package. The client for this system is DOS-based and is available in all locations. GAP has a project on the table to migrate from this system to a more current Windows NT-based system later in the year. This system must remain available to the GAP users after the NT and Exchange implementation is complete. Therefore, NT and NetWare will coexist after the messaging implementation and until the accounting/inventory package is migrated.

Remote users dial into headquarters using Novell's NetWare Connect. The clients connect remotely to access file, print, and messaging services. The accounting/inven-tory package isn't currently used by the remote buyers group.

Existing NetWare Servers

The Novell NetWare servers primarily provide file and print services. Table 14.8 lists the file and print servers at each location.

Table 14.8   **Existing NetWare servers and their functions**

Location	Server	Function
Yakima, WA	3 Novell NetWare 4.11	Remote communication
	1 Novell NetWare Connect	Communication
	1 cc:Mail SMTP Gateway	File and print
Taipei, Taiwan	2 Novell NetWare 4.11	File and print
Hong Kong, China	2 Novell NetWare 4.11	File and print
Los Angeles, CA	1 Novell NetWare 4.11	File and print
Kansas City, KS	1 Novell NetWare 4.11	File and print
Newark, NJ	1 Novell NetWare 4.11	File and print
Munich, Germany	1 Novell NetWare 4.11	File and print
Lima, Peru	1 Novell NetWare 4.11	File and print
Cape Town, South Africa	1 Novell NetWare 4.11	File and print

These servers are running on a variety of Pentium-class computers. As mentioned, these servers will remain in service until the accounting/inventory application is retired.

Existing Administrative Structure

Within the information systems department are two groups: administrators and operators. The administrators are responsible for managing and supporting the overall systems configuration. These systems include desktop configuration, messaging system configuration and support, and accounting/inventory system configuration and support. The second group consists of operators responsible for help desk services, creating and deleting user accounts and mailboxes, and back-up-and-restore services.

Internet Services

GAP provides Internet messaging services to all its users through the cc:Mail system. Only a few users at headquarters can browse the Internet. Administration has decided that only administration and the Information Systems group will be allowed Internet Web services.

Existing Messaging Architecture

GAP has used cc:Mail for several years. As a messaging system, cc:Mail has served them well. The Information Systems group is familiar with and comfortable managing and troubleshooting cc:Mail. They are anxious about implementing Windows NT and a messaging system that is new to them. The next sections discuss this current cc:Mail architecture.

Post Office Topology

There are a total of nine cc:Mail post offices throughout the GAP organization. Each facility has a single post office, residing on the local NetWare server that serves those local users. The headquarters location has the cc:Mail router, which acts as an MTA for the transfer of messages between all cc:Mail post offices. The cc:Mail router is a single point of failure in this cc:Mail network. The cc:Mail topology is shown in Figure 14.5.

All mail between nonheadquarters sites travels through the headquarters site. They don't take advantage of the intersite WAN connections between Taipei and Hong Kong or between Munich and Cape Town.

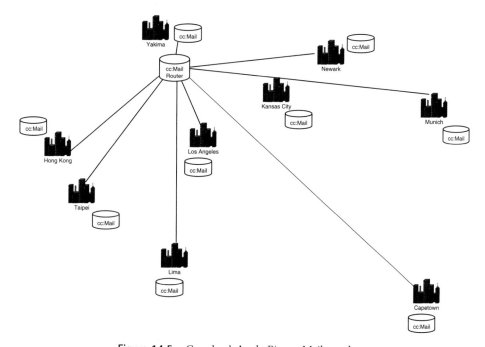

Figure 14.5 Grandma's Apple Pies cc:Mail topology.

SMTP Services

Although there are currently two Internet connections, only one SMTP mail gateway exists in the current GAP messaging configuration. The cc:Mail SMTP gateway is located in Yakima. It is configured as a relay agent, forwarding all SMTP mail to the ISP's SMTP host. The ISP SMTP host then resolves the domain name using DNS and delivers the message.

For inbound SMTP mail, the ISP is configured to forward all SMTP mail to the cc:Mail gateway on the GAP network. The MX records for `gapies.com` are shown in Figure 14.6.

The firewall is configured to allow only the cc:Mail gateway to initiate SMTP sessions to the Internet. The firewall is also configured to allow only SMTP sessions from the Internet to the SMTP gateway, using address translation.

Administrative Structure

All cc:Mail post offices are managed by Information Systems administrators and operators groups. The operators create, change, and delete user accounts as needed. The administrators are responsible for supporting and configuring the cc:Mail post offices.

Automated Services That Use the Messaging System

The accounting/inventory system creates a report nightly that is saved to a text file on the NetWare servers. Every morning, a custom batch file is run to email these reports to a set of GAP managers and administrators. The recipients of this message are defined in a distribution list hosted on cc:Mail. This functionality will have to be moved to Exchange.

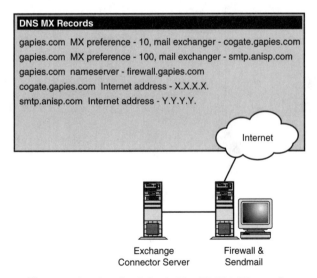

Figure 14.6 Grandma's Apple Pies DNX MX records.

Remote User Services

The buyers group of remote users dials into the network through the NetWare Connect server. In most cases, they incur long-distance charges with each call. The cost of this long-distance remote support ranges from $20 to $100 per month.

Once dialed in, the remote users typically access email. They use email to deliver their order status and delivery status email.

Occasionally, users travel to pie-tasting contests and bakers' conventions. Currently, these users don't utilize remote services while traveling. This functionality is desired.

Recipient Group Structure

There are several groups in cc:Mail that users email on a regular basis. Even more groups are seldom used. Table 14.9 lists the groups that are to be migrated to distribution lists in Exchange.

Table 14.9 **Groups to be migrated to distribution lists in Exchange**

Everyone	Help Desk	Buyers
Order status report recipients	Delivery status report recipients	Production managers
Distribution managers	Bakers	Peelers
Facility maintenance	Human Resources	Information Systems
All Europe	All Africa	All Asia

Bulletin Board Structure

Several cc:Mail bulletin boards have been created over the years. Few are for business use. Most are for employee interaction, such as want ads and movie reviews. It has been decided that these bulletin boards don't contain information that needs to be migrated. Additionally, the experience with the cc:Mail bulletin boards has highlighted the need to have specific usage policies for public forums and the expiration of messages.

Windows NT Architecture

Since Grandma's Apple Pies doesn't have an existing production NT architecture, it is necessary to include one in the project. Microsoft Exchange depends on the NT architecture for its functionality. In many respects, the Exchange implementation can be limited in reliability and efficiency by the NT architecture. This section defines not only the NT domain that Exchange will rely on, but the NT architecture to which the company's information systems will eventually be migrated. Therefore, it is important to design a system that will be extensible to support additional Windows NT server applications as well as file and print and messaging services.

Domain Approach

The GAP environment requires only a single domain because of the central administration team and number of users. With the current version of NT available, Windows NT 4.0, a single domain is advantageous for several reasons. One of the primary reasons is that the eventual migration to Windows NT 5.0 will be made simpler by having only one domain. For more information on NT domains, see page 108.

Grandma's Apple Pies' Windows NT domain will be called GAP.

Domain Controller Physical Locations

The Windows NT Primary Domain Controller (PDC) for GAP will be in Yakima, along with a single Backup Domain Controller (BDC). The backup domain controller will balance the authentication load with the PDC when both are operating. Both the PDC and the BDC can handle the authentication load if the other fails. This redundancy is necessary in a physical location with this many users. Every other site in the organization will have a single BDC to provide local authentication and redundancy in case the WAN circuit fails. The server topology is shown in Figure 14.7.

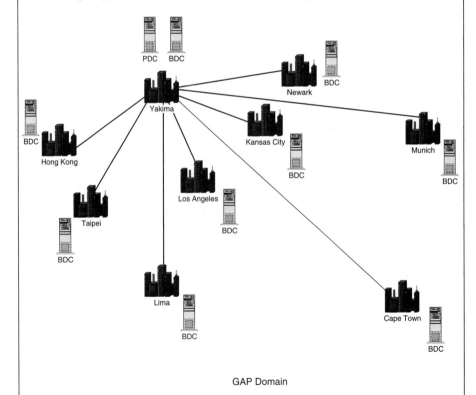

GAP Domain

Figure 14.7   Windows NT server locations

BDC Implementation Policies

If any additional local area networks are added to the WAN, and these networks will participate in the GAP domain, at least one BDC for each new network should be considered. The additional BDC will increase network authentication and browsing performance.

When, through the use of Performance Monitor, it is determined that the BDCs can't keep up with the authentication requests on a network, an additional BDC will be added to the network. It is also possible to move some of the network services that the existing BDCs support, such as DHCP, DNS, and WINS, to other Windows NT servers in the enterprise if that is a more appropriate means of reducing the server load.

Trusts

With a single domain, no trusts are necessary.

Naming Conventions

Resources in a network are given names so that they will be easier to use and manage. Naming schemes are most efficient when they follow easy-to-understand conventions. All computers, printers, users, and most other network objects can be given names. The naming convention defined here is a continuation and extension of the GAP naming convention already in place.

NetBIOS Names

Microsoft Windows operating systems use NetBIOS (Network Basic Input/Output System) with their networking protocols. Network resources are identified and located by a unique NetBIOS name. NetBIOS names can be up to 15 characters long and may contain a variety of alphanumeric characters. Because GAP will also be using Internet resources, it is recommended that the NetBIOS name also be compatible with DNS (Domain Name Service) host names. DNS names are restricted to a to z, A to Z, 0 to 9, and the hyphen. DNS names may not contain blank spaces. For these reasons, the format defined in the following sections is recommended.

Workstation Names

Workstation names will consist of a three-letter city code defined in Table 14.10, then a hyphen, and then a unique four-digit number.

Format: *<city code><-><unique four-digit number>*

Examples: YKM-0001, MUC-0100

Table 14.10   **Three-letter codes for the computer-naming convention**

City	Abbreviation	City	Abbreviation
Yakima	YKM	Hong Kong	HKG
Los Angeles	LAX	Taipei	TPE
Kansas City	KCK	Munich	MUC
Newark	EWR	Cape Town	CPT
Lima	LIM		

Server Names

Server names will consist of a three-letter server code defined in Table 14.11, then a three-character abbreviation denoting server function, and then a unique two-digit number. Hyphens, although X.500- and DNS-compliant, won't be implemented in server names because of support issues with SQL Server.

Format: *<server location><server function><increment>*

Examples: LIMBDC04, EWREXC01, YKMPDC01

Table 14.11 **Application codes for the server-naming convention**

Application	Abbreviation
Domain Controller	PDC/BDC
Exchange	EXC
SQL Server	SQL
Communications	COM
Backup/Archive	BUS
File and Print Server	FPS

Host Names

The host name is the native TCP/IP name given to a workstation or host. Host names will be the same as the computer NetBIOS name in lowercase characters. Windows NT Servers will also have the GAP domain name `gapies.com` configured as the TCP/IP domain name. The Fully Qualified Domain Name (FQDN) for each Windows NT server will then be *servername*`.gapies.com`.

Printer Names

When network printing services are migrated from NetWare to Windows NT, two pieces of information will be necessary to print to a network printer. First, the user must know where the printer is, or to which department it belongs. Second, the user might need to know the model of printer. This information can be useful should the user need to install a local printer driver. Due to browser constraints from Windows 95 workstations, the share name length should be limited to 12 characters. The server that is hosting the printer queue will define the city the printer is in. The printer share name will define the department and model of the printer.

Format: *<department abbreviation><model number descriptor><-><unique three-digit number>*

Example of share name: ADMINLJ4-002

Example of network path: \\KCKFPS01\ADMINLJ4-002

This path shows that this printer is in the Administration department of the Kansas City office.

To further assist users while choosing a printer, the share description field will be used to elaborate on the printer's description. A label will be affixed to each printer with its share name.

User Names

All users of the GAP network who want access to domain resources such as Exchange will log on to the domain GAP with their own account. Account names will be derived from the user's name. When two or more people have the same name, the middle initial will be used to ensure a unique NT account name.

Full name format: *Last name, first name middle initial.*

Example: Smith, John D.

Username format (NT account name): *<first initial first name><last name>*

Example: Jsmith

This format matches the current NetWare naming convention.

Miscellaneous Names

Other network components, such as hubs, switches, routers, and even patch panel ports, will be given logical names on an ad-hoc basis.

DNS

DNS is the method of translating host names into IP addresses. An example of a DNS name is `www.microsoft.com`. In this example, `microsoft.com` is the domain, and `www` is the host. DNS services provide resolution for internal services such as intranet hostname resolution. For more information on DNS, see page 106.

Currently, GAP has no internal DNS host name resolution. Instead, all DNS host name resolution is for *external* IP addresses. This external host name resolution is performed by the DNS server, which runs on the firewall. Any DNS request for an Internet host that is unknown or not cached by the firewall's DNS services is then forwarded to one of the root DNS servers on the Internet.

Microsoft Windows NT offers DNS services. These services will play a much more important role in the Microsoft Windows network with the next version of Windows NT (5.0). Therefore, it is recommended that DNS be implemented to some degree in the GAP *internal* environment. This will help ease the migration to Windows NT 5.0 while helping familiarize the IS staff with the management of DNS.

The Microsoft Windows NT DNS will be installed and configured on the BDC server at headquarters (YKMBDC01) and the BDC server in Hong Kong (HKGB-DC01). All DNS servers will be configured to integrate with the local WINS server. The DNS server closest to each subnet will be the primary DNS server for that subnet. The other server will be configured as the secondary DNS server.

The DNS servers will forward requests for external host IP addresses (Internet addresses) to the firewall DNS. This DNS configuration is shown in Figure 14.8.

DNS Domain

GAP has a single DNS domain, `gapies.com`, which is registered with InterNIC.

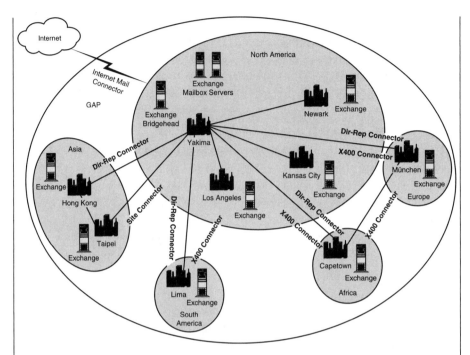

Figure 14.8 GAP DNS topology.

Zone

GAP will continue to have one zone, `gapies.com`. One zone is sufficient to serve the number of hosts and clients at Grandma's Apple Pies.

Primary Name Server

The *primary name server* manages the data for the zone(s) it is authoritative for.

Yakima

The primary Windows NT name server will be located in Yakima and will replicate with the authoritative server, located on the firewall, for the `gapies.com` zone. This name server will also be configured as a forwarder to resolve external DNS requests to the Internet, forwarding those requests to the firewall.

Other LANs

All other LANs will be configured to resolve to the DNS server closest to their LAN.

Secondary Name Servers

The *secondary name server* gets its data from the primary name server at startup. A secondary name server allows for local name resolution that reduces WAN traffic and provides redundancy.

Hong Kong

Hong Kong will have DNS installed and configured on the Hong Kong BDC server. The Hong Kong name server will replicate with the Yakima name server. Hosts in Hong Kong will first request host name resolution from the Hong Kong DNS. The Hong Kong name server will be configured to integrate with WINS.

Time to Live (TTL)

GAP will have a long TTL configuration on its name servers because the domain information will be mostly static—especially for non-Windows hosts that typically are servers. Windows hosts won't have their names registered in DNS, but will be resolved via WINS integration. The long TTL will also help reduce server load and wide area network traffic. In preparation for host changes, IP readdressing, and other changes that affect the DNS database, the TTL will temporarily be set to a small value so that the clients won't cache incorrect data.

WINS Integration

For WINS-capable machines that don't have static entries in the DNS database, such as machines that have dynamic IP addresses, WINS integration with DNS will provide friendly-name services. The name servers will be configured to refer to the WINS database for requests that can't be resolved in the DNS database.

WINS integration provides two major benefits. First, in addition to DNS entries, all WINS-capable computers can be referred to by friendly host names. Secondly, the WINS database is a dynamic database, where hosts register their names and IP addresses upon startup. Alternatively, the DNS database is a static database where changes must be made manually. Because DNS can query WINS, it enjoys the same dynamic workstation registration features as WINS.

To provide interoperability between DNS and WINS, a new record will be defined as part of the zone database file. The WINS record is specific to Windows NT and may be attached *only* to the zone root domain. The presence of a WINS record instructs the name server to use WINS to look up any requests for hosts in the zone root that don't have static addresses in the IP database.

Format: *<domain>* IN WINS *<IP address of WINS server>*

Example: @ IN WINS 10.10.1.3

This feature can also be set using the DNS user interface.

Dynamic Host Control Protocol (DHCP)

GAP currently assigns static TCP/IP addresses to hosts. This project will replace this strategy with DHCP. DHCP is a protocol by which a computer with no

TCP/IP configuration information can contact a DHCP server and lease IP address settings. These settings include the subnet mask, default gateway, and WINS and DNS server IP addresses.

Server Addressing

All GAP servers, both NetWare and NT, will have statically assigned IP addresses. The server IP address range will be excluded from the DHCP server pool(s).

Scope Ranges

There will be two active DHCP servers on the GAP LAN. Since DHCP servers don't share leasing information, each server will offer leases from a unique IP address pool.

DHCP Server Redundancies

There will be a DHCP server in Yakima and one in Hong Kong. The DHCP scopes will be split 90/10. Ninety percent of the IP addresses in a scope will be configured on the closest DHCP server, and the other 10 percent of the scope will be on the other DHCP server. If one DHCP server fails or is shut down, the other DHCP server will be available to lease IP addresses.

Option Assignments

The DHCP servers will provide clients with the options listed in Table 14.12.

Table 14.12 **DHCP option assignments**

Option Number	Description	Assigned Value
1	Subnet mask (enabled by default)	255.255.255.0
3	Router	Address of the nearest router
6	DNS servers	Addresses of DNS servers in descending order of priority
15	Domain name	gapies.com
44	WINS/NBNS servers (primary and secondary will be different for each DHCP server)	Each subnet scope will specify the WINS server for that subnet as the primary WINS server. The secondary WINS server will be the PDC at headquarters.
46	WINS/NBT node type	0×8 (hybrid node)
51	Lease time value (enabled by default)	21 days

DHCP Server Location

A DHCP server will be hosted in both Yakima and Hong Kong. The DHCP server in Yakima, on the BDC, will lease IP addresses for all subnets except Hong Kong and Taipei. The DHCP server in Hong Kong, on the BDC, will lease IP addresses for Hong Kong and Taipei. This DHCP strategy is shown in Figure 14.9.

Windows Internet Naming Service (WINS)

Windows networking uses NetBIOS names to identify nodes on the network. In a TCP/IP environment, these NetBIOS names need to be resolved to IP addresses before communication can take place. GAP will use WINS to maintain NetBIOS name registrations and provide NetBIOS-name-to-IP-address resolution for client workstations. For more information on WINS, see page 107.

WINS Server Distribution

It is important that WINS servers can accommodate the number of NetBIOS name resolution requests issued, as well as replicate their respective databases between WINS servers at other locations. The following sections define the locations and responsibilities of the WINS server in GAP.

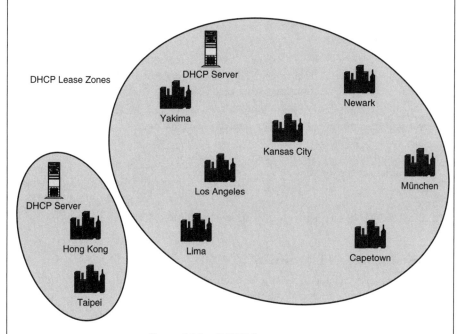

Figure 14.9 DHCP lease strategy.

Yakima

There will be two WINS servers in Yakima that will serve as primary and secondary WINS servers for the headquarters. The PDC (YKMPDC01) will be the primary WINS server, and the BDC (YKMBDC01) will be the secondary WINS server. In Yakima, the PDC WINS server will be defined as the primary WINS server, and the BDC WINS server will be defined as the secondary WINS server. This will be configured on the DHCP scopes defined in the preceding section.

Hong Kong

An additional WINS server will be located on the Hong Kong BDC (HKGB-DC01). The DHCP servers will lease the IP addresses for the Hong Kong and Taipei subnets, with the Hong Kong WINS server defined as the primary WINS server and the Yakima BDC WINS server defined as the secondary WINS server.

Other Facilities

All LANs other than Yakima and Hong Kong will use the WINS server in their region. For the Los Angeles, Kansas City, Newark, Lima, Munich, and Cape Town locations, the WINS services will be provided by the Yakima WINS server. For Taipei, the WINS services will be provided by the Hong Kong WINS server. The DHCP servers at headquarters will lease WINS-configured IP addresses that will designate themselves as WINS servers.

Server Replication

All WINS servers will replicate their databases with the WINS server on the PDC at headquarters. The primary WINS server in Yakima (PDC) will replicate through a push/pull relationship to the secondary WINS server in Yakima.

Replication between the Yakima PDC WINS server and the Hong Kong WINS server will be a pull replication. Because the majority of services are provided locally to each WINS server (and associated remote offices), it isn't necessary to update the databases more than once every eight hours. The pull replication time will be set for 6 p.m. GMT in Yakima and 7 p.m. GMT in Hong Kong. This configuration should optimize the replication to occur after the clients have registered with the WINS servers and also during off-hours for network traffic. The WINS server topology is shown in Figure 14.10.

Browsing the NT Domain

The PDC in Yakima also acts as the domain master browser and will synchronize browse lists between itself and the master browsers in Yakima, as well as the master browsers of the other subnets. The Yakima PDC, as the domain master browser, along with the other master browsers and backup browsers, will also provide browse lists to workstations that are browsing network shares on the Yakima LAN.

The backup domain controllers on each LAN will be the master browsers of those subnets. They will provide browse lists to workstations that are browsing network shares on their prospective LANs.

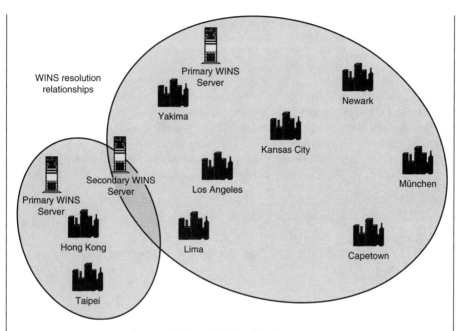

Figure 14.10 WINS replication strategy.

NT Accounts

Two types of NT accounts are necessary to support the Exchange architecture: user accounts and device accounts. These accounts are defined in the following sections.

User Accounts

One of the challenges of network administration is to provide secure network resources with minimum inconvenience to users. A major benefit of a correctly architected domain model is that users use only one user account and password to access all NT-based network resources. This simplifies the task of securing the network from external attack.

A domain user account will be created for all users of the network. To protect the utility of the security audit log, users won't log in using shared accounts or device accounts (see the following section). During the creation of user accounts, the following standards will be observed:

- User accounts for contingent workers will have a preset expiration date.
- User account creation will be automated to ensure consistency and accuracy of all user options. NT accounts will be automatically created during the cc:Mail migration by the Exchange Migration Wizard. A two-step migration can be used if account names need to be modified.

- The Description field will be used to identify the user's position or title, and other relevant information as appropriate.

- All users, including administrators, will be members of the Domain Users global group.

- Currently, Novell NetWare is the primary network service. Windows NT accounts will be set to expire at a slightly longer interval than the NetWare accounts. However, when Windows NT assumes the primary network server, Windows NT networking provides several mechanisms designed to increase the security of a user's password. Password policies will be set as follows:

  - Passwords must be at least six characters long.
  - Passwords will expire after 90 days.
  - There will be no minimum password age.
  - The system will remember the last five passwords.
  - After three unsuccessful login attempts, the account will be disabled for five minutes.

Device Accounts

Accounts that exist for use by applications or processes are considered a special case. Wherever possible, device accounts should be local users, not domain users. If they must be domain users, login rights will be limited to only the few necessary machines. Such accounts will be set with strong passwords that never change or expire. "Strong" means that the password should have at least 10 characters and should not resemble any intelligible word or acronym. Computer-generated random strings are preferred. Such account passwords should be documented and stored in a physically secure location. Such accounts shouldn't be members of Domain Users or any other group populated by real users. Where appropriate, the account will be granted rights directly to resources or objects. This is an exception to the general rule that only groups are assigned rights to resources or objects. The Exchange service account is an example of a device account.

Policies and Profiles

The policies and profiles made possible with Windows NT help manage the desktop and extend user options such as roaming to Windows 95, Windows 98, and Windows NT Workstation desktop users. For more information on policies and profiles, see page 109.

Profiles

User profiles will be stored both locally on the workstation's hard drive and on the server in the user's private directory. The Domain User profile will retain user settings such as Exchange mailbox settings, desktop color preferences, and bookmarks. The profile will contain shortcuts only. Users are not to place files on their desktops, only shortcuts to files located on network file servers. This is to ensure that files are backed up, because there is no current workstation backup process.

Policies

Configuration policies for Windows 95 haven't been implemented. Upon release of Windows 98 and NT Workstation 5, GAP will reexamine the benefit of policies to see if the Microsoft Zero Administration Windows (ZAW) will help reduce workstation administration.

Login Scripts

All users will execute a login script upon successful authentication from a domain controller. The login scripts will be maintained by the GAP Information Systems staff. Although Novell NetWare is the primary server service, the login scripts will do the following:

- Synchronize the workstation's clock with a network time reference.
- If the user is connected via Ethernet, the workstation will be updated with the latest virus signature files and will perform any additional management tasks.

Once Microsoft Windows NT takes the role currently held by NetWare on the GAP network, the NT login script will provide additional functionality currently achieved by the GAP NetWare login script.

Network drive mappings may be added to the login script on an as-needed basis.

Once migration from Novell NetWare to Microsoft NT begins, a formal login script should be developed. This login script should be written for the Kixtart32 interpreter—a scripting tool created and provided by Microsoft on the NT Server Resource Kit. This script and all supporting files will be replicated between all domain controllers. This script is aware of users who are connecting remotely and won't perform virus updates due to speed limitations. The login script is very extensible and can be used to perform a variety of future functions as required. This script is stored centrally on the PDC and is replicated to all BDCs using NT's Directory Replication Service. Because the file is located centrally and all users process the same script, changes can be made globally from one location.

CHECKRAS is a utility included in the Microsoft Windows NT resource kit that will be used in the script to determine if the user is on a high-speed network or a remote dial-up connection. Based on the results of this test, certain procedures will or won't be run during the login script.

In addition, the script will connect the workstation to printers based on the subnet of the IP address leased from the DHCP server. This will allow roving laptop users to print locally when they travel from office to office.

Server Security

Aside from policies and profiles, other rights relate to an NT Server environment. Such rights include the right to log on locally, to access the server from the network, to shut down, and to change the server's time. The following changes will be made to the default NT permissions on the servers:

The right Access this computer from Network will be changed from the Everyone group to the Domain Users group. Administrators will remain on this Access Control List (ACL), even though they should also receive this right through membership in the Domain Users group. This will prevent anonymous users from accessing share lists, user lists, and the Registry.

Non-IS staff won't have permission to log on locally to servers. This means that nonadministrative personnel won't be able to use the server's console.

The Server Operators local group will be allowed to take ownership of files.

Auditing will be enabled with the settings shown in Figure 14.11 on all domain controllers.

Administrator Account

A built-in Administrator account has total control over the system. In the case of the domain SAM, the administrator has total control over all domain controllers, as well as over all member computers via the Domain Admins global group. Every NT computer that isn't a domain controller also has a local Administrator account. The Administrator account won't generally be used. Its password should be very strong, documented, and stored in a physically secure location. The Administrator password will ensure that the organization can take full control of the network in the event of IS staff changes. If the Administrator account is used, the password should be changed and the appropriate documentation updated at least once a year. Additionally, a common industry practice is to give the Administrator account a unique name, such as AdminGAP. This makes the account more secure, because someone who tries to break into the system won't be able to guess the username for the administrative account.

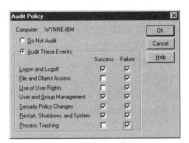

Figure 14.11   The auditing settings used for all domain controllers in the GAP domain.

Every administrator should use his own account that is a member of the Domain Admins group to log on. The AdminGAP account shouldn't be used for several reasons:

- Auditing will log privileged access to the network according to user name. Using the Administrator account allows effectively anonymous access and defeats accountability.

- Any means of communicating a password is a security exposure. Whether it is whispered or scribbled on a piece of paper, there is a risk that it could be intercepted.

- If several people know the administrative password, it is compromised whenever one person leaves the organization. When this happens, a new password should be chosen and communicated to each administrator. This represents a significant security exposure.

- For performing administrative functions, appropriate user accounts will be granted elevated permissions through strategic group assignments.

Share-Level Security

Security at the share level can further restrict, but not expand, rights granted at the file level. Generally, industry practice doesn't advise implementing share-level security, except in special cases. By default, domain users and administrators will have full control at the share level. Security will be applied on the file system level, not the network share level.

Group Assignment

Industry experience has developed a methodology that has proven to make ideal use of the user-to-group assignment features in domain security. It is called the UGLR paradigm: **U**ser **G**lobal **L**ocal **R**ights.

Users are members of **G**lobal groups.

Global groups are members of **L**ocal groups.

Local groups are assigned **R**ights to resources.

As networks grow, the sheer number of users and files becomes unmanageable. To simplify security administration, groups are used to aggregate several similar objects into a single object. Figure 14.12 describes how the UGLR paradigm greatly simplifies security administration.

NetWare File and Print Services

Though initially Novell NetWare will continue to provide file and print services to the GAP network, it is important to adhere to the following practices at the inception of this Windows NT network. These practices are as important as other aspects of the Windows NT architecture, regardless of the timing of file and print services deployment.

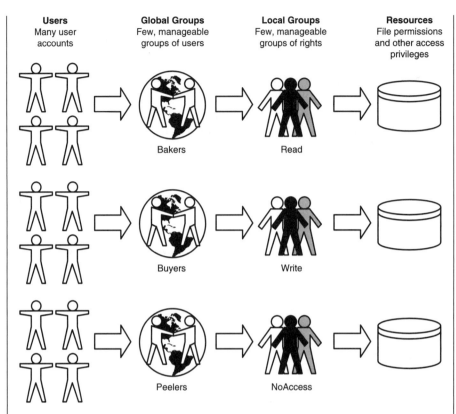

Users	Global Groups	Local Groups	Resources
Many user accounts	Few, manageable groups of users	Few, manageable groups of rights	File permissions and other access privileges

Figure 14.12   NT group strategy.

Remember that *global groups* are groups of *users,* and they should reflect the company's organizational structure. *Local groups* are groups of *privileges,* and they should reflect the network resources in general terms.

Here are two notable exceptions to the UGLR paradigm:

- In the user's private network directory, the user account will be directly assigned permissions on the directory.
- The local group Administrators should be listed with full control on all groups.

File Security Guidelines

Following the *need to know/need to use* rule as defined in the UGLR paradigm, access will be given as conservatively as practical. The following guidelines will apply as general rules and are based on the capabilities of the Windows NT File System (NTFS):

- The Administrators local group will always have full control, even of private user directories. This is a recommendation and can be configured otherwise. If the Administrator groups don't have permissions on the user directories, an administrator would have changed permissions to view or manipulate the directory. This change of permissions would be reflected in the security log.

- The NT group Everyone won't appear in any Access Control List (ACL). This will protect against unauthorized access to sensitive data.

- Only the IS administrative local groups will have full control. Users shouldn't be able to modify permissions or take ownership of files—even files in their own private directories.

- Custodians, who are designated users/owners of files, will have read/write/change/delete permissions.

- Users, who are designated users of files, will have read permissions.

- Execute permissions will never be coupled with write/change/delete, except for elevated accounts *and* within private directories. For obvious security reasons, execute permissions are very powerful and should never be given where normal users can also create files. To minimize the network's exposure to malicious attack or viral infection, only qualified IS staff will place executable files on the server.

Other guidelines will be implemented as situations dictate.

Client Software Installation Points

The Outlook client software will be stored on a NetWare file and print server in each location.

Backup Services

All server drives will be backed up to a magnetic tape device. The backup tapes will be stored in a secure place on GAP premises with a tape periodically taken to a secure remote location.

Each LAN will have its own backup device that can back up the entire server on a single tape during off-hours. Additional Windows NT servers will be backed up from a common backup server or individually to a local backup device, depending on the amount of data to be backed up.

Seven tapes will be kept in rotation for each backup device. This will allow restorations as far back as seven days. Once a month, a tape will be taken out of the rotation and stored in a secure remote location. Then a new tape will be put into the rotation.

The backup software will be configured to notify an administrator of a backup failure. This notification will be in the form of an email. The server console will also receive a notification that the backup has failed. The local backup operator will check this when the tape is being changed. For more information on backing up and restoring, see page 197.

Backup Software

Backup software needs to be evaluated before being selected. Any backup software used should have support for Microsoft Exchange and Microsoft SQL Server (to support the accounting software package that will be implemented in the future).

Backup Schedule

With the use of Digital Linear Tape devices, each server should be able to complete a full backup overnight. If this is proven incorrect, incremental or differential backups can be performed.

Restoration Strategy

To restore a server, the most recent full backup will be used. If incremental or differential backups are being performed, the most recent full backup will be restored, along with the appropriate differential or incremental backups.

Twice a year, a backup will be restored on a blank server in a lab environment (not connected to the GAP network). This will ensure that the backup tapes are in good order, that the necessary system software is available, and that the Information Systems personnel are familiar with the restoration procedures. This process will be completed for each location.

A disaster recovery plan will be put in place no later than six months after implementation.

NetWare Integration

Grandma's Apple Pies plans on migrating from their current accounting/inventory system, which relies on Novell NetWare, to a Windows NT-based system later in the year. This means that Windows NT and Novell NetWare must co-exist during that time. To ease administration and provide the most functionality, the following strategies and products are recommended.

Novell Administrator for NT

Novell Administrator for Windows NT includes a snap-in to the NetWare Administrator console that allows for integration between the GAP Windows NT Domain and Novell NetWare network. By delivering a single point of administration for users and groups in a mixed environment, it simplifies the entire network administration process, thus reducing the cost of owning and managing the GAP's heterogeneous network during the migration to Windows NT. Furthermore, GAP IS administrators are familiar with the Novell Administrator console.

NetWare Client for Windows NT

It is recommended that the Novell NetWare client for Windows NT and Windows 95 be implemented during migration. This client enables password synchronization between the Windows NT domain and NDS.

Network Management

Network management in an organization such as GAP is essential and affordable.

SNMP Manager

GAP will deploy a centralized management platform to monitor network activity. Network components have been installed in the GAP environment that are

SNMP-enabled. To ensure consistency with these active network components and optimum *management information base* (MIB) compliance, a network management application such as HP Openview should be evaluated.

NT Server Management

Both Windows NT Server and Workstation have an SNMP agent included with the standard product. The SNMP agent for Windows NT will respond to *gets* from the SNMP manager and can send alerts when thresholds are exceeded.

All Windows NT servers will have their SNMP agent installed and configured so that they are visible to the SNMP manager.

Things such as *available disk space* thresholds will be set. If an Exchange server's available disk space drops below 500MB, an alert will be sent to the SNMP manager.

Exchange Management

Microsoft Exchange 5.5 comes with an MIB named MADMAN (RFC 1566) that lets the SNMP manager monitor Exchange resources. Some SNMP objects available in the Exchange MIB are defined in Table 14.13. The SNMP manager will monitor all Exchange services on each Exchange server. In addition, traps will be set for queue length on the MTAs for each computer and the IMS on the Connector server. Exchange Server provides service-monitoring functionality that will be implemented per the Exchange architecture.

Table 14.13 **Available SNMP Exchange objects**

Object	RFC Description	Exchange IMC	Exchange MTA	Suggested Value
MtaStoredVolume	The total volume of messages currently stored in the MTA, measured in kilo-octets	Total bytes queued	Work queue bytes	10MB
MtaLoopsDetected	Counts the number of times the MTA has detected such a situation since initialization. May indicate a routing problem.	Total loops detected	Total loops detected	50

continues

Table 14.13 **Continued**

Object	RFC Description	Exchange IMC	Exchange MTA	Suggested Value
TotalMessagesQueued	Total of the queued inbound and outbound counters at all times	Total messages queued	50	

Several additional counters exist that may be applicable to the GAP environment.

The Grandma's Apple Pies Exchange Architecture

With the existing corporate environment and NT architecture just defined, it is possible to define the Exchange architecture. From the information gathered from Grandma's Apple Pies, we build an Exchange architecture that will become the foundation for collaborative applications and enterprise messaging.

Overview

GAP is currently using cc:Mail to provide internal and external messaging services, including an SMTP gateway for Internet email. In an effort to strengthen the feature set and increase functionality, Grandma's Apple Pies will implement Exchange Server 5.5 and Outlook 98 during the next year.

Architecture Overview

Exchange will initially provide support for four primary services: email, scheduling, public folders, and external connectivity. This Exchange architecture will also establish the infrastructure for additional services specific to workgroup applications and collaboration. The Exchange design will use five sites to serve the GAP organization. The migration is deliberate and can be phased in so that hardware and software purchases and implementation are spread throughout the period rather than front-loaded. Because of its more-robust character, most functionality will migrate to Exchange in the earlier migration phases. In this architecture, Exchange provides the Internet Mail Service and can provide faxing and paging solutions. The actual migration process is outlined in a separate document. Coexistence will be highlighted in a later section.

Implementation Approach

After the architecture is approved by the project team, implementation will proceed based on a methodical set of steps designed to validate all elements and protect current capabilities. These steps include a lab and a pilot. They continue with general migration of all users and conclude after the end of migration as the final elements of cc:Mail are removed.

During the lab, server hardware will be configured and tested, the Exchange Server application will be installed and configured, and testing in a lab environment will be conducted. During the pilot, a small workgroup will be migrated. This workgroup will be selected on the basis of its general similarity to most users and its ability to test a wide variety of elements of the environment. The pilot tests migration processes and integration of the Exchange system into the existing cc:Mail and Novell NetWare environment. At the end of this pilot, all necessary infrastructure to support Exchange will be in place, tested, and verified as functional—and therefore will be ready for a production implementation.

This messaging architecture provides a first step in an Exchange implementation. It lays the foundation for the lab and pilot. Following migration, as users become dependent on Exchange as a preferred form of communication, it will be prudent to reevaluate the number of servers in the primary site necessary to support the GAP messaging environment.

Naming Conventions

Naming conventions in Microsoft Exchange are critical to a successful implementation and need to be defined before implementation. Some of the names, such as the organization name, can't easily be changed after installation. For this reason, it is important to establish naming standards before any implementation.

Organization

The Exchange organization name defines the boundaries of the Exchange X.500 address space and is the root of the name tree. You should select a name that is very unlikely to change. Grandma's Apple Pies has selected GAP as the Exchange organization name. This name can't be changed without reinstalling Exchange on all servers in the organization. It's also case-sensitive.

Site Names

Within the Exchange organization, there can be one or more sites. Network bandwidth or administrative policies typically define site boundaries. The GAP Exchange organization will be implemented with five sites. Site names will be North America, South America, Europe, Africa, and Asia.

Server Names

Exchange server names are inherited from the Windows NT server on which Exchange is installed. The Windows NT server names are listed in Table 14.14.

Table 14.14   **Exchange server names for the GAP organization**

Location	Name
Yakima	YKMEXC01 and YKMEXC02
Los Angeles	LAXEXC01
Kansas City	KCKEXC01
Newark	EWREXC01
Taipei	TPEEXC01
Hong Kong	HKGEXC01
Munich	MUCEXC01
Cape Town	CPTEXC01
Lima	LIMEXC01

User Mailboxes

User mailboxes have several different names associated with them. These include the SMTP aliases, display names, and cc:Mail addresses.

Mailbox Alias

Each mailbox has its own mailbox alias. This alias name is usually associated with the NT user name and is the field that Exchange tries to associate with NT if it isn't creating a new NT account. The GAP mailbox alias will be the same as the NT user name, defined as the user's first initial followed by his complete last name.

Mailbox alias (NT account name): *<first initial first name><last name>*

Example: Jsmith

SMTP Alias

SMTP aliases provide the unique element of the user SMTP address, as in `alias@gapies.com`. SMTP aliases will be the user's first initial followed by his complete last name. When two or more people have the same name, the middle initial will be used to assure a unique SMTP address.

SMTP alias: *<first initial first name><last name>*@gapies.com

Example: `jsmith@gapies.com`

Display Name

Mailbox display names are the normal representation of user names. They define the presentation of the name in the address book. The mailbox display name is constructed from the user's first name, middle initial, and last name.

Display name: *<first name> <middle initial>. <last name>*

Example: John B. Smith

cc:Mail Addresses

Exchange will maintain cc:Mail addresses that correspond to the existing user addresses.

cc:Mail format: *<last name>, <first name> <middle initial>* at *<post office>*

Example: Smith, John B at YAKLANC1

Exchange Service Account

In order for Exchange Server to function correctly, it uses a domain account with special access rights. All servers in an Exchange site must use the same service account. In the case of GAP, which has a single domain, trust relationships to use this account won't be an issue. This account is necessary for communication between Exchange servers and between Exchange and NT services and shouldn't be the NT Administrator account. This account will be named !exchange. The password for this account will be a 10-character cryptic password that never expires. This password will be kept in a secure location and won't be shared among Exchange administrators.

The Exchange service account is automatically granted Login as Service rights, as well as other rights. These rights shouldn't be altered.

Site Characteristics

The Microsoft Exchange organization is built on a hierarchical object tree (based on the X.500 standard). At the top of the tree is the organization. Within the organization are the Global Address List, Exchange folders (both public and system folders), and sites. Sites contain servers, configuration information, and recipient containers. All servers in a single site automatically share the same directory information and communication over high-bandwidth permanent and synchronous connections. The primary configurable elements of the site include the site/organization topology, public folders, distribution lists, custom recipients, and mailboxes. For more information on sites and drawing site lines, see page 69.

Topology

As noted, the GAP Exchange organization will be built with five sites. The Asia site will include users in Taipei and Hong Kong. The remaining four sites are North America, South America, Europe, and Africa. The North America site will act as the hub for messaging communications. All sites will be connected with X.400 and directory replication connectors over TCP/IP, except for the Asia site. The Asia site will be connected using the site connector because of the larger available bandwidth between the Asia locations and Yakima. An Exchange server in Yakima will provide intrasite and external messaging connectivity. For more information on Exchange connectors, see page 72. Figure 14.13 shows the GAP Exchange organization topology.

North America

The North America site will hold mailboxes for approximately 500 users in Yakima, 50 users in Los Angeles, 50 users in Kansas City, and 50 users in Newark. One Class A mailbox server in Yakima will initially accommodate their required number of mailboxes. All the other locations will have one Class B mailbox server. Each server will host public folders for their respective locations.

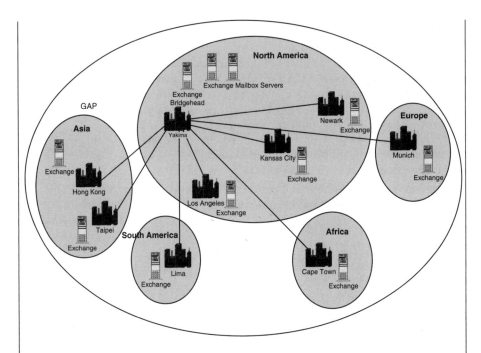

Figure 14.13   The site topology of the GAP organization.

GAP will monitor the growth of the mailbox server's private store to identify when it approaches 15GB in size. If the store reaches this size, an additional mailbox server will be added to the location. Daily maintenance is the primary reason for limiting the information store size to 15GB. Currently, cc:Mail stores run approximately 10MB per user, and the initial store size will be approximately 5 to 7GB.

An additional Connector/Bridgehead server will serve as the North America Bridgehead server. This Connector server will be responsible for delivering messages from North America to other sites, as well as passing messages along from one non-headquarters site to another non-headquarters site. This Connector server will also be responsible for delivering and receiving messages from foreign messaging systems, such as the Internet.

Isolating these services on a separate server, or Connector server, will provide improved performance. Equally important, this server separation allows for server maintenance and downtime. When the Connector server is offline for maintenance, the Yakima users will still have mailbox access. When the Yakima mailbox server is offline, intersite and foreign messaging connectivity won't be affected.

South America

The South America site will contain a single Class B server. This server will contain mailboxes for approximately 25 users, as well as the X.400 connector and directory replication connector to North America. The South America server will also store public folders for the South America site, as well as replicated public folders from other sites.

Europe

The Europe site will contain a single Class B server. This server will contain mailboxes for approximately 25 users, as well as the X.400 connector to North America and Africa. The directory replication connector will be configured to North America. The Europe server will also store public folders for the Europe site, as well as replicated public folders from other sites.

Africa

The Africa site will contain a single Class B server. This server will contain mailboxes for approximately 25 users, as well as the X.400 connector to North America and Europe. The directory replication connector will be configured to North America. The Africa server will also store public folders for the Africa site, as well as replicated public folders from other sites.

Asia

The Asia site will contain two Class A servers—one in Taipei and one in Hong Kong. These servers will contain mailboxes for approximately 100 users each, as well as the site connector for North America. The directory replication connector will be configured to North America. The Asia servers will also store public folders for the Asia site, as well as replicated public folders from other sites. The connector topology is shown in Figure 14.14.

Connectors

Sites within the GAP Exchange organization will be connected in a hub-and-spoke manner with site and X.400 connectors that use a TCP/IP MTA transport stack. For all sites other than Asia, the X.400 connector is appropriate when physical connections between sites have limited available bandwidth. The X.400 connector is more durable and tunable than the site Connector in WAN environments such as GAP.

As mentioned earlier, a Connector Exchange server will be implemented in Yakima. This server will host no mailboxes but will be responsible for transferring messages between Exchange sites and the Internet. The X.400 connectors between North America and all sites connected with an X.400 connector will have bridgehead relationships with the Connector server in Yakima. This means that the X.400 connectors will be configured on the remote site's Exchange servers and the Yakima Connector Exchange server.

The Asia site has enough available bandwidth to support the site connector. The site connector will be configured with a bridgehead relationship with the Connector Exchange server in Yakima. The servers in Taipei and Hong Kong won't be configured as bridgehead servers—just the Yakima Connector server. This means that when users in those locations send messages outside the Asia site, the server will open the RPC association with the recipient server and deliver the message. All messages going to the Asia site will be funneled through the Yakima bridgehead server.

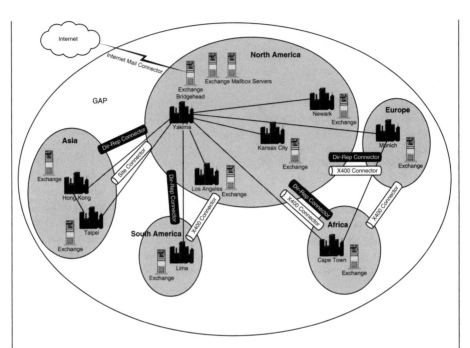

Figure 14.14 Connector topology.

The X.400 and site connectors will be named for the sites to which they connect and the protocol they connect over.

Format: *<messaging protocol>* over *<transport protocol>* to *<destination site>*

Example: X.400 over TCP/IP to Lima

Directory Replication Connectors

Exchange utilizes a multimaster X.500-like directory replication design. The Directory Replication Connectors pass Exchange directory information between Exchange sites so that each server in each site will have a complete copy of the total organizational directory.

Directory Replication Connectors are only necessary between sites. Replication between servers in a site occurs automatically and isn't scheduled by the administrator. Within a multi-server site, replication will occur within five minutes of a directory change.

Directory Replication Connectors will be named for the site to which they connect.

Format: DirRep Connector to *<destination site>*

Example: DirRep Connector to Lima

The directory replication configuration topology is shown in Figure 14.15.

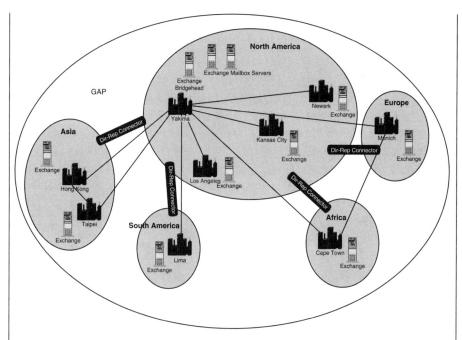

Figure 14.15   The GAP organization topology with directory replication connectors.

Exchange Information Store Protocols

The Exchange information stores can be accessed by numerous protocols in addition to the native RPC/MAPI client, including POP3, IMAP4, LDAP, and HTTP through the IIS. These protocols are all enabled at the site, server, and mailbox levels, except for the HTTP and LDAP protocols, which are only enabled at the site and server levels.

POP3, IMAP4, LDAP, and HTTP

At the time of the Exchange rollout, GAP will enable HTTP access to the Exchange servers through the IIS for all sites and servers to accommodate remote users. There isn't an existing client installed on any of the GAP workstations for the other protocols, so they won't be enabled. For more information on these services, see page 85.

Custom Recipients

Custom recipients are email recipients who have a foreign (external) address entry in the directory. For example, a customer contact may have a custom recipient address list entry that refers all mail to the customer's SMTP address on the Internet. This address would let any Exchange user send mail to that recipient without having to know the customer's Internet address.

Custom recipients will have a recipient container in the North America site and will appear in the global address list for the entire organization.

Custom Recipient Creation Policy

Custom recipient entries will be configured only for vendors and customers. There won't be entries for former employees or personal friends. This policy helps to keep the maintenance of the global address list to a minimum.

Distribution List Strategy

Distribution lists are also recipients that can receive mail. This means that all distribution lists have a valid SMTP address that is addressable from the Internet. Typically, it is good practice to remove the SMTP address of all distribution lists except those that need to be addressed from the Internet. This reduces the possibility of mistaken or malicious efforts affecting the Exchange organization. For example, if GAP had an Everyone distribution list, anyone on the Internet could send a message to everyone@gapies.com, and the message would be sent to every member of the distribution list. If it is required that some Internet users be able to send messages to a distribution list, this can be allowed by leaving the SMTP address on the distribution list and including the Everyone distribution list along with the individual Internet Custom Recipient in the Accept Messages From section of the Delivery Restrictions property of the distribution list.

By default, no distribution list will receive Out Of Office (OOF) messages. This is necessary for very large distribution lists. If someone were to send a message to the Everyone distribution list, and 50 users had their OOFs enabled, the sender would receive 50 Out Of Office messages. In some situations, however, it is prudent to enable the OOF message for a distribution list. If the distribution list is a group of managers for which the sender wants to know if a manager doesn't get the message, enabling this feature would tell the sender who on the distribution lists had their OOF enabled. This option will be enabled for small distribution lists on a case-by-case basis.

Distribution List Structure

GAP will establish a distribution list hierarchy. Each department will have a distribution list, and any groups within departments will have distribution lists. There will be an Everyone distribution list that includes all department distribution lists. All group distribution lists will be members of their department distribution list. With this nested implementation of distribution lists, users need only be maintained in the lists specific to their department or group. For example, if you add Jane Doe to the A/R distribution list, which already belongs to the Finance distribution list, Jane Doe will also be a member of Finance and Everyone.

The distribution lists created at the time of the Exchange migration will reflect all the current cc:Mail distribution lists that are currently actively used.

Figure 14.16 shows the distribution list hierarchy.

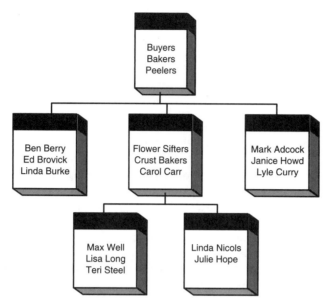

Figure 14.16 The nested distribution list hierarchy for the GAP organization.

Distribution List Creation Policy

Distribution lists will be created only by administrators. Management/ownership of the distribution list will then be assigned to the requestor of the distribution list so that the lists will be maintained by a participant of the list. No distribution lists will be created for nonbusiness interests such as "Everyone interested in running." This policy will help reduce maintenance of the global address list.

Mailboxes

Mailboxes are the most common recipients of the messaging system. They contain objects, organized into one or more folders, and are formatted by the client. Only NT users with permissions on the mailbox may view its objects.

Microsoft Exchange is a single-instance store. This means that when multiple recipients receive the same message, only a single copy of the message is stored in the Exchange database. If a message is designated for recipients on more than one server, each server gets a single copy of the message.

Policies

Each mailbox must be associated with a GAP NT domain account. Exchange utilizes NT security to control access to any object in the Exchange directory. Only the NT account associated with a mailbox will be able to log on as that mailbox. That user can then permit other users to access areas of the mailbox as needed.

Mailbox Limits

A mailbox quota will be established during the GAP Exchange implementation. For large organizations, a 50MB message store limit is a typical limit imposed on Exchange users. Within cc:Mail, GAP users average 10MB of storage. It is recommended that a mailbox quota of 50MB be set on the GAP Exchange servers. Despite the mailbox quota, the message store may eventually grow beyond what should be contained on a single server. When the compacted Exchange information store on a mailbox server exceeds 15GB, an additional server will be added to the location, and approximately one-half of the mailboxes will be moved to the new server. For more information on mailbox limits, see page 120.

One mailbox server in the Yakima location serving 500 mailboxes at 50MB per mailbox results in a potential 25GB mail store.

Because Exchange is a single-instance store, it is highly unlikely that an Exchange server will ever reach its calculated maximum store limit. This is due to multiple mailboxes having their quotas calculated from the same messages. Additionally, most organizations have median mailbox sizes that are much lower than the mailbox limit. For an organization such as GAP with consistent but limited mailbox usage, it is expected that there will be about 30 to 50 users at, near, or over the mailbox limit at any time, but the median mailbox size will be approximately 15MB.

Deleted Item Retention Policy

Exchange 5.5 provides the ability to maintain copies of deleted messages so that users can recover mistakenly deleted items. During the period in which these deleted items are retained, they would continue to be present on backups. GAP will enable the deleted items retention time for three days and will also allow items to be kept until the information store has been backed up. This will ensure that the deleted items will be present on at least one backup. This policy will add about 1GB of data storage on the Yakima server, with incrementally less on the other locations' servers.

Templates

To aid in the creation of mailboxes for employees, mailbox templates will be created for each site. The template mailboxes will be configured with site-specific information, such as business addresses and phone numbers. Using the templates when creating new accounts reduces data entry time and ensures consistent information for each account. Mailbox templates will normally remain hidden from the address book so that they won't get mail. Template names will begin with *x-location*.

Mailbox Cleanup Agent

The Mailbox Cleanup Agent, available in the Microsoft BackOffice Resource Kit, will be used to move messages based on age limits. Within each recipient container in a site, age limits will be set on the user's Inbox, Sent Items folder, Deleted Items folder, and all other folders as a group. Outdated messages will be moved to the Deleted Items folder or to a special private folder so that users can process the messages at their own discretion. After the Mailbox Cleanup Agent has cleaned out a mailbox, it sends a message to the user, describing the cleanup operations that were performed. This utility also logs information for administrators to the Windows NT Server Event Log.

To enforce when deleted items are permanently deleted, this feature can be set to delete items from the Deleted Items folder. To allow GAP users to control which messages are deleted, the Mailbox Cleanup Agent will be configured to move messages to the System Cleanup folder. If the System Cleanup folder doesn't already exist when Cleanup is run, the Mailbox Cleanup Agent creates it. The System Cleanup folder is a private folder in the user's mailbox that can remind users to delete outdated messages. It doesn't actually delete the messages. Users can keep messages moved to the System Cleanup folder by dragging and dropping them into a personal folder file (.pst file).

The System Cleanup folder contains subfolders for each folder that is cleaned. For example, if you configure the Mailbox Cleanup Agent to move messages in Sue's mailbox to the System Cleanup folder, the folder hierarchy might look like this:

Inbox

Sent Items

Sue's folder

System Cleanup folder

Inbox

Sent Items

Sue's folder

The age limit policy for the GAP organization is outlined in Table 14.15.

Recipient Containers

Exchange organizes recipients into containers. Recipients include mailboxes, custom recipients, public folders, and site-specific distribution lists. All recipients will be held in the default Recipients container for their respective servers. The North America site will have additional containers to hold non-GAP employees (that is, custom recipients) and organization-wide distribution lists. Each site will have a specific recipient container for resources such as conference rooms, video equipment, and so on. No recipient containers will be created to subdivide the mailboxes on any site. This is because it isn't possible to move mailboxes between containers (with Exchange 5.5), so any move would require all the mail to be downloaded to a .pst file, account deletion from the original recipient container, account creation in the new recipient container, and upload of messages to that new account.

Table 14.15 **Age limits for the mailbox folders**

Folder	Age Limit
Inbox	180 days
Sent Items	90 days
Deleted Items	45 days
All other folders	180 days

Public Folders

Public folders act as a central, shared location of information. The public folder hierarchy is replicated automatically throughout the organization. The Exchange administrators configure where in the organization the contents of public folders are replicated and thus available to clients.

Public Folder Hierarchy

A public folder hierarchy policy will be established. The general GAP organization will have a single top-level public folder. Each department and site will also have a single top-level public folder. This hierarchy provides for easier maintenance and administration. For more information on public folder design, see page 92.

Public Folder Administration

Only Exchange administrators will be allowed to create top-level folders. Any new top-level folder will be evaluated by the Exchange administrators for necessity.

At least one user from each department or site will be granted permissions on that department's or site's top-level public folder. This user is dubbed the folder administrator. The folder administrator can create subfolders and apply permissions to those folders. This includes granting other users similar permissions.

Figure 14.17 illustrates a recommended structure for GAP's public folder directory.

Public Folder Recipients

Public folders don't typically need configuration in order to be email recipients. By adding a public folder as a member of a distribution list, you can keep a record of all messages sent to a distribution list. Public folders can also be recipients for Internet *list services*. If there is an industry-specific list service on the Internet, a public folder can subscribe to that list service. All messages originating from that list service will be sent to the public folder, which in turn is available to the Exchange organization.

Replicas and Affinity

By default, public folders reside only on the server on which they were created and, given necessary permissions, are only visible to Outlook clients within the same site. Users in other sites can be granted access to a site's public folder information one of two ways—affinity or replica.

When public folder affinity is configured, a user anywhere in the organization who has sufficient rights to the folder can access the public folder's contents by reaching out across the WAN to open the public folder. For public folders that change frequently but are accessed infrequently, public folder affinity is the most efficient means of access. For more information on public folder affinity, see page 100.

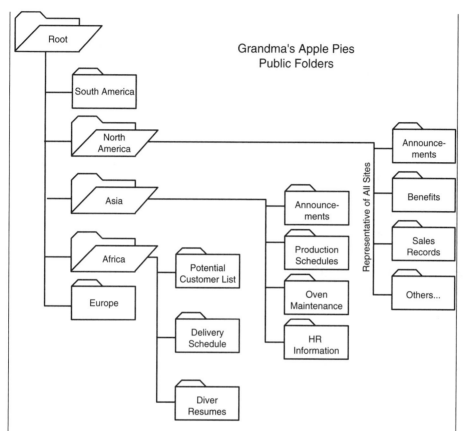

Figure 14.17 The public folder directory structure for Grandma's Apple Pies.

Public folder replication is performed between Exchange servers on selected folders. The Exchange administrators will decide, based on user access and the nature of the public folder, which public folders will be replicated. When a folder is replicated, its contents are replicated from one server to another. Users accessing the data can then retrieve the contents of the public folder from the local site and don't have to reach out across the WAN to find the content of the public folder. For more frequently accessed folders or public folders containing large documents, public folder replication reduces the total burden on the WAN. For more information on public folder replication, see page 100.

One organization-wide top-level public folder will be created and replicated to each site if required. Site-specific folders will only be replicated as necessary. Analysis of activity on other folders should provide information on which to base decisions of whether or not to replicate.

The replication schedule, by default, will be set to once every hour. On a folder-by-folder basis, the replication schedule can be shortened or lengthened based on the content of the public folder and the necessity of up-to-date information.

For public folder access beyond what is available in the site, public folder affinity will be configured between the Europe, South America, and Africa sites because of the similarity of data and function between those locations.

System Folders/Offline Address Book

Exchange provides an offline address book for use by mobile users. It can be configured in an object contained in the system folders. Typically, the book is regenerated daily during off-peak hours. By using the Global Address List as the data source for the offline address book, all laptop users will have the ability to communicate with anyone listed in the GAP address book.

The GAP offline address book will be updated once a day.

External Connectivity

The GAP organization currently uses only Internet connectivity to communicate with users outside GAP. This will be the same connectivity provided with Exchange messaging.

Internet Mail Service (IMS)

The Internet Mail Service operates as an SMTP host that allows Exchange users as well as other foreign mail users to send mail to, and receive mail from, the Internet, either directly or through a firewall proxy. For more information on the IMS, see page 125.

In the absence of a firewall proxy, when the Exchange server receives a message destined for the Internet, it uses DNS to resolve the SMTP domain to an IP address and then opens a TCP/IP port 25 session to that host and delivers the message.

Currently, GAP receives Internet messages with the SMTP cc:Mail gateway. The firewall at GAP is configured to pass SMTP packets to the cc:Mail gateway. The *Mail eXchanger* (MX) records registered on the Internet point to the GAP domain. The GAP MX records look like this:

```
gapies.com    MX preference = 10, mail exchanger =
➥ccgate.gapies.com
gapies.com    MX preference = 100, mail exchanger =
➥smtp.anisp.com
gapies.com    nameserver = firewall.gapies.com
ccgate.gapies.com  internet address = X.X.X.x
smtp.anisp.com internet address = Y.Y.Y.Y
```

The GAP domain (`gapies.com`) will have an MX DNS record that will allow Internet SMTP hosts to resolve GAP recipients to the Yakima bridgehead Exchange server's external IP address. All inbound SMTP mail, including that destined for Asia, will come into the IMS (SMTP) connector and then be delivered to the user through the Exchange system.

A secondary MX record will be registered to the Hong Kong Exchange server running the Internet Mail Service. A third MX record will again point to the ISP Sendmail host. If for some reason the Exchange Connector server in Yakima can't receive an Internet message, the sending SMTP host will deliver the message to the secondary (next-highest-cost) MX record, and the message will be delivered to Hong Kong. If both servers are unavailable, the message will be delivered to the ISP. If the Asia Exchange server receives the inbound message, it will deliver the message to its destination. If the ISP host receives the messages, it will continue to try and deliver the message until the server is again available.

The MX records will be modified to look like this:

```
gapies.com    MX preference = 10, mail exchanger =
➥ykmexc0X.gapies.com
gapies.com    MX preference = 20, mail exchanger =
➥hkgexc0X.gapies.com
gapies.com    MX preference = 100, mail exchanger =
➥smtp.anisp.com
gapies.com    nameserver = firewall.gapies.com
ykmexc0X.gapies.com internet address = X.X.X.X
hkgexc0X.gapies.com internet address = X.X.X.X
smtp.anisp.com internet address = X.X.X.X
```

The firewalls will be configured to restrict SMTP traffic to the associated Exchange Internet Mail Service server—the Yakima Exchange Connector server for the Yakima firewall and the Hong Kong Exchange server for the Hong Kong firewall. This will allow SMTP traffic to be received by the Exchange Connector servers and will allow SMTP traffic to originate only from the Exchange Connector servers, as shown in Figure 14.18. The firewalls will have their SMTP proxy enabled.

Internet Messaging Protocols

Exchange supports IMAP4, POP3, LDAP, and NNTP protocols. Exchange also supports Web access via HTTP protocol through the Internet Information Server, which comes with Windows NT. These protocols give users a variety of methods to access mail and resources from the Internet. In addition, by enabling these protocols, non-Windows mail clients, such as UNIX clients, can have mailboxes on the Exchange server and can participate in the Exchange organization. Initially, GAP won't enable POP3, IMAP4, NNTP, or LDAP protocols. The HTTP protocol will be enabled to support remote and roving users.

These protocols are typically used in heterogeneous environments where Unix and Windows coexist using TCP/IP. Popular messaging clients for Unix use these Internet messaging protocols.

LDAP will be used by Windows NT 5.0 for access to the Windows NT 5.0 directory.

Administration Strategy

The administration of the Exchange organization will be similar to the cc:Mail administration practices currently in place. The two IS groups, administrators and operators, will continue to maintain the Exchange organization from the central Yakima location.

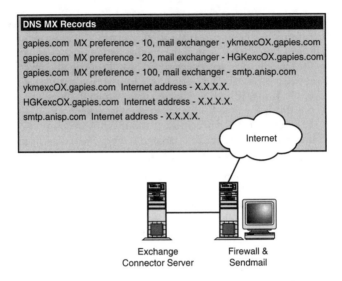

Note: OX denotes the assigned server number

Figure 14.18   The Internet connectivity configuration for the GAP organization.

Administrators and Permissions Administrators

The administrators workgroup will be responsible for configuring, upgrading, and troubleshooting the Exchange organization. This workgroup will be assigned permissions administration rights for the Exchange organization.

The operators workgroup will be responsible for creating and deleting Exchange objects. These users will be assigned to an NT group that has Exchange administration rights but that doesn't have permissions administration rights so that they can't change permissions for objects within the organization.

Third-Party Services

Fax and pager gateways for Exchange aren't part of the current Exchange messaging project scope. After the deployment of Exchange, the GAP IS department will investigate these options.

Client Strategy

The client strategy for GAP is simplified because of the rather homogeneous nature of the clients. Although there are still a few instances of 16-bit Windows in the organization, all computers are Windows-based, and the organization's direction is toward a unified desktop operating system.

Outlook

Clients will use Outlook 98 to connect to Exchange 5.5. In general, Outlook capabilities will be loaded by default, but all services might not be installed immediately. The Outlook information services listed in Table 14.16 will be installed. For more information on Outlook client design, see page 121.

In addition, the offline message store will be configured on each workstation. This will enhance performance with Outlook 98 and enable mailbox message access for folders that have been synchronized during Exchange outages. Performance is enhanced because Outlook 98 first checks the local Offline Message Store (OST) when opening a message before calling the server, thus acting as a cache.

Remote Client

As noted earlier, Exchange provides a robust collection of protocols to enable remote access. These protocols are enabled by default. GAP will disable POP3, IMAP4, and LDAP protocols at the server. HTTP (Web) will be enabled, and its supporting services, contained in IIS, will be configured. With this protocol enabled and with the necessary configuration of the firewall, remote users will be able to connect to Exchange 5.5 via Outlook Web Access with any JavaScript- and frames-enabled HTML browser. The Outlook Web Access client provides almost all the functionality of the standard client, including access to email, folders, calendar, contacts, and scheduling. With SSL (Secure Sockets Layer) enabled, communications with the Web Access client can be encrypted. This will secure users' information as it passes through the Internet.

Outlook Web Access

Outlook Web Access will be used to provide additional messaging services for the GAP organization, as shown in Figure 14.19.

Table 14.16 **Message store and address book services to be configured on the user's Outlook client**

Service Name	Description
Exchange Server	Message store and address book information service used to communicate with the Exchange server. This service also makes journaling, group calendaring, and server task storage possible.
Outlook address book	Address book information service used to access contact email addresses during email name resolution
Personal address book	Address book information service used to store and access addresses in a local file (.pab). This will primarily be used to store personal distribution lists, because they aren't currently possible using contacts.

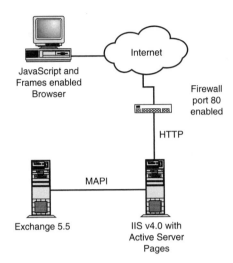

Figure 14.19   Outlook Web Access for the GAP organization.

Outlook Web Access is best suited to non–Windows users, remote users, and roving users and will be installed in the GAP organization.

Remote users will have two choices for remote Exchange connectivity: Outlook Web Access or Outlook 98 client access. It is recommended that traveling users, and perhaps home users, take advantage of the built-in remote functionality of the standard Outlook client. With a configured Offline Message Store (OST), Outlook users can work offline and then dial up to send and receive mail. Remote users will be able to connect to Exchange with their standard Outlook client after a RAS solution is put into place. Remote Outlook sessions use RPCs that can be configured for 40-bit encryption. For users who are accessing the organization from a workstation that doesn't have the Outlook client installed or from a network that won't allow RPC connectivity with the GAP Exchange servers, Outlook Web Access is the preferred connectivity method.

cc:Mail Coexistence

GAP has selected Exchange 5.5 Enterprise to replace the aging and increasingly unstable cc:Mail system. The current system provides for email and bulletin board services. The migration will take place in several phases over several months. As a result, the Exchange and cc:Mail systems will coexist for an extended period. To improve performance and reliability as quickly as possible, external connectivity capabilities will be moved to Exchange, and the cc:Mail router (routing messages) will be removed as Exchange is implemented. For more information on cc:Mail migration and coexistence, see page 150.

cc:Mail Connector Architecture

As migration progresses, the Exchange system will be integrated with the cc:Mail system using a cc:Mail connector in each location.

In Yakima, a cc:Mail connector will link the Exchange connector server to ccYAK, the primary cc:Mail messaging hub. Initially, the cc:Mail connector between ccYAK and the Exchange bridgehead server YKMEXC01 will route messages and synchronize directory information between the two systems.

The connectors in the other sites will link the local Exchange server with the local cc:Mail post office. During configuration of coexistence, each cc:Mail connector will only be responsible for message flow between the two local systems and will be set up only during the period when the site is migrating—perhaps for as short a period as two weeks. Once the Exchange server is installed and the cc:Mail connectors are configured, all cc:Mail will be routed through the Exchange system. Exchange will deliver messages to other cc:Mail post offices and Exchange users.

Directory Synchronization

Directory synchronization will be supported across the cc:Mail connector in the Yakima site. All cc:Mail addresses synchronized to the Exchange directory will be placed in a cc:Mail Users recipient container in the North America site. This recipient container will replicate throughout the Exchange organization. Hence, all Exchange users will be able to address all cc:Mail users. From cc:Mail, the Exchange server will look like an additional post office. ADE will move this post office directory information about Exchange users to the other cc:Mail post offices. Synchronization should be scheduled daily in the evening after backups are complete.

Recipient Groups

A recipient container for cc:Mail users will be created in the North America site. It will hold all cc:Mail directory information delivered by the cc:Mail connector. This container will be named cc:Mail Users.

Bulletin Boards

There is no built-in synchronization between cc:Mail bulletin boards and Exchange public folders. Due to GAP's limited dependence on cc:Mail bulletin boards, it is recommended that synchronization not be attempted. Instead, the cc:Mail users should be informed that migrated Exchange users will no longer have access to the cc:Mail bulletin boards. Furthermore, users should be informed that cc:Mail users won't have access to the Exchange public folder system.

Foreign Messaging System Coexistence

When coexistence between Exchange and cc:Mail is configured, cc:Mail users can benefit from the foreign messaging systems that Exchange is connected to. Therefore, all foreign messaging systems currently supported by the cc:Mail environment will be migrated to Exchange. Both Exchange users and cc:Mail users will utilize these connectors.

Internet Mail Service

SMTP addresses will remain unchanged when the gateway is moved from the cc:Mail host to Exchange. The MX records in DNS will be changed to reflect the Exchange server's SMTP IP address. One of the first Exchange services to migrated from cc:Mail to Exchange will be the SMTP service.

Maintaining the Messaging Organization

Once Exchange servers have been implemented in the GAP organization, even for a pilot implementation, it is necessary to provide maintenance for the messaging environment. The processes necessary for maintaining the GAP Exchange environment are described in the following sections.

Exchange Backup

Exchange stores all message and directory information in databases. These database files are locked to the file system and missed during normal backups. Backups of Exchange are mainly for disaster recovery, because they readily recover the entire database. There are currently no backup products that are well-suited to restoring individual pieces of email or individual mailboxes.

The leading backup software vendors offer Exchange-enabled backup agents for their backup software. These agents allow the backup software to back up the online message and directory stores. It is recommended that Wadeware's Backup Da-Disk be installed and configured on all Exchange mailbox servers in the GAP organization. It is also recommended that Wadeware's Backup Da-Disk Agent for Microsoft Exchange Server be installed on each server responsible for backups. This agent allows Da-Disk to back up the Exchange databases online.

Exchange database circular logging will be disabled on the Exchange servers. This will allow for differential and incremental backups and restores and provides more backup flexibility. Backups of the Exchange server must be made daily and verified periodically. Restoration exercises should include all steps of disaster recovery—rebuilding the server software, restoring the data, and verifying that the owners can retrieve their messages.

Message Tracking

GAP will track all message transfers within the organization to ensure system availability. Message tracking will be enabled for the information stores, the cc:Mail connectors, and the Internet Mail Service for all Exchange sites. The tracking logs will be kept for the default seven days. For more information on message tracking, see page 170.

Link Monitors

Link monitors will be configured to monitor the SMTP connection to the Internet and the X.400 connectors to all sites from North America. When a link doesn't respond within 15 minutes, an alert will be sent to the Exchange console, and an email will be sent to the Exchange Administrators distribution list. A paging mechanism can also be configured when paging services become available. For more information on link monitors, see page XXX.

Server Monitors

Server monitors will be configured to monitor Exchange Server services with the proper alerts and actions configured for each Exchange server. If an Exchange service stops on an Exchange server, an alert will be sent to the Exchange server console, and an email will be sent to the Exchange Administrator's distribution list. The server monitor will attempt to start the service. If the service doesn't start on the first attempt, the server monitor will do nothing on subsequent attempts. For more information on server monitors, see page 162.

Periodic Maintenance

The following matrix describes a schedule for recommended maintenance activities.

Daily Operations

Table 14.17 outlines the activities to be performed on a daily basis.

Table 14.17 **Daily maintenance activities**

Activity	Description
Back up	Perform a full back up of the Exchange databases if possible. Perform an incremental or differential backup otherwise.
Scan Event Log	Use the Resource Kit utility to regularly monitor the event log for errors and alerts.
Monitor disk space	Use network management to ensure that disk space on Exchange servers isn't reaching critical.
MTA queue monitoring	Monitor queue lengths on the connector server to confirm that there are no message queue buildups.

Weekly Operations

Table 14.18 outlines the activities to be performed on a weekly basis.

Table 14.18 **Weekly maintenance activities**

Activity	Description
Full backup	If incremental or differential backups become necessary, perform a full backup over the weekend.
Check replication activity	Check directory replication and synchronization using the Event Log.
Public folder replication configuration	Make sure public folders have not been replicated unnecessarily.
Gather statistics	Gather statistics to monitor the utilization of the Exchange server. Over time, this will show trends in server utilization and allow for the planning of additional servers or hardware.

Periodic Operations

Table 14.19 outlines the activities to be performed on a periodic basis. "Periodic" is loosely defined as monthly or biquarterly. This definition may fluctuate, depending on the maturity of the Exchange implementation.

Securing the Messaging Organization

The security of the messaging organization is crucial to maintaining available services and the integrity of the system. The following sections discuss how GAP will secure the messaging organization.

Table 14.19 **Periodic maintenance activities**

Activity	Description
Offline defragmentation (quarterly or biannually)	Elapsed time will depend on store size, CPU, and disk speed. Requires double the store size in disk space. Back up stores before and after defragmentation.
Confirm Mailbox Cleanup Agent is functioning	Do this by reviewing the Event Log.
Run disaster recovery exercise	Recover a server from backup to validate backup media, location of software, and necessary recovery procedures. Have a disaster recovery white paper as part of a larger Disaster Recovery document.
Install service packs	Install service packs that have been released for 60 to 90 days.
Lab environment	Configure an environment for the following activities: Connected to the organization Runs new software Used by a selected group of users Duplicates essential elements of the production environment
Perform six-month review	Assess technical development and their potential effects on the following: Windows NT design Network design Exchange organization design Client desktop environment Operational practices Review statistics and predict growth patterns: Identify bottlenecks Install additional hardware or servers before this is required

NT and Exchange Security

Exchange is tightly tied to the NT security system. To access a mailbox, a user must have an NT account linked to his mailbox. All Exchange objects are controlled by permissions. The tight integration of NT and Exchange also lets NT groups be specified in Exchange permissions. This is a mechanism that GAP can use to manage permissions on the Exchange directory.

Permissions

By default, permissions are assigned at three levels of an Exchange organization—organization, site, and configuration (within a site). Permissions flow within each of these levels but don't flow through them. In other words, when a group is assigned permissions on the Exchange organization, that group needs to be assigned permissions in *each* level. Additionally, permissions can be set on any object by exception. By assigning permissions at one, but not all, levels, access can be more finely controlled. Two levels of administration highlight the GAP permissions structure. Windows NT global groups will define these two types of Exchange administrators. Each global group will be granted appropriate permissions on both permissions levels.

Exchange Permissions Administrators

The Exchange Permissions Administrators group is a very limited group of administrators. It is recommended that not more than two or three administrators be defined as Exchange Permissions Administrators.

Exchange Permissions Administrators can alter the permissions on an object. Hence, they can grant themselves or someone else permissions on anyone's mailbox, and then enter that mailbox and view mail. Administrators with just Administrator permissions can't alter permissions.

Exchange Permissions Administrators have complete control over the directory. The Permissions Administrators NT global group will be granted Permissions Administrator permissions on the organizations, all three sites, and all three site-configuration objects.

Exchange Administrators

The Exchange Administrators group can administer all elements of the Exchange organization, including changing connectors, site and server configurations, and public folder organization.

The Exchange Administrators group has all the permissions that the Permissions Administrator has, except the ability to change permissions on an object. The typical Exchange administrator will be assigned to this group.

The Exchange Administrators global group will be granted Administrator permissions on the organization, all three sites, and all three site-configuration objects in the Exchange directory.

Service Account

The Exchange service account will be named *!exchange*. The password for this account will adhere to the service account password policies defined in the Windows

NT architecture. The password will be a 10-character strong password kept in a secure location and won't be shared among all Exchange administrators. The password won't expire.

If it becomes necessary to change the Exchange service account password, it must only be changed from within the Exchange Administrator program.

During installation, the Exchange service account is granted Service Account Admin permissions on all objects in the Exchange directory. This too won't change or be altered.

Messaging Service

One of the many advantages of Microsoft Exchange is its ability to connect and coexist with many different messaging and information systems. The following are some of the messaging services Exchange can use to fulfill the GAP messaging requirements.

Electronic Forms

Electronic forms enable formatted display or the capture of information in Exchange. They can be created with Exchange Forms Designer and can be used to post items in public folders or process routine actions such as vacation requests.

Microsoft Outlook is equipped with a powerful forms development environment. These forms can be purely developed in the Outlook environment or coupled with Visual Basic or C++ controls and services.

Electronic forms can also be developed for use by a Web browser using HTML and active server pages. These electronic forms can take advantage of Exchange services and transports.

With Exchange 5.5 and the Collaborative Data Objects environment, powerful workgroup applications can be developed. Included in this environment is a rendering engine that converts an Outlook electronic form into a Web form, for similar functionality from both clients and reduced development cycles.

Virus Protection

As part of the virus protection section of the Windows NT architecture, a virus protection system is recommended for Exchange.

WynneShield for Exchange, from the makers of WynneFree anti-virus products, is one product on the market that can protect an Exchange server. The WynneShield SMTP component scans incoming SMTP messages for viruses.

Faxing

Several third-party companies offer faxing software for Microsoft Exchange. This software lets Exchange users send—and, in some cases, receive—faxes through the Exchange server. Custom recipients can be set up for commonly faxed clients, and Exchange users can send "one-off" faxes by sending the message to the fax number.

Paging

Several third-party companies offer alphanumeric paging software for Microsoft Exchange. A user can have both a paging address and a mailbox address. Such a solution allows Exchange users to send a page through the Exchange system. It also gives a properly configured pager the ability to receive alphanumeric messages as well as alarms and other automated messages. Such functionality allows Exchange or MAPI-aware programs to automatically dispatch a page when a monitored server or service becomes unavailable or changes.

Crystal Reports

To more easily and accurately provide statistical information on Exchange usage and performance, use the Crystal Reports tools. Daily, weekly, and monthly reports can be generated in the areas of individual client use, overall traffic patterns, and specific traffic patterns (Internet, individual site, and so on). Sample tools are included in the Exchange 5.5 Resource Kit. Crystal Reports is a third-party product.

The Grandma's Apple Pies Migration Strategy

This document defines the migration strategy for Grandma's Apple Pies.

Overview

The cc:Mail migration assumes that the recommended Exchange organization structure has been fully implemented across the GAP enterprise. In addition, this cc:Mail migration document assumes that coexistence between cc:Mail and the Exchange organization is established and stable. An Exchange Implementation Plan should outline the steps and parameters necessary to implement Exchange and Exchange coexistence with cc:Mail, as described in the NT/Exchange Architecture Design document. For more information on implementation plans, see page 179.

cc:Mail Migration

cc:Mail directory and mailbox data for users will be migrated at the time the user is moved to the new Exchange environment. GAP staff will migrate users at a rate of 25 per day unless experience allows for a more aggressive pace. With approximately 500 users in the Yakima facility, the migration will last approximately five weeks. During this time, coexistence between the Exchange system and the cc:Mail system will have to be monitored and maintained.

Because other facilities have fewer users, they will migrate in much less time due to their smaller size and remote location.

Verify Coexistence

As part of the Exchange implementation, cc:Mail connectors will be installed at all locations. Once Exchange is fully operational and the cc:Mail connectors are installed and configured, directory synchronization between the Exchange organization and the cc:Mail system will be configured in the North America site.

Reconfigure cc:Mail Routing

The strategy for migrating users in the Europe, South America, and Africa offices is to complete the process within two weeks of starting. Given the short time frame for migration at these sites, the routing between cc:Mail post offices won't be altered. However, the cc:Mail connectors at the Taipei and Hong Kong offices will be reconfigured to route cc:Mail through the Exchange organization during migration. Directory synchronization between Exchange and cc:Mail in those offices will be achieved by the Yakima cc:Mail connector.

Reconfigure SMTP Mail Routing

Exchange will support delivery and receipt of SMTP mail to and from the Internet. There are two advantages to enabling Exchange as the SMTP gateway for the GAP enterprise. First, the Exchange SMTP host is very fast and reliable. Second, by having the Exchange server act as the SMTP host, messages will flow between the cc:Mail system and Exchange, thus exercising the cc:Mail connector. It is recommended that Exchange be configured as the SMTP host for cc:Mail prior to the migration to validate the configuration of the cc:Mail connectors.

Pilot Migration

GAP should conduct a pilot test of the migration process prior to the production migration. The pilot will be valid only if the complete Exchange environment is in place according to the NT/Exchange Architecture Design. The users who participate in the pilot should be willing to endure service outages and a learning curve.

Furthermore, the pilot users should represent various departments in the GAP organization. From this pilot group, migration scripts can be fine-tuned, client issues can be addressed, and data migration can be validated. For more information on conducting Exchange pilots, see page 184.

Migration Steps

After the pilot group issues have been successfully resolved, the main migration can begin. Three main tasks need to take place for each user concurrently. The granular steps in each of these tasks will be defined in an Exchange Implementation Plan. Some of these steps will also be discovered during the pilot. Table 14.20 outlines the steps for the migration.

Table 14.20 **Migration steps**

Step	Description
Workstation configuration	The Exchange user workstations need to be configured with both Microsoft Networking and Outlook 98.
Training	The user needs to attend Outlook training.
cc:Mail mailbox migration	The user's cc:Mail mailbox information will be migrated to Exchange using the Exchange Migration Wizard utility that comes with Exchange 5.5. This process is executed from the server.

Coexistence Issues and Strategy

Coexistence between cc:Mail and Exchange is described in the NT/Exchange Architecture Design. However, once a user has migrated from cc:Mail to Exchange, certain tasks need to be performed manually to complete the migration.

cc:Mail Custom Recipients to Exchange Mailboxes

The cc:Mail connector will synchronize all cc:Mail addresses into an Exchange recipient container named cc:Mail Users in the form of a custom recipient. This custom recipient, by design, has the same SMTP address as the cc:Mail user. When Exchange receives an SMTP addressed message, it forwards that message down the cc:Mail connection to the SMTP recipient. Before the user is migrated, it is important to delete that custom recipient from the cc:Mail Users recipient container. This allows the new user to be assigned the proper SMTP address.

Mailing Lists and Distribution Lists

Another area of attention during migration is that of mailing lists and distribution lists. When a user is migrated from cc:Mail to Exchange, it is important to add him to the proper Exchange distribution lists.

cc:Mail Addresses for Exchange Users

Another important reason for deleting the custom recipient from the cc:Mail Users recipient container is so that the migrated Exchange user keeps the same cc:Mail address.

Training

No matter how eloquent the server deployment, if users are unable to operate the client, they will view the migration as a failure. Hence, one of the most important components of a migration is end-user training. For more information on training, see page 186.

Administrator

Microsoft Exchange is a more complex messaging environment than other store-and-forward messaging systems. With this complexity comes the necessity for administrators to understand the basic principles that Exchange is based on, as well as the daily, weekly, and periodic tasks an Exchange administrator must perform.

It is recommended that the GAP Information Systems staff responsible for messaging attend Microsoft Official Curriculum Exchange training.

End-User

GAP employs qualified training staff. This training staff will be responsible for providing end-user Outlook training to Exchange users while their workstations are being configured and their cc:Mail accounts are being migrated.

15

Case Study: Medium–Large Organization

THIS CHAPTER PRESENTS A SAMPLE ARCHITECTURE for a medium–large-sized organization of 4,900 users. The design document encompasses all the requirements and decisions necessary to implement Exchange in a medium-large organization.

Company Profile

Vaporwear Systems (VWS) is a medium-sized Internet software company leading the electronic commerce industry with its flagship product, *call-em*. Vaporwear Systems has approximately 5,000 employees spread across four locations in the Western United States. The locations and employee distribution are listed in Table 15.1.

Table 15.1 **Vaporwear Systems locations and employee distribution**

Location	Main Function	Number of Users
Seattle, WA	Headquarters, Development	3,000
Portland, OR	Development	500
Denver, CO	Development	900
Phoenix, AZ	Support	500
Remote	Investor Relations	100

The two largest groups of users at VWS are development and marketing. The developers are sophisticated users who, by the nature of their title, depend on email in their collaboration with users in other offices. The marketing group is comprised of beginning users who are being encouraged to depend on computers more for reporting, communications, and marketing.

The other users are management and administration, finance, human resources, and investor relations. The investor relations group consists of about 100 users who work from home. They depend on email as their primary means of communication and consider email a mission-critical application.

Corporate Direction

Currently, VWS takes advantage of a Windows NT domain that is configured in a multi-master domain structure. VWS users primarily use Windows 95, but a large number of developers use Windows NT workstation.

Vaporwear has been using Microsoft Mail for their messaging system. The MSMail system has been useful, and the VWS IS staff is comfortable supporting users and directory synchronization. However, the IS staff has been spending more and more time dealing with issues of corruption of the MSMail system and mailboxes as the organization and number of mailboxes have grown. Additionally, VWS recognizes that users could work more efficiently, especially across sites, if a more groupware-capable system were implemented. Vaporwear Systems has decided that Microsoft Exchange is more reliable and will be the foundation upon which they will build their collaborative applications.

Business Case for Exchange

Although the budget had not been allocated at the beginning of the 1998 fiscal year for a messaging system upgrade, the need for a new messaging system became apparent when the CEO couldn't access his mail for 48 hours because the message file was corrupt. That emergency spawned the process of analyzing the current messaging system operations and support costs. At the end of this analysis, four prevalent reasons emerged that identified the need for Exchange:

- Of the 4,900 users on MSMail, almost 30 percent had experienced or were experiencing ongoing corruption problems that resulted in downtime.

- The mail administrators group was spending the majority of their messaging support time on restorations, troubleshooting directory synchronization issues, and other reactive support issues.

- Having a consistent front-office and back-office software vendor will ensure feature consistency and supportability into the future.

- The ability of Exchange to scale and tune for both the small and large locations would reduce the organization's administrative and maintenance costs.

Network Architecture

The VWS network architecture is very up-to-date. The network infrastructure was identified early on as a critical piece of the cost of doing business and has been well maintained and tuned.

This section describes the existing local area networks that make up the VWS enterprise, as well as the wide area network used to connect these LANs. The Exchange architecture will be built based on this understanding of the network infrastructure.

WAN Environment

Although server resources are available in each of the locations, there is a significant need for WAN connectivity between the locations because of the distributed nature of the workgroups.

Geographic Profile

The VWS WAN uses frame relay services for connectivity between each site. All offices are connected to the frame relay service provider, although the access rate varies. The connection to the frame cloud from each office is shown in Figure 15.1. This figure also shows the access rates from each location to the frame relay cloud.

WAN Circuit Type and Available Bandwidth

As shown in Figure 15.2, three Permanent Virtual Circuits (PVCs) are currently configured to support interoffice communication. Seattle has a PVC to Denver, and Portland has a PVC to Denver and Phoenix.

Table 15.2 summarizes the PVC committed information rate and available bandwidth average for each configured PVC. For more information on total bandwidth and available bandwidth, see page 102.

This configuration results in a logical topology, as shown in Figure 15.2, with the CIRs for each link.

Table 15.2 **PVC committed information rate and available bandwidth**

City	Committed Information Rate	Available Bandwidth
Seattle to Denver	512KB	256KB
Portland to Denver	256KB	128KB
Portland to Phoenix	256KB	384KB

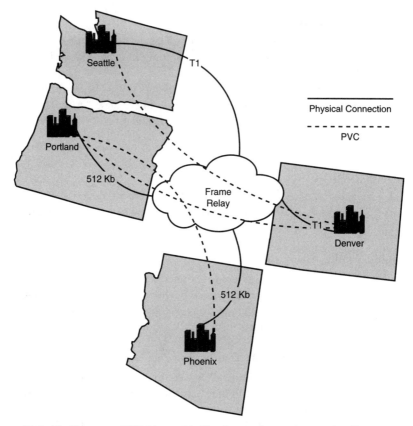

Figure 15.1 The Vaporwear WAN is provided by frame relay services. Each office is connected to the cloud with varying access rates and PVCs.

The Exchange design of two sites, NW and SW, as described in the section "Existing Messaging Architecture," requires that additional PVCs be configured to optimize the messaging traffic over the network routes. This will require a PVC between Seattle and Denver, a PVC between Seattle and Portland, a PVC between Phoenix and Seattle, and a PVC between Denver and Phoenix. The new PVC configuration and the associated CIRs are shown in Figure 15.3.

The result will be a full-mesh topology that will work optimally with the site connector because a network path will be available to support server-to-server RPC connections. The resulting logical topology is shown in Figure 15.3.

LAN Topology

This section describes the existing local area networks that make up the VWS enterprise offices. This information will be used to determine placement of servers and services as well as help optimize client-to-server connectivity.

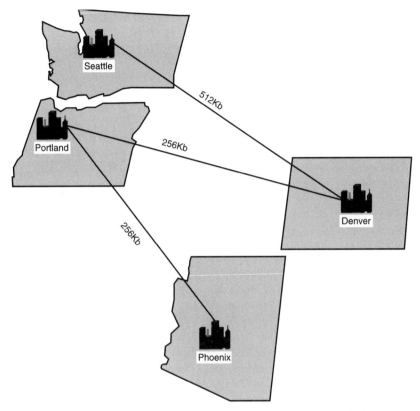

Figure 15.2 The resulting logical topology for the Vaporwear WAN. Speeds shown are the CIRs for each circuit.

Protocols

The Vaporwear network is primarily a TCP/IP network. As an e-commerce solution provider, TCP/IP has been the strategic direction for their external product as well as their internal networking.

LAN Segmentation

This section describes the status of the LAN at each location, including initiatives that will be occurring during the same time frame as the messaging project.

Seattle LAN

The Seattle location has the largest number of users and, consequently, the largest number of network segments. The network is divided into 50 segments. Twenty-five of these segments support developers and are 100MB Ethernet. The other 25 are 10MB Ethernet. These segments tie into several high-speed switches in the central network location. All workstations that will support the Outlook client will have TCP/IP connectivity to the Exchange server(s).

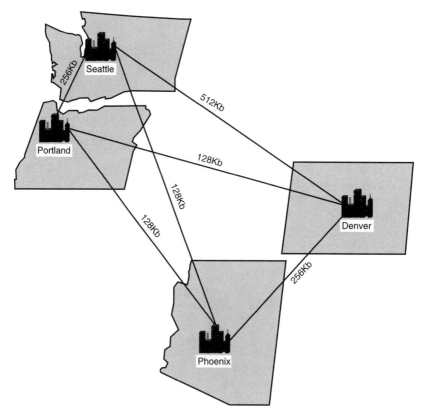

Figure 15.3 The logical topology resulting from the recommended PVC configuration is a full-mesh topology.

There are 30 NT servers in Seattle. This number of servers supports the NT domain topology, messaging post offices, and network services such as WINS, DHCP, and file and print sharing. The developers require a large amount of server disk space storage.

Other Locations

The other locations in Vaporwear have the local area networks defined in the following list:

- **Portland LAN.** The Portland LAN supports 500 users and seven servers. It is divided into 8 to 10MB Ethernet network segments.

- **Denver LAN.** The Denver LAN has 12 network segments to support its 900 users and 10 NT servers. Eight of the network segments are 100MB Ethernet, and four are 10MB Ethernet. All network segments are connected to a high-speed switch on the collapsed backbone.

- **Phoenix LAN.** The Phoenix LAN has four 10MB Ethernet network segments that support the 500 users and five servers at that location.

Existing Server and Workstation Hardware Specifications

The inventory of existing server and workstation hardware specifications is necessary to determine the client architecture needs for the entire organization, as well as to decide on the reuse of server hardware.

Workstations

Most of the workstations in the Vaporwear organization were purchased in the last two years and are running Windows 95 or Windows NT Workstation 4.0. A few developers run PC-based UNIX versions. VWS is dedicated to keeping the workstation hardware up-to-date and standardized across the organization because of the demanding needs of the developers and the increased cost of supporting multiple hardware profiles. Table 15.3 shows the breakdown of the workstation hardware and software configuration.

Servers

The hardware for the Exchange servers will be purchased new. There will be two classes of servers, depending on which services and in which location they will be installed. For more information on sizing servers, see page 136.

Class A Exchange Server

This class of server, defined in Table 15.4, is configured to host several mailboxes and public folder content. This class of server will be installed in each of the VWS locations, because each location will host several hundred Exchange clients. An additional Class A Exchange Server will be added to the site when one of two thresholds is reached:

Table 15.3 **Vaporwear workstation hardware and software configuration**

	Windows 95 Computers	**Windows NT Computers**	**UNIX Computers**
Number of workstations	1,280	2,500	120
Processor	Pentium/166	Pentium II/266	Pentium II/266
RAM	64 MB	128 MB	128 MB
Hard drive space	4 GB	8 GB	8 GB
Average hard drive space free	2 GB	300 MB	200 MB
TCP/IP installed?	Yes	Yes	Yes
Microsoft client installed?	Yes	Yes	Yes

- The size of an information store exceeds 50GB. Exchange can support information stores in the terabytes, but maintenance and recovery of these very large information stores becomes cumbersome and impractical. When a compacted information store exceeds 50GB, it is recommended that an additional Class A Server be added to the site and that users be moved to that server. The number of users moved will be proportional so that an equal number of users exist on each server.

- The performance of the server is not acceptable. When slow performance is being experienced at the Outlook client, a performance audit should be performed. This audit will expose the cause of the poor performance. If the cause is determined to be overutilized CPUs or excessive paging, and additional resources can't be added to remedy the symptoms, an additional Class A server will be added to the site (see Table 15.4).

Class B Exchange Server

The second class of server, Class B (see Table 15.5), is configured to fit two roles in the VWS organization:

- A Connector server for the Seattle facility. A Connector server complements large mailbox servers because it offloads the responsibility of moving messages between sites, MSMail post offices, and the Internet. Furthermore, the Connector server can be restarted without affecting the users, which adds to the total uptime of an Exchange organization. A single Connector server is recommended for the Seattle facility.

- An Exchange server for the test lab. The test lab servers are available for testing new versions, performing mailbox restorations, and for restoration fire drills.

TCP/IP Strategy and Topology

The TCP/IP strategy for the VWS organization has been defined and implemented. VWS uses the private Class A IP address space of 10.x.x.x for all of their LAN and WAN addresses. The firewalls perform Network Address Translation (NAT) for all packets coming from and going to the Internet.

Table 15.4 **Class A Exchange Server specifications**

Resource	Specification
CPU	3 266Mhz Pentium Pro
RAM	512MB
HDD	Hardware RAID 5; 126GB (14×9) for 112GB available
Tape	DLT

Table 15.5 **Class B Exchange Server specifications**

Resource	Specification
CPU	2 200Mhz Pentium
RAM	256MB
HDD	Hardware RAID 5; 12GB (3×4) for 9GB available
Tape	DLT

Subnets

For the LAN and WAN subnets, VWS has used the first three octets for the network portion and the last octet for the host portion, creating a subnet mask of 255.255.255.0 for all addresses within the organization. Table 15.6 shows the allocation for the LAN and WAN subnets.

DNS

DNS services are currently being provided by a UNIX server at the Seattle location. This DNS server is authoritative for the `vaporwear.com` domain and has records for the MSMail SMTP gateway, all servers in the organization, and the Vaporwear external Web servers.

Internet Connectivity

The Internet connection for the organization determines the design for the SMTP mail and the service offerings to clients inside and outside the organization.

WAN Connection to Internet

Vaporwear has two Internet connections—one from the Seattle location and one from the Denver location. The bandwidth of the Seattle Internet connection is 45MB (DS3), and the bandwidth of the Denver Internet connection is 1.536MB (T1).

Table 15.6 **LAN and WAN IP address allocation for the Vaporwear network**

IP Subnet	Allocation
10.10.1.x to 10.10.49.x	Seattle LAN
10.10.50.x	Seattle WAN
10.10.51.x to 10.10.99.x	Portland LAN
10.10.100.x	Portland WAN
10.10.101.x to 10.10.149.x	Denver LAN
10.10.150.x	Denver WAN
10.10.151.x to 10.10.199.x	Phoenix LAN
10.10.200.x	Phoenix WAN

Firewalls

The Vaporwear organization has a firewall for each of its Internet connections. Both of these firewalls are running firewall software that does packet filtering, logging, and network address translation. Each firewall has two ISP-provided Class C IP address segments to use for public address translation.

Web Services

Vaporwear has five IIS servers that support their e-commerce application and host the VWS company Web site.

Internet Client Access Methods

Although the MSMail messaging system doesn't currently provide Internet client access, several POP3 servers have been implemented by the developers. The deployment of the Exchange messaging system will support these POP3 services and eliminate the need for the UNIX POP3 servers.

With Exchange, the remote users are migrating their remote access to an Internet Service Provider dial-up account and then will be accessing their mail through their Outlook client.

Security Policies

The security policy at VWS requires that all passwords sent over the Internet be encrypted. No other security policies are defined at this time.

Existing Network Services

Vaporwear has used NT for the domain services since the company was founded. This started as a single domain in Seattle and has grown into a multiple master domain architecture as the other locations grew.

Domain Approach

As Vaporwear expanded to other geographical locations to tap the development staff in other job markets and to take advantage of an existing call center location, the IS staff saw the need to divide the network responsibilities and services. The existing architecture is a multiple master domain model with an accounts domain for the NW region, which includes Seattle and Portland, and an accounts domain for the SW region, which includes Denver and Phoenix. Each geographical location has its own resource domain. The accounts domains are named for their respective regions, NW and SW, and the resource domains are named for their respective metropolitan areas—Seattle, Portland, Denver and Phoenix. For more information on NT domains, see page 108.

Domain Controller Physical Locations

The primary domain controller (PDC) and two backup domain controllers (BDCs) for the NW accounts domain reside in Seattle. The Portland location also has a BDC for the NW accounts domain to support local authentication. The PDC and one BDC for the SW accounts domain reside in Denver. The Phoenix location also has a BDC for the SW accounts domain.

Each resource domain has a PDC and a BDC in the location it serves. This server topology is shown in Figure 15.4.

BDC Implementation Policies

If any additional local area networks are added to the WAN, at least one BDC for the respective accounts domain will be installed. The BDC will increase network authentication and browsing performance for the new location.

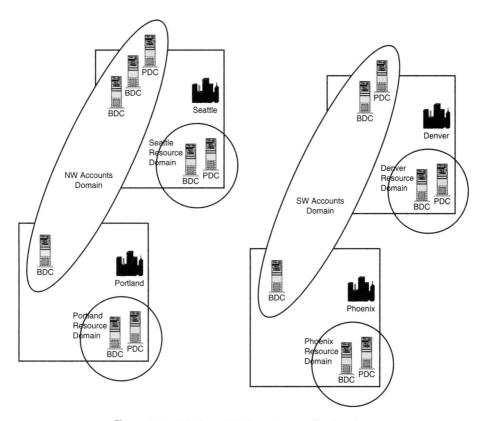

Figure 15.4 Windows NT domain controller locations.

When, through the use of Performance Monitor, it is determined that the BDCs can't keep up with the authentication requests on a network, an additional BDC will be added to the network. It is also possible to move some of the network services that the existing BDCs support—such as DHCP, DNS, and WINS—to other Windows NT servers in the enterprise if that is a more appropriate means of reducing the server load.

Trusts

With this multiple master domain implementation, several trust relationships are necessary. Each accounts domain trusts the other, creating a two-way trust between the accounts domains. For the resource domains, every resource domain trusts both accounts domains. These trust relationships are shown in Figure 15.5.

Naming Conventions

Resources in a network are given names so that they may be easier to use and manage. Naming schemes are most efficient when they follow easy-to-understand conventions. All computers, printers, users, and most other network objects can be given names. The naming convention defined here is a continuation and extension of the Vaporwear naming convention already in place.

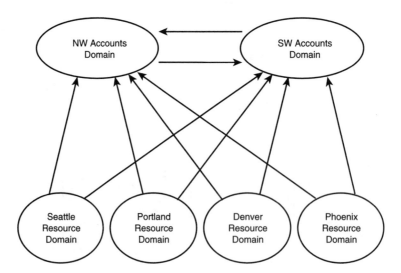

Figure 15.5 The trust relationship necessary to support the Vaporwear multiple master domain model.

NetBIOS Names

Microsoft Windows operating systems use NetBIOS (Network Basic Input/Output System) as their networking protocol. Network resources are identified and located by a unique NetBIOS name. NetBIOS names can be up to 15 characters long and may contain a variety of alphanumeric characters. Because VWS will also be using Internet resources, it is recommended that the NetBIOS name also be compatible with DNS (Domain Name Service) host names. DNS names are restricted to a to z, A to Z, 0 to 9, and the hyphen. DNS names may not contain blank spaces. For these reasons, the formats defined in the following sections are recommended.

Workstation Names

Workstation names consist of a three-letter city code, defined in Table 15.7, a hyphen, and a unique five-character asset number.
> Format: *<city code><-><unique five-character asset number>*
> Examples: SEA-0001S, PDX-0100S

Server Names

Server names consist of a three-letter city code, the server's function (a three-character abbreviation; see Table 15.8), and a unique two-digit number. Hyphens, although X.500- and DNS-compliant, have not been implemented in server names because of support issues with SQL Server.
> Format: *<server location><server function><increment>*
> Examples: PDXaBCD04, DENEXC01, PHXrPDC01

Host Names

The host name is the native TCP/IP name given to a workstation or host. Host names are the same as the computer NetBIOS name in lowercase characters. Windows NT Servers also have the Vaporwear domain name, `vaporwear.com`, configured as the TCP/IP domain name. The Fully Qualified Domain Name (FQDN) for each Windows NT server will then be `servername.vaporwear.com`.

Table 15.7 **Three-letter codes for the computer-naming convention**

City	Abbreviation
Seattle	SEA
Portland	PDX
Denver	DEN
Phoenix	PHX

Table 15.8 **Application codes for the server-naming convention**

Application	Abbreviation
Accounts domain controller	aPDC/aBDC
Resource domain controller	rPDC/rBDC
Exchange: general purpose	EGEN
Exchange Mailbox server	EMBX
Exchange Connector server	ECON
Exchange Public Folder server	EPFS
SQL Server	SQL
Communications	COM
Back up/archive	BUS
File and Print server	FPS

Printer Names

Two pieces of information are necessary to print to a network printer. First, the user must know where the printer is, or to which department it belongs. Second, the user might need to know the model of printer. This information can be useful should the user need to install a local printer driver. Due to browser constraints from Windows 95 workstations, the share name length should be limited to 12 characters. The server that is hosting the printer queue defines which city the printer is in. The printer share name defines the printer's department and model.

Format: *<department abbreviation><model number descriptor><-><unique three-digit number>*

Example of share name: ADMINLJ4–002

Example of network path: `\\PHXFPS01\ADMINLJ4-002`

This path shows that this printer is in the Administration department of the Phoenix office.

To further assist users while choosing a printer, the share description field is used to elaborate on the printer's description. A label is also affixed to each printer with its share name.

User Names

All users of the VWS network who want access to domain resources such as Exchange log on to the account domain with their own account. Account names will be derived from the user's name. When two or more people have the same name, the middle initial is used to ensure a unique NT account name.

Full name format: *Last name, first name middle initial.*

Example: Smith, John D.

Username format (NT account name): *<first initial first name><last name>*

Example: Jsmith

Miscellaneous Names

Other network components, such as hubs, switches, routers, and even patch panel ports, will be given logical names on an ad-hoc basis.

DNS

DNS is the method of translating host names into IP addresses. An example of a DNS name is `www.microsoft.com`. In this example, `microsoft.com` is the domain, and `www` is the host. DNS services provide resolution for internal services such as intranet host-name resolution. For more information on DNS, see page 106.

Currently, VWS has no DNS host name resolution for external services and internal servers. Any DNS request for an Internet host that is unknown or not cached by the UNIX server's DNS services is forwarded to one of the root DNS servers on the Internet.

Windows NT offers DNS services. These services will play a much more important role in the Windows network with the next version of Windows NT (5.0). Therefore, it is recommended that DNS be implemented to some degree in the VWS *internal* environment. This will help ease the migration to Windows NT 5.0 while helping to familiarize the IS staff with the management of DNS.

The Windows NT DNS will be installed and configured on one of the account domain BDC servers at headquarters (SEAaBDC01) and the account domain BDCs at every other location (PDXaBDC01, DENaBDC01, PHXaBDC01). All DNS servers will be configured to integrate with the local WINS server. The DNS server closest to each subnet will be the primary DNS server for that subnet. The other DNS server in that region will be configured as the secondary DNS server.

The DNS servers will forward requests for external host IP addresses (Internet addresses) to the UNIX DNS.

DNS Domain

Vaporwear has a single DNS domain, `vaporwear.com`, which is registered with InterNIC.

Zone

Vaporwear will continue to have one zone, `vaporwear.com`. One zone is sufficient to serve the number of hosts and clients at VWS.

Primary Name Server

The *primary name server* manages the data for the zone(s) it is authoritative for.

Seattle

The primary Windows NT name server will be located in Seattle and will replicate with the authoritative server, located on the UNIX DNS, for the `vaporwear.com` zone.

This name server will also be configured as a forwarder to resolve external DNS requests to the Internet, forwarding those requests to the firewall.

Secondary Name Servers

The *secondary name server* gets its data from the primary name server at startup. A secondary name server allows for local name resolution that reduces WAN traffic and provides redundancy.

Portland, Denver, and Phoenix

The Portland, Denver, and Phoenix DNS servers will have DNS installed and configured on their respective account domain BDC servers. These will be secondary name servers and will replicate with the Seattle name server. Hosts in each city will first request host name resolution from their local DNS. The secondary name servers will be configured to integrate with WINS.

Time to Live (TTL)

Vaporwear will have a long TTL configuration on its name servers, because the domain information will be mostly static—especially for non-Windows hosts that typically are servers. Windows hosts won't have their names registered in DNS. Instead, they will be resolved via WINS integration. The long TTL will also help reduce server load and wide area network traffic. In preparation for host changes, IP readdressing, and other changes that affect the DNS database, the TTL will temporarily be set to a small value so that the clients won't cache incorrect data.

WINS Integration

For WINS-capable machines that don't have static entries in the DNS database, such as machines that have dynamic IP addresses, WINS integration with DNS will provide friendly-name services. The name servers will be configured to refer to the WINS database for requests that can't be resolved in the DNS database.

WINS integration provides two major benefits. First, in addition to DNS entries, all WINS-capable computers can be referred to by friendly host names. Secondly, the WINS database is a dynamic database, where hosts register their names and IP addresses at startup. The DNS database is a static database, where changes must be made manually. Because DNS can query WINS, it enjoys the same dynamic workstation registration features as WINS.

To provide interoperability between DNS and WINS, a new record will be defined as part of the zone database file. The WINS record is specific to Windows NT and may be attached *only* to the zone root domain. The presence of a WINS record instructs the name server to use WINS to look up any requests for hosts in the zone root that don't have static addresses in the IP database.

Format: *<domain>* IN WINS *<IP address of WINS server>*
Example: @ IN WINS 10.10.1.3
This feature can also be set using the DNS user interface.

Dynamic Host Control Protocol (DHCP)

Vaporwear currently uses DHCP to dynamically allocate IP addresses and IP settings. These settings include the subnet mask, default gateway, and WINS and DNS server IP addresses. DHCP greatly simplifies the administration of large numbers of workstations by delegating the tedious task of managing hundreds of host TCP/IP settings to a simple protocol.

Server Addressing

All VWS servers have statically assigned IP addresses. The server IP address range has been excluded from the DHCP server pool(s).

Scope Ranges

There are five active DHCP servers on the VWS network. They reside on the BDCs for the respective accounts domain. Since DHCP servers don't share leasing information, each server offers leases from a unique IP address pool.

DHCP Server Redundancies

Each subnet has its addresses split up between two DHCP servers in a 75/25 configuration. If one DHCP server fails, or is shut down, the other DHCP server is available to lease IP addresses.

For Seattle, the addresses are split between the two local BDCs. For all other locations, the addresses are split between the local BDC and the other BDC in the respective region. This DHCP server subnet division is shown in Table 15.9.

Option Assignments

The DHCP servers provide clients that have the options listed in Table 15.10.

Windows Internet Naming Service (WINS)

Windows networking uses NetBIOS names to identify nodes on the network. In a TCP/IP environment, these NetBIOS names need to be resolved to IP addresses before communication can take place. VWS will use WINS to maintain NetBIOS name registrations and provide NetBIOS-name-to-IP-address resolution for client workstations. For more information on WINS, see page 107.

Table 15.9 **DHCP server subnet division for Vaporwear**

Server	Scope	Backup Scope Server
SEAaBDC01	75% of the first half of the Seattle subnets	SEAaBDC02
SEAaBDC02	75% of the second half of the Seattle subnets	SEAaBDC01
PDXaBDC01	75% of all of the Portland subnets	SEAaBDC02
DENaBDC01	75% of all of the Denver subnets	PHXaBDC01
PHXaBDC01	75% of all of the Phoenix subnets	DENaBDC01

Table 15.10 **DHCP option assignments**

Option Number	Description	Assigned Value
1	Subnet mask (enabled by default)	255.255.255.0
3	Router	Address of the nearest router
6	DNS servers	Addresses of DNS servers in descending order of priority
15	Domain name	vaporwear.com
44	WINS/NBNS servers (primary and secondary are different for each DHCP server)	Each subnet scope specifies the WINS server for that subnet as the primary WINS server. The secondary WINS server is the corresponding WINS server for the region.
46	WINS/NBT node type	0×8 (hybrid node)

WINS Server Distribution

It is important that WINS servers be able to accommodate the number of NetBIOS name resolution requests issued, as well as replicate their respective databases between WINS servers at other locations. WINS services are installed on all account domain controller BDCs at each location.

Seattle

Two WINS servers in Seattle will serve as primary and secondary WINS servers for headquarters. The BDC SEAaBDC01 is the primary WINS server, and the BDC SEAaBDC02 is the secondary WINS server. The DHCP servers will designate the primary and secondary WINS servers for each location.

Portland, Denver, and Phoenix

The other WINS servers are distributed among the physical locations. The DHCP servers for those locations lease the IP addresses for the location subnets. The local WINS server will be defined as the primary WINS server, and the other respective BDC WINS server for that region will be defined as the secondary WINS server.

Server Replication

All WINS servers will replicate their databases with the WINS server on the PDC at headquarters. The primary WINS server in Seattle (SEAaBDC01) will replicate through a push/pull relationship with the secondary WINS server in Seattle.

Replication between the Seattle BDC01 WINS server and the other WINS servers will be a pull replication. Because the majority of services are provided locally to each WINS server (and associated remote offices), it isn't necessary to update the databases more than once every four hours. The pull replication times between the Seattle primary WINS server the WINS servers in the other locations will be set for after the morning authentication activity. This configuration will optimize the replication to occur after the clients have registered with the WINS servers and also during off-hours for network traffic. Figure 15.6 shows the WINS replication strategy.

Browsing the NT Domains

The PDC for each NT domain will act as the domain master browser and will synchronize browse lists between itself and the other master browsers in the same location, as well as the master browsers of the other subnets. The domain master browser and the other master browsers and backup browsers will also provide browse lists to workstations that are browsing network shares on the LANs.

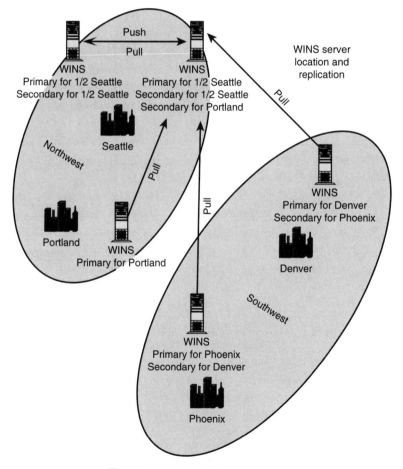

Figure 15.6 WINS replication strategy.

The backup domain controllers on each LAN will be the master browsers of those subnets. They will provide browse lists to workstations that are browsing network shares on their respective LANs.

NT Accounts

Two types of NT accounts, user accounts and device accounts, are necessary to support the Exchange architecture. These accounts are defined in the following sections.

User Accounts

One of the challenges of network administration is to provide secure network resources with minimum inconvenience to users. A major benefit of the multiple master domain model with the appropriate trust relationships configured is that users use only one user account and password to access all NT-based network resources. This simplifies the task of securing the network from external attack.

Every user has a domain account. To protect the utility of the security audit log, users won't log in using shared accounts or device accounts (see the following section). During the creation of user accounts, the following standards will be observed:

- User accounts for contingent workers will have a preset expiration date.

- The Description field will be used to identify the user's position or title, and other relevant information as appropriate.

- All users, including administrators, will be members of the Domain Users global group.

- Passwords must be at least six characters long.

- Passwords will expire after 90 days.

- There is no minimum password age.

- The system will remember the last five passwords.

- After three unsuccessful login attempts, the account will be disabled for five minutes.

Device Accounts

Accounts that exist for use by applications or processes are considered a special case. Wherever possible, device accounts should be local users, not domain users. If they must be domain users, login rights will be limited to only the few necessary machines. Such accounts will be set with very strong passwords that never change. "Very strong" means that the password should have at least 10 characters and should not resemble any intelligible word or acronym. Computer-generated random strings are preferred. Such account passwords should be documented and stored in a physically secure location. Device account passwords never expire. Such accounts shouldn't be members of Domain Users or any other group populated by real users. Where appropriate, the account will be granted rights directly to resources or objects. This is an exception to the general rule that only groups are assigned rights to resources or objects. The Exchange service account is an example of a device account.

Policies and Profiles

The policies and profiles made possible with Windows NT help manage the desktop and extend user options such as roaming to Windows 95, Windows 98, and Windows NT Workstation desktop users. For more information on policies and profiles, see page 109.

Profiles

User profiles will be stored both locally on the workstation's hard drive and on the server in the user's private directory. The Domain User profile will retain user settings such as Exchange mailbox settings, desktop color preferences, and bookmarks. The profile will contain shortcuts only. Users are not to place files on their desktops, only shortcuts to files located on network file servers. This is to ensure that files are backed up, because there is no current workstation backup process.

Policies

Configuration policies for the workstations haven't been implemented. The development environment and mind-set have dictated a lack of desktop restriction in company policy.

Login Scripts

All users will execute a login script upon successful authentication from a domain controller. The login scripts will perform some basic functions and will be maintained by the VWS Information Systems staff. The login scripts will do the following:

- Synchronize the workstation's clock with a network time reference.
- If the user is connected via Ethernet, the workstation will be updated with the latest virus signature files.

CHECKRAS is a utility included in the Microsoft Windows NT Resource Kit that is used in the script to determine if the user is on a high-speed network or a remote dial-up connection. Based on the results of this test, certain procedures will or will not run during the login script.

In addition, the script will connect the workstation to printers based on the subnet of the IP address leased from the DHCP server. This will allow roving laptop users to print locally when they travel from office to office.

Server Security

Aside from policies and profiles, other rights relate to an NT Server environment. Such rights include the right to log on locally, to access the server from the network, to shut down, and to change the server's time. A recent audit of the VWS servers revealed that these rights haven't been maintained to a standard within the organization. Therefore, the following changes will be made to the default NT permissions on the existing and new servers:

The right to access this computer from Network will be changed from the Everyone group to the Domain Users group. Administrators will remain on this Access Control List (ACL), even though they should also receive this right through membership in the Domain Users group. This will prevent anonymous users from accessing share lists, user lists, and the Registry.

Non-IS staff won't have permission to log on locally to servers. This means that nonadministrative personnel won't be able to use the server's console.

The Server Operators local group will be allowed to take ownership of files.

Auditing will be enabled with the settings shown in Figure 15.7 on all domain controllers.

Administrator Account

A built-in Administrator account has total control over the system. In the case of the domain SAM, the administrator has total control over all domain controllers, as well as over all member computers via the Domain Admins global group. Every NT computer that isn't a domain controller also has a local Administrator account. The Administrator account won't generally be used. Its password should be very strong, documented, and stored in a physically secure location. The Administrator password will ensure that the organization can take full control of the network in the event of IS staff changes. If the Administrator account is used, the password should be changed and the appropriate documentation updated at least once a year.

Every administrator should use his own account that is a member of the Domain Admins group to log on. The Administrator account shouldn't be used for several reasons:

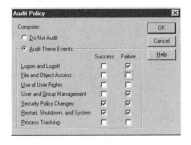

Figure 15.7 The auditing settings used for all domain controllers in the Vaporwear domain.

- Auditing will log privileged access to the network according to user name. Using the Administrator account allows effectively anonymous access and defeats accountability.

- Any means of communicating a password is a security exposure. Whether it is whispered or scribbled on a scrap of paper, there is a risk that it could be intercepted.

- If several people know the administrative password, it is compromised whenever one of the people leaves the organization. When this happens, a new password should be chosen and communicated to each administrator. This represents a significant security exposure.

- For performing administrative functions, appropriate user accounts will be granted elevated permissions through strategic group assignments.

Share-Level Security

Security at the share level can further restrict, but not expand, rights granted at the file level. Generally, industry practice doesn't advise implementing share-level security, except in special cases. Share-level security hasn't been implemented on the VWS domain resources, and Domain Users and Administrators have full control at the share level. Security will be applied on the file system level, not the network share level.

Group Assignment

Industry experience has developed a methodology that has proven to make ideal use of the user-to-group assignment features in domain security. It is called the UGLR paradigm: **U**ser **G**lobal **L**ocal **R**ights.

Users are members of **G**lobal groups.

Global groups are members of **L**ocal groups.

Local groups are assigned **R**ights to resources.

As networks grow, the sheer numbers of users and files becomes unmanageable. To simplify security administration, groups are used to aggregate several similar objects into a single object. Figure 15.8 describes how the UGLR paradigm greatly simplifies security administration.

Remember that *global groups* are groups of *users,* and they should reflect the company's organizational structure. *Local groups* are groups of *privileges,* and they should reflect the network resources in general terms.

Here are two notable exceptions to the UGLR paradigm:

- In the user's private network directory, the user account will be directly assigned permissions on the directory.

- The local group Administrators should be listed with full control on all groups.

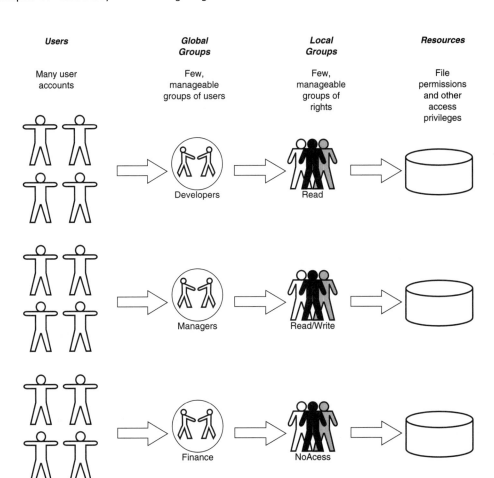

Figure 15.8 NT group strategy.

In an account domain/resource domain configuration, there are a couple of placement issues to note:

- The global groups are configured in the account domain.
- The local groups are configured in the resource domain or on member servers.
- If the local group has been defined on a domain controller, the group will be available to all domain controllers.
- If the local group has been defined on a member server, the group will only be available to that server.
- The Exchange service account will reside in the appropriate accounts domain for the site.

File Security Guidelines

Following the *need to know/need to use* rule as defined in the UGLR paradigm, access is given as conservatively as is practical. The following guidelines apply as general rules and are based on the capabilities of the Windows NT File System (NTFS):

- The *Administrators* local group will always have full control, even of private user directories. This is a recommendation and can be configured otherwise. If the Administrator groups don't have permissions on the user directories, an administrator would have to change permissions to view or manipulate the directory. This change of permissions would be reflected in the Security Log.

- The NT group Everyone won't appear in any Access Control List (ACL). This will protect against unauthorized access to sensitive data.

- Only the IS administrative local groups will have full control. Users shouldn't be able to modify permissions or take ownership of files—even files in their own private directories.

- Custodians, who are designated users/owners of files, will have read/write/change/delete permissions.

- Users, who are designated users of files, will have read permissions.

- Execute permissions will never be coupled with write/change/delete, except for elevated accounts *and* within private directories. For obvious security reasons, execute permissions are very powerful and should never be given where normal users can also create files. To minimize the network's exposure to malicious attack or viral infection, only qualified IS staff will place executable files on the server.

Other guidelines will be implemented as situations dictate.

Client Software Installation Points

The Outlook client software will be stored on a file and print server in each location.

Backup Services

All server drives will be backed up to a magnetic tape device. The backup tapes will be stored in a secure place on VWS premises with a tape periodically taken to a secure remote location.

Each LAN has its own backup device that can back up the entire server on a single tape during off-hours. Additional Windows NT servers will be backed up from a common backup server or individually to a local backup device, depending on the amount of data to be backed up.

Seven tapes are kept in rotation for each backup device. This allows for restorations as far back as seven days. Once a month, a tape will be taken out of the rotation and stored in a secure remote location. Then a new tape will be put into the rotation.

The backup software is configured to notify an administrator of a backup failure. This notification is in the form of an email. The server console will also receive a notification that the backup has failed. The local backup operator will check this when the tape is being changed. For more information on backing up and restoring, see page 197.

Backup Schedule

With the use of Digital Linear Tape devices, each server should be able to complete a full backup overnight. If this is proven incorrect, incremental or differential backups can be performed.

Restoration Strategy

To restore a server, the most recent full backup will be used. If incremental or differential backups are being performed, the most recent full backup will be restored, along with the appropriate differential or incremental backups.

Twice a year, a backup will be restored on a blank server in a lab environment (not connected to the VWS network). This is not a current VWS procedure and has led to some confusion when restorations have been necessary. The test restoration will ensure that the backup tapes are in good order, that the necessary system software is available, and that the Information Systems personnel are familiar with the restoration procedures. This process should be completed for each location.

A disaster recovery plan for Exchange will be put in place no later than six months after implementation.

Network Management

Network management in an organization such as Vaporwear is essential and affordable.

SNMP Manager

Vaporwear has deployed a management platform to monitor network activity. Monitoring of the environment occurs from the Seattle and Denver locations.

NT Server Management

Both Windows NT Server and Workstation have an SNMP agent included with the standard product. The SNMP agent for Windows NT will respond to *gets* from the SNMP manager and can send alerts when thresholds are exceeded.

All Windows NT servers will have their SNMP agent installed and configured so that they are visible to the SNMP manager.

Things such as *available disk space* thresholds will be set. If an Exchange server's available disk space drops below 500MB, an alert will be sent to the SNMP manager.

Exchange Management

Microsoft Exchange 5.5 comes with an MIB named MADMAN (RFC 1566) that lets the SNMP manager monitor Exchange resources. Some SNMP objects available in the Exchange MIB are defined in Table 15.11. The SNMP manager will monitor all Exchange services on each Exchange server. In addition, traps will be set for queue length on the MTAs for each computer and the IMS on the Connector server. Exchange Server provides service-monitoring functionality that will be implemented per the Exchange architecture.

Several additional counters exist that may be applicable to the Vaporwear environment, depending on the VWS environment and how it grows.

Existing NT Servers

The NT servers provide file and print services as well as host the MSMail post offices. The NT servers at each location are listed in Table 15.12.

These servers are running on a variety of Pentium and Pentium Pro class computers.

Table 15.11 **Available SNMP Exchange objects**

Object	RFC Description	Exchange IMC	Exchange MTA	Suggested Value
MtaStoredVolume	The total volume of messages currently stored in the MTA, measured in kilo-octets	Total bytes queued	Work queue bytes	10MB
MtaLoopsDetected	Counts the number of times the MTA has detected such a situation since initialization. May indicate a routing problem.	Total loops detected	Total loops detected	50
TotalMessagesQueued	Total of the queued inbound and outbound counters at all times	Total messages queued	50	

Table 15.12 **Existing servers**

Location	Servers	Function
Seattle	25 NT 4.0 SP3 file, print, and messaging servers. 3 NT 4.0 SP3 account domain controllers. 2 NT 4.0 SP3 account resource domain controllers.	File, print, and MSMail. Account domain authentication. Resource domain authentication.
Portland	4 NT 4.0 SP3 file, print, and messaging servers. 1 NT 4.0 SP3 account domain controller. 2 NT 4.0 SP3 account resource domain controllers.	File, print, and MSMail. Account domain authentication. Resource domain authentication.
Denver	6 NT 4.0 SP3 file, print, and messaging servers. 2 NT 4.0 SP3 account domain controllers. 2 NT 4.0 SP3 account resource domain controllers.	File, print, and MSMail. Account domain authentication. Resource domain authentication.
Phoenix	2 NT 4.0 SP3 file, print, and messaging servers. 1 NT 4.0 SP3 account domain controller. 2 NT 4.0 SP3 account resource domain controllers.	File, print, and MSMail. Account domain authentication. Resource domain authentication.

Existing Administrative Structure

The IS organization at Vaporwear is divided into two major geographical groups: Seattle and Denver. The Seattle IS network support organization has 20 staff members responsible for maintaining the network services at the Seattle and Portland locations. The Denver IS network support organization has 10 staff members responsible for maintaining the network services at the Denver and Phoenix locations.

Internet Services

Vaporwear provides Internet messaging services to all its users through the MSMail SMTP gateway and through the POP3/SMTP UNIX servers. All users have full Internet access.

Existing Messaging Architecture

Vaporwear has used MSMail since the company was founded. As a messaging system, MSMail has served them well until the last year. The Information Systems group is familiar with and comfortable managing and troubleshooting MSMail, but they are eager to move to a more sophisticated and robust messaging system. The next sections discuss this current MSMail architecture.

Post Office Topology

There is a total of 15 MSMail post offices throughout the Vaporwear organization. Each facility has a single bridgehead post office that is responsible for connectivity to the other post offices. The headquarters location has the SMTP gateway, which delivers and receives all Internet mail. The MSMail SMTP gateway is a single point of failure in this MSMail network. The MSMail topology is shown in Figure 15.9.

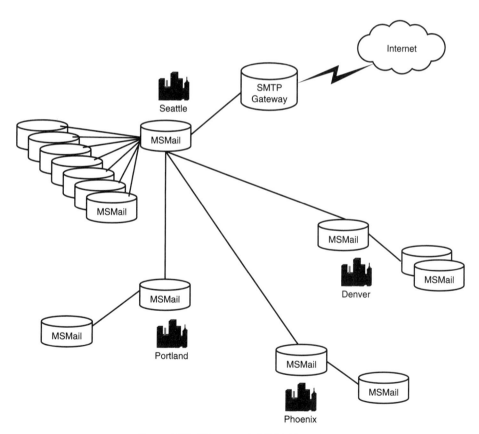

Figure 15.9 Vaporwear's MSMail topology.

SMTP Services

Although there are currently two Internet connections, only one SMTP mail gateway exists in the current Vaporwear messaging configuration. The MSMail SMTP gateway is located in Seattle. It is configured as a relay agent, forwarding all SMTP mail to the ISP's SMTP host. The ISP SMTP host then resolves the domain name using DNS and delivers the message.

For inbound SMTP mail, the ISP is configured to forward all SMTP mail to the MSMail gateway on the Vaporwear network. The MX records for `vaporwear.com` are shown in Figure 15.10.

The firewall is configured to allow only the MSMail gateway to initiate SMTP sessions to the Internet. The firewall is also configured to allow only SMTP sessions from the Internet to the SMTP gateway, using address translation.

Administrative Structure

All MSMail post offices are managed by Information Systems administrators and operators groups. The operators create, change, and delete user accounts as needed. The administrators are responsible for supporting and configuring the MSMail post offices.

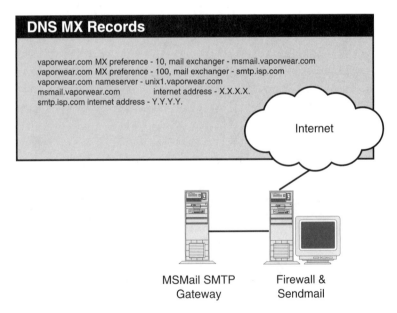

Figure 15.10 Vaporwear's DNX MX records.

Automated Services That Use the Messaging System

An automated service runs nightly and delivers reports to a group of developers. This system runs on a UNIX workstation and delivers mail using SMTP services.

Remote User Services

The investor group of remote users dials into the network through two RAS servers located in Seattle. Because these users are working from home and are located in the Seattle area, all phone charges are local. However, the modems have been unreliable, and support of the dial-in system for 100 users has been a burden on the IS staff.

Once dialed in, the investors typically access email services. Occasionally the management staff travels to off-site investor meetings. They are then configured to dial into an ISP and use POP3 messaging services. The different email client and the division of the sent message items between the services isn't working well for the management users.

Distribution List Structure

All the MSMail distribution lists are used heavily. These distribution lists can be large and are critical to the messaging system. Table 15.13 lists the groups that can be migrated to distribution lists in Exchange.

Shared Folders Structure

The shared folders structure in MSMail has grown to an unreasonable size. There was no control of the top-level folder creation, and most folders have been created by owners who no longer use the folders or who have left the company. The shared folders will not be migrated to Exchange. Additionally, the experience with the MSMail shared folders has highlighted the need to have specific use policies for public forums and the expiration of messages.

Table 15.13 **MSMail groups to be migrated**

Everyone	**Management Committee**	**IS NW Region**
All Seattle	Developers	IS SW region
All Portland	Training	UNIX bitheads
All Denver	Support	Marketing
All Phoenix	All IS	Operations
Finance	Human Resources	Investor relations

Windows NT Architecture

Vaporwear has been relying on Windows NT for its authentication and networking services since the company was founded. The NT architecture that has developed is sound and will work to support the Exchange architecture.

The Vaporwear Exchange Architecture

With the existing corporate environment and the existing NT architecture just defined, it is possible to define the Exchange architecture. From the information gathered from VWS, we build an Exchange architecture that will become the foundation for collaborative applications and enterprise messaging.

Overview

Vaporwear Systems is an organization made up primarily of software developers and other technical personnel. These users spend a considerable amount of their day in front of the computer, using its tools to do their job. One of these tools is electronic mail. Email at VWS is a business-critical application that is used across the organization.

VWS is currently using MSMail to provide internal and external messaging services, including an SMTP gateway for Internet email. The store-and-forward architecture employed by MSMail is no longer meeting their messaging requirements. VWS needs more efficient and elaborate messaging to keep their growing employee base productive in the groups they are assigned to.

As VWS has grown, groups of developers have started to collaborate both within the group and between groups. Their current messaging system doesn't provide the platform necessary to do this.

In an effort to strengthen this feature set and increase functionality to meet the growing collaboration demands of VWS users, VWS will implement Exchange Server 5.5 and Outlook 98 over the next several months.

Necessary Changes to the WAN Infrastructure

Additional frame relay Permanent Virtual Circuits (PVCs) will be defined between Portland and Seattle and between Denver and Phoenix, as shown in Figure 15.11. These PVCs will allow for direct TCP/IP sessions between Exchange servers in those locations. This is necessary because the Exchange servers in those locations will be in the same site. Servers in the same site communicate often. Having these additional PVCs will reduce the load on the routers in Seattle and Portland as well as the bandwidth consumption of those circuits to the frame cloud.

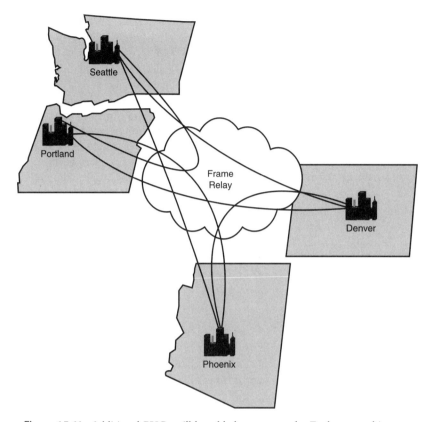

Figure 15.11 Additional PVCs will be added to support the Exchange architecture.

Architecture Overview

Exchange will initially provide support for four primary services: email, scheduling, public folders, and external connectivity. This Exchange architecture will also establish the infrastructure for additional services specific to workgroup applications and collaboration. The Exchange design will use two sites to serve the VWS organization. The migration is deliberate and can be phased in so that hardware and software purchases and implementation are spread throughout the period rather than front-loaded. Because of its more-robust character, most functionality will migrate to Exchange in the earlier migration phases. In this architecture, Exchange provides the Internet Mail Service and can provide faxing and paging solutions. The actual migration process is outlined in a separate document. Coexistence will be highlighted in a later section.

Implementation Approach

After the architecture is approved by the project team, implementation will proceed based on a methodical set of steps designed to validate all elements and protect current capabilities. These steps include a lab and a pilot. They continue with general migration of all users and conclude after the end of migration as the final elements of MSMail are removed.

During the lab, server hardware will be configured and tested, the Exchange Server application will be installed and configured, and testing in a lab environment will be conducted. During the pilot, a small workgroup will be migrated. This workgroup will be selected on the basis of its general similarity to most users and its ability to test a wide variety of the environment's elements. The pilot tests migration processes and integration of the Exchange system into the existing MSMail environment. At the end of this pilot, all necessary infrastructure to support Exchange will be in place, tested, and verified as functional—and therefore will be ready for a production implementation.

This messaging architecture provides a first step in an Exchange implementation. It lays the foundation for the lab and pilot. Following migration, as users become dependent on Exchange as a preferred form of communication, it will be prudent to reevaluate the number of servers in the primary site necessary to support the VWS messaging environment.

Naming Conventions

Naming conventions in Exchange are critical to a successful implementation and need to be defined before implementation. Some of the names, such as the organization name, can't easily be changed after installation. For this reason, it is important to establish naming standards before any implementation.

Note that this section defines only the naming conventions.

Organization

The Exchange organization name defines the boundaries of the Exchange X.500 address space and is the root of the name tree. You should select a name that is very unlikely to change. Vaporwear has selected Vaporwear as the Exchange organization name. This name can't be changed without reinstalling Exchange on all servers in the organization. It's also case-sensitive.

Site Names

Within the Exchange organization, there can be one or more sites. Network bandwidth or administrative policies typically define site boundaries. The VWS Exchange organization will be implemented with two sites. Site names will be Northwest and Southwest.

Server Names

Exchange server names are inherited from the Windows NT server on which Exchange is installed. Exchange servers can have different responsibilities within the VWS organization. The name of the Exchange server will reflect the server's primary responsibility, as shown in Table 15.14.

Table 15.14 **Exchange server naming conventions**

Exchange Server Function	Abbreviation
General purpose (mailboxes, public folders, connectors)	EGEN
Mailbox server	EMBX
Connector server	ECON
Public Folder server	EPFS

The Windows NT server names will reflect the city the server is located in (as discussed earlier in this chapter). This, coupled with the server responsibility and a two-digit server number, will make up the Exchange server names. For the initial implementation, the Exchange server names will be the ones listed in Table 15.15.

User Mailboxes

User mailboxes have several different names associated with them. These include the mailbox alias, SMTP aliases, mailbox display names, and MSMail addresses. The naming conventions for these properties are defined in the following sections.

Mailbox Alias

Each mailbox has its own mailbox alias. This alias name is usually associated with the NT user name and is the field that Exchange tries to associate with NT when creating a new NT account. The VWS mailbox alias will be the same as the NT user name, defined as the user's first initial followed by his complete last name.

Mailbox alias (NT account name): *<first initial first name><last name>*
Example: Jsmith

SMTP Alias

SMTP aliases provide the unique element of the user SMTP address, as in `alias@vaporwear.com`. SMTP aliases will be the user's first initial followed by his complete last name. When two or more people have the same name, the middle initial will be used to ensure a unique SMTP address.

SMTP alias: *<first initial first name><last name>*@vaporwear.com
Example: `jsmith@vaporwear.com`

Table 15.15 **Exchange server names for the VWS organization**

Location	Name
Seattle	SEAEMBX01 SEAEMBX02 SEAEMBX03
	SEAECON01
	SEAEPFS01
Portland	PDXEGEN01
Denver	DENEMBX01
	DENEPFS01
Phoenix	PHXEGEN01

Display Name

Mailbox display names are the normal representation of user names. They define the presentation of the name in the address book. The mailbox display name is constructed from the user's first name, middle initial, and last name.

Display name: *<first name> <middle initial>. <last name>*
Example: John B. Smith

MSMail Addresses

Exchange will maintain MSMail addresses that correspond to the existing user addresses.

MSMail format: *network/post office/alias*
Example: vaporwear/seattle1/jsmith

Exchange Service Account

In order for Exchange Server to function correctly, it uses a domain account with special access rights. All servers in an Exchange site must use the same service account. In the case of VWS, which has two accounts domains, there will be two Exchange service accounts—one in each accounts domain.

This account is necessary for communication between Exchange servers and between Exchange and NT services and should not be the NT Administrator account. This account will be named !exchange in each accounts domain. The password for these accounts will be the same: a 10-character strong password that never expires. This password will be kept in a secure location and won't be shared among Exchange administrators.

The Exchange service account is automatically granted Login as Service rights, as well as other rights. These rights shouldn't be altered.

Site Characteristics

The Exchange organization is built on a hierarchical object tree (based on the X.500 standard). At the top of the tree is the organization. Within the organization are the Global Address List, Exchange folders (both public and system folders), and sites. Sites contain servers, configuration information, and recipient containers. All servers in a single site automatically share the same directory information and communication over high-bandwidth permanent and synchronous connections. The primary configurable elements of the site include the site/organization topology, public folders, distribution lists, custom recipients, and mailboxes. For more information on drawing site lines, see page 69.

Topology

As mentioned earlier, the Vaporwear Exchange organization will be built with two sites. The Northwest site will include users in Seattle and Portland. The

Southwest site will include users in Phoenix and Denver. The two will be connected with a site connector and directory replication connectors over TCP/IP. For more information on Exchange connectors, see page 72.

VWS has enough available WAN bandwidth to be in a single Exchange site. However, the division in administrative responsibilities between Seattle and Denver requires two sites. Having two sites will let two groups of administrators have independent permissions on their respective sites. The site connector is a high-bandwidth connector that will be configured by default to allow any server in one site to initiate communications with any server in the other site. This will ensure fast message transfer, with no intermediate hops between sites, while allowing for the separate administrative structures.

The Exchange connector server in Seattle will provide external connectivity to the Internet for the Northwest. The Exchange public folder server in Denver will provide Internet connectivity for the Southwest. The routes of these Internet Mail Connectors will be configured to replicate between sites to allow each IMS to act as a backup for the other, in case of an outage. Furthermore, the support facility in Phoenix has requested X.400 connectivity to support some of their clients who use the X.400 global network. An X.400 connector will be configured in Phoenix. Figure 15.12 shows the VWS Exchange organization topology.

Northwest

The Northwest site will hold mailboxes for approximately 3,000 users in Seattle and 500 users in Portland.

■ Seattle will have a total of five Exchange servers. To support the 3,000 Seattle users, there will be three Class A Exchange mailbox servers. There will be one Class A public folder server and a Class B connector server.

■ Portland will have a single Class A server to host Portland's 500 users and public folders.

The names of these servers are defined in the previously mentioned server naming section under naming conventions.

VWS will monitor the growth of the mailbox server's private store to identify when it approaches 50GB in size. VWS will have a mailbox quota of 100MB per user, but it is expected that few users will reach this limit. Hence, there will be a potential of 100GB of store disk consumption. When the store reaches 50GB in size, an additional mailbox server will be added to the location. Daily maintenance is the primary reason for limiting the information store size to 50GB. Currently, MSMail post offices run approximately 10MB per user, and the initial store size will be approximately 10GB.

The public information store on the mailbox servers will be deleted. The private information store object on these servers will be configured to associate the public folder server as the source of public folder information for the mailbox server users.

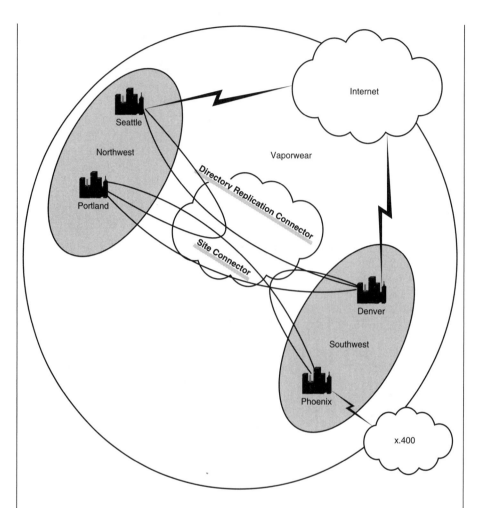

Figure 15.12 The site topology of the Vaporwear organization.

The Connector Exchange server will serve as the Internet Mail server for the Northwest and as the MSMail connector server for Seattle. This Connector server will be responsible for delivering messages from the Northwest to the Internet, as well as passing along messages from Exchange to MSMail in Seattle. The Exchange server in Portland will have an MSMail connector configured to deliver messages between Exchange and MSMail in Portland.

Isolating Internet mail services on a separate connector server in Seattle will provide improved performance. Equally important, this server separation allows for maintenance and downtime of the Internet Mail Server. When the Connector server is offline for maintenance, the Seattle users will still have mailbox access. When the Seattle mailbox servers is down, Internet messaging connectivity for the Northwest won't be affected.

Southwest

The Southwest site will hold mailboxes for approximately 900 users in Denver and 500 users in Phoenix.

- Denver will initially have two Exchange mailbox servers to support the 900 Denver users. In addition, there will be one Class A public folder server.
- Phoenix will have a single Class A server to host Phoenix's 500 users and public folders.

The names of these servers are defined in the previously mentioned server naming section under naming conventions.

VWS will monitor the growth of the mailbox server's private store to identify when it approaches 50GB in size. VWS will have a mailbox quota of 100MB per user, but it is expected that few users will reach this limit. Hence, there will be a potential of 45GB of store disk consumption. When the store reaches 20GB in size, an additional mailbox server will be added to the location. Daily maintenance is the primary reason for limiting the information store size to 20 GB. Currently, MSMail post offices run approximately 10MB per user. The initial store size will be approximately 4.5GB.

Connectors

The two sites within the VWS Exchange organization will be connected using a site connector that uses RPC associations over TCP/IP. These RPC associations are encrypted with 128-bit encryption. By default, site connectors are configured so that any server in one site can communicate directly with any server in another site. VWS will not change this default configuration.

With the site connector in this configuration, when a user in one site sends a message to a user in another site, the sender's server will open an RPC association directly with the recipient's server and deliver the message. This reduces the number of MTA hops and increases efficiency in inter-site message delivery.

The site connectors will be named for the sites to which they connect and the protocol they connect over:

Format: <*messaging protocol*> over <*transport protocol*> to <*destination site*>

Example: Site Connector over TCP/IP to Southwest

It is quite possible that, in the future, with the growth of the organization, additional sites and connectors will be added. By establishing this format and policy now, connectors added in the future will be distinguishable from one another.

Directory Replication Connectors

Exchange utilizes a multi-master X.500-like directory replication design. The Directory Replication Connector passes Exchange directory information between Exchange sites so that each server in each site will have a complete copy of the organizational directory.

Replication connectors are only necessary between sites. Replication between servers within a site occurs automatically and is not scheduled. Within a multi-server site, replication is automatically conducted every five minutes. This means that the Seattle and Portland Exchange servers, as well as the Denver and Phoenix servers, will replicate changes to their directories within 300 seconds. Replication between the two sites will be handled and scheduled by the Directory Replication connector.

The Directory Replication Connectors will be named for the site to which they connect.

Format: DirRep Connector to *<destination site>*

Example: DirRep Connector to Southwest

Exchange Information Store Protocols

The Exchange information services can be accessed by numerous protocols in addition to the native RPC/MAPI client, including POP3, IMAP4, LDAP, and HTTP through the IIS. These protocols are all enabled at the site, server, and mailbox levels, except for the HTTP and LDAP protocols, which are only enabled at the site and server levels.

POP3, IMAP4, LDAP, and HTTP

At the time of the Exchange rollout, VWS will enable the HTTP protocol for all sites and servers to accommodate remote users. Several developers use UNIX workstations. These users have Eudora installed on their UNIX hosts and connect using POP3 to a UNIX server running sendmail. They have been unable to interact with the MSMail users other than through the SMTP gateway. This means that the UNIX users haven't had the benefit of a dynamic corporate email directory.

With Exchange, UNIX workstation users will have the choice of using Eudora to connect to their mailboxes on the Exchange server or to use the Outlook Web client by installing a frames- and JavaScript- enabled browser. The Eudora client, when configured to use LDAP, will enable access to the Exchange directory. Therefore, POP3, IMAP4, HTTP, and LDAP will be enabled on the sites. For more information on Exchange services, see page 85.

Custom Recipients

Custom recipients are email recipients who have a foreign (external) address entry in the directory. For example, a customer contact may have a custom recipient address list entry that refers all mail to the customer's SMTP address on the Internet. This address would let any Exchange user send mail to that recipient without having to know the customer's Internet address.

Custom recipients will have a recipient container in both the Northwest and Southwest sites.

Custom Recipient Creation Policy

Custom recipient entries will be configured only for vendors and customers. There won't be entries for former employees or personal friends. This policy helps to keep the maintenance of the global address list to a minimum. Each site's administrative group will be responsible for maintaining that site's custom recipient list.

Distribution List Strategy

Distribution lists are also recipients that can receive mail. This means that all distribution lists have a valid SMTP address that is addressable from the Internet. Typically, it is good practice to remove the SMTP address of all distribution lists except those that need to be addressed from the Internet. This reduces the possibility of mistaken or malicious efforts affecting the Exchange organization. For example, if VWS had an Everyone distribution list, anyone on the Internet could send a message to everyone@vaporwear.com, and the message would be sent to every member of the distribution list. If it is required that some Internet users be able to send messages to a distribution list, this can be allowed by leaving the SMTP address on the distribution list and including the Everyone distribution list along with the individual Internet Custom Recipient in the Accept Messages From section of the Delivery Restrictions property of the distribution list.

By default, no distribution list will receive Out Of Office (OOF) messages. This is necessary for very large distribution lists. If someone were to send a message to the Everyone distribution list, and 50 users had their OOFs enabled, the sender would receive 50 Out Of Office messages. In some situations, however, it is prudent to enable the OOF message for a distribution list. If the distribution list is a group of managers for which the sender wants to know if a manager doesn't get the message, enabling this feature would tell the sender who on the distribution lists had their OOF enabled. This option will be enabled for small distribution lists on a case-by-case basis.

Distribution List Structure

VWS will establish a distribution list hierarchy. Each site will have a distribution list that contains the cities in that site, as well as any site-specific distribution lists. Each department will also have a distribution list, and any groups within departments will have distribution lists. There will be an Everyone distribution list that includes all department distribution lists. All group distribution lists will be members of their department distribution list. With this nested implementation of distribution lists, users need only be maintained in the lists specific to their department or group. For example, if you add Jane Doe to the A/R distribution list, which already belongs to the Finance distribution list, Jane Doe will also be a member of Finance and Everyone.

The distribution lists created at the time of the Exchange migration will reflect all the current MSMail distribution lists that are currently actively used.

Figure 15.13 shows the VWS distribution list hierarchy.

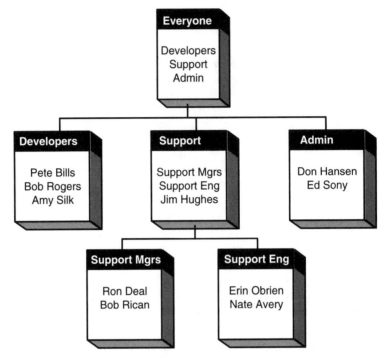

Figure 15.13 The nested distribution sample list hierarchy for the VWS organization.

Distribution List Creation Policy

Distribution lists will be created only by administrators in each site. Management/ownership of the distribution list will then be assigned to the requestor of the distribution list so that the lists will be maintained by a participant of the list. No distribution lists will be created for non-business interests such as "Everyone interested in running." This policy will help reduce maintenance of the global address list.

Mailboxes

Mailboxes are the most common recipients of the messaging system. They contain objects that are organized into one or more folders and are formatted by the client. Only users validated by the NT domain and with permissions on the mailbox may view its objects.

Policies

As mentioned earlier, each mailbox must be associated with a VWS NT domain account. Exchange utilizes NT security to control access to any object in the Exchange directory. Only the NT account associated with a mailbox will be able to log on as that mailbox. That user can then permit other users to access areas of the mailbox as needed.

Mailbox Limits

Exchange is a single-instance store. In other words, when multiple recipients receive the same message, only one copy of the message is stored in the Exchange database. If a message is designated for recipients on more than one server, each server gets a single copy of the message.

Despite the advantages of the single instance store, it is still prudent to impose limits on the amount of disk space that an Exchange user may consume. A mailbox quota will be established during the VWS Exchange implementation. This quota, 100MB, will provide ample space for the average user. At the same time, it will keep a single user, or a small group of users, from consuming an inordinate amount of information store space.

With such a liberal mailbox quota, the message store may eventually grow beyond what should be contained on a single server. When the compacted Exchange information store on a mailbox server exceeds 50GB, an additional server will be added to the location, and approximately one-half of the mailboxes will be moved to the new server.

With each mailbox server in the Seattle location serving 1,000 mailboxes, at 100MB per mailbox, the result is a potential of 100GB of mail store.

Because Exchange is a single instance store, it is highly unlikely that an Exchange server will ever reach the calculated maximum store limit. This is due to multiple mailboxes having their quotas calculated off the same messages. Additionally, most organizations have median mailbox sizes that are much lower than the mailbox limit. For an organization such as VWS, which has consistent but limited mailbox usage, it is expected that there be about 30 to 50 users at, near, or over the mailbox limit at any time and that the median mailbox size will be approximately 15MB. For more information on mailbox limits, see page 120.

Deleted Item Retention Policy

Exchange 5.5 provides the ability to maintain copies of deleted messages so that users can recover mistakenly deleted items. During the period in which these deleted items are retained, they would continue to be present on backups. VWS will enable the deleted items retention time for five days and will also allow items to be kept until the information store has been backed up. This will ensure that the deleted items will be present on at least one backup. This policy will add about 2GB of data storage to the Seattle mailbox servers, with incrementally less on the other locations' servers. The 2GB estimation is based on experience.

Templates

To aid in the creation of mailboxes for employees, mailbox templates will be created for each site. The template mailboxes will be configured with site-specific information, such as business addresses and phone numbers. Using the templates when creating new accounts reduces data entry time and ensures consistent information for each account. Mailbox templates will normally remain hidden from the address book so that they won't get mail. Template names will begin with *x-location*.

Recipient Containers

Exchange organizes recipients into containers. Recipients include mailboxes, custom recipients, and site-specific distribution lists. All recipients will be held in the default Recipients container for their respective servers. Both sites will have additional containers to hold non-VWS employees (that is, custom recipients) and site-oriented distribution lists. Each location will have a specific recipient container for resources such as conference rooms, video equipment, and so on.

There will also be a recipient container created for the MSMail users. Exchange will populate this recipient container during directory synchronization with MSMail.

Public Folders

Public folders act as a central, shared location of information. The public folder hierarchy is replicated automatically throughout the organization. Public folder content is available to users either in their local site or through public folder affinity, depending on where the public folder originated and if it is replicated.

Public Folder Hierarchy

A public folder hierarchy policy will be established. The general VWS organization will have a single top-level public folder. Each department and location will also have a single top-level public folder. This hierarchy provides for easier maintenance and administration. For more information on public folder strategies, see page 92.

Public Folder Administration

Only Exchange administrators will be allowed to create top-level folders. Any new top-level folder will be evaluated for necessity.

At least one user from each department or site will be granted permissions on that department's or site's top-level public folder. This user is dubbed the folder administrator. The folder administrator can create subfolders and apply permissions to them. This includes granting other users similar permissions.

Figure 15.14 illustrates a recommended structure for VWS's public folder directory.

Public Folder Recipients

Public folders don't typically need configuration in order to be email recipients. By adding a public folder as a member of a distribution list, you can keep a record of all messages sent to a distribution list. Public folders can also be recipients for Internet *list services*. If there is an industry-specific list service on the Internet, a public folder can subscribe to that list service. All messages originating from that list service will be sent to the public folder, which in turn is available to the Exchange organization.

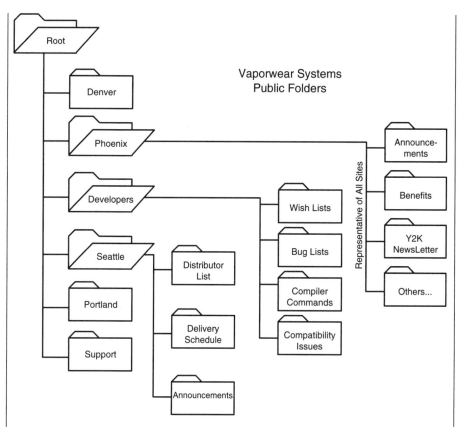

Figure 15.14 The public folder directory structure for Vaporwear Systems.

Replicas and Affinity

By default, public folders reside only on the server on which they were created and, given necessary permissions, are only visible to Outlook clients within the same site. Users in other sites can be granted access to a site's public folder information in one of two ways—affinity or replica.

When public folder affinity is configured, a user anywhere in the organization who has sufficient rights to the folder can access the public folder's contents by reaching out across the WAN to open the public folder. For public folders that change frequently but are accessed infrequently, public folder affinity is the most efficient means of access. For more information on public folder affinity, see page 100.

Public folder replication is performed between Exchange servers on selected folders. When a folder is replicated, its contents are replicated from one server to another. Users accessing the data can then retrieve the contents of the public folder from the local site and don't have to reach out across the WAN to find the content of the public folder. For more frequently accessed folders or public folders containing large documents, public folder replication reduces the total burden on the WAN. For more information on public folder replication, see page 100.

One organization-wide top-level public folder will be created and replicated to each site if required. Site-specific folders will only be replicated as necessary. Analysis of activity on other folders should provide information on which to base decisions of whether or not to replicate.

The replication schedule, by default, will be set to once every hour. On a folder-by-folder basis, the replication schedule can be shortened or lengthened based on the content of the public folder and the necessity of up-to-date information.

For public folder access beyond what is available in the site, public folder affinity will be configured between the Northwest and Southwest sites to give users full access to the public folder system.

Public Folder Servers

Both Seattle and Denver will have a public folder server. This server is responsible for providing public folder services to the clients in the site and the organization.

The public information store on the mailbox servers will be deleted. The private information store object on these servers will be configured to associate the public folder server as the source of public folder information for the mailbox server users.

This configuration has two major advantages:

- It reduces the overhead on the mailbox servers by offloading public folder responsibilities to another server.
- It centralizes public folder resources on a single server. When a client opens a public folder, the client must search several servers when looking for the content of a public folder.

System Folders/Offline Address Book

Exchange provides an offline address book for use by mobile users. It can be configured in an object contained in the system folders. Typically, the book is regenerated daily during off-peak hours. By using the Global Address List as the data source for the offline address book, all laptop users will have the ability to communicate with anyone listed in the VWS address book.

The VWS offline address book will be updated three times a day.

Organizational Forms Library

Exchange clients can share customized electronic forms. This is accomplished by installing the forms into a special Exchange public folder. This public folder is then replicated around the organization. When a user needs to use an electronic form, the Outlook client can access the organizational public forms library and open the form.

Each location in VWS will have the organizational forms library available through a replicated copy on one of the servers in its site.

External Connectivity

The VWS organization currently uses Internet connectivity to commuicate with users outside VWS. However, the support group in Phoenix has a number of clients who communicate using the X.400 global network. They have requested that the X.400 connector be configured to support this client requirement.

Internet Mail Service (IMS)

The Internet Mail Service is an SMTP host that allows Exchange users as well as other foreign mail users to send mail to and receive mail from the Internet, either directly or through a firewall proxy. For more information on the IMS, see page 125.

In the absence of a firewall proxy, when the Exchange server receives a message destined for the Internet, it uses DNS to resolve the SMTP domain to an IP address and then opens a TCP/IP port 25 session to that host and delivers the message.

Currently, VWS receives Internet messages with the MSMail SMTP gateway. The firewall at VWS is configured to pass SMTP packets to the MSMail gateway. The *Mail eXchanger* (MX) records registered on the Internet point to the VWS domain. The VWS MX records look like this:

```
vaporwear.com     MX preference = 10, mail exchanger =
➡msmail.vaporwear.com
vaporwear.com     nameserver = unix1.vaporwear.com
msmail.vaporwear.com internet address = X.X.X.X
```

The VWS domain (vaporwear.com) will have an MX DNS record that will allow Internet SMTP hosts to resolve VWS recipients to the Seattle Exchange connector server's external IP address. All inbound SMTP mail, including that destined for Southwest, will come into the IMS (SMTP) connector and then be delivered to the user through the Exchange system.

A secondary MX record will be registered to the Denver Exchange Public Folder server running the Internet Mail Service. A third MX record will point to the ISP's Sendmail host. If for some reason the Exchange Connector server in Seattle can't receive an Internet message, the sending SMTP host will deliver the message to the secondary (next-highest-preference) MX record, and the message will be delivered to Denver. If both servers are unavailable, the message will be delivered to the ISP. If the Southwest Exchange server receives the inbound message, it will deliver the message to its destination. If the ISP host receives the messages, it will continue to try and deliver the message until the server is again available.

The MX records will be altered to look like this:

```
vaporwear.com     MX preference = 10, mail exchanger =
➡seaecom01.vaporwear.com
vaporwear.com     MX preference = 20, mail exchanger =
➡denepfs01.vaporwear.com
vaporwear.com     MX preference = 100, mail exchanger =
➡smtp.isp.com
vaporwear.com     nameserver = firewall.vaporwear.com
```

```
seaecom01.vaporwear.com internet address = X.X.X.X
denepfs01.vaporwear.com internet address = X.X.X.X
smtp.isp.com internet address = X.X.X.X
```

The firewalls will be configured to restrict SMTP traffic to only the associated Exchange Internet Mail Service server—the Seattle Exchange Connector server for the Seattle firewall and the Denver Exchange server for the Denver firewall. This will allow SMTP traffic to be received by the Exchange Connector servers and will allow SMTP traffic to originate only from the Exchange Connector servers. The firewalls will have their SMTP proxy enabled.

Internet Messaging Protocols

As mentioned earlier, Exchange supports IMAP4, POP3, LDAP, NNTP, and HTTP protocols. Exchange also supports Web access through the Internet Information Server, which comes with Windows NT. VWS will enable POP3, IMAP4, and LDAP to give their UNIX clients a variety of options as to the type of client they want to use to access their Exchange mailbox. The HTTP protocol will be enabled to support remote and roving users in addition to UNIX users.

The UNIX sendmail host that acts as a post office for the UNIX clients will now be disabled and the users migrated to Exchange.

The UNIX clients will be able to access their mailbox using POP3 or IMAP4 and the directory using LDAP. However, they will be given full calendaring and contacts functionality by using Outlook Web Access through a browser and HTTP.

LDAP will also be used in the next version of Windows NT for directory access.

Server Strategy

To determine the type and number of servers to use when implementing Exchange, the following metrics are used.

User Classification

The typical user at VWS is an advanced messaging user by most standards. This is due in part to the nature of the VWS business and the need to collaborate using the computer. Yet when comparing users within VWS to one another, they do fit into three categories—light, medium, and heavy messaging users.

Definition of Light, Medium, and Heavy Messaging Users

For this architecture in the VWS environment, users are defined as shown in Table 15.16.

Table 15.16 **User classification**

User Type	Messages Sent Per Day	Messages Received Per Day
Light users	15	10
Medium users	25	25
Heavy users	35	35

The Vaporwear Exchange Architecture 325

Number of Light, Medium, and Heavy Users Per Physical Location

Based on the information listed in Table 15.16, the users at each location are divided into the categories listed in Table 15.17.

Table 15.17 **User classification by location**

Type of User	Percentage of Users	Seattle	Portland	Phoenix	Denver
Light	15	500	100	50	100
Medium	63	2,100	200	250	600
Heavy	22	500	200	200	200

Type of Messaging Traffic and Load

From the data listed in Table 15.17, we can conclude that there is considerable load on the messaging system. The server candidate will have to be able to provide efficient communication with this required load.

Server Candidate

The server candidate will be a large Class A server.

Server Candidate Validation Method

The server candidate will be validated by using Loadsim from the Exchange Resource Kit. Loadsim will be configured to simulate the number of defined users, sending and receiving the prescribed number of messages while being monitored for performance. The candidate server will need to show acceptable performance with 1,000 users. Fifteen percent of these users will be defined as light users, 63 percent medium users, and 22 percent heavy users. All will send and receive their defined number of messages simultaneously.

Administration Strategy

The administration of the Exchange organization will be similar to the MSMail administration practices currently in place. The Northwest and Southwest sites will be the two administrative structures. These administrative structures will be split into two IS groups: administrators and operators. The Northwest administrators and operators will maintain the Northwest Exchange site from Seattle. The Southwest administrators and operators will maintain the Southwest Exchange site from Denver.

Administrators and Permissions Administrators

The administrators workgroup will be responsible for configuring, upgrading, and troubleshooting the Exchange organization. This workgroup will be assigned Permissions Administrator rights for the Northwest and Southwest Exchange sites.

The operators workgroup will be responsible for creating and deleting Exchange objects. These users will be assigned to an NT group that has Exchange Administrator rights but that doesn't have Permissions Administrator rights so that they can't change permissions for objects within the organization.

Each accounts domain will have a separate ExchangeAdmin and ExchangeOPs group. Messaging staff will be assigned to their appropriate groups. To keep with VWS administration strategy, these groups will only be assigned permissions on the Exchange site they are associated with.

Client Strategy

The client strategy for VWS is simplified because of the rather homogeneous nature of the clients. Although there are still a few UNIX workstations in the organization, all computers are Windows-based, and the organization's direction is toward a unified desktop operating system.

Outlook

Clients will use Outlook 98 to connect to Exchange 5.5. In general, Outlook capabilities will be loaded by default, but all services might not be installed immediately. The Outlook information services listed in Table 15.18 will be installed. For more information on the Outlook client, see page 121.

In addition, the offline message store will be configured on each workstation. This will enhance performance with Outlook 98 and enable mailbox message access for folders that have been synchronized during Exchange outages.

Table 15.18 **Message store and address book services to be configured on the user's Outlook client**

Service Name	Description
Exchange Server	Message store and address book information service used to communicate with the Exchange server. This service also makes journaling, group calendaring, and server task storage possible.
Outlook address book	Address book information service used to access contact email addresses during email name resolution
Personal address book	Address book information service used to store and access addresses in a local file (.pab). This will primarily be used to store personal distribution lists, because they aren't currently possible using contacts.

Remote Client

As noted earlier, Exchange provides a robust collection of protocols to enable remote access. These protocols are enabled by default, and VWS will leave them enabled. HTTP (Web) will also be enabled, and its supporting services, IIS and Active Server pages, will be configured. With this protocol enabled and with the necessary configuration of the firewall, remote users will be able to connect to Exchange 5.5 via Outlook Web Access with any JavaScript- and frames-enabled HTML browser. The Outlook Web Access client provides almost all the functionality of the standard client, including access to email, folders, and calendar and scheduling. With SSL (Secure Sockets Layer) enabled, communications with the Web Access client can be encrypted. This will secure users' information as it passes through the Internet.

Outlook Web Access

Outlook Web Access will be used to provide additional messaging services for the VWS organization, as shown in Figure 15.15.

Outlook Web Access is best suited to non-Windows users, remote users, and roving users and will be installed in the VWS organization. The UNIX workstations will get the most functionality from the messaging system by using Outlook Web Access. Although other protocols will be enabled for their use, Outlook Web Access is the preferred tool of UNIX workstation users.

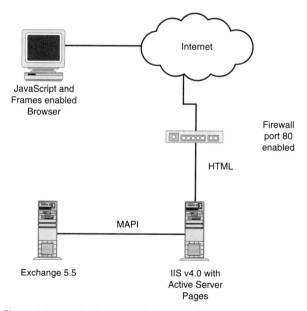

Figure 15.15   Outlook Web Access for the VWS organization.

Remote users will also have many choices for remote Exchange connectivity: Outlook Web Access, POP3, IMAP4, LDAP, or Outlook 98 client access. It is recommended that traveling users, and perhaps home users, take advantage of the built-in remote functionality of the standard Outlook client. With a configured Offline Message Store (OST), Outlook users can work offline and then dial up to send and receive mail. Remote users will be able to connect to Exchange with their standard Outlook client after a RAS solution is put into place. Remote Outlook sessions use RPCs that can be configured for 40-bit or 128-bit encryption. For users who are accessing the organization from a workstation that doesn't have the Outlook client installed or from a network that won't allow RPC connectivity with the VWS Exchange servers, Outlook Web Access is the preferred connectivity method.

MSMail Coexistence

VWS has selected Exchange 5.5 Enterprise to replace the aging and increasingly unstable MSMail system. The current system provides for email and shared folder services. The migration will take place in several phases over several months. As a result, the Exchange and MSMail systems will coexist for an extended period. To improve performance and reliability as quickly as possible, external connectivity capabilities will be moved to Exchange, and the MSMail MTA (external) will be removed as Exchange is implemented. For more information on MSMail coexistence and migration, see page 144.

MSMail Connector Architecture

As migration progresses, the Exchange system will be integrated with the MSMail system using several MSMail connectors, one in each location.

Each location has an MSMail hub. Each of these hubs is downstream from the MSMail hub in Seattle, as shown in Figure 15.9.

The MSMail connector will be configured between the MSMail hub and the Exchange Connector server in Seattle.

The MSMail hub in Seattle is also the dirsync server for the MSMail network. The Exchange connector server will initially be just another requestor to this hub. After coexistence is established by installing MSMail connectors at each site, the dirsync server will be reconfigured so that the Exchange connector server is the dirsync server.

The connectors in the other sites will link the local Exchange server with the local MSMail post office. During configuration of coexistence, each MSMail connector will only be responsible for message flow between the two local systems and will be set up only during the period when the site is migrating—perhaps for as short a period as two weeks. Once the Exchange server is installed and the MSMail connectors are configured, all MSMail will be routed through the Exchange system. The existing routes between MSMail post offices and the MSMail hub post office in Seattle will be removed (as denoted by the dotted lines in Figure 15.16). Exchange will deliver messages to other MSMail post offices and Exchange users, as shown in Figure 15.16.

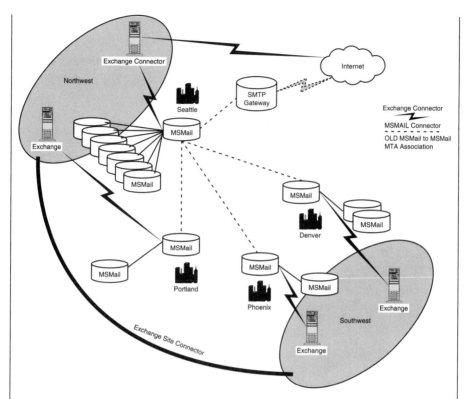

Figure 15.16 MSMail and Exchange coexistence strategy.

Directory Synchronization

Currently, the MSMail hub in Seattle is the MSMail dirsync server, and all other post offices in the network are requestors. This system is working without any significant problems. Because of this, the Exchange connector server will be configured as another requestor. All Exchange user information from both sites will be synchronized with the MSMail hub post office. The Exchange connector server requestor will be configured to export both sites' recipient containers only. No other recipient containers will be included in directory synchronization.

If dirsync were unstable, it would be possible to reconfigure the entire MSMail network to use the Exchange connector server as the dirsync server. However, because the current system is reliable, there is no reason to change the configuration.

Recipient Container

A recipient container for MSMail users will be created in the Northwest site. It will hold all MSMail directory information delivered by the MSMail connector. This container will be named MSMail Users.

MSMail Groups

All MSMail groups that are used for business functions will be incorporated into the Exchange Distribution list hierarchy. Maintaining these groups during the migration will be time-consuming. The fewer there are to maintain, the better.

Shared Folders

There is no built-in synchronization between MSMail shared folders and Exchange public folders. Due to VWS's limited dependence on MSMail shared folders, it is recommended that synchronization not be attempted. Instead, the MSMail users should be informed that migrated Exchange users will no longer have access to the MSMail shared folders. Furthermore, users should be informed that MSMail users won't have access to the Exchange public folder system.

Foreign Messaging System Coexistence

When coexistence between Exchange and MSMail is installed and configured, MSMail users can benefit from the foreign messaging systems to which Exchange is connected. Therefore, all foreign messaging systems currently supported by the MSMail environment will be migrated to Exchange. Both Exchange users and MSMail users will utilize these connectors.

Internet Mail Service

SMTP addresses will remain unchanged when the gateway is moved from the MSMail host to Exchange. The MX records in DNS will be changed to reflect the Exchange server's SMTP IP address. One of the first Exchange services to be migrated from MSMail to Exchange will be the SMTP service. It is important that directory synchronization be configured and working before the MX record is changed.

Maintaining the Messaging Organization

Once Exchange servers have been implemented in the VWS organization, even for a pilot implementation, it is necessary to provide maintenance for the messaging environment. The processes necessary for maintaining the VWS Exchange environment are described in the following sections.

Exchange Backup

Exchange stores all message and directory information in databases. These database files are locked to the file system and missed during normal backups. Backups of Exchange are mainly for disaster recovery, because they readily recover the entire database. There are currently no backup products that are well-suited to restoring individual pieces of email or individual mailboxes.

The leading backup software vendors offer Exchange-enabled backup agents for their backup software. These agents allow the backup software to back up the online message and directory stores. It is recommended that Wadeware's

SpeedyBackup be installed and configured on all Exchange mailbox servers in the VWS organization. It is also recommended that Wadeware's SpeedyBackup Agent for Exchange Server be installed on each server responsible for backups. This agent allows SpeedyBackup to back up the Exchange databases online.

Exchange database circular logging will be disabled on the Exchange servers. This will allow for differential and incremental backups and restores and provides more backup flexibility. Backups of the Exchange server must be made daily and verified periodically. Restoration exercises should include all steps of disaster recovery—rebuilding the server software, restoring the data, and verifying that the owners can retrieve their messages.

Message Tracking

VWS will track all message transfers within the organization to ensure system availability. Message tracking will be enabled for the information stores, the MSMail connectors, and the Internet Mail Service for all Exchange sites. The tracking logs will be kept for the default seven days. For more information on message tracking, see page 170.

Link Monitors

Link monitors will be configured in Seattle to monitor connectivity between Seattle and all other locations. Additional link monitors will be configured to monitor the SMTP connection to the Internet and the X.400 connector to the X.400 provider. When a link doesn't respond within 15 minutes, an alert will be sent to the Exchange console, and an email will be sent to the Exchange Administrators distribution list. A paging mechanism can also be configured when paging services become available. For more information on link monitors, see page 164.

Server Monitors

Server monitors will be configured to monitor Exchange Server services with the proper alerts and actions configured for each Exchange server. If an Exchange service stops on an Exchange server, an alert will be sent to the Exchange server console, and an email will be sent to the Exchange Administrator's distribution list. The server monitor will attempt to start the service. If the service doesn't start on the first attempt, the server monitor will do nothing on subsequent attempts. For more information on server monitors, see page 162.

Periodic Maintenance

The following tables describe a schedule for recommended maintenance activities.

Daily Operations

Table 15.19 outlines the activities to be performed on a daily basis.

Table 15.19 **Daily maintenance activities**

Activity	Description
Back up	Perform a full back up of the Exchange servers if possible. If not, perform the appropriate differential or incremental backups.
Scan Event Log	Use the Resource Kit utility to scan the Event Log for errors and alerts.
Monitor disk space	Use network management to ensure that disk space on Exchange servers isn't depleted to dangerous levels.
MTA queue monitoring	Monitor queue lengths on the connector server to confirm that there are no message queue buildups.

Weekly Operations

Table 15.20 outlines the activities to be performed on a weekly basis.

Table 15.20 **Weekly maintenance activities**

Activity	Description
Full backup	If incremental or differential backups become necessary, perform a full backup over the weekend.
Check replication activity	Check directory replication and synchronization using the Event Log. Confirm that directory information is being replicated across the organization.
Public folder replication configuration	Make sure public folders have not been replicated unnecessarily. Confirm that the public folders that exist on thepublic folder servers are there by design.
Gather statistics	Gather statistics to monitor the utilization of the Exchange server(s). Over time, this will show trends in server utilization and allow for the planning of additional servers or hardware.

Periodic Operations

Table 15.21 outlines the activities to be performed on a periodic basis.

Table 15.21 **Periodic maintenance activities**

Activity	Description
Compress stores with ESEUTIL	Periodically (quarterly or biannually), the information stores may need to be defragmented offline. This can increase performance and reduce the information store file size. ■ Elapsed time will depend on store size, CPU speed, and disk speed. ■ Requires double the store size in disk space. ■ Back up stores before and after defragmentation.
Run disaster recovery exercise	In the lab, recover a server from backup to validate backup media, location of software, and necessary recovery procedures. Have a disaster recovery white paper as part of a larger Disaster Recovery document.
Install service packs	Install service packs that have been released for 60 to 90 days.
Lab environment	Confirm that the lab environment is configured for the following activities: ■ Connected to the organization ■ Runs new software ■ Used by a selected group of users ■ Duplicates essential elements of the production environment
Perform a six-month review	Assess technical development and its potential effects on the following: ■ Windows NT design ■ Network design ■ Exchange organization design ■ Client desktop environment ■ Operational practices Review statistics collected during weekly operations and predict growth patterns: ■ Identify bottlenecks. ■ Install additional hardware or servers before it's required.

Securing the Messaging Organization

The security of the messaging organization is crucial to maintaining available services and the integrity of the system. The following sections discuss how VWS will secure the messaging organization.

NT and Exchange Security

Exchange is tightly tied to the NT security system. To access a mailbox, a user must have an NT account linked to his mailbox. All Exchange objects are controlled by permissions. The tight integration of NT and Exchange also lets NT groups be specified in Exchange permissions. This is a mechanism that VWS can use to manage permissions on the Exchange directory.

Permissions

By default, permissions are assigned at three levels of an Exchange organization—organization, site, and configuration (within a site). Permissions flow within each of these levels but don't flow through them. In other words, when a group is assigned permissions on the Exchange organization, that group needs to be assigned permissions for *each* level. Additionally, permissions can be set on any object by exception. By assigning permissions at one, but not all, levels, access can be more finely controlled. Two levels of administration highlight the VWS permissions structure. Windows NT global groups will define these two types of Exchange administrators. Each global group will be granted appropriate permissions on both permissions levels.

VWS has two master accounts domains—one for the Northwest, named NW, and one for the Southwest, named SW. Each domain has an ExchangeAdmins and ExchangeOPs global group. These groups will be configured with the permissions on the Exchange directory objects listed in Table 15.22.

Exchange Permissions Administrators

The Exchange Permissions Administrators group is a very limited group of administrators. It is recommended that not more than two or three administrators be defined as Exchange Permissions Administrators.

Table 15.22   **Permissions to be assigned on the VWS directory**

Group	Object	Permission
NW/ExchangeAdmins	Organization Vaporwear	Permissions Administrator
SW/ExchangeAdmins	Organization Vaporwear	Permissions Administrator
NW/ExchangeOPs	Organization Vaporwear	Administrator
SW/ExchangeOPs	Organization Vaporwear	Administrator
NW/ExchangeAdmins	Site Northwest	Permissions Administrator
SW/ExchangeAdmins	Site Southwest	Permissions Administrator
NW/ExchangeOPs	Site Northwest	Administrator
SW/ExchangeOPs	Site Southwest	Administrator
NW/ExchangeAdmins	Configuration Northwest	Permissions Administrator
SW/ExchangeAdmins	Configuration Southwest	Permissions Administrator
NW/ExchangeOPs	Configuration Northwest	Administrator
SW/ExchangeOPs	Configuration Southwest	Administrator

Exchange Permissions Administrators can alter the permissions on an object. Hence, they can grant themselves or someone else permissions on anyone's mailbox, and then enter that mailbox and view mail.

Exchange Permissions Administrators have complete control over the directory. The Permissions Administrators NT global group will be granted Permissions Administrator permissions on the organizations, their respective sites, and their respective site-configuration objects.

Exchange Administrators

The Exchange Administrators group can administer all elements of the Exchange organization, including changing connectors, site and server configurations, and public folder organization.

The Exchange Administrators group has all the permissions that the Permissions Administrator has, except the ability to change permissions on an object. The typical Exchange administrator will be assigned to this group.

The Exchange Administrators global group will be granted Administrator permissions on the organization, their respective sites, and their respective site-configuration objects.

Service Account

The Exchange service account will be named *!exchange*. The password for this account will adhere to the service account password policies defined in the Windows NT architecture and the service account section of the previously mentioned naming convention section.

In each master accounts domain, an exchange service account will be created. Each site will use the service account from its respective accounts domain. The password for each service account will be a 10-character strong password kept in a secure location and won't be shared among all Exchange administrators. The password for each service account will be the same and won't expire.

If it becomes necessary to change the Exchange service account password, it must only be changed from within the Exchange Administrator program and will be done in both sites using the NT Administrator account.

During installation, the Exchange service account is granted Service Account Admin permissions on all objects in the Exchange directory. This too won't change or be altered.

Messaging Service

One of the many advantages of Exchange is its ability to connect and coexist with many different messaging and information systems. The following are some of the messaging services Exchange can use to fulfill the VWS messaging requirements.

Electronic Forms

Electronic forms enable formatted display or the capture of information in Exchange. They can be created with Exchange Forms Designer and can be used to post items in public folders or process routine actions such as vacation requests.

As specified in the public folder section of this chapter, an organizational forms library will be created and replicated to all public folder information stores.

Microsoft Outlook is equipped with a powerful forms development environment. These forms can be purely developed in the Outlook environment or coupled with Visual Basic or C++ controls and services.

Electronic forms can also be developed for use by a Web browser using HTML and active server pages. These electronic forms can take advantage of Exchange services and transports.

With Exchange 5.5 and the Collaborative Data Objects environment, powerful workgroup applications can be developed. Included in this environment is a rendering engine that converts an Outlook electronic form into a Web form, for similar functionality from clients and reduced development cycles.

Virus Protection

As part of the virus protection section of the Windows NT architecture, a virus protection system is recommended for Exchange.

WynneShield for Exchange, from the makers of WynneFree anti-virus products, is one product on the market that can protect an Exchange server. The WynneShield SMTP component scans incoming SMTP messages for viruses.

Faxing

Several third-party companies offer faxing software for Exchange. This software lets Exchange users send—and, in some cases, receive—faxes through the Exchange server. Custom recipients can be set up for commonly faxed clients, and Exchange users can send "one-off" faxes by sending the message to the fax number.

Paging

Several third-party companies offer alphanumeric paging software for Exchange. A user can have both a paging address and a mailbox address. Such a solution allows Exchange users to send a page through the Exchange system. It also gives a properly configured pager the ability to receive alphanumeric messages as well as alarms and other automated messages. Such functionality allows Exchange or MAPI-aware programs to automatically dispatch a page when a monitored server or service becomes unavailable or changes.

Crystal Reports

To more easily and accurately provide statistical information on Exchange usage and performance, use the Crystal Reports tools. Daily, weekly, and monthly reports can be generated in the areas of individual client use, overall traffic patterns, and specific traffic patterns (Internet, individual site, and so on). Sample tools are included in the Exchange 5.5 Resource Kit. Crystal Reports is a third-party product.

The Vaporwear Systems Migration Strategy

This document defines the migration strategy for Vaporwear Systems.

Overview

The MSMail migration assumes that the recommended Exchange organization structure has been fully implemented across the VWS enterprise. In addition, this MSMail migration document assumes that coexistence between MSMail and the Exchange organization is established and stable. An Exchange Implementation Plan should outline the steps and parameters necessary to implement Exchange and Exchange coexistence with MSMail, as described in the Exchange Architecture document. For more information on developing an implementation plan, see page 179.

MSMail Migration

MSMail directory and mailbox data for users will be migrated at the time the user is moved to the new Exchange environment. VWS staff will migrate users at a rate of 25 per day unless experience allows for a more aggressive pace. With approximately 3,000 users in the Seattle facility, the migration will last approximately 24 weeks. During this time, coexistence between the Exchange system and the MSMail system will have to be monitored and maintained.

Verify Coexistence

As part of the Exchange implementation, MSMail connectors will be installed at all locations. Once Exchange is fully operational and the MSMail connectors are installed and configured, directory synchronization between the Exchange organization and the MSMail system will be configured in the Northwest site. As mentioned earlier, the Seattle Exchange connector server will be a requestor to the MSMail dirsync server. The Exchange connector server will be responsible for exchanging directory information with the MSMail network.

Reconfigure MSMail Routing

Due to the number of users at each location, the coexistence with MSMail just described will be completed before any users are migrated. Once the MSMail connectors are put into place at each location, the routing of MSMail messages will be reconfigured at each location to go through the Exchange system. This will entail configuring the MSMail post offices to connect to the upstream post offices indirectly through the Exchange MSMail connector.

Reconfigure SMTP Mail Routing

Exchange will support delivery and receipt of SMTP mail to and from the Internet. There are two advantages to enabling Exchange as the SMTP gateway for the VWS enterprise. First, the Exchange SMTP host is very fast and reliable.

Second, by having the Exchange server act as the SMTP host, messages will flow between all the MSMail post offices and Exchange, thus exercising the MSMail connectors. It is recommended that Exchange be configured as the SMTP host for MSMail prior to the migration to validate the configuration of the MSMail connectors.

Pilot Migration

VWS should conduct a pilot test of the migration process prior to the production migration. The pilot will be valid only if the complete Exchange environment is in place according to the Exchange Architecture document. The users who participate in the pilot should be willing to endure service outages and a learning curve. Furthermore, the pilot users should represent various departments in the VWS organization. From this pilot group, migration scripts can be fine-tuned, client issues can be addressed, and data migration can be validated. For more information on conducting an Exchange pilot, see page 184.

Migration Steps

After the pilot group issues have been successfully resolved, the main migration can begin. Three main tasks need to take place for each user concurrently. The granular steps in each of these tasks will be defined in an Exchange Implementation Plan. Some of these steps will also be discovered during the pilot. Table 15.23 outlines the steps for the migration.

Coexistence Issues and Strategy

Coexistence between MSMail and Exchange is described in the Exchange Architecture document. However, once a user has migrated from MSMail to Exchange, certain tasks need to be performed manually to complete the migration.

Table 15.23 **Migration steps**

Step	Description
Workstation configuration	The Exchange user workstations need to be configured with both Microsoft Networking and Outlook 98.
Training	The user needs to attend Outlook training.
MSMail mailbox migration	The user's MSMail mailbox information will be migrated to Exchange using the Exchange Migration Wizard utility that comes with Exchange 5.5. This process is executed from the server.

MSMail Custom Recipients to Exchange Mailboxes

The MSMail connector on the Seattle Exchange Connector server will synchronize all MSMail addresses into an Exchange recipient container named MSMail Users in the form of a custom recipient. This custom recipient, by design, has the same SMTP address as the MSMail user. When Exchange receives an SMTP addressed message, it forwards that message down the MSMail connector to the SMTP recipient. Before the user is migrated, it is important to delete that custom recipient from the MSMail Users recipient container. This allows the new user to be assigned the proper SMTP address.

Mailing Lists and Distribution Lists

Another area needing attention during migration is that of mailing lists and distribution lists. When a user is migrated from MSMail to Exchange, it is important to add him to the proper Exchange distribution lists.

MSMail Addresses for Exchange Users

Another important reason for deleting the custom recipient from the MSMail Users recipient container is so that the migrated Exchange user has only one address in the Global Address Book. Otherwise, the user will have an Exchange address and a custom recipient address, causing confusion and bounced messages.

Training

No matter how eloquent the server deployment, if users are unable to operate the client, they will view the migration as a failure. Hence, one of the most important components of a migration is end-user training. For more information on training, see page 186.

Administrator

Exchange is a more complex messaging environment than other store-and-forward messaging systems. With this complexity comes the necessity for administrators to understand the basic principles that Exchange is based on, as well as the daily, weekly, and periodic tasks an Exchange administrator must perform.

It is recommended that the VWS Information Systems staff responsible for messaging attend Microsoft Official Curriculum Exchange training.

End-User

VWS employs qualified training staff. This training staff will be responsible for providing end-user Outlook training to Exchange users while their workstations are being configured and their MSMail accounts are being migrated.

16

Adapting the Exchange Architecture for Growth

THIS BOOK HAS FOCUSED ALMOST EXCLUSIVELY on small- and medium-sized organizations. We haven't attempted to address any of the complex issues that arise when Exchange is deployed in a large organization. We do recognize, however, that you might need to be aware of some of the issues faced by large organizations when they deploy Exchange. Your organization might be growing, and you might be the person assigned to prepare for that growth. Or you might be considering a career move to another organization that falls into the large organization category. Whatever the case may be, we are concluding this book with a brief discussion of some of the issues faced by large organizations that use Exchange—large in both the number of users and geographically.

It is important to consider scalability when designing your Exchange architecture, no matter what the size of your organization. Three types of scalability need to be addressed when you're designing an Exchange architecture:

- Scalability in the number of recipients utilizing the Exchange system
- Scalability of the Exchange system across a broader geographic area
- Scalability in the usage of the Exchange system as users become acquainted with its full functionality

Due to the nature of business today, the first type of scalability, the number of Exchange users, is practically unavoidable for most organizations. No matter what the size of your organization, it will grow over time. It may not grow to include 200,000 recipients around the world, but it will grow beyond the number of recipients included when the Exchange system was implemented.

In addition to growth in the number of recipients who utilize the Exchange system, growth will occur on a geographic scale. Most companies today provide services to or require services from organizations outside of their immediate geographic area. This means that it will be necessary to scale the Exchange system to provide services to multiple locations. In many of the examples in this book, we have addressed the complexities of designing an Exchange architecture that includes a distributed server environment. This chapter discusses some of the challenges faced when the geographic scope of the system grows after it has been implemented.

The third type of growth in Exchange systems is often the most common. It is a growth in the actual utilization of the Exchange system by the people in the organization. This type of growth is a natural result of an effective Exchange system. Once you provide your users with a messaging system that has more functionality, greater potential for collaboration, and better integration with their desktop environment, they will take advantage of that system. This means that more data will be transferred by e-mail than was transferred before Exchange was implemented. It also means that users will begin to use the system for more than simple messaging. They will implement collaborative computing solutions and will discover ways to utilize the system that you never planned for. Consequently, the size of the information stores on your Exchange servers will grow, and the processor and memory will be affected by server-based applications. All of this means that you should spend some time now thinking about growing your Exchange architecture to support the future needs of your users and your organization.

Growing Your Architecture

One of the primary goals of this book has been to identify the critical elements that are common across all Exchange architectures, regardless of the size of the organization in which Exchange is being implemented. As you grow your Exchange architecture, these common elements will serve as guideposts in a changing landscape. Many of the elements that are essential to a small-to-medium-size implementation of Exchange will also be essential to a large-scale implementation.

200,000 Seats Across the U.S.

Not everyone will be responsible for implementing and managing an Exchange organization comprised of 200,000 seats spread across an entire continent. However, there are some lessons to be learned when considering an implementation of that size. These lessons fall into three separate categories:

- Server hardware scalability
- Local and distributed network requirements
- User service requirements

Server Scalability

Server hardware scalability is one of the most critical issues to plan for when growing your Exchange architecture. Server hardware scalability isn't as simple an issue as it may appear at the outset.

The first step in developing a plan for addressing expanded server hardware requirements in your Exchange organization is to take inventory of what hardware is currently in place. When compiling that inventory, you should answer several questions about the hardware:

- What is the existing hardware profile of each server in the organization?
- Is the existing server hardware extensible, including the number of processors, memory, and fixed media storage space?
- Can the servers' drive arrays be expanded or replaced dynamically online, or do the systems need to be shut down?
- What is the available bandwidth on the network segments that support the servers? Can the server hardware support the maximum available bandwidth?
- Does the existing server hardware support failover and/or clustering? If not, can it be reconfigured to do so?

Once you have identified the nature of the server hardware and the extensibility of it, the next step is to determine if the server resources such as RAM and disk space should be expanded, or if instead new servers should be added to the organization. There are some initial questions that can help you determine the best approach to take:

- How many recipients are currently located on each server?
- How large are the public and private information stores on each server?
- How many geographic locations are included in the Exchange organization, and how many servers are in each location?

With this information, you can determine if new servers should be added or if the existing hardware should be expanded. If, for example, there are fewer than 500 recipients on a server and the size of the public and private information stores on that server are kept small because of limited drive space, it might be appropriate to expand the drive array. However, if the information stores are large in size or several thousand recipients are located on the same server, you should consider adding more servers to offload some of the recipients.

In addition, if the Exchange organization services several geographic locations but doesn't have servers configured in all of those locations, it might be necessary to configure servers for placement throughout the organization. As part of this configuration process, it is important to consider time and network bandwidth to complete the initial replication of the organization directory. If bandwidth between geographic locations is limited and the directory for the organization is large, it might be prudent to consider building servers for distributed locations online in a central location. This is an effective way to build servers for remote geographic locations without affecting the network. Here are the steps involved:

1. Deliver all server hardware to a central location at which the main Exchange servers are located (typically the headquarters for the organization).

2. Configure each server with a local IP address (if TCP/IP is the network protocol being utilized).

3. Build each server with Exchange in the proper site configuration for the organization according to the architecture.

4. Once Exchange has been loaded and the directory has been replicated, change the IP address to be a valid address for the network where the server will ultimately reside.

5. Shut down the server and ship it to the remote location.

6. Install the server at the remote location and verify services and connectivity to the Exchange organization.

This approach to distributing servers in a large and growing organization is also effective when there aren't enough system administrators skilled in Exchange at each geographic location to oversee the installation of servers. If the servers are sent out prebuilt, a less-skilled administrator can install the server and boot it up. Then, an Exchange administrator at a central location can continue with the server's configuration.

Network Requirements

The second element of any Exchange architecture that will need to be modified is the underlying physical network. As organizations expand, the physical networks that link distributed locations—and, in some cases, the local networks as well—become inadequate. The networks typically either don't have the bandwidth to support the increased traffic that Exchange will require or won't provide connectivity to new geographic areas into which the organization has expanded.

Implementing new networks to meet these growing needs is relatively straightforward. The challenge can arise in growing the physical Exchange organization to meet the needs of all the recipients. As discussed in the preceding section, you might face challenges in finding an adequate number of skilled administrators who have the time to travel to several distributed locations to install servers.

Multiple Information Stores

With versions of Exchange later than 5.5, it will be possible to configure multiple information stores on a single server. This will mean that thousands of recipients can be configured on a single server and that the size of any single private or public information store can be limited to a manageable size.

In addition to finding an adequate number of administrators, you will also face a challenge in securing an adequate budget for implementing the necessary network topology for Exchange. Senior-level managers might find it hard to justify additional expenditures for network infrastructure and bandwidth simply for e-mail. If you meet that type of opposition, it's best to once again emphasize the collaborative computing aspect of Exchange and help the managers involved to fully understand the productivity gains offered by implementing Exchange. These managers might not realize that several of the organization's workflow processes and collaborative applications might depend on Exchange for their functionality. If the performance of the messaging system suffers from lack of resources, these applications will also suffer. This might have an overall effect on productivity. If you document these facts, you could easily justify the additional resources.

Although it may be relatively easy to implement increased network bandwidth in most locations, what do you do when you're faced with an Exchange implementation at a location where it isn't possible to obtain high-speed network services? Your organization might be opening a branch office in a location where the only network access is via asynchronous dial-up or ISDN. In situations like this, Exchange is well-suited to provide dial-on-demand connectivity between sites.

To provide dial-up connectivity between Exchange servers, you have two choices:

■ Purchase dial-on-demand routers that will dial the destination site when a packet is received for that site. With this configuration, Windows NT and Exchange Server don't know that the destination site isn't permanently connected. However, to configure domain replication for such a connection to domains, one at each site would be configured if the domains are large. If a single domain is to be used, the *replication governor* would be configured to control replication to the remote BDC.

■ If dial-on-demand routers aren't purchased, two domains would be created, and the Internet Mail Service would be configured as the connector between Exchange sites (see Figure 16.1). The Internet Mail Service can be configured to dial between sites to deliver user and replication messages.

Obviously, throughout any network expansion project, you should work closely with what your network providers, such as the local telephone companies, to coordinate network outages and service implementation. That will help guarantee a smooth and successful transition with as little disruption as possible to the end-user. As with every other step of an Exchange implementation, the end client should remain the focus of the project team.

User Services

As your organization grows larger, user services will also need to be expanded. User services can be grouped into two broad categories: server-based and workstation-based.

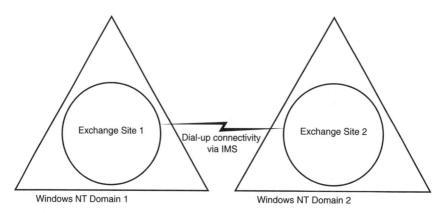

Figure 16.1 In a large distributed environment, you can provide dial-up connectivity between sites. However, you need to configure separate Windows NT domains between sites. Consequently, each site will utilize a separate Exchange service account.

Server-based services include public folder resources, access methods to server information, server-based agents, directory information, and mailbox quotas.

Workstation-based services include client functionality components that come with current and new versions of Outlook. Workstation-based services can expand dramatically with collaborative applications that provide access to network resources, databases, and groupware functionality.

Increase of Message Flow and Usage

The most obvious aspect of an Exchange organization that grows is that the message flow and usage within the organization will also grow. If you add a person to the organization, you add more message traffic. However, message flow and usage also grow as people utilizing the system begin to fully explore and utilize all aspects of Exchange functionality. Attachments are typically the first aspects of increased usage, followed by simple and then more-complex e-forms. Finally, people begin utilizing server-based agents for processing workflow applications. With the increased load on the system, it is important that the system continue to meet expected performance metrics. In addition, managing large-scale information stores can prove challenging.

Maintaining Performance Requirements

Performance requirements for the Exchange system are typically documented in a server-level agreement that is established between the user community and the Exchange system administrators. Service-level agreements define the levels of service that users can expect. Your performance requirements should encompass, but might not be limited to, the following:

- Maximum acceptable message delivery time between Exchange recipients
- Maximum acceptable message delivery time between Exchange and any external messaging environment. Environment is defined as a group of systems such as the Internet. The agreement should define the boundaries of the organization's responsibility and influence
- Maximum allowable size for private mailboxes
- Maximum allowable size for public folders
- Server-based agent execution time
- Public folder replication schedules

As Exchange organizations grow, the performance of many of the parameters just listed will decline. As more messages are delivered between Exchange recipients, delivery times will increase. As more messages are transferred between Exchange and external messaging systems, delivery times will increase. The maximum size of private and public information stores will grow. In addition, the time it takes server-based agents to execute will increase. The amount of time it takes to replicate public information between servers will also increase.

There are several ways to address these performance issues. The most important is to communicate effectively and openly with your users. Notify your users as soon as possible if you anticipate that performance will be affected due to an increase in the use of the Exchange system.

Managing Large-Scale Information Stores

Perhaps one of the most challenging aspects of growing an Exchange organization is managing large information stores. As people begin to fully understand and utilize the functionality of Exchange, the amount of data stored in the information stores will grow. With this growth comes some unique challenges.

Consider, for example, the challenge faced by backing up and restoring a large information store. You can restore an information store that is less than 10 GB in a reasonable amount of time. If you're restoring from a DLT tape, you can complete the restoration in a few hours. However, if you're restoring an information store of more than 20 GB, it could take a day or more to restore the data.

With the current release of Exchange, version 5.5, it isn't possible to have multiple private or public information stores on the same server. Consequently, it is prudent to maintain fewer users on each server than the hardware can support in order to keep the information store size small. This will change with the next release of Exchange. The design specification for the next release includes the capability to segment multiple information stores on the same server. Thus, it will be possible to build multiple private information stores on a single server and keep them all less than 10 GB in size. The same will hold true for public information stores.

Scaling External Connectivity

As message traffic internal to an Exchange organization increases, so will traffic between Exchange users and mail recipients external to the organization. Consequently, it is critical to maintain focus on expanding external connectivity at the same time you expand internal server capacity, network infrastructure, and user services. External connectivity will typically include at a minimum a connection to the Internet. In addition, external connectivity may also include commercial X.400 connections over X.25 or IP, and proprietary point-to-point connections to external vendors or partners.

The main metric you should measure when evaluating whether or not the current external connectivity is sufficient should be the maximum amount of time it takes messages to be delivered to and from recipients on the Internet or any other external system. While it may be possible to accurately measure end-to-end delivery times on proprietary systems, such as X.400-based systems, it isn't as easy to measure between destinations on the Internet. In lieu of end-to-end delivery, you can measure the maximum amount of time that messages remain in the outbound queue in the Internet Mail Service. If the amount of time that messages remain in the outbound queue begins to dramatically increase, it may be time to increase connectivity speed to the outside world.

When you're addressing external Internet connectivity, remember that small-to-medium-sized organizations typically initiate connectivity with the Internet with a fractional T-1 connection of less than 1.54 Mbps. It is most likely the case, however, that the telecom organization that installed the server implemented a physical connection that can support 1.54 Mbps speed but has only a limited number of 64 Kbps channels activated. Consequently, it can be a simple matter to increase the circuit speed between the Internet and the Exchange system.

Other connections can be more complicated to upgrade. If your organization has implemented a secure connection to an external organization via X.400 over X.25, it can be costly and time-consuming to upgrade the circuit speed. Depending on the type of X.25 PAD you have installed on your end of the circuit, you may be required to upgrade your hardware. If you have implemented X.400 over IP, the upgrade should be simpler. X.400 over IP often enters an organization via the same circuit as the Internet connection.

If your external connectivity is via a proprietary point-to-point connection to an external vendor or partner, you may be required to install a completely new circuit in order to expand connectivity speeds. This will most likely also require an additional hardware investment.

In addition to actual connectivity speed with the outside world, it is important to monitor the server hardware on which the IMS or X.400 connector is configured. As the load on the external connection increases, it may be necessary to improve the configuration of the server hardware by adding RAM, processors, or drive space.

Expanding the Messaging Services

We began this book with a discussion of how to sell Exchange within your organization as a collaborative computing platform rather than just a messaging solution. As your Exchange organization grows, it is appropriate to once again turn your focus to expanding messaging services beyond the traditional realm of e-mail. This includes examining the way in which your organization is delivering collaborative computing applications on top of Exchange. In addition, you should address some of the other aspects of expanded messaging servers, including the concept of a universal inbox and extended Internet connectivity.

Collaborative Computing

As organizations grow, collaborative applications grow in complexity. Complexity can include both the level of detail and the number of tasks that these applications perform, as well as the distributed nature of the applications. Both of these factors can drastically affect the performance of collaborative applications and, consequently, the continued acceptance of these applications by the end-user community.

Complexity of applications directly affects end-user performance by increasing the impact on the server hardware. More-complex applications will increase the load on server CPU and memory resources. Consequently, you should monitor the maximum processor utilization and memory usage on your Exchange application servers and adjust or add to resources as appropriate.

Universal Inbox

Another aspect of extended messaging services is the concept of the universal inbox. The universal inbox includes all types of data and messaging in the Exchange inbox, including regular electronic messaging, fax data, and voice message data. Several third-party products provide integration of these data types. For a complete listing of these solutions, go to `http://www.microsoft.com/exchange`.

Extended Internet Connectivity

As your organization grows, you may also need to address extending the scope of the connectivity between your organization and the Internet. Most typical small-to-medium-sized organizations initiate connectivity to the Internet with a single connection. This connection services all inbound and outbound message queues. As organizations grow, however, especially if they grow geographically to international locations, they will need to implement additional connections to the Internet.

As an example, an initial connection to the Internet might include an IMS that services all inbound mail with an MX record in DNS for the company, such as `excell.com`. As the company expands to an international location, it might be necessary to implement a second Internet connection in the new location with an MX record that is appropriate for the host country, such as `excell.co.uk`. Organizations should register an appropriate domain name for the host country.

When your organization grows from a medium-sized company to a large company, your information systems must grow too. The larger organizations get, the more difficulty communication becomes. Therefore, an investment in keeping the messaging system reliable and efficient is considered money well spent as organizations grow.

Index

N

T

Books for Networking Professionals

New Riders

Windows NT Titles

Windows NT TCP/IP

By Karanjit Siyan
1st Edition Summer 1998
500 pages, $29.99
ISBN 1-56205-887-8

If you're still looking for good documentation on Microsoft TCP/IP, then look no further—this is your book. *Windows NT TCP/IP* cuts through the complexities and provides the most informative and complete reference book on Windows-based TCP/IP. Concepts essential to TCP/IP administration are explained thoroughly, then related to the practical use of Microsoft TCP/IP in a real-world networking environment. The book begins by covering TCP/IP architecture, advanced installation and configuration issues, then moves on to routing with TCP/IP, DHCP Management, and WINS/DNS Name Resolution.

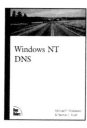

Windows NT DNS

By Michael Masterson,
Herman L. Knief, Scott Vinick
and Eric Roul
1st Edition Summer 1998
325 pages, $29.99
ISBN 1-56205-943-2

Have you ever opened a Windows NT book looking for detailed information about DNS only to discover that it doesn't even begin to scratch the surface? DNS is probably one of the most complicated subjects for NT administrators, and there are few books on the market that really address it in detail. This book answers your most complex DNS questions, focusing on the implementation of the Domain Name Service within Windows NT, treating it thoroughly from the viewpoint of an experienced Windows NT professional. Many detailed, real-world examples illustrate further the understanding of the material throughout. The book covers the details of how DNS functions within NT, then explores specific interactions with critical network components. Finally, proven procedures to design and set up DNS are demonstrated. You'll also find coverage of related topics, such as maintenance, security, and troubleshooting.

Windows NT Registry

By Sandra Osborne
1st Edition Summer 1998
500 pages, $29.99
ISBN 1-56205-941-6

The NT Registry can be a very powerful tool for those capable of using it wisely. Unfortunately, there is very little information regarding the NT Registry, due to Microsoft's insistence that their source code be kept secret. If you're looking to optimize your use of the registry, you're usually forced to search the Web for bits of information. This book is your resource. It covers critical issues and settings used for configuring network protocols, including NWLink, PTP, TCP/IP, and DHCP. This book approaches the material from a unique point of view, discussing the problems related to a particular component, and then discussing settings, which are the actual changes necessary for implementing robust solutions. There is also a comprehensive reference of registry settings and commands, making this the perfect addition to your technical bookshelf.

Windows NT Performance Monitoring

By Mark Edmead

1st Edition Fall 1998

400 pages, $29.99

ISBN 1-56205-942-4

Performance monitoring is a little like preventative medicine for the administrator: no one enjoys a checkup, but it's a good thing to do on a regular basis. This book helps you focus on the critical aspects of improving the performance of your NT system, showing you how to monitor the system, implement benchmarking, and tune your network. The book is organized by resource components, which makes it easy to use as a reference tool.

Windows NT Terminal Server

By Ted Harwood

1st Edition Winter 1998

500 pages, $29.99

ISBN 1-56205-944-0

It's no surprise that most administration headaches revolve around integration with other networks and clients. This book addresses these types of real-world issues on a case-by-case basis, giving tools and advice on solving each problem. The author also offers the real nuts and bolts of thin client administration on multiple systems, covering such relevant issues as installation, configuration, network connection, management, and application distribution.

Windows NT Security

By Richard Puckett

1st Edition Winter 1998

600 pages, $29.99

ISBN 1-56205-945-9

Swiss cheese. That's what some people say Windows NT security is like. And they may be right, because they only know what the NT documentation says about implementing security. Who has the time to research alternatives; play around with the features, service packs, hot fixes and add-on tools; and figure out what makes NT rock solid? Well, Richard Puckett does. He's been researching Windows NT Security for the University of Virginia for a while now, and he's got pretty good news. He's going to show you how to make NT secure in your environment, and we mean really secure.

Windows NT Administration Handbook

By Eric Svetcov

1st Edition Winter 1998

400 pages, $29.99

ISBN 1-56205-946-7

Administering a Windows NT network is kind of like trying to herd cats—an impossible task characterized by constant motion, exhausting labor and lots of hairballs. Author Eric Svetcov knows all about it—he's administered NT networks for some of the fastest growing companies around Silicon Valley. So we asked Eric to put together a concise manual of best practices, a book of tools and ideas that other administrators can turn to again and again in administering their own NT networks. Eric's experience shines through as he shares his secrets for administering users, for getting domain and groups set up quickly and for troubleshooting the thorniest NT problems. Daily, weekly and monthly task lists help organize routine tasks and preventative maintenance.

Planning for Windows NT 5

By David Lafferty & Eric K. Cone
1st Edition Spring 1999
400 pages, $29.99
ISBN 0-73570-048-6

Windows NT 5 is poised to be one of the largest and most important software releases of the next decade, and you are charged with planning, testing, and deploying it in your enterprise. Are you ready? With this book, you will be. *Planning for Windows NT 5* lets you know what the upgrade hurdles will be, informs you how to clear them, guides you through effective Active Directory design, and presents you with detailed rollout procedures. MCSEs David Lafferty and Eric K. Cone give you the benefit of their extensive experiences as Windows NT 5 Rapid Deployment Program members, sharing problems and solutions they've encountered on the job.

MCSE Core Essential Reference

By Matthew Shepker
1st Edition Fall 1998
500 pages, $19.99
ISBN 0-7357-0006-0

You're sitting in the first session of your Networking Essentials class and the instructor starts talking about "*RAS*" and you have no idea what that means. You think about raising your hand to ask about *RAS*, but you reconsider—you'd feel pretty foolish asking a question in front of all these people. You turn to your handy *MCSE Core Essential Reference* and find a quick summary on *Remote Access Services*. Question answered. It's a couple months later and you're taking your Networking Essentials exam the next day. You're reviewing practice tests and you keep forgetting the maximum lengths for the various commonly used cable types. Once again, you turn to the *MCSE Core Essential Reference* and find a table on cables, including all of the characteristics you need to memorize in order to pass the test.

BackOffice Titles

Implementing Exchange Server

By Doug Hauger, Marywynne Leon, and William C. Wade III
1st Edition Fall 1998
450 pages, $29.99
ISBN 1-56205-931-9

If you're interested in connectivity and maintenance issues for Exchange Server, then this book is for you. Exchange's power lies in its ability to be connected to multiple email subsystems to create a "universal email backbone." It's not unusual to have several different and complex systems all connected via email gateways, including Lotus Notes or cc:Mail, Microsoft Mail, legacy mainframe systems, and Internet mail. This book covers all of the problems and issues associated with getting an integrated system running smoothly and addresses troubleshooting and diagnosis of email problems with an eye towards prevention and best practices.

SQL Server System Administration

By Sean Baird, Chris Miller et al.
1st Edition Fall 1998
400 pages, $29.99
ISBN 1-56205-955-6

How often does your SQL Server go down during the day when everyone wants to access the data? Do you spend most of your time being a "report monkey" for your co-workers and bosses? *SQL Server System Administration* helps you keep data consistently available to your users. This book omits the introductory information. The authors don't spend time explaining queries and how they work. Instead they focus on the information that you can't get anywhere else, like how to choose the correct replication topology and achieve high availability of information.

Internet Information Server Administration

By Kelli Adam, et. al.
1st Edition Winter 1998
300 pages, $29.99
ISBN 0-73570-022-2

Are the new Internet technologies in Internet Information Server 4.0 giving you headaches? Does protecting security on the Web take up all of your time? Then this is the book for you. With hands-on configuration training, advanced study of the new protocols in IIS 4, and detailed instructions on authenticating users with the new Certificate Server and implementing and managing the new e-commerce features, *Internet Information Server Administration* gives you the real-life solutions you need. This definitive resource also prepares you for the release of Windows NT 5 by giving you detailed advice on working with Microsoft Management Console, which was first used by IIS 4.

Unix/Linux Titles

Solaris Essential Reference

A Reference for the User
By John Mulligan
1st Edition Winter 1998
350 pages, $19.99
ISBN 0-7357-0230-7

Looking for the fastest, easiest way to find the Solaris command you need? Need a few pointers on shell scripting? How about advanced administration tips and sound, practical expertise on security issues? Are you looking for trustworthy information about available third-party software packages that will enhance your operating system? Author John Mulligan—creator of the popular Unofficial Guide to Solaris Web site (sun.icsnet.com)—delivers all that and more in one attractive, easy-to-use reference book. With clear and concise instruction on how to perform important administration and management tasks, and key information on powerful commands and advanced topics, *Solaris Essential Reference* is the reference you need when you know what you want to do and you just need to know how.

Linux System Administration

By James T. Dennis
1st Edition Winter 1998
450 pages, $29.99
ISBN 1-56205-934-3

As an administrator, you probably feel that most of your time and energy is spent in endless firefighting. If your network has become a fragile quilt of temporary patches and workarounds, then this book is for you. For example, have you had trouble sending or receiving your email lately? Are you looking for a way to keep your network running smoothly with enhanced performance? Are your users always hankering for more storage, more services, and more speed? *Linux System Administration* advises you on the many intricacies of maintaining a secure, stable system. In this definitive work, the author addresses all the issues related to system administration, from adding users and managing files permission to internet services and Web hosting to recovery planning and security. This book fulfills the need for expert advice that will ensure a trouble-free Linux environment.

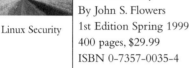

Linux Security

By John S. Flowers
1st Edition Spring 1999
400 pages, $29.99
ISBN 0-7357-0035-4

New Riders is proud to offer the first book aimed specifically at Linux security issues. While there are a host of general UNIX security books, we thought it was time to address the practical needs of the Linux network. In this definitive work, author John Flowers takes a balanced approach to system security, from discussing topics like planning a secure environment to firewalls to utilizing security scripts. With comprehensive information on specific system compromises, and advice on how to prevent and repair them, this is one book that every Linux administrator should have on the shelf.

Linux GUI Application Development

By Eric Harlow
1st Edition Spring 1999
400 pages, $34.99
ISBN 0-7357-0214-7

We all know that Linux is one of the most powerful and solid operating systems in existence. And as the success of Linux grows, there is an increasing interest in developing applications with graphical user interfaces that really take advantage of the power of Linux. In this book, software developer Eric Harlow gives you an indispensable development handbook focusing on the GTK+ toolkit. More than an overview on the elements of application or GUI design, this is a hands-on book that delves deeply into the technology. With in-depth material on the various GUI programming tools, a strong emphasis on CORBA and CGI programming, and loads of examples, this book's unique focus will give you the information you need to design and launch professional-quality applications

Lotus Notes and Domino Titles

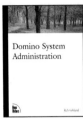

Domino System Administration

By Rob Kirkland
1st Edition Winter 1998
500 pages, $29.99
ISBN 1-56205-948-3

Your boss has just announced that you will be upgrading to the newest version of Notes and Domino when it ships. As a Premium Lotus Business Partner, Lotus has offered a substantial price break to keep your company away from Microsoft's Exchange Server. How are you supposed to get this new system installed, configured, and rolled out to all of your end users? You understand how Lotus Notes works—you've been administering it for years. What you need is a concise, practical explanation about the new features, and how to make some of the advanced stuff really work. You need answers and solutions from someone like you, who has worked with the product for years, and understands what it is you need to know. *Domino System Administration* is the answer—the first book on Domino that attacks the technology at the professional level, with practical, hands-on assistance to get Domino running in your organization.

Lotus Notes and Domino Essential Reference

By Dave Hatter & Tim Bankes
1st Edition Winter 1998
500 pages, $19.99
ISBN 0-7357-0007-9

You're in a bind because you've been asked to design and program a new database in Notes for an important client that will keep track of and itemize a myriad of inventory and shipping data. The client wants a user-friendly interface, without sacrificing speed or functionality. You are experienced (and could develop this app in your sleep), but feel that you need to take your talents to the next level. You need something to facilitate your creative and technical abilities, something to perfect your programming skills. Your answer is waiting for you: *Lotus Notes and Domino Essential Reference.* It's compact and simply designed. It's loaded with information. All of the objects, classes, functions and methods are listed. It shows you the object hierarchy and the overlaying relationship between each one. It's perfect for you. Problem solved.

Networking Titles

Cisco Router Configuration and Troubleshooting

By Pablo Espinosa and
Mark Tripod
1st Edition Winter 1998
300 pages, $34.99
ISBN 0-7357-0024-9

Want the real story on making your Cisco routers run like a dream? Why not pick up a copy of *Cisco Router Configuration and Troubleshooting* and see what Pablo Espinosa and Mark Tripod have to say? They're the folks responsible for making some of the largest sites on the Net scream, like Amazon.com, Hotmail, USAToday, Geocities, and Sony. In this book, they provide advanced configuration issues, sprinkled with advice and preferred practices. You won't see a general overview on TCP/IP—we talk about more meaty issues like security, monitoring, traffic management, and more. In the troubleshooting section, the authors provide a unique methodology and lots of sample problems to illustrate. By providing real-world insight and examples instead of rehashing Cisco's documentation, Pablo and Mark give network administrators information they can start using today.

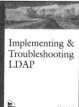

Implementing and Troubleshooting LDAP

By Robert Lamothe
1st Edition Spring 1999
400 pages, $29.99
ISBN 1-56205-947-5

While there is some limited information available about LDAP, most of it is RFCs, white papers and books about programming LDAP into your networking applications. That leaves the people who most need information—administrators—out in the cold. What do you do if you need to know how to make LDAP work in your system? You ask Bob Lamothe. Bob is a UNIX administrator with hands-on experience in setting up a corporate-wide directory service using LDAP. Bob's book is NOT a guide to the protocol; rather, it is designed to be an aid to administrators to help them understand the most efficient way to structure, encrypt, authenticate, administer and troubleshoot LDAP in a mixed network environment. The book shows you how to work with the major implementations of LDAP and get them to co-exist.

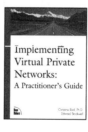

Implementing Virtual Private Networks

A Practitioner's Guide
By Tina Bird and Ted
Stockwell
1st Edition Spring 1999
300 pages, $29.99
ISBN 0-73570-047-8

Tired of looking for decent, practical, up-to-date information on virtual private networks? *Implementing Virtual Private Networks* by noted authorities Dr. Tina Bird and Ted Stockwell, finally gives you what you need—an authoritative guide on the design, implementation, and maintenance of Internet-based access to private networks. This book focuses on real-world solutions, demonstrating how the choice of VPN architecture should align with an organization's business and technological requirements. Tina and Ted give you the information you need to determine whether a VPN is right for your organization, select the VPN that suits your needs, and design and implement the VPN you have chosen.

New Riders | How to Contact Us

Visit our Web site

www.newriders.com

On our Web site you'll find information about our other books, authors, tables of content, indexes, and book errata. You can also place orders for books through our Web site.

Email us

newriders@mcp.com

Contact us at this address:

- if you have comments or questions about this book
- to report errors that you have found in this book
- if you have a book proposal to submit or are interested in writing for New Riders
- if you would like to have an author kit sent to you
- if you are an expert in a computer topic or technology and are interested in being a technical editor who reviews manuscripts for technical accuracy

international@mcp.com

To find a distributor in your area, please contact our international department at the address above.

pr@mcp.com

For instructors from educational institutions who wish to preview Macmillan Computer Publishing books for classroom use. Email should include your name, title, school, department, address, phone number, office days/hours, text in use, and enrollment in the body of your text along with your request for desk/examination copies and/or additional information.

Write to us

New Riders
201 W. 103rd St.
Indianapolis IN 46290-1097

Call us

Toll-free (800) 571-5840 + 9 + 4557
If outside U.S. (317) 581-3500 ask for New Riders

Fax us

(317) 581-4663

We want to know what you think

To better serve you, we would like your opinion on the content and quality of this book. Please complete this card and mail it to us or fax it to 317-581-4663.

Name _____

Address _____

City _____ State _____ Zip _____

Phone _____

Email Address _____

Occupation _____

Operating System(s) that you use _____

What influenced your purchase of this book?

❑ Recommendation   ❑ Cover Design

❑ Table of Contents   ❑ Index

❑ Magazine Review   ❑ Advertisement

❑ Reputation of New Riders   ❑ Author Name

How would you rate the contents of this book?

❑ Excellent   ❑ Very Good

❑ Good   ❑ Fair

❑ Below Average   ❑ Poor

How do you plan to use this book?

❑ Quick reference   ❑ Self-training

❑ Classroom   ❑ Other

What do you like most about this book?
Check all that apply.

❑ Content   ❑ Writing Style

❑ Accuracy   ❑ Examples

❑ Listings   ❑ Design

❑ Index   ❑ Page Count

❑ Price   ❑ Illustrations

What do you like least about this book?
Check all that apply.

❑ Content   ❑ Writing Style

❑ Accuracy   ❑ Examples

❑ Listings   ❑ Design

❑ Index   ❑ Page Count

❑ Price   ❑ Illustrations

What would be a useful follow-up book to this one for you?_____

Where did you purchase this book?_____

Can you name a similar book that you like better than this one, or one that is as good? Why?_____

_____

_____

How many New Riders books do you own? _____

What are your favorite computer books?_____

_____

What other titles would you like to see us develop? _____

_____

Any comments for us? _____

_____

_____

_____

_____

Fold here and scotch tape to mail

New Riders
201 W. 103rd St.
Indianapolis IN 46290

EXCELL

EXCELL DATA CORPORATION

You've read the experts,
Now join their team!

Be a part of the team that wrote this book. It's all possible by joining the premiere Microsoft Certified Solution Provider Partner in the Western U.S.

Excell Data offers unparalleled opportunities for our consultants. You'll get the chance to work with new technologies from Microsoft clients that offer unique challenges on projects throughout North America, our staff of consultants and technology experts providing an unmatched environment for professional growth. If you have skills in the following areas, then you should seriously consider joining our team:

- Application Development
- Enterprise Networking
- Enterprise Messaging
- Project Management

- Internet Security
- Web Development
- Database Design
- Business Analysis

Take this opportunity to work with the experts.
Visit our web site for current positions, or email your resume today!

http://www.excell.com   excell@excell.com